A PIECE
OF BLUE SKY

A PIECE OF BLUE SKY

Scientology, Dianetics
and L. Ron Hubbard Exposed

by Jon Atack

A LYLE STUART BOOK
Published by Carol Publishing Group

A Lyle Stuart Book
Published by Carol Publishing Group

Editorial Offices   Sales & Distribution Offices
600 Madison Avenue   120 Enterprise Avenue
New York, NY 10022   Secaucus, NJ 07094

In Canada: Musson Book Company
A division of General Publishing Co. Limited
Don Mills, Ontario

Manufactured in the United States of America

Library of Congress Cataloging-in-Publication Data

Atack, Jon.
    A piece of blue sky : Scientology, Dianetics, and L. Ron Hubbard
exposed / by Jon Atack.
      p.   cm.
    "A Lyle Stuart book."
    Includes bibliographical references and index.
    ISBN 0-8184-0499-X : $19.95
    1. Scientology—Controversial literature.   2. Dianetics—
Controversial literature.   3. Hubbard, L. Ron (La Fayette Ron),
1911- .   4. Church of Scientology—History. I. Title.
BP605.S2A83   1990
299'.936'092—dc20   89-77666
                                                          CIP

It was 1950, in the early, heady days of Dianetics, soon after L. Ron Hubbard opened the doors of his first organization to the clamoring crowd. Up until then, Hubbard was known only to readers of pulp fiction, but now he had an instant best-seller with a book that promised to solve every problem of the human mind, and the cash was pouring in. Hubbard found it easy to create schemes to part his new following from their money. One of the first tasks was to arrange "grades" of membership, offering supposedly greater rewards, at increasingly higher prices. Over thirty years later, an associate wryly remembered Hubbard turning to him and confiding, no doubt with a smile, "Let's sell these people a piece of blue sky."

Acknowledgments

My particular thanks are due to my three good friends Mitch Beedie, Lawrence Kristiansen and George Shaw. Mitch Beedie has been a constant source of encouragement, support and editorial insight throughout six years of research and writing. Lawrence Kristiansen has proved to be an invaluable resource, sharing freely his knowledge and understanding of Scientology. His meticulous research, and his painstaking editing, helped me to focus ever more closely on the subject matter. George Shaw also signed up as an unpaid (and exceptional) researcher, gave me the benefit of his considerable knowledge of Scientology, and provided fascinating perspectives on Hubbard's character and motives.

This book is based upon statements made by over 150 individuals whether in interviews, correspondence, taped talks, published accounts, affidavits or sworn testimony. Those of my sources whose statements were made publicly, and those who have given permission, are named in the reference summary. I am grateful to them all and to the many people who have asked to remain anonymous, for reasons which the book should make clear.

In return for access to my manuscript and my collaboration as a consultant, Russell Miller made his interview notes available to me, and for this and our friendly working relationship I am most grateful.

I also wish to express my thanks to Dave Walters and the staff of the Montana Historical Society; to Ron Neuman for access to his collection of Hubbard letters and first editions; and to Brenda Yates and Carol Kanda for ensuring that I received the 28 volumes of the transcript of the Armstrong case. Without Brenda these vital documents would not have become available in the first place.

Gratitude is also due to those authors whose work made my own less daunting: the late Joseph Winter, Martin Gardner, the late Helen O'Brien, George Malko, Pauletter Cooper, Cyril Vosper, Bob Kaufman, the late Christopher Evans, C.H. Rolph, John Forte and most especially Roy Wallis for *The Road to Total Freedom*. I am also in debt to the *St. Petersburg Times* and the *Clearwater Sun* for their excellent coverage of Scientology.

I am grateful to the many friends who have revived my sometimes flagging spirits on the long road to publication. Gratitude is due especially to: Robyn, Joy, Fiona, Joyce, Marcia, Sam, Gail, Hana, Gay, John, Greg, Sarge, Marcus, Lew, Chris, Callan, Otto, my parents, my brother Andrew, and my wife, Noella.

The litigious nature of the Scientologists has frightened most publishers into silence. Lyle Stuart and Steven Schragis were not intimidated, and I am extremely grateful to them. Finally, my thanks to our attorney, Mel Wulf, for his patient attention to detail; to my editor Bob Smith; and to all at Carol Publishing Group for making this book a published reality.

—JON ATACK

Contents

Scientology is both immoral and socially obnoxious . . . it is corrupt, sinister and dangerous. It is corrupt because it is based upon lies and deceit and has as its real objective money and power for Mr. Hubbard, his wife and those close to him at the top. It is sinister because it indulges in infamous practices both to its adherents who do not toe the line unquestioningly and to those who criticize or oppose it. It is dangerous because it is out to capture people, especially children and impressionable young people, and indoctrinate and brainwash them so that they become the unquestioning captives and tools of the cult, withdrawn from ordinary thought, living and relationships with others.—JUSTICE LATEY, ruling in the High Court in London in 1984

As soon as one's convictions become unshakeable, evidence ceases to be relevant—except as a means to convert the unbelievers. Factual inaccuracies . . . are excusable in the light of the Higher Truth.—P.H. HOEBENS

What Is Scientology?

Scientology is among the oldest, largest, richest, and most powerful of contemporary cults. The "Church" of Scientology, first incorporated in 1953, claims to have seven million members, and reserves of a thousand million dollars. There are nearly 200 Scientology "Missions" and "Churches" spread across the globe.

During the 1970's, cults became big business and big news. Yet in the welter of books published about these "new religious movements," there has been no real history of Scientology. This is rather surprising, because the history of Scientology is at turns outrageous, hilarious and sinister. Accurate information about Scientology is scarce because the cult is both secretive and highly committed to silencing its critics.

A few sociologists have argued that involvement in any cult is usually short-lived and sometimes beneficial. However, after four years of research, including interviews with over a thousand former cult members, researchers Conway and Siegelman came to very different conclusions about Scientology: "The reports we have seen and heard in the course of our research . . . are replete with allegations of psychological devastation, economic exploitation, and personal and legal harassment of former members and journalists who speak out against the cult."[1] Making a comparison with the tens of other cults in their study, they said: "Scientology's may be the most debilitating set of rituals of any cult in America."[2]

Scientology, a peculiar force in our society, escapes tidy definition. The "Church" of Scientology claims religious status; yet at times Scientology represents itself as a psychotherapy, a set of business techniques, an educational system for children or a drug rehabilitation program. Officers of the Church belong to the largely landbound "Sea Organization," and wear pseudo-Naval uniforms, complete with campaign ribbons, colored lanyards, and badges of rank, giving Scientology a paramilitary air. Although Scientology has no teachings about God, Scientologists sometimes don the garb of Christian ministers. The teachings of Scientology are held out not only as scientifically proven, but also as scriptural, and therefore beyond question. Scientology was also the first cult to establish itself as a multinational business with marketing, public relations, legal and even intelligence departments.

Scientology is also unusual because it is not an extension of a particular traditional religion. It is a complex and apparently complete set of beliefs, techniques and rituals assembled by one man: L. Ron Hubbard. During the 36 years between the publication of his first psychotherapeutic text and his death in 1986, Hubbard constructed what appears to be one of the most elaborate belief systems of all time. The sheer volume of material daunts most investigators. Several thousand Hubbard lectures were tape-recorded, and his books, pamphlets and directives run to tens of thousands of pages.

In 1984, judges in England and America condemned both Hubbard and Scientology. Justice Latey, in a child custody case in London, said: "Deprival of property, injury by any means, trickery, suing, lying or destruction have been pursued [by the Scientologists] throughout and to this day with the fullest vigour," and further: "Mr. Hubbard is a charlatan and worse as are his wife Mary Sue Hubbard . . . and the clique at the top privy to the Cult's activities."

In America, dismissing a case brought against a former member by the Scientologists, Judge Breckenridge said: "In addition to violating and abusing its own members' civil rights, the organization over the years . . . has harassed and abused those persons not within the Church whom it perceives as enemies. The organization clearly is schizophrenic and paranoid, and this bizarre combination seems to be a reflection of its founder LRH [L. Ron Hubbard]. The evidence portrays a man who has been virtually a pathological liar when it comes to his history, background and achievements. The writings and documents in evidence additionally reflect his egoism, greed, avarice, lust for power, and vindictiveness and aggressiveness against persons perceived by him to be disloyal or hostile."

The evidence cited by Judge Breckenridge consisted of some 10,000 pages of material forming part of Hubbard's personal archive, including his teenage diaries, a black magic ceremony called the "Blood Ritual," and hundreds of personal letters to and from his three wives. Some of these documents were read into the record, and others released as exhibits. The picture they reveal is very different from Hubbard's representations about his life.

Nevertheless, Hubbard's personal history is one of the great adventure stories of the 20th century. A penny-a-word science-fiction writer who created an immense and dedicated organization to act out his grandiose ideas on a global scale, Hubbard commanded the devotion of his followers, who revere him as the greatest man who has ever lived. At the height of his power, Hubbard controlled a personal intelligence network which successfully infiltrated newspapers, medical and psychiatric assocations throughout the world, and even a number of United States government agencies. Eleven of Hubbard's subordinates, including his wife, received prison sentences for their part in these criminal activities.

There is also something tantalizing in the psychotherapeutic techniques which are at the core of Scientology. Cult devotees are sometimes seen as adolescent, half-witted zombies easily coerced into joining an enslaving group because of their inadequacy. But Scientology has attracted medical doctors, lawyers, space scientists and graduates of the finest universities in the world. One British and two Danish Members of Parliament once belonged to Scientology. Even psychologists, psychiatrists and sociologists have been enthusiastic practitioners of Hubbard's techniques. And such people have often parted with immense sums of money to pay for Scientology counselling which can cost as much as $1,000 per hour.

Hubbard's ideas have inspired many imitators, and several contemporary ''psycho-technologies'' and New Age movements derive from Scientology (est, eckancar and co-counselling, for example).

Any assessment of Scientology is further complicated because it has demonstrably been the target of harassment. A Tax Court judge admitted in a ruling that the IRS had investigated Scientologists solely because they were Scientologists. Governments have panicked and over-reacted: for example, for several years in three Australian states the very practice of Scientology was an imprisonable offence.

The secret inner workings of Scientology have long been zealously guarded, but in 1982, two years after Hubbard disappeared into complete seclusion, a purge began and the Church began to disintegrate. Hundreds of long-term Scientologists, many of whom had held important positions within the Church, were excommunicated and expelled. They were placed under the interdict of ''Disconnection,'' whereby other Scientologists were prohibited from communicating with them in any way. At a rally in San Francisco, young members of the new management harangued and threatened executives of Scientology's franchised "Missions." While the newly created International Finance Dictator spoke, his scowling, black-shirted International Finance Police patrolled the aisles. Huge amounts of money were demanded from the Mission Holders. In the following weeks, Scientology's Finance Police swooped down on the Missions collecting millions of dollars and almost bankrupting the entire network.

Hubbard had styled himself the "Commodore" of his "Sea Organization," and by 1982, the new leaders, some still in their teens, were members of the "Commodore's Messenger Organization." Many of these youngsters had been raised in Scientology, separated from their parents, originally working as Hubbard's personal servants.

Anonymous letters describing incredible events circulated among Scientologists. We read about Gilman Hot Springs, a 500 acre estate in south California, surrounded by high fences, patrolled by brown-shirted guards, and protected by an elaborate and expensive security system. We heard accounts of bizarre punishments meted out at this supposedly secret headquarters. A group of senior Church executives had been put on a program where they ran around a tree in near desert conditions for twelve hours a day, for weeks on end. Some Scientologists gave accounts of their treatment at the hands of the International Finance Police, where they had been abused verbally and physically, sometimes signing over huge amounts of money before coming to their senses.

During this reign of terror, thousands of Scientologists left the Church, believing that Hubbard was either dead or under the control of the Messengers. These new "Independent" practitioners of Scientology were subjected to prolonged and extensive harassment and litigation. Private Investigators followed important defectors, sometimes around the clock for months. The Church widely distributed scandal sheets packed with fabricated libels concerning defectors.

The essential question which plagued Scientologists who had left the Church was whether Hubbard knew what was happening. By the time Hubbard's death was announced in January 1986, many Scientologists believed his body had been deep-frozen for several years. Others believed he was still alive, that the coroner had been bribed, and that his death had been staged to escape the net of the Criminal Investigation Branch of the Internal Revenue Service, which was investigating the transfer of hundreds of millions of dollars of Church funds into Hubbard's personal accounts.

As part of its campaign to stem the tide of defectors, Scientology brought law suits against several former members. In return, multi-million dollar counter-suits were filed against Scientology. In 1986, a Los Angeles jury awarded $30 million in damages to a former Church member. On the last day of 1986, a group of over 400 former members initiated a billion dollar suit against the Church.

Former highly-placed Hubbard aides broke silence for the first time. The documentary evidence referred to by Judge Breckenridge pierced the self-created fantasy of Hubbard's past. The sinister reality beneath the smiling mask of the Church of Scientology was at last revealed.

P A R T   O N E

INSIDE SCIENTOLOGY
1974–1983

This is useful knowledge. With it the blind again see, the lame walk, the ill recover, the insane become sane and the sane become saner. By its use the thousand abilities Man has sought to recover become his once more.—L. RON HUBBARD, *Scientology: A History of Man*, 1952

CHAPTER ONE

My Beginnings

It was 1974 and I was nineteen. I had just returned to England after a disastrous tour of the South of France only to find that my girlfriend, with whom I had been living for over a year, had been sleeping with one of my friends and was going to live with him in New Zealand.

A few weeks later while alone at a friend's house, I found a copy of Hubbard's book *Science of Survival*. After reading 200 pages, I was hooked.

I was impressed by Hubbard's insistence that his "Dianetics" was not dependent on faith, but was completely scientific. The book began with an impressive array of graphs purportedly depicting increases in IQ and betterment of personality through Dianetics, which appeared to have undergone extensive testing.

Dianetics claimed to be an extension of Freudian therapy. By re-experiencing unconfronted traumas it was allegedly possible to unravel the deep-seated stimulus-response patterns which ruin people's lives. Hubbard departed from Freud by denying that sexual repressions were basic to human aberration. He promised a new and balanced emotional outlook through the application of Dianetics.

It seemed that Dianetics had been absorbed by Scientology. *Science of Survival* contained an out-dated list of Scientology Churches. Eventually I found a phone number for the "Birmingham Mission of the Church of Scientology." After a few minutes of conversation, the receptionist insisted that I take a train immediately. About three hours later, after a complicated journey, I arrived at the "Mission." It was over a launderette in Moseley village, at that time the dowdy home of the Birmingham hippy community.

The receptionist sat behind an old desk at the head of the steep stairs. It was just after six in the evening, and the rest of the Mission staff had gone home to take a break before returning for the evening session. The receptionist was in her early twenties, and had abandoned a career in teaching to become a full-time Scientologist. She was cheerful and self-assured, and she looked me straight in the eye. She exuded confidence that Scientology was the stuff of miracles. I mentioned my interest in Buddhism, so she gave me a Scientology magazine called *Advance!*, which claimed that Scientology was its modern successor. I was passionately interested, but she would not trust me to take a copy of Hubbard's *Dianetics: The Modern Science of Mental Health*, and pay the next day.

Perhaps to her surprise, I did return the next day and bought the book. I spent the Christmas season locked away with my misery and "Dianetics." The 400 pages took ten days to read. The book was turgid and difficult, but I was not interested in Hubbard's style, I was interested in Dianetic therapy.

Hubbard claimed to have found the source of all human unhappiness. Dianetics would eradicate depression, and the seventy percent of all ailments which Hubbard claimed are mentally generated, or "psychosomatic." According to Hubbard's book, each of us has a stimulus-response mind which records all trauma. This "Reactive Mind" is hidden from the conscious or "Analytical Mind." When elements of an environment resemble those of an earlier traumatic incident, the Reactive Mind cuts in and enforces irrational behavior upon the individual. The Reactive Mind is idiotic, and tries to resolve present situations by regurgitating a jumble of responses from its recording of the traumatic incident. Failing to see the cause of this irrational behavior, the Analytical Mind justifies it, in exactly the way a hypnotized subject justifies his enactment of implanted suggestions.

According to Hubbard, the deepest personal traumas were moments of unconsciousness or pain, which he called "engrams." By relieving engrams an individual could erase the Reactive Mind and become well-balanced, happy and completely rational. The earliest engram would have occurred before birth, and would be the "basic" of all subsequent engrams. Those who had relieved this original engram, and consequently erased their Reactive Mind, Hubbard called "Clears."

People receiving Dianetics were "Preclears." I began to absorb this elaborate and complex new language.

More recent incidents would have to be relieved before the Preclear would be capable of reliving his birth and his experiences in the womb. I was wary of Hubbard's constant assertion that most parents try to abort their children, but glossed over it, thinking his initial research must have been done on rather strange people.

What severe "engrams" had I received? Because so much emphasis was put on birth and the prenatal period, I asked my mother about her pregnancy. Her answers horrified me. After an emergency operation to treat a twisted ovary, the doctor had told her she was pregnant. The doctor said he had held the evidence (me) in his hand. A very nasty "prenatal engram" indeed; perhaps explaining my backache, my slight near-sightedness, or my current intense depression.

I was a romantic teenager, deeply upset by the end of a love affair. I wanted help and I thought that L. Ron Hubbard could provide that help. A year before, a Zen teacher had warned me to join only groups where *all* the members had something I wanted. The people I met at the Scientology "Mission" all seemed unusually cheerful. They were confident and positive about life. Qualities I sorely needed. I had met Moonies, Hare Krishnas, and Children of God, but Scientologists had an easy cheerfulness, not the hysterical euphoria I had seen in these "cult" converts.

Within a few weeks, I moved into the house where most of the Mission staff lived. I asked my Scientologist roommate if he had any pet hates. He smiled broadly and said, "Only wogs." I was startled, and launched into a defense of dark-skinned people. He laughed, and explained that "wog" was a Hubbardism for all "non-Scientologists." This gave me pause for thought, but I dismissed it as an unfortunate turn of phrase. I thought that Hubbard probably did not realize how racially offensive the term is in Great Britain.

I became intrigued by the many claims Hubbard had made about himself. In the 1930s he had been an explorer. A trained nuclear physicist, he had applied the rigorous precision of Western science to the profound philosophy of the East, which he had encountered at first hand in his teens in China, Tibet and India. One of Freud's disciples had trained him in psychoanalysis. During the Second World War Hubbard had distinguished himself as a squadron commander in the U.S. Navy, sinking U-boats and receiving no less than 27 medals and awards.[1] The end of the war found him in a military hospital, "crippled and blinded."[2] Applying scientific method to Eastern philosophy, and combining the results with Freudian analysis, Hubbard claimed to have cured himself completely. Out of this miracle cure came Dianetics. Because of his experience of "man's inhumanity to man" in the war, he had continued his research and brought Scientology into being.[3]

The young woman who ran the Scientology Mission was attractive, intelligent, and bubbling with enthusiasm. She was a "Clear," having "erased" her Reactive Mind, and seemed living proof of the efficacy of the system. The five Mission staff members generated a friendly atmosphere. They listened to whatever I had to say and steered me towards a more optimistic state of mind. I was convinced that they were genuinely interested in my well-being, and found their positive attitude very helpful.

Scientology Organizations are eager to make new converts, and all Scientologists who are not Organization staff members are designated "Field Staff Members," or FSMs, and are expected to recruit new people. Desperately wanting to help, I became a full-time FSM. Before I really knew anything about Scientology, I was recruiting everyone I could. I did "body-routing" from the street, which is to say "routing" people's "bodies" into the Mission.

I was "drilled" step by step, by an experienced Scientologist. Pretending to be a member of the public, the coach dreamed up situations. If I made a mistake the coach would say "flunk," and the mistake would be explained. Then the coach would repeat the phrase and the gestures I had mishandled. Through the drills I was meant to become confident in real life situations. The drills often took strange turns. One coach asked if I wanted to "screw" her. I was flunked for not simply excusing myself. She explained that we were not trying to interest prostitutes in Scientology. Homosexuals, Communists, journalists and the mentally deranged were not to be approached either. Scientology's goal was to "make the able more able."

I would introduce myself to someone on the street as if I was conducting a survey. I would ask "What would you most like to be?" then "most like to do?" then "have?" The questions were purely a device to start people talking. As soon as they did, I would slip into Hubbard's "Dissemination drill"[4] by saying I was a Scientologist, and dealing with any negative response by attacking the person's source of information. If someone said, "Didn't the Australians ban Scientology?" I would say, "Where did you hear that?" They would almost inevitably say, "In the newspapers." This could often be dismissed with "Well, you can't believe *anything* you read in the papers," diverting attention from the complaint. It sounds remarkable, but many people would agree and abandon their criticism. This trained tactic underlies Scientology's self-defense: divert the critic, attack the source not the information.

Next, I was told to direct the person to their "ruin": whatever they thought was ruining their life. I would keep asking questions until they showed genuine emotion about some aspect of their life. Then I was supposed to "bring them to understanding" by letting them know that *whatever* their problem was, there was a Scientology course that dealt with it. "You're frightened of dying? Scientology has a course that can help you!" "Oh, yes, Scientology can help you with your asthma!" I was told to say these things, and I believed what I was saying. The course which would help their problem, from obesity to pre-menstrual tension, was always the "Communication Course."

I would take an interested person to the Mission, and hand them over to a "Registrar" to be given a lengthy Scientology personality test, or a free introductory lecture. I took many strangers into the Mission, and most of my friends. Several started courses, though most drifted away without finishing.

The yellow walls of the Mission were covered with small notices, newspaper clippings about Scientology "wins," testimonials ("Success Stories"), and Hubbard quotes: "Scientology leads to success in any walk of life," for instance. The Mission consisted of a course room, an office, a tiny kitchen, a lavatory, and two counselling rooms. The course room could hold about 30 people, but most of the time only a few students were present. The receptionist doubled as a Course Supervisor. In the evenings seasoned Scientologists would arrive to take more advanced courses. Among these were a bank manager and his wife, who held a senior position with the county Health Authority. I also did drills with the managing director of an engraving business, and with an active Quaker. They were all very encouraging about the benefits they felt they had experienced because of Scientology.

I expected to take a short course in Dianetics, and then start shifting my engrams around. This was not to be. In the quarter century since the publication of *Dianetics: The Modern Science of Mental Health*, Hubbard had allegedly conducted a great deal of research, and the original procedure was now outmoded. A rigidly defined series of steps constituted the Scientology "Bridge." It was possible to receive counselling for a fee, or to train as a counselor and co-counsel with another student for free. There were several courses involved, but before Mission staff would even discuss the cost, they insisted that I do the Communication, or "Comm," Course.

The Comm Course is the beginning of most Scientology careers. Hubbard claimed to have been the first person to scientifically dissect communication. The Comm Course drills are called Training Routines, or TRs.[5]

The first two TRs are similar to meditation. They are supposed to help you focus your attention on the person you are talking to. Two people sit facing each other, without speaking or moving. In the first drill (OT TR-O) they sit with their eyes closed, in the second (TR-O) open and staring at one another. These drills are often done for hours without pause, and form part of most Scientology courses. As with meditation, I hallucinated while doing the open-eyed TR-O. My coach explained vaguely that people who had taken drugs often experienced this. In fact, hallucination is not unusual for anyone who stares fixedly for long enough, but I did not realize this, and was genuinely concerned.

The next step is "TR-O Bullbait." One student baits the other, verbally and through gestures, trying to disturb the recipient's motionless composure. If the recipient moves, laughs, speaks, or even blinks excessively, the coach "flunks" him. It is presumed that something the coach said or did provoked the reaction, so the drill is restarted, and the coach tries to repeat the earlier stimulus exactly. This is done until there is no reaction from the recipient.

I was first "bullbaited" by a dour, middle-aged house painter who had little time for me. In "bullbaiting," the coach can do anything save leave his chair; so he sat and insulted me, told obscene jokes, and pulled faces until I stopped responding. The idea is to find "buttons" which when pushed force an immediate reaction and, through drilling, to overcome these reactions, allowing a more considered response to real-life stimuli. His main approach was to insist that because I had long hair I must be a homosexual. It took about two hours before I attained immobility in the face of this onslaught. I felt a tremendous sense of accomplishment.

The next Training Routine, TR-1, is supposed to teach the student to speak audibly and coherently, and to teach him to ask written questions in a natural way. In TR-1, the student reads lines at random from Lewis Carroll's *Alice in Wonderland*; he "makes the line his own," and then repeats it to the coach. The coach must hear clearly what is said, and feel it was intended that he hear it. A course room full of people declaiming, "Off with his head!" or "Contrariwise" is one of many surreal experiences Scientology provides.

TR-2 deals with acknowledgments. In counselling it is necessary to show you've heard, so you say "Good," "Thank-you," "Okay," or something similar. This ends what Hubbard calls a "cycle of communication," and prepares the way for a new "cycle." The coach reads a line from *Alice in Wonderland* and the student acknowledges it.

By the time the student comes to TR-3, he has learned to concentrate on the person in front of him and not be thrown by his reactions. The student has also learned to make sure that he is clearly audible, and to show he has heard what is said to him. The lessons of the earlier TRs must be retained throughout the course. In TR-3, the student learns to repeat an unanswered question without variation. TRs were designed for Scientology counsellors, and Hubbard's counselling questions are exactly worded. To prevent the drilling from turning into counselling, two non-sensitive questions are used: either "Do birds fly?" or "Do fish swim?" If the coach answers, the student accepts the answer by acknowledging it. If the coach does anything else, the student says, "I'll repeat the question," and does so.

TR-4, the last Training Routine on the Comm Course, drills the student to "handle originations" made by the coach, and to return his attention to the original question. For example:

Student: Do birds fly?
Coach: It's hot in here!
Student: I'll open the window (opens window). Okay, I'll repeat the question, do birds fly?

Over the years I persuaded about 20 people to do the Communication Course. I instructed some of them, or in Scientology terms "supervised," as Hubbard's course materials do all the talking, and the supervisor adds nothing by way of explanation or comment. He meets the confused student's queries with, "What do your materials state?" This is supposed to ensure that Hubbard's materials are not altered by personal interpretations.

The Comm Course helps people to hide, though not overcome, their nervousness, and to look people "right in the eye." It also inculcates persistence with questions until they are answered. It can have a positive effect, generating self-confidence. Of course, people on the receiving end sometimes feel intimidated. Critics of Scientology usually mention the "relentless stare" which for the great majority of Scientologists is habitual.

After completing the Comm Course, I was allowed a few pounds against the "Hubbard Qualified Scientologist Course" for all the people I had brought in. Scientology usually pays a 10 or 15 percent commission for recruitment. I was already too involved in Scientology to realize I had been working for the Mission for several weeks without pay.

The Hubbard Qualified Scientologist (HQS) Course packages many of the basic ideas of Scientology. The student does the Comm Course Training Routines again, and four additional Training Routines called the "Upper Indoctrination TRs." These drill the student to maintain control of someone through physical contact, but more so through "intention," or sheer will power—really by having a very determined approach.

On the HQS course I learned about several of Hubbard's many "Scales," among them the key Scale of Scientology: the "Emotional Tone Scale." Hubbard believed that there is a natural progression of emotional states, and that any individual can be led through these simply by conversation. The purported idea of Scientology counselling is to permanently raise the Preclear on the "Tone Scale." The scale rises from Death through Apathy, to Grief, to Sympathy, to Fear, to Hostility, to Boredom, to Cheerfulness, to Enthusiasm. Scientology seeks to take someone who is apathetic, miserable, anxious, or antagonistic and make of him someone cheerful and positive.

While on the HQS Course, I had my first stab at "auditing," or counselling. A friend and I drilled the procedures using an over-size rag doll as the Preclear receiving counselling. One of us would be the "Auditor," and the other the coach, making verbal responses on the rag doll's behalf.

Despite painstaking drilling, my first Auditor collapsed while giving me a session. He was asking me to touch objects in the room, one by one, and suddenly crumpled against the wall, sinking to the floor in uncontrollable laughter. The artificial atmosphere of auditing was too much for him. I was unprepared for this, and felt dizzy and confused. A seasoned Auditor gave me a "Review," asking questions about the session and "earlier similar incidents." After 20 minutes I felt better. To me it seemed to prove Scientology's validity.

Considering myself a Zen Buddhist, I readily accepted Hubbard's ideas about reincarnation. He said that during counselling so many people had spontaneously volunteered "past life" incidents that he had had to accept it as a reality. Auditing is virtually impossible without such a belief.

By the time I became involved in Scientology, "Clear" was no longer the ultimate attainment; now there were levels beyond. Hubbard used the word "thetan" to describe the spirit, the "being himself," and beyond "Clear" were the "Operating Thetan"(OT) levels. Here the individual would purportedly break away from the limitations of human existence. Having completed the "OT levels" one would be able to remember all of one's earlier lives, to "exteriorize" from the body at will and perform miraculous feats.

Such ideas were completely foreign to me. Interest in psychic abilities is frowned upon in the Zen community as a distraction from the road to wisdom. What I wanted from Scientology was emotional equilibrium, so I could win my girlfriend back, make a successful career in the Arts, and concentrate on achieving Enlightenment. But gradually I was absorbed into the pursuit of the state of "Operating Thetan."

By this time I had a fairly well developed picture of Lafayette Ronald Hubbard. His voice on tape was rich and jocular. Photographs of Hubbard in Scientology magazines and on the walls of the Mission showed a smiling man, not a dry philosopher, but a man of action with a tremendous love for humanity, who had devoted his life to the solution of other men's ills. Hubbard seemed to be a true philanthropist; a learned man with a grasp of science and a comprehension of the mysteries. Hubbard had a sense of humor, and was given to anecdotes. He was not trying to impress anyone with his intellect, instead he wanted you to help yourself, and all mankind, by using the subject he had developed. This view of Hubbard is shared by all devoted Scientologists.

By the summer of 1975 I was coming back onto an even keel. My life revolved around Scientology, and I had put my ex-girlfriend out of mind, although the subject had never been addressed in my counselling. I had abandoned those of my friends who were not interested in Scientology, because my lifestyle had changed so much, and I had made new friends—all of them Scientologists.

I had a powerful feeling of comradeship for the Mission staff, and wanted to become one of their number. I knew that they took only a day off each week, and worked all the weekday evenings too. From their comments it was obvious that the pay was very low. Even so, I wanted to work with them. I was told that I would have to "petition" the Guardian's Office of the Church to obtain permission to join the Mission staff and that I would also have to become more highly qualified in Scientology.

In order to qualify for staff, I would have to do Auditor training courses which were only available at a "Church of Scientology," or "Org" (for "Organization"). The nearest was in Manchester, and was in a partially condemned building in the Chinese district. Some of the walls had just been painted purple to try and brighten up the remarkably dingy premises. There was only one student there. The "Registrar" was too insistent, even belligerent. He seemed to take an immediate dislike to me. I decided to go to Saint Hill instead.

CHAPTER TWO

Saint Hill

My purpose is to bring a barbarism out of the mud it thinks conceived it and to form, here on Earth, a civilization based on human understanding, not violence.

That's a big purpose. A broad field. A star-high goal.

But I think it's your purpose, too.—L. RON HUBBARD, *Scientology 0–8*

Ron Hubbard bought Saint Hill Manor from the Maharajah of Jaipur in 1959. The Manor is on the edge of the hamlet of Saint Hill, a few miles from the small Sussex town of East Grinstead, 30 miles south of London. For eight years Saint Hill was the axis of the Scientology world, and many of Hubbard's research "breakthroughs" were made there. Following Hubbard's departure in 1967, Saint Hill remained a major Scientology center. I visited Saint Hill in August, 1975, to see whether to commit myself to six months of study there.

Saint Hill Manor, a large gray-stone building set in about 50 acres, was built by a retired soldier in the early eighteenth century. The house has a solid military severity, largely devoid of Georgian charm. By the time I arrived, students no longer studied in the Manor, but in the "castle," a peculiar folly on which construction had started in the mid-1960s and which was eventually finished in 1985. The word "castle" conjures images of an imposing Norman fortress, but Saint Hill "castle" is only a castle in the sense that it is faced with yellow stone and has a few turrets. As castles go, it is very small, especially considering the score of years invested in its construction. By 1975, only one single-story wing was finished. The castle is a monstrosity; a hybrid of breeze-blocks, leaded windows and battlements under a flat, tarmac roof. However, I was not interested in Hubbard's architectural taste.

The place buzzed with smiling people, many in pseudo-naval uniforms. Although I had encountered "Sea Org" members before, it was strange seeing them en masse. At Saint Hill they wore colored lanyards and campaign ribbons on their navy blue blazers. A religion run by sailors? I pushed the thought aside.

An attractive brunette whisked me around, carefully avoiding the Manor, which housed the mysterious "Guardian's Office." Between the Manor and the castle there was an encampment of huts occupied by busy Sea Org members. The expensive canteen was also housed in a corrugated hut, as were the book-store and several of the administrative offices. The "castle" housed the course-rooms and the public parts of the Organization. My tour ended in the office of the "Registrars" (the sales staff), where I was treated as royalty. I handed over what seemed to me a fortune (some £400), borrowed only after repeated assurances that I would make money easily after taking the Auditor training courses.

Despite my insistence that I was only visiting, I was ushered into a course-room. Scientology has a tremendous sense of urgency, which took hold of me. I read the "Basic Study Manual" until the evening session ended. I was then told that a Sea Org member wanted to see me. I was surprised as it was eleven o'clock, and I had to find my lodgings. The Sea Org member was a recruiter, who, for the next two hours, tried to persuade me to join that group.

In 1967, Hubbard had put to sea with a group of devoted followers, who became the "Sea Organization." I was shown photos of Hubbard dressed up as the "Commodore." Sea Org Members signed a *billion-year* contract, swearing to return life after life to fulfill "Ron's purpose." They also staffed the four "Advanced Organizations," where the secret upper levels of Scientology were delivered. Saint Hill was one of the four. I had heard much of this before and had already been tempted to join the Sea Org and work at the Publications Organization in Denmark. I saw the Sea Org as the monastic order of Scientology, something like the Knights Templar, perhaps. I felt guilty, because I was not ready to renounce everything for the good of the cause. I doggedly insisted that I wanted to train as an "Auditor," and "go Clear" before deciding whether to join the Sea Org. I was going to be a full-time student, and felt that as a trained Auditor I would be far more useful to the Sea Org.

Eventually the recruiter showed me a "confidential" Sea Org issue, which claimed that the governments of the world were on the verge of collapse. The Sea Org would survive and pick up the pieces. Her attempt to stir up a sense of impending doom failed miserably. I wanted no part of it. Hubbard had said elsewhere that Scientology was non-political. I was interested in Scientology as a therapy, nothing more. As a therapy I felt it might have a world-changing impact.

Completely exasperated, the recruiter retreated into the argument that anyone who did not join the Sea Org was insane. I was flustered, not understanding that I was her last chance to reach her weekly quota of recruits. Moreover, I did not know that her pay, her self-esteem and the esteem of her fellow staff members all depended upon increasing her quota each week.

The Sea Org was a bemusing aspect of Scientology. It was difficult to reconcile the military appearance of its members with religion or psychotherapy. However, I was convinced that Scientology was a valid and potent therapy, so I accepted the existence of the Sea Org.

I moved to East Grinstead in September 1975, living with my new girlfriend in a rented room. All three bedrooms of the small house were occupied, as was one of the two downstairs rooms. There were eight of us living there, including a baby. The couple who ran the house rented it from another Scientologist. They were both Sea Org members who were "living out," away from the house run by the Scientology Church. They worked incredibly long hours (the husband from eight in the morning to midnight Sunday to Friday, as well as Saturday afternoons). They were American, although the 1968 use of the Aliens Act prohibited non-UK residents from studying or working for Scientology in Great Britain. They bought their clothes from rummage sales, as do most Sea Org members in Britain. They always looked gray and exhausted. Somehow they managed to support their baby, though seeing little of him. In spite of it all, they were usually cheerful.

The husband was supposedly a Clear, and had done three levels *beyond* Clear. He often hinted at his psychic abilities, but excused himself from any demonstration, in case it "overwhelmed" me. He claimed to be able to back the right horse, which is how he spent his only free morning. Nonetheless, he continued to live below the poverty line.

I went to Saint Hill daily and applied myself to my studies. Scientology courses are run in a similar way to correspondence courses. The student is given a "checksheet," which has the written materials, Hubbard tapes, and practical work listed in strict sequence on it. The student signs off each completed step. I sailed through the Basic Study Manual, and went onto the Hubbard Standard Dianetics Course.

On the Dianetics Course I learned how to use the "Hubbard Electropsychometer," or "E-meter," which shows changes in a person's electrical resistance through movements of a needle on a dial. The person receiving counselling holds two electrodes (in fact, empty soup cans) and the E-meter is supposed to show changing states of mind, or the "movement of mental mass." A "fall" or "read" (rightward needle movement) shows that a subject is "charged." A "floating needle" is "a rhythmic sweep of the dial at a slow, even pace." This supposedly happens when there is no emotional "charge," or after any "charge" has been released. So areas of upset are found with the "fall" of the needle, and their resolution is shown by a "floating needle."[1]

The E-meter is used in most auditing. Lists of questions are checked for responses. A "floating needle" is one of the indications that an auditing "process" or procedure is complete.

I had been given my "Original Assessment" at Birmingham. Dianetic auditing is supposed to dig out buried memories, so it seemed reasonable that the first step should be an E-metered questionnaire about my background. This included questions about my relationships with everyone in my family; anyone I knew who was antagonistic to Scientology; my education; and a complete alcohol and drug history (including all medicines), listing every occasion of use. My Auditor asked for precise information about emotional losses, accidents, illnesses, operations, my present physical condition, whether I had any family history of insanity, any compulsions and repressions I felt I was suffering from, whether I had a criminal record, and if so the details, and my involvement with "former practices," which in my case included Zen meditation.[2]

This "Original Assessment" is the beginning of the "Preclear folder," which contains notes taken during auditing sessions. Auditors keep a running record of the Preclear's more significant comments during each session.

At that time, Dianetic auditing first addressed the psychological effect of drugs. This procedure was called the Dianetic Drug Rundown, and it followed a very exact pattern, which has changed little to this day. The Auditor reads out the list of drugs given by the Preclear, looking for the most marked E-meter reaction. He then asks for attitudes associated with taking that drug. If an attitude given by the Preclear "reads" on the E-meter, the Auditor sets about "running" Dianetics on it.[3]

Having asked the Preclear to locate an incident of the given attitude, the Auditor directs the Preclear to "move to the beginning of the incident," and then go through it. When the E-meter shows that enough "charge" has been released from the incident, the Preclear is directed to find an "earlier similar incident." In theory the Preclear will at first give conscious moments of this attitude (called "Locks"). Then he will usually run into an Engram. The Auditor asks for earlier and earlier incidents, and the Preclear almost invariably goes into "past lives." When the earliest Engram is found and relieved, the Preclear is supposed to have a realization ("cognition") about its effect upon him, "Very Good Indicators" (VGIs), which is to say a grin, and a "floating needle." From then on, the Preclear should be free from the effects of the Engram chain.

The whole drug list is treated painstakingly in this way. Going through every attitude, emotion, sensation and pain associated with each drug. Then the drug list is checked on the E-meter until nothing on it "reads" any more. I remember Victory-V cough sweets being a persistent "item" on my drug list. I spent hours trying to think of some attitude, emotion, sensation or pain associated with Victory-Vs.

I was disappointed with my Dianetic auditing, because I did not experience any real change. My back-ache and my near-sightedness remained. A few times, inexplicably powerful images of what seemed to be "past lives" rushed into mind. At one point, I had the very vivid sensation of being burned at the stake. But for the most part I could not quite believe it. Not because I doubted Dianetics, but because I felt that I was not yet capable of fully contacting my past.

After the Dianetics Course, I did several Scientology Auditor courses. As well as receiving Dianetic auditing, the Preclear was meant to go through eight "Release Grades" before doing the "Clearing Course," and then the mysterious "Operating Thetan" levels. As a Scientology Auditor, I learned how to audit the first three of these "Release Grades." These were meant to deal with memory, communication and problems.

During this time, I had my first brush with Saint Hill "Ethics." The "Ethics Officer" would try to resolve disputes, and to remove any obstacles to a resolute practice of Scientology. I had arrived at Saint Hill with the remainder of a small court fine to pay. The papers had been transferred to one office and I had been told to deal with another, so I received a summons for non-payment.

The morning I received the summons I went to the Saint Hill "Ethics Officer," an intense, overweight Australian, who wore knee-length boots with her dishevelled Sea Org uniform. I requested a morning off to attend the court-hearing. She insisted I tell her all the details. I explained that the remainder of the fine was less than £40, and that it was all due to an administrative mix-up. I was amazed when she told me that she was removing me from the course because I was a "criminal." She insisted that even if a fine were the result of a parking ticket, the offender would be barred from Scientology courses until it was paid.

Saint Hill was very different from the Birmingham Mission where there was an easy-going attitude. The Ethics Officer there would apologise for having to "apply Policy." At Saint Hill, the Ethics Officers were daunting, overworked and unsmiling. Saint Hill Registrars (salesmen or, more usually, saleswomen) were a little too sugary, and it was obvious that they wanted money. The constant and unavoidable discussions with Sea Org recruiters at Saint Hill were wearing. Virtually everyone there was too busy trying to save the world to create any genuine friendships.

The advantages of "going Clear" still loomed large for me. I did not think of leaving Scientology, just going back to the friendlier atmosphere of Birmingham—which I finally decided to do. My decision was accelerated by continuing price rises.

In November 1976, the price of Scientology auditing and training began to rocket. Until then auditing had been £6 an hour ("co-auditing" between students was free). My Dianetics Course had cost

£125. Beginning in November 1976, the prices were to go up at the rate of 10 percent a *month*, allegedly to improve staff pay and conditions. I did not object to that goal, but I did object when the prices continued to go up with each new month. The price rises were to continue for the next four years.

CHAPTER THREE

On to OT

In September 1977, I started Art college, and did no more Scientology courses for over two years. I did not question the "workability" of Scientology, but had serious reservations about the increasingly high prices and the incompetence of the organization. I simply could not understand how Hubbard's extensive research into administration had created such a bumbling and autocratic bureaucracy which churned out inane advertising. BUY NOW! was a favorite slogan. Although staff worked themselves to a frazzle, they seemed to achieve very little. Then there were the little Hitlers who used their positions to harass anyone who did not fit neatly into their picture of normality. But I was puzzled rather than embittered.

Like most Scientologists, I presumed that Hubbard was "off the lines," busily involved in "research." The price increases and the failure to attract throngs of new people had to be the fault of the caretaker management. I waited for Hubbard's return to management while my girlfriend and I ran a Scientology group one evening a week from our home.

We heard very little about the July 1977 FBI raids on the Scientology "Guardian's Offices" in Los Angeles and Washington, D.C. I had virtually no contact with the Guardian's Office ("GO"). The GO was supposed to deal with all attacks on Scientology, and to create a good public image. The GO was established so that Scientology Orgs would not be distracted from providing Scientology services. Public Relations and Legal were major functions of the GO. If Scientology was sued, the GO would deal with it. Beyond that the Guardian's Office was meant to create socially useful programs such as Narconon to help addicts get off drugs. The GO also campaigned against electric shock treatment and psychiatric brain surgery, as well as for Freedom of Information in Britain.

There was scant mention of the FBI raids in British newspapers and the GO only commented on the subject when forced to do so by the few reports that did emerge. After nearly two years, top Scientology officials admitted to having taken documents from United States government offices. I was uneasy about this, but was told government agencies had failed to release information which should have been available via the Freedom of Information Act. We were told nine GO staff members were being indicted for "theft of photocopy paper." It was argued that they had the right to the information they had copied, but had made the mistake of using government photocopiers, thereby stealing the paper.

I had not even heard of the raids when the new Executive Director of the Manchester Org came to see me in 1979. He was a veteran Sea Org member who had taken Manchester from the verge of collapse, and turned it into a thriving Organization with 38 staff. He listened to my complaints and reservations about the Church and, to my amazement, agreed with me totally. By sheer force of personality he persuaded me to go back "on course."

In 1978, Hubbard decided that people had been "going Clear" on Dianetic auditing. The Scientology "Clearing Course," given only by the few senior Orgs since 1965, was no longer necessary to achieve the state of "Clear." Hubbard also said that some people had never had a Reactive Mind and were "Natural Clears," supposedly an extremely rare occurrence. The number of Clears leapt from less than 7,000 to over 30,000 in two years. I was told I was a Natural Clear. In fact, as I later learned, in order to be judged a Clear, it was only necessary to reword one of the Scientology dictionary definitions of "Clear" into a personal "realization."

Now I could go almost immediately onto the mysterious "Operating Thetan" (or OT) levels, where I would revive my dormant psychic abilities. All I had to do was earn the money to pay for it, a process which took almost three years.

In November 1979, I learned first-hand how relentlessly Sea Org members work. The Manchester Org was at last moving from its crowded, partially condemned offices into an imposing, five-story building on one of the main streets. I was persuaded to help with its renovation. For four weeks, I worked and slept in the empty building. I would work for twenty-four hours, then sleep for eight. Because I had some experience I became the "Renovations In-Charge." In retrospect, the hours and the conditions were impossible. My workforce consisted largely of tired and inexperienced staff members, who did a twelve hour day before starting work on the building. Fortunately, a few non-staff Scientologist carpenters, a decorator and an electrician volunteered their help. We had to build partitions, completely rewire, put in doors, sand and varnish floors, and decorate the whole place. It was a very large building. Although we were not paid, there was no duress. We did the work willingly. The whole project was undertaken at Scientology's usual breakneck speed. A Sea Org member had been sent to supervise the whole project. He had worked extensively on the building of Saint Hill castle and described various shortcuts taken in its construction. I was horrified, but often had to yield to his use of similar shoddy methods to finish the job on time.

By September 1980, the price of Scientology services had risen far beyond my reach. Auditing, which had been £6 an hour only four years before, was now £100 an hour. The Dianetics Course I bought for £125 had been revised slightly and re-named the "New Era Dianetics" (or NED) Course, and by this time it cost £1,634. Many Scientologists complained bitterly. In October 1980, a new list came out, and the prices had been slashed. The cost of auditing was down to £40 an hour, and the NED Course to £430. These prices still seemed excessive, but at least it was a step in the right direction.

I returned to East Grinstead in May 1982, having handed over about £2,000 for the levels up to OT 3. In March, "OT Eligibility" had been introduced. I had to do a "Confessional" before starting the OT levels, to make sure that I was "ethical." Several "OTs" had apparently given the secret course materials to newspapers in the United States and Holland.

In a Confessional, a list of questions is checked on the E-meter. The questions are supposed to clear away any residual guilt about earlier discreditable activities. Details of a transgression which "reads" on the E-meter are given to the Auditor. If there is no "floating needle," the Auditor asks for "earlier similar" transgressions. This procedure is supposed to bring relief to the Preclear and, especially in "OT Eligibility" Confessionals, to root out any infiltrators or people who might later attack the organization.

I had only three and a half hours of auditing left in my account for "OT Eligibility." I was told I had to buy thirty-seven and a half more auditing hours at an extra cost of about £2,400. I protested and the estimate was reduced to twenty-five hours. I still refused, so, finally, my Confessionals were started. There were a few embarrassing episodes, since my Auditor was a friend's wife. I had received Confessionals at Manchester a short time before and felt the procedure was largely unnecessary. I certainly did not gain anything by it, but I was glad that it took only the three and a half hours I had on account.

At last I was allowed into the "Advanced Organization" (AO), the Holy of Holies, prohibited to all but OTs. The AO course room was rather scruffy, with peg-board partitions and decrepit furniture, but I did not mind. At last I was here, among the gods.

Most of the Operating Thetan levels are "Solo-audited," which requires yet more training. On "Solo part 1" I had already learned how to hold the two tin cans (electrodes) "solo," separated by a piece of plastic, in my left hand, while working the E-meter and keeping session notes with my right. At Saint Hill I did "Solo Part 2": a series of simple auditing procedures which I "solo-audited."

At last I was starting the OT levels! After nearly seven years in Scientology I was going to discover the hidden secrets of *myself*. I would be able to "exteriorize" from my body at will, read minds, change conditions purely through my intention, and so much more. I would perceive the truth directly and at last be free of the need to speculate or to rely on belief. But most of all, I would be able to help others to free themselves.

In the 1970s, the Church of Scientology became cagey about the promised results of the OT levels. Nonetheless, references to the "End Phenomena" of the OT levels were not hard to come by. The purported "End Phenomenon" of OT 1 is: "Extroverts a being and brings about an awareness of himself as a thetan in relation to others and the physical universe."[1]

Section 1 of the OT Course was presented to me in a pink cardboard folder. I was instructed not to read anything but the very next "process." I went back to my lodgings in East Grinstead, carrying the folder in a locked bag, a compulsory precaution with all OT material. Shut away in my auditing room I opened the folder. The first OT1 "process" consisted of walking about counting people until you had a "win" (i.e., felt good). I remember counting somewhere over 600 people before deciding I must have failed to notice the "win." Back at my lodgings, the E-meter seemed to confirm my suspicions.

All of the OT1 processes are similar. I could not understand the secrecy. No one could hurt themselves doing this. But it was a preparation for OT2 and OT3, after all.

The "End Phenomenon" of OT2 is supposed to be the "Rehabilitation of intention; ability to project intention." Even the Course Supervisor admitted that the materials were confusing. OT2 is an extension of the "confidential" Grade 6 and the Clearing Course. Since "Dianetic" and "Natural" Clear, few people had done these courses. I had to cross reference to the earlier materials and watch Hubbard's 20-year-old Clearing Course films. These were very poor quality black and white and were barely audible.

According to Hubbard, when an individual is caught up between two opposed possibilities he becomes confused and incapable of decision or action. Long ago, Thetans (spirits) were trapped, and "Implanted" with contradictory suggestions while being tortured. These contradictions reduced most Thetans to blank apathy. The Implant commands were very simple, and a ready example is provided by Hamlet's famous question, "To be or not to be." As Implant commands the statement would be split into "To be" and "Not to be." Apparently Thetans who have been cowed into inaction in this way are more susceptible to control, more malleable, being next to incapable of making up their minds. Implants are the true foundation of the Reactive Mind.

The OT2 materials consist of tens, perhaps hundreds, of pages of such Implant commands in Hubbard's writing, forming a wad over an inch thick. My heart dropped at the thought of auditing my way through all of this. It would take months.

Using the E-meter as a guide, the "Pre-OT" is supposed to strip away the "charge" of these Implants. He is instructed to focus on particular areas of his body, read off the next Implant command (which might be as simple as the word "create"), to sense the shock that accompanies the Implant command, and sometimes to "spot the light" which shone simultaneously with the shock.

OT2 is actually a continuation of the Clearing Course. Originally both were done ten times through. One of my friends did *600* hours of auditing on OT2 when it was first released in 1966. I was more fortunate. I spent about three days on it and started to feel rotten. I had the suspicion that it was doing precisely nothing. I began to wonder if I was really ready for OT2. Maybe I had skimped OT1? Maybe I wasn't really Clear? I did not question the efficacy of the "Technology" itself.

I made an E-metered statement to the Advanced Org's "Director of Processing," a wizened seventy-year-old Sea Org veteran and was taken into session by an OT Review Auditor. He asked whether I had "over-run" (gone past) the end of the process. The needle obviously floated, as the Auditor told me I had indeed "over-run" OT2. I was never able to pinpoint any tangible benefit from doing OT2, but for the rest of that day I was as pleased as Punch.

At last I was ready for OT3. After "Clear," OT3 is the most significant level to Scientologists. In a 1967 tape announcing the release of OT3 Hubbard had this to say:

> I have probably done something on the order of a century of research in the very few years since 1963, and can advise you now that I have completed any and all of the technology required from wog [non-Scientologist] to OT . . .
>
> The mystery of this universe and this particular area of the universe has been, as far as its track [history] is concerned, completely occluded . . . it is so occluded that if anyone tried to penetrate it, as I am sure many have, they died. The material involved in this sector is so vicious that it is carefully arranged to kill anyone if he discovers the exact truth of it. So, in January and February of this year I became very ill, almost lost this body and somehow or other brought it off, and obtained the material and was able to live through it. I am very sure that I was the first one that ever did live through any attempt to attain that material.

The purported "End Phenomenon" of OT3 is "Return of full self determinism: freedom from overwhelm." Before being allowed onto the OT3 Course I had to sign a waiver, to the effect that any damage incurred during the auditing was my own responsibility. The mystique was being poured on with a ladle and I loved every moment of it.

In the Advanced Org course room I signed out the OT3 folders. Behind a thin partition at the back of the course room I opened the dog-eared, pink cardboard folder. A few pages in I came to a photocopy of the handwritten instructions for OT3.

The story was fragmented, little more than a series of notes. Hubbard asserted that some 70 million years ago, our planet, then called Teegeeack, had been one of the 76 planets of the Galactic Confederation. The Confederation was badly overpopulated, with hundreds of billions on each planet. Xenu (also called "Xemu" by Hubbard), the president of the Confederation, ruled that the excess population should be sent to Teegeeack, put alongside volcanoes and subjected to nuclear explosions. The spirits, or Thetans, of the victims were then "implanted" with religious and technological images for 36 days. They were then sent to either Hawaii or Las Palmas to be stuck together into clusters. Human beings, so Hubbard said, are actually a collection of Thetans, a cluster of "Body Thetans." Xenu was rounded up six years after the event and imprisoned in a mountain. According to Hubbard, anyone remembering this material would die.

I was reminded of Colin Wilson's novel *The Mind Parasites*, where invisible creatures from outer space attach themselves to human beings and feed off their emotions. Not that I disbelieved any of it. In seven years, I had come to trust Hubbard implicitly.

The proof would come in the auditing, but I felt a tremendous sense of relief. Here at last was the remedy for my problems! My body was inhabited by a mass of "Body Thetans" which had formed into "Clusters" and were influencing my thoughts, my feelings, my behavior. This at last explained why, although I was Clear, I still felt depressed occasionally, lost my temper sometimes, and did not have a perfect memory. It explained my back-ache and my near-sightedness. Body Thetans!

OT3 also addressed an earlier incident of some four *quadrillion* years ago. This was an implant which was supposedly the gateway to our universe. The unsuspecting Thetan was subjected to a short, high-volume crack, followed by a flood of luminescence, and then saw a chariot followed by a trumpeting cherub. After a loud set of cracks, the Thetan was overwhelmed by darkness.

Back at my lodgings I carefully locked my auditing room door, unlocked my bag, and placed the OT3 folders on the table. I did not think about the ramifications of what I was doing. I simply wanted to find a Body Thetan. This was done by thinking about parts of the body, and seeing if there was a reaction on the E-meter. Then with "a very narrow attention span" (so as not to upset any other Body Thetans in the vicinity) the Body Thetan would be audited through Incident 2 and then Incident 1, at which point it should unstick and go on its way. If a "Cluster" of Body Thetans (or "BTs") was discovered the incident that made it a Cluster had to be audited, and then the individual BTs that formed it run through the Incidents.

A list of volcanoes was checked to see where the BT had received Incident 2. Although I did not stop to think if this was self-induced schizophrenia, nor to consider the parallels to demon exorcism, I did wonder if I was inventing the whole thing. It suddenly seemed too far-fetched. But the E-meter responded, so I put my doubts aside and got on with it.

Originally Scientologists had taken months, even years, of auditing on OT3, but since the late 1970s the emphasis was on moving on to OT5 quickly. I finished OT3 in a week. Again I felt euphoric. I waited to see whether any new and miraculous powers became evident. I expected to "exteriorize" from my body at any moment. Two days after finishing, I felt awful. I was worried that I had "falsely attested," although the Auditor who checked me out had failed to find any more "Body Thetans." Still, I was worried I might have to go back onto OT3, which would mean paying for the course again. It had cost me £800 earlier that year and by now was considerably more expensive.

I told the Senior Case Supervisor that I was disappointed that I had not achieved anything spectacular on OT3. To my surprise, he con-fided that many people did not. I expected to be sent to Ethics for even daring to make such a suggestion, so I was relieved to hear that most people got what they wanted on the New OT4. This was also known as the "OT Drug Rundown" and was supposed to free one from the cumulative effects of drugs taken in past lives.

At the Senior Case Supervisor's insistence, I borrowed £1,000. On OT3, I had supposedly rid myself of Body Thetans, so I was dismayed to discover that OT4 was also solely a matter of Body Thetans. This time it was Body Thetans that had been Clustered through drug incidents.

The Senior Case Supervisor visited me again. I again expressed reservations about the results I had obtained. Now he said that OT5 did the trick for most people. He had the sort of eccentricity I enjoy and we got on well together. He was living on a diet of nothing but bananas, because he had heard that Hubbard was researching carbohydrate diets. Before Scientology, the Case Supervisor had studied at one of the prestigious Art Colleges, so we had topics of mutual interest. He even asked me to put one of my paintings aside for him. He arrived at midnight one night, with a Scientologist moneylender. I held the £7,000 cheque for several minutes before seeing the insanity of borrowing so much money, especially at over 30 percent per year interest.

A few days later, the Senior CS spent thirteen hours solid with my business partner and I, to convince us to pay for me to have twenty-five hours of OT5. The Supervisor claimed that when I had completed the auditing, our business would flourish and it would be easy for us to pay back what we had borrowed, and to pay for my partner and my wife to do their OT5. My whole life would be transformed and everything I touched would turn to gold. It is no secret that Scientology Registrars take courses to learn hard-sell techniques.

OT5 was called "the living lightning of life itself" in the promotional material. Its "End Phenomenon" was given as "Cause over Life." I borrowed £2,500 and began. When I opened the "indoctrination pack" I was dismayed to find that it too dealt wholly, solely and only with Body Thetans.

I did not do well on OT5. The sessions are very short, often just ten minutes, so twenty-five hours of auditing took weeks to finish. About three days into the auditing, I developed a pain in my shoulder. You are required to report any aches and pains which "turn on" during auditing and I dutifully did so. For the next several days, we concentrated on Body Thetans in my shoulder. To no avail.

While on OT5, I was involved in the most insistent Registrar interview I experienced in Scientology. An ex-Sea Org member was working on a "project" to get people onto OT7 in Florida. She tried to talk me into borrowing about £50,000. I half-heartedly looked into borrowing the money.

I was displeased with the auditing and expressed my reservations to my Auditor. OT5 had been sold to me with the understanding that the results were nothing short of miraculous. I was given a one-hour lecture, the essence of which was that OT5 was simply a preparatory action prior to doing the *real* OT levels. I should not have expected to make any gains. I would have to wait until OT8 and beyond for that. OT8 had not yet been released.

I had used the last of my paid hours, so I quietly "routed out" of Saint Hill. I had not hidden anything from the Org about my attitude and it was considered "unethical" to talk about any personal problem or dissatisfaction with Scientology to anyone but the auditing staff of the Org. So I kept quiet. I had more or less decided that it was my own fault. After all, no one I had met who had done OT5 had complained and their written "success stories" were usually pretty remarkable.

CHAPTER FOUR

The Seeds of Dissent

During 1982, a stream of "Suppressive Person Declares" poured out from Church management.[1] Labelling someone a "Suppressive Person" (SP) is Scientology's ultimate condemnation. According to Hubbard, SPs make up about two and a half percent of the world's population. Unlike other people, SPs are intent upon the destruction of everything good, valuable or useful. In Hubbard's philosophy, association with SPs is the ultimate explanation for all illness and failure. Hubbard also called SPs "merchants of chaos" and "anti-social personalities." They are synonymous with anti-Scientologists, of course. I had been involved in Scientology for eight years, and although occasionally I heard of people being "Declared SP," no-one I knew was among them. In 1983, however, a close friend with whom I was working was Declared. I was summoned to the Ethics Office at Saint Hill, and shown a Scientology Policy Directive which reintroduced the practice of "Disconnection."

Hubbard had introduced the policy of Disconnection in 1965. Once someone was labelled Suppressive, no Scientologist was allowed to communicate with that person in any way. This policy had caused problems with several governments, and in 1968 Hubbard had acquiesced to demands that the policy be cancelled.

Now the policy was back.[2] I was told not to communicate with my friend. I did not have the choice, my friend was still a "good" Scientologist, and insisted that I disconnect.

Losing my friend was not the only cause for concern; monthly price rises were re-introduced in January 1983. At the same time, a newsletter was broadly distributed, which contained extracts from a conference held in October 1982, at the San Francisco Hilton. For the first time we heard of David Miscavige, who seemed to hold a high position in the Sea Org. The newsletter announced the "get-tough attitude of the 'new blood in management.' " It also introduced the "International Finance Dictator."

Inside Scientology, complaints must only be addressed to the relevant section of the Organization, and mentioning dissatisfaction to anyone else is frowned upon. I wrote letters complaining about the ridiculous prices and the Declare of my friend and, by inference, all other recent Declares. After each evasive reply, I wrote to the person on the next rung of the organizational ladder. The curious titles of these Scientology officials say a great deal: the "Special Unit Mission In-Charge," the "International Justice Chief," the "Executive Director International." It took me seven months to climb all the way to the "Standing Order Number One Line."

The Church of Scientology routinely reprinted "Standing Order Number One." It gave the idea that anyone could write to Ron Hubbard, and receive a reply from him. Although I did not believe this, it was nevertheless the last recourse in Scientology. So I wrote to "Ron," fastidiously enclosing my earlier petition to the Executive Director International, and a copy of his reply.

At first I believed that my references to the violations of Hubbard's Policy Letters would suffice, and that the Organization would automatically correct itself. By this time I was not so sure. It was rumored that Scientology had been taken over by young Sea Org members. I thought I was witnessing an overreaction to an internal plot on the part of some of those who had been "Declared." But I was amazed at the genuine fear expressed by some Scientologists I knew, who privately said it was pointless to complain.

In September 1983, I visited a friend who had been in Scientology for 20 years. She showed me a letter from David Mayo that had just been broadly circulated among Scientologists. Mayo had been the "Senior Case Supervisor International," and Hubbard's heir apparent. Mayo had been declared "Suppressive" earlier that year. With the reintroduction of Disconnection, Scientologists were not supposed to read his letter. Even so, many did.

Mayo described his background in Scientology from his first involvement in 1957. He had been a staff-member from that time, joining the Sea Org in 1968, shortly after its inception. He had been trained by Hubbard personally, and was one of a handful of top-grade "Class 12" Auditors. From the early 1970s Mayo had supervised Hubbard's own auditing. He had worked with Hubbard on OT 5, 6 and 7 (NOTs and Solo NOTs) and was Hubbard's Auditor in 1978. He was one of the very few people privy to the many as yet unreleased OT levels.

Mayo claimed that Hubbard had appointed him his successor in a "long and detailed letter" in April 1982. Hubbard had said he was going to "drop the body" (his expression for dying). Mayo would be responsible for the "Technology" of Scientology until Hubbard's next incarnation.

Mayo wrote that a group of young Sea Org members had cut his line to Hubbard, who was in seclusion by this time, and that "after all my efforts to rectify matters internally, I left in February 1983." He had started an independent Scientology group called the "Advanced Ability Center" in Santa Barbara, California.

Mayo's letter had a tremendous impact on me. My complaints to the management were getting nowhere, so I decided to have a straight talk with a Sea Org member I knew well, who had just returned from Scientology's Florida headquarters. He enthused about his experiences there and assured me that Scientology management was in better shape than ever before. He had worked briefly in the Ethics Office at the Florida "Flag Land Base" and, to my surprise, said that resignations from the Church were pouring in. He said this in an attempt to reassure me that the Church was aware of the situation. I was far from reassured. I had only heard of one resignation, an Australian, John Mace, who lived in East Grinstead. Pouring in?

How could David Mayo, who had worked so closely with Hubbard for so many years, suddenly turn out to be "Suppressive"? Surely, Hubbard should be pretty good at spotting Suppressives. Why had it taken him twenty years to spot Mayo?

I asked my Sea Org friend to tell me who was actually running Scientology, having heard about a mysterious group called the "Watchdog Committee" for some time. He said they ran the Church, but although he was a long-term Sea Org member, he had no idea who was on the Watchdog Committee. Worse yet, he did not care. I grew heated and said I was not willing to be ordered to Disconnect from friends, least of all by these anonymous people. I wanted to know who they were. I told him that I would write to my "Declared" friend if the reply I received from "Ron" was unsatisfactory. I had followed "Policy" to the letter and my genuine grievances were being ignored. I was unwilling to lose a close friend because of the whims of bureaucrats.

The following day I received my reply from "Ron." It was as evasive as the earlier replies. I was completely dismayed. Again my request had been ignored. It did not matter that Hubbard's published Policy was being flaunted. I could do nothing more inside the Church: the "highest authority" had denied my request. The next day I wrote to my Declared friend, who had been a senior Church executive, and expressed my lack of confidence in the new management. I asked him what was really going on.

A few days later I received a copy of a Church "Executive Directive" called "The Story of a Squirrel: David Mayo." "Squirrel" is one of the most disparaging terms in the Scientology vocabulary. It means someone who alters Scientology in some way, the most heinous of crimes. Squirrels are profiteers who pervert Scientology because of their inability to correctly apply it.

"The Story of a Squirrel" was written by Mayo's replacement, the new Senior Case Supervisor International, Ray Mithoff. It was full of fatuous statements, many of which were attributed to Hubbard:

> Mayo was simply a bird-dog. The definition of a bird-dog is: "Somebody sent in by an enemy to mess things up." (LRH) [sic] . . . The actual situation is that you had a bird dog right in the middle of the control room: David Mayo. He was sabotaging execs [executives] by wrecking their cases [destroying their psychological well-being]. None of this was by accident or incompetence. Of all the crazy, cockeyed sabotage I've ever seen, man, he was at it. He was not doing Dianetics and Scientology. He was just calling it that and using the patter. His obvious intention was to wreck all cases of persons who could help others.

What shocked me most was the carping tone of the issue. It seemed to be the product of a deranged mind. It gave me the distinct idea that the faceless "Watchdog Committee" was a self-interested power group, intent upon destroying the Church, and all that I thought the Church stood for.

I was suffering from a severe bout of influenza and went to Saint Hill for a counselling "assist." Instead, I was interrogated about my, at that time non-existent, connections with people who had resigned from the Church of Scientology, most especially John Mace.

The following afternoon I was summoned back to Saint Hill. Having denied all of the supposed connections, and bearing in mind my physical condition, I expected to receive counselling. To my surprise, I was subjected to an Ethics interview. I sat there for over an hour, with a raging temperature, trying to keep my distance so that no-one would catch the virus, and besieged by a series of half-smiling, half-menacing justifications of the excesses of Scientology management. All the Ethics Officer unwittingly persuaded me to do was to ignore the taboo, and ask questions of those who might know: the "Suppressives."

The next day I phoned John Mace. The Church was clearly frightened of him and its insistent criticism determined me to hear his story. Mace said I would probably be "Declared" for seeing him. I did not care, I wanted to know the truth and to assert my right to communicate with whomsoever I chose. Mace probably thought I was a Church agent. He said later that several copies of tapes had disappeared during visits from people ostensibly upset with the Church. The tapes were by various Declared Scientologists and described events leading up to an alleged take-over by Miscavige and his cronies.

I listened to tapes and read newsletters and resignations that had been passing from hand to hand in the Scientology world. The message was clear. The Church had been taken over. Hubbard was dead or incapacitated. The new rulers were fanatics intent on completely taking over all power within the Church. To do this they had "Declared" hundreds of people suppressive.

When John Mace left for Australia a few weeks later, I found myself at the center of the burgeoning English Independent Scientology movement. I helped to establish the first Independent group to deliver auditing, but mostly concentrated on finding out what had caused the schism and on persuading people either to make their complaints against the Church thoroughly known, or to leave and help to create an Independent movement.

People I had known for years suddenly stopped talking to me. I came under pressure from the Church's new Guardian's Office, redubbed the "Office of Special Affairs." I was followed by Private Investigators, who snapped photos of me in the street. I became the target of a whispering campaign. A Scientologist who once worked for me called my friends and acquaintances and told them lies about me; for example, claiming that I had undergone electric shock treatment.

For months, I was inundated with calls and visits by frightened and confused Scientologists. I devoted all of my time to helping them escape the clutches and some of the conditioning of the Church. During this time in November 1983, a friend left me 700 pages of material relating to Hubbard and the Church.

In that mass of documents were affidavits by former members of Hubbard's personal staff; affidavits by ex-Guardian's Office staff about their criminal activities while working for the Church; and 100 pages about Hubbard's past, including his college reports, an abstract of his naval record and letters answering enquiries about his supposed achievements. Each and every Hubbard claim about his past seemed to have been false.

One of the affidavits was by Anne Rosenblum, who joined the Sea Org in June, 1973. By the end of 1976, she was in the "Commodore's Messenger Organization." The following spring she was finally assigned to Hubbard's personal retinue at his California hide-out. This is Rosenblum's description of Hubbard (she calls him "LRH"):

> He had long reddish-grayish hair down past his shoulders, rotting teeth, a really fat gut . . . He didn't look anything like his pictures. . . .
>
> The Messengers went everywhere with LRH. We chauffeured him, we followed him around carrying his ashtray and cigarette lighter, and we also lit his cigarettes for him. LRH would explode if he had to light his own cigarette.
>
> I found LRH was very moody, and had a temper like a volcano. He would yell at anybody for something he didn't like, and he seemed mad at one thing or another 50% of the time. He was a fanatic about dust and laundry. The Messengers, at the time I was there, were also doing his laundry. There was hardly a day that he wouldn't scream about how someone used too much soap in the laundry, and his shirts smelled like soap, or how terrible the soap was that someone used (though it was the same soap used the day before), so someone must have changed the soap . . . I was petrified of doing the laundry.
>
> He is also a fanatic about cleanliness. Even after his office had just been dusted top to bottom, he would come in screaming about the dust

and how "you are all trying to kill me!" That was one of his favorite lines—like if dinner didn't taste right—"You are trying to kill me!"

In another affidavit, former Hubbard aide Gerald Armstrong alleged that Hubbard had received millions of dollars from Scientology, despite his public protestations to the contrary.[3]

My idea of Hubbard as a compassionate philosopher-scientist, a man of great honesty and integrity, was shaken to the core. Even so, for several months I retained my belief in the "Technology," or auditing procedures, of Scientology. I started a newsletter called *Reconnection*, which was read by thousands of Scientologists, but my belief was evaporating. I finally realized that I had taken much of this "Science" on trust.

By the summer of 1984, I had drifted away from the "Tech," but was still caught up in the quest for the truth about Hubbard and his organization. What follows is the fruit of that quest.

PART TWO

BEFORE DIANETICS
1911–1949

Appoint Amongst you
Some small few
To tell about me lies
And invent wicked Things
And spread out infamy
Abroad and Within
And to stand before
Our altars
And insult and
Lie and tell
Evil rumors about us all.

—L. RON HUBBARD, *Hymn of Asia*

CHAPTER ONE

Hubbard's Beginnings

To be free, a man must be honest with himself and with his fellows.
—L. RON HUBBARD, "Honest People Have Rights Too"

Novelists often elaborate their own mundane experience into fictional adventures. Hubbard did not confine his creativity to his fictional work. He reconstructed his entire past, exaggerating his background to fashion a hero, a superhero even. Although Hubbard wrote many imaginative stories, his own past became his most elaborate work of fiction.

Hubbard's works are peppered with references to his achievements. He often broke off when lecturing to relate an anecdote about his wartime experience or his Hollywood career. Even before he generated a following he would tell tall stories to anyone who cared to listen. He stretched his tales to the ridiculous, claiming he broke broncos at the age of three and a half, for example. Most Scientologists believe these tales. Few have bothered to compare the anecdotes or the many and varied biographical sketches published by Hubbard's Church, so the many discrepancies pass largely unnoticed. The pattern of Hubbard's reconstructed past is the translation of the actual, sometimes mediocre, sometimes sordid, reality into a stirring tale of heroic deeds.

Even critics of Scientology occasionally swallow part of the myth. Paulette Cooper, in her penetrating exposé of Scientology, assured her readers, quite erroneously, that Hubbard was "severely injured in the war . . . and in fact was in a lifeboat for many days, badly injuring his body and his eyes in the hot Pacific sun.''

But Hubbard's accounts are not the only source of information. By the summer of 1984, the fabric of his heroic career had been badly torn, largely through the work of two men: Michael Shannon and Gerald Armstrong.

In July 1975, on a muggy evening in Portland, Oregon, Michael Shannon stood waiting for a bus. A young man approached him, and asked if he wanted to attend a free lecture. Shannon went along, thinking that at least the lecture room would be air-conditioned (it was not). He listened to a short, plausible talk about ''Affinity, Reality and Communication,'' and after a brief sales pitch signed up for the ''Communication Course.''

Many Scientologists' stories begin this way. Shannon's soon took a different turn. The next day he decided he did not want to do the Communication Course and, after a ''brief but rather heated discussion,'' managed to get his money back. He kept and read the copy of *Dianetics: The Modern Science of Mental Health* which kindled his curiosity, not for Dianetics, but for its originator.

> I started buying books. Lots of books. There was a second hand bookstore a few blocks away and they were cheaper, and I discovered they had books by other writers that were about Scientology—I happened on the hard to find *Scandal of Scientology* by Paulette Cooper. Now I was fascinated, and started collecting everything I could get my eager hands on—magazine articles, newspaper clippings, government files, anything.

By 1979, Shannon had spent $4,000 on his project and had collected ''a mountain of material which included some files that no one else had bothered to get copies of—for example, the log books of the Navy ships that Hubbard had served on, and his father's Navy service file.'' Shannon intended to write an exposé of Hubbard.

After failing to find a publisher, Shannon sent the most significant material to a few concerned individuals and ducked out of sight, fearful of reprisals. Five years later, he was still in hiding and my efforts to contact him failed. The hundred pages Shannon sent out included copies of some of Hubbard's naval and college records, as well as responses to Shannon's many letters inquiring into Hubbard's expeditions and other alleged exploits.

The "Shannon documents" also found their way to Gerald Armstrong. Armstrong had been a dedicated Sea Org member for nearly ten years when he began a "biography project" authorized by Hubbard. Much of the immense archive collected by Armstrong consisted of Hubbard's own papers, not the forgeries that Hubbard claimed had been created by government agencies to discredit Scientology. The archive largely confirmed Shannon's material. Armstrong and Shannon reached the same eventual destination from opposed starting points.

To complete the picture has taken a great deal more research, but the foundations were well laid by Armstrong and Shannon. Let us compare Scientology's changing versions of the life of L. Ron Hubbard with the truth.

There is *some* agreement between all concerned on at least one fact: Lafayette Ronald Hubbard was born in Tilden, Nebraska, on March 13, 1911; despite one of his later claims, it was not *Friday* the 13th.[1]

His Birth Certificate also shows that Ron was born in Dr. Campbell's Hospital on Oak Street with S.A. Campbell "in attendance."

His mother, Ledora May Hubbard, had returned to the town of her birth to bring her son into the world. His father was Harry Ross Hubbard. Although Ron boasted about his paternal ancestry, the famous Hubbard name, in fact, Harry Hubbard had been an orphan and was born Henry August Wilson. L. Ron had not a drop of Hubbard blood in him.[2]

Ron claimed that he was born the son of a U.S. Navy Commander. Harry Hubbard had served a four year stint in the Navy as an enlisted man until 1908. He re-enlisted when America entered World War I, when his son was six. Harry Hubbard eventually did become a Lieutenant Commander, but not until 1934.

From this point, the Scientology accounts of Hubbard's life are usually at variance with the facts and often at variance with one another. We are told that when Ron was six months old (or three weeks, in another Hubbard account)[3] his family moved to Oklahoma. In fact, the first account is nearly accurate: the Hubbard family spent the Christmas season in Oklahoma, with Ron's maternal grandparents, then moved on to Kalispell, Montana.[4]

Before he was a year old, one Scientology version continues, Hubbard was sent to his maternal grandparents, the Waterburys, because his "father's career kept the family on the move." His grandparents owned an enormous cattle ranch, "one quarter of Montana." Shannon found no record of the Waterbury ranch, because he looked for it in Helena. But Ron's grandfather did briefly own 320 acres (a half-section) west of Kalispell, where he pastured horses.[5] Montana amounts to 94 million acres.

Ron supposedly learned to ride before he could walk and was breaking "broncos" at the age of three and a half, at which age he could also read and write. He became a bloodbrother of the Blackfoot Indians in 1915 (aged four at most) and remained with his grand-parents, the Waterburys, until he was ten.

Hubbard described his early years thus: "Until I was ten, I lived the hard life of the West, in a land of 40-degree-below blizzards and vast spaces."

The City Directories published in many U.S. towns listed the inhab-itants, their jobs, addresses, and the value of their taxable assets. In the 1913 Kalispell Directory, Lafayette Waterbury was assessed at $1,550. He was comfortable, but by no means rich.

In truth, when Ron's grandfather moved to Kalispell and bought his half-section, he continued to earn his living as a veterinarian. By 1917, he was living in Helena, running the Capital City Coal Company. Ron's father, Harry, had left his job on a Kalispell newspaper to become manager of the Family Theater in Helena, Montana, in 1913. Between 1913 and 1916 he was working as a book-keeper at the Ives Smith Coal and Cattle Company. The next year, when Ron was six, Harry was working at the same place as a wagon-driver. Harry Hub-bard helped his father-in-law set up the Capital City Coal Company before re-enlisting in the U.S. Navy on October 10, 1917, where he remained until his retirement in 1946. Ron's mother did clerical work for government agencies.

There is actually no way of checking whether Ron, or anyone else, became a "bloodbrother" of the Blackfeet in 1915. There are no records. It seems unlikely, as the Piegan reservation was over sixty miles from the Waterbury half-section, and over 100 from Helena, where Ron was living with his parents in 1915. A Scientologist eighth-blood Blackfoot, having failed to find any record, recently admitted Hubbard without the Blackfoot nation's approval. In the 1930s Hubbard admitted that what he knew of the Blackfeet came second hand from someone who really had been a bloodbrother.

Hubbard was certainly an enthralling story-teller. He once told an audience that when he was six, his neighborhood was terrorized by a twelve-year-old bully called Leon Brown, and by "the five O'Connell kids," aged from seven to fifteen. Ron learned "lumberjack fighting" from his grandfather, and took on the two youngest O'Connell kids one after the other. The O'Connell kids "fled each time I showed up . . . Then one day I got up on a nine foot high board fence and waited until the twelve-year-old bully passed by and leaped off on him boots and all and after the dust settled that neighborhood was safe for every kid in it."[6]

Shannon located school registration cards for five Helena boys called O'Connell. When Ron was six, the oldest O'Connell boy was sixteen, and the youngest five. Shannon did not find Leon Brown, but he did exist, living a few doors away from Ron, and he was twelve in 1917. Ron Hubbard must have been a very tough six-year-old!

Ron's grandfather's coal company in Helena had failed by 1925, and the Helena City Directory listed him as the owner of an automobile spare parts business. By 1929, Waterbury had returned to veterinary work. He died two years later, still at 736 Fifth Avenue, Helena. His obituary made no mention of his having been a rancher.

Ron Hubbard claimed he had been raised by his maternal grandparents. In fact, he was with both of his parents until his father rejoined the Navy, in 1917. Even then his mother stayed put with her family until 1923, when she joined her husband, taking Ron with her. Ron was part of a tolerant and joyful family community.

The young Hubbard probably spent a few weeks on his grandfather's small stud farm. To a three-year-old boy those 320 acres near Kalispell probably seemed like a quarter of Montana. He undoubtably met cowboys, and perhaps even Blackfoot Indians (possibly on the rail journey from Helena to Kalispell). There is nothing wrong with any of this, except, from Hubbard's point of view, the scale. It was all far too small. To be revered as the most amazing man who had ever drawn breath, Hubbard would have to do far better.

Hubbard claimed that his interest in the human mind was sparked by a meeting with one Commander Thompson when Hubbard was twelve. According to Hubbard, they met during a trip through the Panama Canal en route to Washington, DC. Thompson was a Navy doctor, with an abiding interest in psychoanalysis, supposedly "a personal student of Sigmund Freud." From Thompson, Hubbard "received an extensive education in the field of the human mind." In a 1953 publication Hubbard claimed that his "research" began when he met Thompson.[7] The claim has the romantic ring of Hubbard's pulp fiction.

Commander "Snake" or "Crazy" Thompson (as Hubbard called him) is something of an enigma. Neither Shannon nor Armstrong discovered anything about him. During the Armstrong case in 1984, Scientology Archivist Vaughn Young at least proved "Snake" Thompson's existence. Young had spoken to Thompson's daughter, who attested her father's love of snakes. A library catalogue listing several papers by Thompson on the subjects both of snakes and the human mind, and a postcard from Freud to Thompson were produced. His death certificate showed that he had indeed been a Commander in the U.S. Navy.

For Scientology Archivist Young, an educated man with a master's degree in Philosophy, Thompson's existence, evidence of his nickname, and a postcard were sufficient proof of Hubbard's claims to have been tutored in the Freudian mysteries by this Navy doctor, at the age of twelve. Hubbard's extensive teenage diaries make no mention of either Thompson or Freud. Nor do they contain any material which supports the idea that the juvenile Hubbard was "researching" the human mind.

Scientologists claim Ron became the youngest Eagle Scout in America at the age of twelve, in Washington, DC, and that he was a "close friend of President Coolidge's son, Calvin Jr., whose early death accelerated L. Ron Hubbard's precocious interest in the mind and spirit of Man."

In a diary, written when he was about nineteen, Hubbard recalled his acquisition of the Boy Scout Eagle. A photograph taken at the time shows Hubbard in uniform, all freckles and acne, with the twenty-one necessary merit badges stitched on to a sash. There is no way of knowing whether he was the *youngest* Eagle Scout in America. The Boy Scouts place no value on the age at which a boy becomes an Eagle Scout, and have never kept a record, nor was there any way that Hubbard could find out. But the Boy Scouts do have a record of a Ronald Hubbard who became an Eagle Scout in Washington DC, and was a member of Troop 10. The Eagle was actually awarded on March 28, 1924, some two weeks after L. Ron Hubbard's thirteenth birthday.

In the same diary, Hubbard recollected a meeting with President Coolidge. He was one of some forty boys. The meeting consisted of Hubbard telling his name to the President and a handshake. Rank Pathe took newsreel film of the boys.[8] Out of this meeting blossomed the supposed close relationship with Coolidge's son, Cal Jr., whose early death was to spur Hubbard's "research." The relationship existed only in Hubbard's mind, which is confirmed by comparing Cal Jr.'s movements to Hubbard's. Moreover, there is no mention of Cal Jr. in Ron's teenage diaries. In March 1924, a few days after Ron shook the President's hand, the Hubbard family left Washington, DC., moving across the country to the state of Washington.

CHAPTER TWO

Hubbard in the East

As a still very young man, with the financial support of his wealthy grandfather, L. Ron Hubbard traveled throughout Asia. He studied with holy men in India and Northern China, learning at first hand the inherited knowledge of the East.—L. RON HUBBARD, *Hymn of Asia*

Hubbard added to his mystique by making believe that he had spent his teens communing with the great masters of Asia. Some part of Hubbard's authority rests on his alleged journeys in China, India and Tibet, because Scientology is supposedly a reformulation of the mystic truths he learned there. By applying the rigorous discipline of Western scientific method to the secrets of Eastern mysticism, Hubbard later claimed to have isolated the laws of life itself.

Quite typically, Scientology accounts of Hubbard's sojourn in the East are packed with contradictions. In one we are told his father was sent to Asia in 1925, and that Ron travelled extensively between 1925 and 1929. Hubbard allegedly spent a considerable period of time in the western hills of Manchuria, and while in China visited many Buddhist monasteries.

In his book *Mission into Time*, Hubbard claimed he had studied with Holy men in Northern China and India. In *What Is Scientology?* Hubbard's life is depicted in a series of amateurish paintings, amongst them one of three fur-clad Tibetan bandits, with the caption: "In the isolation of the high hills of Tibet, even native bandits responded to

52

Ron's honest interest in them and were willing to share with him what understanding of life they had.'' We can only speculate how Hubbard incorporated facets of Tibetan bandit ''philosophy'' into his science of the mind and spirit.

If provoked, the Scientologists hand out an article, allegedly from a Helena newspaper (though the paper does not exist in the Helena records). In the article, Hubbard described a ''trip to the Orient'' lasting from April 30, when he left San Francisco, to September 1, when he returned to Helena to stay with his maternal grandparents and attend high school. The year was 1927, not 1925. Scientology accounts say Hubbard returned to the U.S. upon the death of his maternal grandfather, but the clipping the Church provides says he was again living with this same grandfather, who in fact died in 1931. In the article Hubbard said he had visited Guam, the Philippines, Wake Island, Hong Kong and ''Yokohoma.''

In a short autobiography written for *Adventure* magazine in 1935, Hubbard said: ''it was not until I was sixteen [in 1927] that I headed for the China Coast. . . . In Peiping . . . I completely missed the atmosphere of the city, devoting most of my time to a British major who happened to be head of the Intelligence out there. In Shanghai, I am ashamed to admit that I did not tour the city or surrounding country as I should have. I know more about 181 Bubbling Wells Road and its wheels than I do about the history of the town. In Hong Kong—well, why take up space?''

So, we are led to believe that Hubbard travelled extensively in China, Tibet and India between 1925 and 1929, though by his own account he did not leave the U.S. until 1927. He purportedly learned the wisdom of the East, yet was ashamed of his lack of inquisitiveness while there.

Shannon dredged up Ron's school records, from which we learn that Ron spent the school year 1925–1926 at Union High School, Bremerton, Washington, while his father was stationed at nearby Puget Sound. At the start of the school year 1926–1927, Ron enrolled at Queen Anne High School, in Seattle. Harry Hubbard's naval record shows that his first shore duty outside the U.S. began on April 5, 1927, when he was assigned to the U.S. Naval Station on the island of Guam, in the western Pacific. Ron left Queen Anne High School in April 1927.

Hubbard recorded two short visits to China in his teenage diaries. The first in 1927, en route to Guam, and the second the following year.

The 1927 diary describes a round trip to Guam, with summaries of the people and places Hubbard saw. The summaries are brief, as was Hubbard's time in the China ports. The *President Madison*, on which he and his mother sailed, was a transport, not a cruise liner.

The *President Madison* visited Hawaii, where Hubbard watched young men diving for coins. Hubbard was unimpressed with Yokohama, Shanghai and Hong Kong. Any sympathy he felt for the people who lived in the squalor his diary records quickly evaporated, and was displaced by a contempt which permeates all of his descriptions of the natives of the places he visited. The *President Madison* took Ron and his mother to the Philippines, where he complained about the idleness and stupidity of the inhabitants. In Cavite, where they joined the Navy transport USS *Gold Star*, a Lieutenant McCain told Ron that under a derelict cathedral crawling with snakes were tunnels full of gold. Hubbard vowed to his diary that he would return.

Ron and his mother left Cavite on the *Gold Star* for the rough seven day passage to Guam. In his diary, Hubbard gave his analysis of the natives of Guam, the Chamarros. He considered them more intelligent than the inhabitants of the Philippines, but felt they had hardly been touched by civilization. They did not compare favorably with American youngsters. Hubbard's dislike of the Spanish inhabitants of Guam was even more pronounced.

Hubbard had been warned that his red hair would generate considerable interest; as it was he claimed that the Chamarros fell silent at his approach.

Hubbard spent about six weeks on Guam in 1927. On July 16, he left on the USS *Nitro*, leaving his parents behind. The pages covering the journey back to the U.S. preserve his only philosophical speculation of the trip. Hubbard and a young friend were perplexed by a book about atheism, so much so that Hubbard decided he would have to wait until his return home before resolving this difficult issue.

Ron was the first to sight Hawaii. An officer told him to wake the lookout, and Hubbard described his perilous climb to the crow's nest. The *Nitro* docked at Bremerton, Washington, on August 6th, 1927.

According to his later accounts, Hubbard's diary was the product of a sixteen-year-old who had studied Freudian analysis, read most of the world's great classics, and started to isolate the rudiments of a philosophical system some four years earlier. In fact, none of these subjects is even touched on in the diary.

Hubbard was at Helena High School from September 6, 1927 to May 11, 1928. While there he joined the 163rd Infantry unit of the Montana National Guard.

In a notebook written when he was nineteen, Hubbard described the events which led him to leave school and make his second trip to Guam. These accounts show that Hubbard had a fanciful imagination even then.

On May 4, 1928, the inhabitants of Helena celebrated a holiday. Hubbard described the procession of clowns and pirates along Main Street. After the parade, he was driving two friends around in his 1914 Ford, when he was struck on the head by a baseball. Hubbard pulled up and started a fight with his assailant, claiming to have broken four of the bones in his right hand in the process (though later medical records give no indication of this). The fight supposedly took place a few days before school examinations, so Hubbard failed to collect the necessary credits toward graduation. As it was, he had been doing badly, having had to repeat the first semester's geometry and physics.[1]

Hubbard visited his aunt and uncle in Seattle, and from there, in June, revisited the Boy Scouts' Camp Parsons. After a week or two, he grew restless and went off on a lone hike. The first night, he made camp about two miles beyond Shelter Rock. While asleep he fell fifty feet, and when he recovered consciousness found blood gushing from his left wrist.

At the end of June, Hubbard learned that the USS *Henderson* would be leaving for the Philippines on July 1, and on impulse decided to join her. He would return to his parents on Guam. Hubbard raced to San Francisco only to discover that the USS *Henderson* had already left port. He decided to sign on as an ordinary seaman with the *President Pierce*, which was China bound. but at the last minute changed his mind and went chasing after the *Henderson* again. He caught up with her in San Diego.

According to Hubbard's notebook, the *Henderson's* Captain said he would need permission from Washington to join the ship. Time was running out. Washington said Harry Hubbard's consent would be needed. An answer from Guam usually took two days, but Hubbard was in luck. Permission came an hour before the *Henderson* sailed. Meanwhile, Ron's trunk had been lost en route. He did not recover it for a year, but in spite of this, Hubbard thoroughly enjoyed the voyage.

There are two accounts of this trip in the same notebook. Although they are within a few pages of one another, they differ in detail. Ron was already making a habit of elaborating his past, and the accounts teach us to question the veracity of any Hubbard claim. The *Henderson*'s passenger list shows that rather than having been allowed aboard only an hour before, Ron was aboard fully 24 hours before she sailed.

On Guam, the seventeen-year-old Ron was tutored by his mother, a qualified teacher, for what should have been his twelfth or senior high school grade. He was being prepared for the Naval Academy examination.

During this period, Ron made his second trip to China, this time with both parents. China was still in the throes of civil war, and travel there was limited. Hubbard kept a diary of his trip aboard the USS *Gold Star*. The ship docked at Tsingtao on October 24, 1928, and stayed there for six days before putting to sea for Ta-ku. The Hubbards then travelled inland to Peking, where they spent about a week.

In his diary, Hubbard gave a fairly elaborate description of the sights, probably seen on tours given by the Peking YMCA. He was unimpressed by the marvels of Chinese architecture, and the only building which won his vote was the Rockefeller Foundation. Even the Great Wall failed to elicit more than a comment about its possible use as a roller coaster. Two years later, in another notebook entry, hindsight had transformed the visit to the Great Wall into a far more romantic experience, but that was Hubbard's way.

Hubbard's opinion of the Chinese was consistently low. Among many other criticisms, he said the Chinese were both stupid and vicious and would always take the long way round.

While in Peking, Hubbard visited a Buddhist temple. He was later to say that Scientology was the western successor to Buddhism, yet his only comment at the time was that the devotees sounded like frogs croaking.

After Peking came Cheffoo and then Shanghai. Ron made little comment about Shanghai. It was cold, and the native part of the city had only been reopened to foreign nationals two weeks earlier. Then came Hong Kong, again with little comment, and by December 15, the Chinese adventure was over and the *Gold Star* was back at sea.

The deep understanding of Eastern philosophy acquired by Hubbard in China was boiled down to a single statement in one of his diaries. He said that China's problem was the quantity of "chinks." Inscrutable, but hardly a compendium of the great thoughts of the Buddhist, Taoist and Confucian masters.

Hubbard was seventeen and this was his last visit to China. In his diary, he made no reference to any meeting in Peking with "old Mayo, last of a line of magicians of Kublai Khan," mentioned in one of his Scientology books.[2] *David* Mayo would turn up far later in Hubbard's life, as one of the rebels who split Scientology apart in the 1980s. But he is a New Zealander and makes no claims of ties to Kublai Khan.

There is no record of Hubbard's supposed travels in Tibet, the western hills of China or India. A flight change at Calcutta airport in 1959 seems to have been his only direct contact with the land of Vedantic philosophy. Indeed, in one of his early Dianetic lectures he dismissed his teenage journeys, saying "I was in the Orient when I was young. Of course, I was a harum-scarum kid. I wasn't thinking about deep philosophical problems."[3]

By Christmas 1928, Hubbard was back in Guam. He took the Naval Academy entrance examination, failing the mathematics section.[4]

In August 1929, Harry Hubbard and his family returned to the U.S. Harry was posted to Washington, DC, and Ron enrolled at the Swavely Prep School, in Manassas, Virginia, for intensive study to prepare him for the Naval Academy. His mother returned to her parents in Helena.

In December 1929, Hubbard acted in the school play. By this time he had developed eyestrain and his near-sightedness prevented him from qualifying for the Naval Academy.

Hubbard enrolled at the Woodward School for Boys on February 30, 1930, and graduated that June. Woodward was a school run mainly for difficult students and slow learners. At nineteen, Hubbard was a year late in graduating from high school.

At Woodward, Hubbard won an oratory contest. He was always a great talker. The set subject was apt for a man later to be accused of entrapping his followers in a brainwashing cult: "The Constitution: a Guarantee of the Liberty of the Individual."

Hubbard's book *Mission into Time* says he enlisted in the 20th Marine Corps Reserve while a student at George Washington University. Shannon obtained Hubbard's Marine service record which confirms that Hubbard actually joined the Reserve in May of 1930, four months before enrolling at the University. Within two months, he had been promoted to First Sergeant, a leap of six ranks. When Shannon asked the Marine Corps Headquarters they were as baffled as he was by such rapid peacetime promotion. The answer is quite simply that the 20th was actually a Reserve training unit connected to George Washington University. Hubbard later explained his promotion by saying it was a newly formed regiment and his superiors "couldn't find anybody else who could drill."[5]

On October 22, 1931, Hubbard received an honorable discharge from the Marine Reserve. In his service record, there is a handwritten note under the character reference: "Excellent." In another hand beneath this is written, "Not to be re-enlisted." There is no explanation of either statement. Hubbard's discharge followed on the heels of criticism of his poor academic performance.

Differing claims have been made in Scientology literature for Hubbard's achievements at George Washington University. It has been said he attended the first courses in nuclear physics, even that he was "one of America's first Nuclear Physicists."[6] The former is unlikely (it was a little late to be the first such course) and the latter is a downright lie. Even Hubbard's last wife, Mary Sue, has admitted that her husband was not a nuclear physicist, though she made the preposterous statement that he had never claimed to be.[7] The claim was excused as a mistake made by over-zealous Scientologists, which remained uncorrected in literature copyrighted to Hubbard for 30 years. In fact, Hubbard made that very claim in a Bulletin called *The Man Who Invented Scientology*, published in 1959.

Hubbard was not a "nuclear physicist" by any stretch of the imagination. He was a student in the School of Engineering at George Washington University, majoring in Civil Engineering. According to his college records, he was enrolled in a course called Molecular and Atomic Physics in the second semester of the 1931–32 college year, receiving an "F" grade in what was certainly an introductory course. By his own admission, Hubbard was poor at mathematics,[8] and his records support this by showing nothing better than a "D." He was later to demonstrate how superficial his understanding of physics was in a book called *All About Radiation*. Ignoring Hubbard's admission, two Scientology biographical sketches say he graduated not only with an Engineering degree, but also a Mathematics degree.

For some time Scientology publications carried the legend "C.E." (Civil Engineer) after Hubbard's name. In fact, Hubbard failed to graduate. At the end of his first year he was put on probation for his poor academic performance, and at the end of the second asked to leave. In 1935, Hubbard wrote: "I have some very poor grade sheets which show that I studied to be a civil engineer in college.'"⁹ Scientology official Vaughn Young says the idea that "C.E." stands for "Civil Engineer" is mistaken. Apparently the initials represents a certificate awarded in the early days of Scientology. The same logic applies to Hubbard's BSc (Bachelor of Scientology), and his self-awarded "Doctor of Divinity."

Hubbard's inflated claims usually have some slim basis in fact. He was an elaborator, not an originator. His much publicized authority as a scientific and philosophical pioneer was founded on his purportedly long, intimate experience of Eastern mysticism, and his training as an engineer and physicist. Hubbard built his house on the very shaky foundation of a two-week vacation in Peking and a Fail grade in Molecular and Atomic Physics.

Behind the prosaic facts was a clever and articulate boy, who did not manage to keep up with his schoolwork. Far from the legend Hubbard was to create, there is little exceptional about Ron Hubbard's childhood and adolescence. Contrary to his later claims, he was with his mother until he was sixteen. The evidence shows he was part of a loving family. His parents were probably upset by his failure to win a place in the Naval Academy or to qualify as an engineer, especially in the dark times of the Great Depression. Ron later said: "My father . . . decreed that I should study engineering and mathematics and so I found myself obediently studying."

Hubbard was already writing in his teens, struggling to generate fiction. His journals are packed with attempts at pulp stories. Even his diary entries were obviously written for an audience, suggesting that even then Hubbard's distinction between fantasy and reality had blurred.

CHAPTER THREE

Hubbard the Explorer

By his own account, Hubbard led his first "expedition" while in college. In fact, the "Caribbean Motion Picture Expedition" set out after Hubbard's last semester at college. Dates vary in the Scientology accounts, but the "expedition" actually took place in the summer of 1932.

The "expedition" is mentioned frequently, but briefly, in Scientology literature. It allegedly provided the "Hydrographic Office" and the University of Michigan with "invaluable data for the furtherance of their research." Hubbard's Church supports these claims with copies of the George Washington newspaper, *The University Hatchet*, of May 1932, and the *Washington Daily News* of September 13, 1932. As ever, the documents support only the basis of Hubbard's story, and completely undermine his inflated claims.

The University Hatchet article preceded the trip, and was enthusiastic about its possible outcome. The headline reads: "L. Ron Hubbard Heads Movie Cruise Among Old American Piratical Haunts," and the article gives considerable detail about the personnel and the objectives of the "expedition." The equipment was to include a light seaplane. Cameras were to be supplied by the University of Michigan. Among the personnel were to be "botanists, biologists and entomologists."

The article continues: "Buccaneers, however, will have the center of the stage. According to Hubbard, the strongholds and bivouacs of the Spanish Main have lain neglected and forgotten for centuries, and there has never been a concerted attempt to tear apart the jungles to

60

find the castles of Teach, Morgan, Bonnet, Bluebeard, Kidd, Sharp, Ringrose and L'Ollanais, to name a few.''

Apparently Hubbard and crew intended to make ''motion pictures'' for Fox Movietone News: ''Down there where the sun is whipping heat waves from the palms, this crew of gentlemen rovers will re-enact the scenes which struck terror to the hearts of the world only a few hundred years ago—with the difference that this time it will be for the benefit of the fun and the flickering ribbon of celluloid. . . . Scenarios will be written on the spot in accordance with the legends of the particular island, and after a thorough research through the ship's library which is to include many authoritative books on pirates.'' Hubbard had become one of the eight Associate Editors of *The University Hatchet* with this issue, so quite possibly he wrote the piece. The style certainly fits.

The voyage took place aboard a 1,000 ton sailing ship, the *Doris Hamlin*, captained by F.E. Garfield. Fifty students were to take part, and the *Hatchet* article gives an impressive list of proposed ports-of-call.

However, the ''expedition'' failed to realize its promise. On his return to the U.S., Hubbard wrote an article for the *Washington Daily News*:

> On June 23, 1932, the chartered fourmaster schooner *Doris Hamlin* sailed from Baltimore for the West Indies with fifty-six men aboard. Exclusive of six old sea dogs the crew consisted of young men between the ages of twenty and thirty who thirsted for adventure and the high seas. A movie camera, scientific apparatus and a radio completed the Caribbean Motion Picture Expedition. . . .
>
> Just twelve hours before the *Doris Hamlin* slipped her whips, ten men cancelled their passage and left us in a delicate financial situation. . . . Our first port of call was Bermuda. The captain was ordered to stand off the island while we landed for mail, but leaky water tanks gave him an excuse to put into the harbor.
>
> Towage, pilotage, and expensive water again depleted the treasury. Two days at sea the water again leaked out and left us with the same amount we had before entering Bermuda. Due to the prevailing direction of the trade winds, it was necessary that we go to Martinique that we might make the more important ports in our itinerary. At Fort de France, Martinique, we put in for mail and supplies.
>
> I refused to turn money over to the captain. Immediately, the crew demanded their wages. I wired home for more money, but before it could arrive the captain told me he had received money from the owners

and that the ship was going back home. I fought the situation as well as I could but the consul at Fort de France allowed a protest to be filed and my hands were tied.

In Bermuda eleven men had become disgusted with the somewhat turbulent seas and had obtained discharges that they might return home. We had fired our cook there . . . and had hired two men from Bermuda. In Martinique we lost several other men who had become disgusted with the situation. When we left Martinique, the whole aspect of the trip had changed. Morale was down to zero.

The *Doris Hamlin* called at Ponce, Puerto Rico, then, on the insistence of its owners, returned to Baltimore. No mention was made of any underwater filming, despite the Scientologists' claim that films made provided the Hydrographic Office and the University of Michigan with "invaluable data." The University of Michigan told Shannon they had no film, and knew nothing of the expedition. Nor is there any mention of the buccaneer film, which was to have been the core of the "expedition." The seaplane, mentioned in the article written before the trip began, has also disappeared in Hubbard's account. The *Doris Hamlin* failed to reach all but three of its sixteen proposed destinations.

A few years later, Hubbard wrote of the "Caribbean Motion Picture Expedition": "It was a crazy idea at best, and I knew it, but I went ahead anyway, chartered a four-masted schooner and embarked with some fifty luckless souls who haven't stopped their cursings yet."[1]

The Captain of the *Doris Hamlin*, who had thirty years of seagoing experience, summed up by saying that it had been "the worst trip I ever made." In an interview published in 1950, Hubbard was quoted as saying "it was a two-bit expedition and a financial bust."[2]

Undeterred, Hubbard undertook his next "expedition" at the end of 1932. In his *Mission into Time* we read: "Then in 1932, the true mark of an *exceptional* explorer was demonstrated. In that year L. Ron Hubbard, aged twenty-one, achieved an ambitious 'first.' Conducting the West Indies Minerals Survey, he made the first complete mineralogical survey of Puerto Rico. This was pioneer exploration in the great tradition, opening up a predictable, accurate body of data for the benefit of others. Later, in other, less materialistic fields, this was to be his way many, many times over."

The Scientologists supply a survey report for manganese, dated January 20, 1933, and signed "L. Ron Hubbard." There is also a letter dated February 16, 1933, headed "West Indies Minerals, Washington, D.C." The letter's author says he was accompanied on a survey by L. Ron Hubbard. Attached to the letter is a crude map entitled "La Plata Mine Assays," and signed with the "LRH" monogram familiar to Scientologists.

As ever, Shannon explored more deeply. He found that a *Bela* Hubbard had made a survey of the Lares district of Puerto Rico in 1923, but the Puerto Rican Department of Natural Resources, the U.S. Geological Survey, and a professor at the University of Puerto Rico, who had prepared the *Geology of Puerto Rico* in 1932–1933, had no knowledge of L. Ron Hubbard.

Armstrong says Hubbard had gone to Puerto Rico to prospect for gold.[3] This is supported by a photograph in Hubbard's *Mission into Time*, with the caption, in his hand, "Sluicing with crews on Corozal River '32." It is possible that Ron fled to Puerto Rico to avoid the legal claims brought against him by members of his Caribbean "expedition."[4]

Long before Scientology, Hubbard told stories about an expedition to South America. Frank Gruber, who knew him in 1934, said Hubbard told him about a four-year expedition to the Amazon. After the War, Hubbard told a fellow writer he had been wounded by native arrows on this supposed expedition.[5] By the time Dianetics came along, this tall story had faded away, to be replaced with others. There is one Scientology biographical sketch which makes a fleeting mention of an "expedition" to *Central* America, made immediately on his departure from college.

Hubbard also claimed to have been a barnstorming pilot (nicknamed "Flash"). Shannon found that for two years Hubbard had a license for gliders, but non for powered aircraft. The barnstorming career seems to have been another student vacation, taken in the summer of 1931 with a friend who was an experienced pilot.

The Scientologists, in a 1989 publication called *Ron the Writer*, claim that having left college Hubbard "went straight into the world of fiction writing and before two months were over had established himself in that field at a pay level which, for those times, was astronomical." Apart from a few contributions to *The University Hatchet Literary Review*, Hubbard's only commercially published article while at the University was for the *Sportsman Pilot*. It was called "Tailwind Willies," and was published in January 1932, and it probably earned little or nothing.

During 1932 and 1933, Hubbard contributed five articles to the *Sportsman Pilot*, including one entitled "Music with Your Navigation,'' and one to the *Washington Star Supplement*, called ''Navy Pets.'' That was his entire commercial output during those years; hardly enough to support himself, let alone produce an ''astronomical'' level of pay.

It was not until 1934 that Hubbard's stories were accepted by pulp magazines such as *Thrilling Adventure, The Phantom Detective*, and *Five Novels Monthly*. His later denials of having written pulp wear thin given some of the titles in question: ''Sea Fangs,'' ''The Carnival of Death,'' ''Man-Killers of the Air,'' and ''The Squad that Never Came Back.'' Hubbard later wrote Western Fiction too.

The Church usually makes no mention of Ron's first two marriages. Upon his return from Puerto Rico, Hubbard married Margaret Louise Grubb, in Elkton, Maryland, on April 13, 1933. He called her ''Polly,'' or ''Skipper,'' and she called him ''Redhead.'' The first child, ''Nibs,'' or more properly Lafayette Ronald Hubbard, Jr., was born prematurely in May 1934. In 1936, Polly bore Hubbard a daughter, Catherine May.

Summer 1934 found Hubbard living in a hotel in New York, where he met Frank Gruber, also an aspiring pulp writer. They spent a lot of time together, and in his book, *The Pulp Jungle*, Gruber told this story:

> During one . . . session Ron began to relate some of his own adventures. He had been in the United States Marines for seven years, he had been an explorer on the upper Amazon for four years, he'd been a white hunter in Africa for three years . . . after listening for a couple of hours, I said, ''Ron, you're eighty-four years old, aren't you?'' He let out a yelp, ''What the hell are you talking about? You know I'm only twenty-six.''

Hubbard was actually twenty-three. Gruber had been taking notes throughout:

> ''Well, you were in the Marines seven years, you were a civil engineer for six years, you spent four years in Brazil, three in Africa, you barn-stormed with your own flying circus for six years . . . I've just added up all the years you did this and that and it comes to eighty-four years. . . .'' Ron blew his stack.

Gruber added: ''I will say this, his extremely vivid imagination earned him a fortune, some years later.''

His Church claims that Hubbard moved to Hollywood in 1935, 1936 or 1937 (depending on which account you read), and while there wrote many major films. Shortly after Gerald Armstrong started working on the Hubbard biographical Archive, he was told that the film *Dive Bomber*, a 1941 Warner Brothers film release, allegedly written by Hubbard, was to be shown to raise money for the legal defense of eleven indicted Scientology staff members. Armstrong started researching the background of the film in February 1980.

I obtained a copy of the short story [Dive Bomber] which Mr. Hubbard had written and had been produced in a pulp magazine in, I believe, 1936. . . . I read through the story and then I went to the Academy of the Motion Pictures Arts and Sciences here in Los Angeles . . . and I obtained a copy . . . of the screen play or, at least, a synopsis or a treatment. And I realized that the two were completely different.

And I also saw that Mr. Hubbard's name was not noted in the credits. And I believe there were a couple of writers noted. . . . I checked their names against other records . . . and confirmed that they couldn't have been him because they were writing on several other movies which he could not possibly have been involved with. So they weren't pseudonyms he was using.

Armstrong was in a quandary: "It would have been embarrassing if someone had said, 'where is your name' and his name wasn't on it. People had paid money. So I thought perhaps I could come up with something else that could be a substitute. . . . I wrote to Mr. Hubbard and let him know what I had found to date . . . he didn't answer me. But he sent down a dispatch."[6]

Hubbard's dispatch, dated February 11, 1980, was sent to the organizer of the showing. It was read into the court record, in the Armstrong case.[7] Hubbard claimed that Warner Brothers had forgotten to put his name on the movie, and had paid him after distribution. He had not cashed the check until the end of the war, when he used the money for a trip to the Caribbean.

Hubbard's most noteworthy work during his brief time in Hollywood was the co-authorship of a 15 part serial called *The Secret of Treasure Island*. He was, however, a successful pulp writer. Many of his stories were published during the 1930s. Among his pseudonyms were Rene Lafayette, Legionnaire 148, Lieutenant Scott Morgan, Morgan de Wolf, Michael de Wolf, Michael Keith, Kurt von Rachen,

Captain Charles Gordon, Legionnaire 14830, Elron, Bernard Hubbel, Captain B.A. Northrup, Joe Blitz and Winchester Remington Colt.

Only his remarkable writing output enabled Hubbard to make a living in those "penny-a-word" days. He wrote a number of "true stories," two of which concerned his alleged experiences in the French Foreign Legion. His first hard-covered book, *Buckskin Brigades*, was published in 1937.

According to Hubbard, his first philosophical breakthrough came in 1938, with the discovery that the primary law of all existence is "Survive!" The notion that everything that exists is trying to survive became the basis of Dianetics and Scientology.

In 1938, Hubbard detailed his supposed insights in a book called *Excalibur*. Hubbard's hints about *Excalibur* are the source of several Scientology myths. It is whispered that the entirety of Scientology was available in the book, but in such a concentrated form that many people would have gone mad had they read it. Indeed, in an early Scientology promotional piece, it was claimed that fifteen copies of *Excalibur* were distributed, but four of the people who read the book went mad as a result, so the manuscript was withdrawn. The book has never been published.

Gerald Armstrong found three different manuscripts of *Excalibur* among Hubbard's personal effects, one of which was between 300 and 400 pages long.[8] Later, someone who had seen a version of *Excalibur* said it was so "dangerous" he would "willingly let his four-year-old daughter read it."

Writer A.E. van Vogt, an important figure in the early Dianetic movement, has said that Hubbard claimed his heart had stopped for six minutes during an operation, in 1938. *Excalibur* was the result of the revelation Hubbard had during this near death experience. Armstrong has said it was a dental extraction under nitrous oxide. Hubbard told his literary agent that a "smorgasbord" of knowledge had been laid out before him. He had absorbed it all, and managed to avoid the command to forget, which was the last part of the incident. *Excalibur* is an expansion of Hubbard's argument that "Survive!" is the basic law of existence. Hubbard's friend and fellow writer, Arthur Burks, saw the book when it was offered to publishers in New York in the summer of 1938. He was impressed, but could not manage to instill his enthusiasm into a publisher. Burks later hinted that he put up money for the book to be published, but that Hubbard returned to Port Orchard in the autumn, dejected that he had failed to find a proper publisher, taking Burks' money with him.[9]

Hubbard often claimed that the only people who understood the value of his research in 1938 were the Russians. In an interview given in 1964, he said that the Russians had offered him $100,000 and laboratory facilities he needed in the USSR, so that he could complete his work. After Hubbard refused, a copy of *Excalibur* was stolen from his hotel room in Miami. Hubbard made no mention of these supposed events when complaining to the FBI about approaches from the Russians in 1951.[10]

In 1938, Hubbard became a science fiction writer, claiming he was "summoned" by the publishing firm of Street & Smith to write for *Astounding Science Fiction*. Hubbard protested that he wrote about people, not machines, and was told that this was precisely what was needed.

Hubbard joined editor John Campbell's circle of friends, and became a major contributor to the reshaping of science fiction which Campbell brought about. Campbell was also to figure in the birth of Dianetics, twelve years later. Recently this pre-war period has been dubbed the Golden Age of Science Fiction. Hubbard's work appeared alongside that of Robert Heinlien, A.E. van Vogt, and Isaac Asimov, each of whom has stated his admiration for Hubbard's stories. Although Hubbard's writing was patchy in places, he certainly had a very inventive imagination. He became a regular contributor to *Astounding*, moving back to New York in the autumn of 1939.

Hubbard's interest in the occult continued, and for six months in 1940 he belonged to the Ancient and Mystical Order Rosae Crucis (AMORC). He completed the first two "neophyte" degrees (probably by mail) before his membership lapsed on July 5, 1940.[11]

In February 1940, Hubbard was accepted as a member of the Explorers' Club of New York (though one Scientology account says 1936). According to his book *Mission into Time*, Hubbard was awarded the Explorers' Club Flag in May 1940, for an expedition to Alaska aboard his ketch, the *Magician*. Hubbard called this trip the "Alaskan Radio Experimental Expedition." Another Scientology account claims the expedition was undertaken for the U.S. Government.

Hubbard seems to have been trying out a new system of radio navigation developed by the Cape Cod Instrument Company. At least the Scientologists provide documentation to that effect. The "expedition'' seems to have consisted of Hubbard and.his first wife, Polly, aboard the 32-foot *Magician*. Some film was sent gratuitously to the U.S. Navy Hydrographic Office. As ever, we are faced with a germ of truth embedded in Hubbard's exaggeration. The habit of a lifetime.

In a letter sent to the *Seattle Star* in November 1940, Hubbard complained that his Alaskan trip had been greatly delayed by frequent failures of the boat's motor. Repairs had been expensive, and Hubbard and his wife were stranded in Ketchikan while he tried to write and sell enough stories to bail them out. Eventually he borrowed $265 from the Bank of Alaska, a debt he blithely forgot as soon he departed.[12]

Hubbard was apparently an accomplished sailor, receiving a License to Master of Steam and Motor Vessels in December 1940, and a License to Master of Sail Vessels (any Ocean), in May 1941.

In 1938, Hubbard had failed to secure a place in the Air Corps, and in 1939 the U.S. War Department turned him down. By the spring of 1941, Hubbard was living in New York, and waging an all-out campaign for a commission in the U.S. Naval Reserve with assignment to intelligence duties.

Hubbard pursued this objective by coaxing his friends to write letters of reference to the U.S. Navy.[13] In March, Jimmy Britton of KGBU radio in Alaska wrote to the Secretary of the Navy, claiming that during a ''ten month'' stay in Alaska, Hubbard had been ''instrumental in bringing to justice a German saboteur who had devised it to be in his power to cut off Alaska from communication with the U.S. in time of war.'' Hubbard does not seem to have mentioned this episode himself, but it is highly likely that Britton heard the story from Hubbard. Hubbard, in a letter to the *Seattle Star* written in 1940, said he had been in Alaska from July to November. Britton said Hubbard had spent ten months in Alaska.

There was a letter from Commander W.E. McCain, of the U.S. Navy which stated: ''I have found him to be of excellent character, honest, ambitious and always very anxious to improve himself, to better himself and become a more useful citizen.'' A letter written in April 1941, by Warren Magnuson of the House of Representatives to President Roosevelt, said: ''An interesting trait is his distaste for personal publicity. He is both discreet and resourceful as his record should indicate.''

One letter, allegedly from a professor at George Washington University, explained that Hubbard's ''average grades in engineering were due to the obvious fact that he had started in the wrong career. They do not reflect his great ability.''

In May came a letter from Robert Ford, also of the House of Representatives, who recommended Hubbard as, ''one of the most brilliant men I have ever known . . . discreet, loyal, honest.'' Ford says that he and Hubbard were close friends at the time, and admits that he probably gave Hubbard some of his note-paper and told him to write whatever he liked.[14]

Lastly, a letter from the editor of *Astounding Science Fiction*, John Campbell, who confined himself mainly to praise of Hubbard's ability to turn in a story on time, but added: ''In personal relationships, I have the highest opinion of him as a thoroughly American gentleman.''

Hubbard stepped up his campaign after he was rejected by the U.S. Navy Reserve in April. His eyesight was inadequate. However, with the expansion of the armed forces due to the growing U.S. committment to the European war, Hubbard's poor eyesight was waived, and he achieved his goal. In July 1941, five months before the attack on Pearl Harbor, the U.S. Navy finally yielded to Hubbard's entreaties, and gave him a commission in the Reserve.

Hubbard As Hero

I do not hesitate to recommend him without reserve as a man of intelligence, courage and good breeding as well as one of the most versatile personalities I have ever known.—JIMMY BRITTON, president KGBU Radio Alaska, of Hubbard in 1941

He is garrulous and tries to give impressions of his importance . . . —U.S. NAVAL ATTACHÉ FOR AUSTRALIA, writing of Hubbard in 1942

Hubbard's claims about his Navy career form a major part of the Superman image he tried to project. He and his followers have claimed he saw action in the Philippines upon the U.S. entry into World War II. Hubbard was supposedly the first returned casualty from the "Far East," and was dispatched immediately to the command of an anti-submarine warfare vessel which served in the North Atlantic. He allegedly rose to command the "Fourth British Corvette" squadron, and then saw service with amphibious forces in the Pacific, ending the War in Oak Knoll Naval Hospital, "crippled and blinded," the recipient of between twenty-one and twenty-seven medals and palms. His exploits were, Hubbard claimed, the basis for a Hollywood movie starring Henry Fonda. As ever, there are inconsistencies between Hubbard's own accounts.

Hubbard also referred to his time in Naval Intelligence, and much is made of this experience by Scientologists. On his U.S. Navy Reserve commission papers, issued in July, 1941, he was designated a volunteer for "Special Service (Intelligence duties)," an assignment he requested. His service record shows that when he was eventually called to permanent active duty in November, he was indeed posted as an "intelligence officer." The expression conjures up cloak and dagger images better associated with the CIA's forerunner, the Office of Strategic Services, which did not exist at that time. Although the U.S. was not yet at war, France had fallen and the Japanese threat was recognized. The U.S. Navy was on a major recruiting drive when Hubbard was commissioned. The duties of intelligence officers at that time were largley routine, including the censorship of letters, and the collection, compilation and distribution of information. Hubbard nominally served in this capacity for five months, spending much of that time either in transit or in training.

After receiving his Naval Reserve commission, Hubbard was not immediately called to active duty. By this time he was employed as a civilian by the Navy in New York City, working with public relations and recruiting. He was only on active duty for two weeks between his commissioning in July and the end of November. He was ordered to the Hydrographic Office, Bureau of Navigation, in Washington, DC. There he annotated the photographs he had taken during his trip to Alaska the year before. A Hydrographic Office memo reads: "These items are all brief, and some are unimportant, but in the aggregate they represent a very definite contribution." The memo adds that Hubbard's information would be used in the 1942 update of the Sailing Directions for British Columbia, section 175, and possibly in section 176. On October 6, he was "honorably released from temporary active duty."

Hubbard was next called to active duty at the end of November, two weeks before the Japanese attack on Pearl Harbor.

In 1984, Captain Thomas Moulton testified in court as a witness for the Scientologists. Moulton had served briefly with Hubbard, and expressed a deep admiration for him. Moulton recounted another of Hubbard's claims of military prowess that the Scientologists probably had not expected.

According to Moulton, on the day the Japanese attacked Pearl Harbor, Hubbard "had been landed, so he told me, in Java from a destroyer named the *Edsall* [misspelt "Edsel" in the Court transcript] and had made his way across the land to Surabaja. . . . When the Japanese came in, he took off into the hills and lived up in the jungle for some time. . . . He was, as far as I know, the only person that ever got off the *Edsall*. . . . She was sunk within a few days after that.'' Hubbard had allegedly been a gunnery officer on the *Edsall*.

Hubbard also told Moulton that he had been hit by machine-gun fire, ''in the back, in the area of the kidneys. . . . He told me he made his escape eventually to Australia. . . . He and another chap sailed a life-raft . . . to West Australia where they were picked up by a British or Australian destroyer . . . on the order of seventy-five miles off Australia. . . . It was a remarkable piece of navigation.'' Sailing over 700 miles in a life-raft is remarkable indeed.

In fact, Hubbard's naval record shows no time on Java. He had been ordered to active duty on November 24, 1941, and, on the day Pearl Harbor was attacked, Hubbard was half a world away from Java in New York. Eight days *after* his supposed landing in Java, Hubbard was receiving instruction at the District Intelligence Office, in San Francisco. Hubbard was en route to the Philippines when the ship's destination was changed to Australia. Hubbard left the ship in Brisbane on January 11. Japanese action against Java began at the end of February. The USS *Edsall* was sunk at the beginning of March (long after Pearl Harbor), and Java surrendered to the Japanese on March 9. On the same day, Hubbard in fact boarded the MV *Pennant*, in Brisbane, Australia, bound for the United States.

When Hubbard arrived in Brisbane in January 1942, he seems to have informally attached himself to a newly landed U.S. Army Unit. Within a few weeks, he was in trouble with his Navy superiors. There had been a mix-up over the routing of a ship, and a copy of a secret dispatch had gone astray. While Hubbard may not have been to blame, he took the undiplomatic course of writing a report about the incident which was openly hostile of his senior officers, including the U.S. Naval Attaché.

The Scientologists offer a document written by Infantry Colonel Alexander Johnson to the Commander of the Base Force, Darwin, Australia, dated February 13, 1942. The document describes Hubbard as ''an intelligent, resourceful and dependable officer.'' The following day the U.S. Naval Attaché to Australia expressed a very different point of view: ''By assuming unauthorized authority and attempting to perform duties for which he has no qualifications, he became the source of much trouble. This, however, was made possible by the representative of the U.S. Army at Brisbane. . . . This officer is not satisfactory for independent duty assignment. He is garrulous and tries to give impressions of his importance. He also seems to think that he has unusual ability in most lines. These characteristics indicate that he will require close supervision for satisfactory performance of any intelligence duty.'' Far from being an important intelligence operative, as the Scientologists fondly believe, Hubbard was simply a nuisance. So much so that after only a month in Australia, orders were prepared for Hubbard's return to the United States.

Twenty years later, Hubbard described his brief time in Australia: ''My acquaintance . . . goes back to being the only anti-aircraft battery in Australia in 1941–42. I was up at Brisbane. There was me and a Thompson sub-machine gun. . . . I was a mail officer and I was replaced, I think, by a Captain, a couple of commanders . . . and about 15 junior officers. . . . They replaced me. I came home.'' He made no mention of his supposed adventures on Java.[1]

A Scientology press release claims that Hubbard was ''flown home in the late spring of 1942 in the Secretary of the Navy's private plane as the first U.S. returned casualty from the Far East.'' Another Scientology account adds that Hubbard ''was relieved by fifteen officers of rank [no longer ''junior officers''] and was rushed home to take part in the 1942 battle against German submarines as Commanding Officer of a Corvette serving in the North Atlantic.'' Yet another Scientology account says he ''rose to command a squadron.''

In reality, after his return by ship to San Francisco at the end of March 1942, Hubbard was hospitalized for catarrhal fever, which he had contracted aboard ship. Being the ''first U.S. returned casualty from the Far East'' seems to have consisted of having a bad cold. A doctor noted that he was ''somewhat preoccupied with himself.'' Upon recovering from his cold, Hubbard was posted to intelligence duties at Naval Headquarters in San Francisco. He immediately requested transfer to New York. After two weeks, he was sent to the Office of the Cable Censor in New York. A dispatch written in April says: ''The Chief Cable Censor is cognizant of the letter from the Naval Attaché, Australia, dated February 14, 1942, and has considered the suggestion made therein. It is therefore recommended that no disciplinary action be taken.''

In New York, Hubbard went on the sick list almost immediately, suffering from conjunctivitis for a few days.

During World War II, junior U.S. Naval Officers were promoted in batches, and in June, Hubbard became a Lieutenant senior grade. This was the highest rank he achieved, which was unusual, as he continued in active service for more than three years beyond this date. When Hubbard was transferred to New York, cable censorship had just ceased to be a function of Intelligence, so Hubbard ceased to be an "intelligence officer." His designation for work in Intelligence was amended to that of a Deck Officer. He requested sea duty in the Caribbean, but was posted to Neponset, Massachusetts, a suburb of Boston, at the end of June 1942. There he was to oversee the conversion of a trawler, the MV *Mist*, into a Navy yard patrol craft, the USS *YP-422*.

A Scientology press release says that the *Mist*, under Hubbard's command, served with British and American anti-submarine warfare vessels in the North Atlantic. The truth is less heroic. The *Mist*, or *YP-422*, put to sea from the Boston Navy Yard on training exercises in August. The exercises lasted twenty-seven hours, in which time *YP-422* fired a few practice rounds, but it saw no action against the enemy under Hubbard's command. Once again Hubbard managed to antagonize his superiors. In a dispatch to the Vice Chief of Naval Operations, the Commandant of the Boston Navy Yard wrote: "Lt. L.R. Hubbard is in command of *YP 422* completing conversion and fitting out at Boston, in the opinion of the Commandant he is not temperamentally fitted for independent command. It is therefore urgently requested that he be detached and that order for relief be expedited in view of the expected early departure of the vessel. Believe Hubbard capable of useful service if ordered to other duty under immediate supervision of a more senior officer."

On October 1, Hubbard was summarily detached from the *YP-422* and ordered to New York. So ended his only command in the Atlantic. Although his record shows no service in the eastern Atlantic, a photograph shows Hubbard wearing the "European and African campaign" ribbon nonetheless. The Scientology tale, doubtless inspired if not written by Hubbard, about his command of a squadron pursuing German submarines is entirely fanciful.

Back in New York, Hubbard wrote to the Bank of Alaska, who had finally caught up with him, explaining that he could not repay the $265 he had borrowed during his 1940 "expedition." This is only one of a number of unpaid debts recorded in his Navy file.

Hubbard again requested sea duty in the Caribbean, but in November 1942 was ordered to the Submarine Chaser Center, in Florida, for training. In a lecture given in 1964, Hubbard talked about his time there: "Fortunately, it was a lovely, lovely warm classroom, and I was shipped for a very short time down into the south of Florida . . . and, boy was I able to catch up on some sleep."[2]

A Scientology publication claims that in 1943 Hubbard became a Commodore of Corvette Squadrons. Whatever else he was, Hubbard was certainly never a Commodore (the rank between Captain and Rear Admiral) in the U.S. Navy; at least until he appointed himself to that rank in his Sea Org, nearly twenty-five years later.

After two months in the warm classrooms of Florida, Hubbard was posted, on January 17, 1943, to the Albina shipyards, in Portland, Oregon. There he was to assist with the fitting out of the *PC 815*, and to assume command when she was commissioned. The *PC 815* was a patrol craft, a "sleek hulled submarine chaser of approximately 280 tons full load," according to *Jane's Fighting Ships*.

Hubbard asked Thomas Moulton, with whom he had studied in Florida, to become his executive officer when the *PC 815* was commissioned. Moulton was posted to Portland in March 1943. He arrived to find Hubbard recovering from another bout of catarrhal fever in the care of his wife, Polly.

Hubbard's eyes troubled him and he wore dark glasses constantly. At a dance at the Seattle Tennis Club, he took off the glasses, and Moulton says Hubbard's eyes reddened and began to water in a matter of minutes. He told Moulton his difficulty was due to the "flash from a large caliber gun . . . on a destroyer he had been on." During a medical examination in 1946, Hubbard attributed his visual trouble to "excessive tropical sunlight." The real problem was a recurrence of his conjunctivitis.

Moulton added: "he frequently complained of pain in his right side and the back in the area of the kidneys which he said was due to some damage from a Japanese machine gun. . . . And from that he had considerable difficulty in urination. And upon at least one occasion I saw him urinating bloody urine."

Attorney Michael Flynn later suggested that Hubbard's difficulty might well have been a "social disease," allegedly mentioned in Hubbard's private papers. Bloody urine can result from an excess of sulfa drugs, commonly used at that time as a treatment for venereal disease. Hubbard later complained about the amount of sulfa drugs he had been fed in the Navy.

When the USS *PC 815* was commissioned on April 21, Hubbard

became her Commanding Officer. The next day, a remarkable article was printed in the *Oregon Journal*. The text is headed with a picture of Hubbard, in dark glasses, and Moulton, and reads in part:

> Lieutenant Commander Ron ("Red") Hubbard, former Portlander, veteran sub hunter of the battles of the Pacific and Atlantic has been given a birthday present for Herr Hitler by Albina Hellshipyard. . . . Hubbard is an active member of the Explorers club, New York city. He has commanded three internationally important expeditions for that organization. In 1934 Hubbard had charge of the Caribbean Motion Picture Expedition and took the first underwater films. He was the first to use the now famous bathosphere [sic] or diving ball [sic!, read "bell"] for this work. In 1935 Hubbard headed a cartographic survey in West Indian waters and in 1939 and 1940, for the navy hydrographic office, led the noted Alaska Radio Experimental Expedition.
>
> Hubbard comes from a long line of naval men: His father is Lieutenant H.R. Hubbard; his grandfather, Captain Lafayette Waterbury; his great grandfather, Captain I.C. De Wolf, all of whom helped to make American naval history.

We are then told that Hubbard spent his youth in Portland, and are given his statement about the "Albina Hellships": "Those little sweethearts are tough. They could lick the pants off anything Nelson or Farragut ever sailed. They put up a sizzling fight and are the only answer to the submarine menace. I state emphatically that the future of America rests with just such escort vessels."

In the *Journal*, Hubbard has been promoted and his father demoted. There is no mention elsewhere of "Captain" Waterbury's naval career, and "I.C. De Wolfe" was the maiden name of Hubbard's maternal grandmother, Ida Corinne. As usual the story was tailored to fit the circumstances, Hubbard had cut his cloth to fit a man of greater stature than himself.

In mid-May 1943, the newly refitted USS *PC 815* sailed from Astoria, on the Oregon coast, into the Pacific on a "shake-down" cruise. Her destination was San Diego. Shortly after leaving Astoria, sonar readings indicated the presence of a submarine; at least according to Hubbard and Moulton in the Action Report they filed at the time.

Strangely enough, Hubbard does not seem to have recounted this story to his followers. Despite many remarkable tales about his naval career, this was the only action which even approached a "battle" in which he took part.

Hubbard's report runs to eighteen typewritten pages. It was written two days after the *PC 815* had returned to Astoria, facing general disbelief, as Hubbard admitted, so he backed up his report with several others from the crew.

Admiral Fletcher, Commander Northwest Sea Frontier who reviewed Hubbard's report found it was "not in accordance with 'Anti-Submarine Action by Surface Ship.' " Fletcher had a point: the action report reads strangely like a short story.

The "battle" took place off Cape Lookout, some fifty miles south of the mouth of the Columbia River. The *PC 815* was in the steamer track, ten or twelve miles off the Oregon coast. After an echo contact had been checked, the *PC 815* laid three depth charges, just before 4:00 a.m., on May 19.

Shortly before 5:00 a.m., Hubbard gave orders to fire on an object that had appeared in the early morning light. In his report he admitted that it was probably a large piece of driftwood, but justified the attack as a means of checking the *PC 815*'s guns.

In the first hour, the *PC 815* made three runs, using nine depth charges. Hubbard had to be more sparing with the remaining three, which were laid one at a time on three successive runs. Hubbard said that his object was to force the submarine to come up, so it could be attacked with the guns.

The *PC 815* was joined by two anti-submarine "blimps" (non-rigid airships) at nine that morning, by which time she had no charges left. The submarine had failed to respond in any way to these attacks. By midday, eight hours into the battle, Hubbard had decided that the submarine could not fire torpedoes. The *PC 815* would have provided an easy target, as, according to Hubbard, the sea was calm (Moulton later contradicted this, saying the sea was sometimes "quite rough").

Hubbard complained that his requests for more depth charges were acknowledged but not answered. For at least four hours, the *PC 815*, which had no depth charges, kept the purported submarine in place. No oil or debris from the submarine had been sighted, so there was no indication of damage. The submarine made no attempt to retaliate or escape. The *PC 815* was joined in the afternoon by the *SC 536* (SCs, or Sub Chasers, were slightly smaller vessels than the *PC 815*). The *SC 536* seems to have had inadequate detection equipment, so had to follow the *PC 815* over the target, and lay her depth charges at the signal of a whistle. In his report Hubbard praised the lieutenant commanding the *SC 536* to the skies.

Later that afternoon the *PC 815*'s soundman found a second submarine. Hubbard said the blimps saw air bubbles, oil and a periscope. The blimps' own reports do not seem to have mentioned this. Throughout the "battle" several oil boils appeared, but the *PC 815* failed to take samples.

The *SC 536* had made three attacks by 4:36 p.m., when a Coast Guard patrol boat delivered twenty-three new depth charges to the *PC 815*. That evening, the USS *CG Bonham* and the *SC 537* arrived. They could not locate a submarine with their detection equipment. Hubbard castigated them for their lack of co-operation, suggesting that the commander of the *Bonham* was afraid he would damage his ship if he fired a depth charge.

On the second day, the "battle" continued at a slower pace. Hubbard was officially given command of the assembly that afternoon. On the third day of this one-sided contest, a periscope was allegedly sighted, but rapidly disappeared when the *PC 815*'s gunners opened fire.

They were joined by the larger *PC 778*, which carried fifty depth charges. She found no indication of submarines, so refused either to lay depth charges, or to supply any to Hubbard. Indeed, Hubbard had such difficulty obtaining more ammunition that Moulton sent a message to the Commander-in-Chief of the Pacific Fleet, in Pearl Harbor, "asking why in thunder we couldn't get any help."

At midnight, on May 21, the *PC 815* was ordered back to Astoria. According to Hubbard's report, the action had lasted for 55 hours, 27 minutes. The *PC 815* had remained in the area searching for a further thirteen hours. They had used a total of thirty-five depth charges, and despite the failure of either of the submarines to respond, they had sustained three minor casualties and shot away their own radio antenna.

In a personnel report attached to his Action Report, Hubbard congratulated his crew without exception for their part in the "battle."

In his summary, Hubbard again sang the praises of Lieutenant Kroepke of the *SC 536*. He criticized the commanding officers of the blimps for their lack of knowledge of anti-submarine warfare.

Hubbard concluded his report with the claim that the *PC 815* had completely immobilized one Japanese submarine, and severely damaged a second.

Another officer, Ensign Walker, mentioned only one submarine in his report. Moulton confirmed Hubbard's report, both at the time and forty years later in court. Admiral Fletcher was not impressed. In his comment on the report of June 8, 1943, he said:

> *SC's 536* and *537, CGC's BONHAM* and *78302*, and blimps *K-33* and *K-39* engaged in this submarine search. Reports have been received from the Commanding Officer of each of these ships in writing and in personal interviews. An oral report has also been received from Lieutenant Commander E.J. Sullivan, U.S.N., Commander Airship Squadron 33, who made a trip to the area during the search on one of the blimps. . . . There is a known magnetic deposit in the area in which depth charges were dropped. . . .
>
> An analysis of all reports convinces me that there was no submarine in the area. Lieutenant Commander Sullivan states that he was unable to obtain any evidence of a submarine except one bubble of air which is unexplained except by turbulence of water due to a depth charge explosion. The Commanding Officers of all ships except the *PC 815* state they had no evidence of a submarine and do not think a submarine was in the area.

It seems that at the time Hubbard managed to win his crew over into believing they had disabled two submarines. They certainly believed in him. One of the reports submitted by the crew included this statement: "But above all the crew, each and every man looks up to and respects the captain, L. Ron Hubbard and everything in every way that the men should respect a leader [sic]. And I might add that the crew thinks that he is one of the best leaders of any ship afloat." And in court Moulton said of Hubbard: "He ran a very competent, extremely competent attack throughout the thing. He did a very fine job."

Hubbard's report, written before Admiral Fletcher had interviewed anyone, was defensive from the start. His statements about those who disagreed with him are interesting: he criticized the very officers who were to deny the submarines' existence. For someone who claimed to have slept during his only course in Anti-Submarine Warfare (ASW), and had not seen action previously, Hubbard's comments about the other commanders' inadequate knowledge of ASW were distinctly high-handed.

On June 28, the *PC 815* put to sea once more for training exercises. At Hubbard's order, she fired three practice rounds from her three-inch gun in the direction of Los Coronados islands. Hubbard had anchored in Mexican waters, and the islands were Mexican territory. Within two days a Board of Investigation was underway. On July 7 a fitness report on Hubbard was written by Rear Admiral Braisted, Commander Fleet Operational Training Command, Pacific. In the "Remarks" section, the Rear Admiral said: "Consider this officer lacking in the essential qualities of judgment, leadership and cooperation. He acts without forethought as to probable results. He is believed to have been sincere in his efforts to make his ship efficient and ready. Not considered qualified for command or promotion at this time. Recommend duty on a large vessel where he can be properly supervised."

As we have seen, this observation about Hubbard's need for supervision had been made by the U.S. Naval Attaché in Australia and by the Commandant of the Boston Navy Yard. This time it was heeded, and Hubbard did not receive another command.

On July 15, 1943, Rear Admiral Braisted wrote a "letter of admonition" to Hubbard and for the record. On the same day, Hubbard complained of epigastric pain and was put on the sick list in San Diego. In his private papers, Hubbard later admitted that his illness was a way of avoiding discipline.[3] He was under observation for nine days for malaria, which he claimed to have suffered from sixteen months before, in a "combat area," according to a doctor's report of Hubbard's statement at the time. Malaria was not diagnosed at this time, nor does diagnosis of malaria appear anywhere in Hubbard's extensive Navy and Veterans Administration medical files, despite his repeated complaints that he was suffering from the symptoms.

Hubbard was on the sick list for a total of seventy-seven days, suffering, it was finally decided, from a duodenal ulcer. At the end of this period, in October 1943, he asked to be ordered to landing vessels, attaching a list of his qualifications to the request which included the command of three expeditions, and a puffed-up account of his brief spell with the Marine Reserve at George Washington University. He also attached a statement seeking to justify the shelling of the Coronados, saying that most of the crew of the *PC 815* had asked to return to his command. He claimed to have been given permission to fire at his own discretion, and complained that other vessels had not been censured for anchoring off the Coronados. Hubbard added, pathetically, that although he knew that he was in the grip of a throat infection at the time, this could not excuse his error.

Hubbard's statement failed to impress. Following the *PC 815* fiasco, it was a year before he put to sea again. In early December 1943, Hubbard was assigned to fitting out and training the crew of the USS

Algol, in Portland. In July 1944, when the *Algol* was commissioned, Hubbard was posted as the "Navigation and Training Officer" aboard the ship, an Attack Cargo Auxiliary Vessel. The *Algol* followed the same initial route as the *PC 815*, south from Portland, but docked at Oakland after training exercises. On Wednesday, September 27, at 4:30 p.m., the Deck Log of the *Algol* shows that the "navigating officer reported to the OOD [Officer of the Deck] that an attempt at sabotage had been made sometime between 1530–1600. A Coke bottle filled with gasoline with a cloth wick inserted had been concealed among cargo which was to be hoisted aboard and stored in No. 1 hold." The log is signed by the navigating officer, L. Ron Hubbard. The FBI and Navy Intelligence were called in to investigate.

The next day's log records a dispatch received at 10:14 on the night of the incident, confirming earlier orders for Hubbard to leave ship. The *Algol* put to sea six days later. It was to play a part in the Okinawa invasion, and by the end of the war had won two battle stars. Hubbard remained safe ashore. He later claimed that the title role in "Mr. Roberts" was based on his experiences aboard the USS *Algol*, with Hubbard's part taken by Henry Fonda. His Commanding Officer, Lieutenant Commander Axton T. Jones (upon whom Hubbard was later to claim the vicious James Cagney character was based), did give Hubbard a generally favorable Fitness Report, but remarked: "Lieutenant Hubbard is a capable and energetic officer, but is very temperamental and often has his feelings hurt. He is an above average navigator and is to be trusted. This officer is of excellent personal and military character. Recommended for promotion when due."

Hubbard responded to a general Navy request for applicants "for intensive training with eventual assignment to foreign duty as civil affairs officers in occupied areas." Commander Jones had earlier approved Hubbard's request for appointment to the School of Military Government. In his application, Hubbard had claimed that he was a trained civil engineer with a knowledge of Spanish, Japanese, Pekin and Shanghai Pidgin, Tagalog and Chamorro. He had also claimed an understanding of the social psychology of the peoples of the Philippines, North China and Japan. Hubbard was one of hundreds of officers who did a three month course in "Military Government" at Princeton. However, his later claims to have studied at Princeton University are misleading. During the war the U.S. Navy had a training establishment on the campus at Princeton, which was not part of the University.

It seems likely that Hubbard was in training for the anticipated post-war occupation of Japan. By his own admission, he failed the examination for overseas posting and became depressed as a consequence.[4] In April 1945, Hubbard's duodenal ulcer flared up, and he spent the next seven months on the sick-list, largely as a patient in Oak Knoll Hospital, Oakland, California.

CHAPTER FIVE

His Miraculous Recovery

Scientology accounts claim that Hubbard, having served in all five theaters of World War II, and received between twenty-one and twenty-seven medals and palms, was taken crippled and blinded to Oak Knoll Naval Hospital. Hubbard's service record presents a different picture: A man who never saw action against the enemy, and received not twenty-one, but four awards, none for combat or wounds.

The Scientologists frequently reissue a Hubbard article called *My Philosophy*, which reads in part:

> Blinded with injured optic nerves, and lame with physical injuries to hip and back, at the end of World War II, I faced an almost non-existent future. My service record states: "This officer has no neurotic or psychotic tendencies of any kind whatsoever," but it also states "permanently disabled physically."
>
> And so there came a further blow—I was abandoned by family and friends as a supposedly hopeless cripple and a probable burden upon them for the rest of my days. Yet I worked my way back to fitness and strength in less than two years, using only what I knew about Man and his relationship to the universe. I had no one to help me; what I had to know I had to find out. And it's quite a trick studying when you cannot see.
>
> I became used to being told it was all impossible, that there was no way, no hope. Yet I came to see again and walk again.

This moving history was designated "Broad Public Issue" by Hubbard, so it is well known to all Scientologists. It is a remarkable story, reinforced by biographical sketches published by his Church. To the Scientologist, Hubbard's miraculous recovery gives hope for his or her own.

Hubbard's *My Philosophy* is not one of the biographical statements containing "errors made by former public relations people who have since been removed," as a high-ranking Scientology official put it, in 1986.[1] There is no doubt that it was written by Hubbard, as the original is in his handwriting, and was admitted into evidence in the Armstrong case.

Documents from Navy and Veterans Administration files tell a very different and far less stirring tale of Hubbard's war wounds. Hubbard did not spend a full year in Oak Knoll Hospital. He was hospitalized for tests in April 1945, took a month's convalescent leave from the end of July, and was again hospitalized (though spent some time as an outpatient) from the end of August until he was mustered out of the Navy on December 6, 1945. In October 1945, a Naval Board gave the opinion that Hubbard was "considered physically qualified to perform duty ashore, preferably within the continental United States." The restriction to duty ashore was due to his chronic ulcer.

The official files give a fairly complete record of Hubbard's medical condition from 1941 well into the 1950s. He was first hospitalized in Vallejo, California, in March 1942, immediately upon his return from Australia. There is no mention there, or anywhere in the extensive records, of "injured optic nerves," or of blindness.

When Hubbard was admitted to Oak Knoll hospital, in 1945, he had 20/20 vision, with glasses. When he was mustered out, that December, his eyesight was 12/20 in the right eye, and 14/20 in the left, again with glasses. The major deterioration coincided with his decision to apply for a disability pension. In a plaintive letter to the Veterans Administration, Hubbard claimed that reading for longer than a few minutes gave him a headache.

Following his accidental attack on one of the Coronados Islands, in June 1943, Hubbard was hospitalized for "stomach trouble," which was diagnosed as a duodenal ulcer. In January 1945, he suffered from arthritis, which he attributed to a climatic change from the tropics to winter in New York. Hubbard had in fact just served for almost a year in Oregon and northern California. He was hospitalized in April 1945, for a recurrence of the duodenal ulcer. The official files support these statements, which were also given by Hubbard to a Veterans Administration doctor in Los Angeles on September 19, 1946, and to the press in 1950.[2] Neither Hubbard nor the examining doctor made any mention of war wounds.

At the time of his separation from the Navy, Hubbard applied to the Veterans Administration for disability benefits. In February 1946, he was awarded a ten percent disability pension of $11.50 per month. His visual deterioration was not considered pensionable. For several years he campaigned, with some success, to have his pension increased. Despite his enormous income in later years, Hubbard continued to draw the pension until his death.

Claims relating to Hubbard's miraculous recovery from his war wounds have been many and various: "Thanks in great part to the unusual discoveries that L. Ron Hubbard made while at Oak Knoll in 1944, he recovered so fully that he was reclassified for full combat duty." "By 1947, overworked and in poverty, he found he had the glimmerings of a workable process." "By 1947 he had recovered fully." "In 1949 Hubbard had had the processes applied to him to the extent that he could again see and sit at a typewriter. He became better physically until he passed a full combat physical—and lost his naval retirement."[3]

In an interview given shortly after the creation of Dianetics, Hubbard was more candid about his war wounds. The December 5, 1950, issue of *Look* magazine quoted him as saying he had been suffering from "ulcers, conjunctivitis, deteriorating eyesight, bursitis and something wrong with my feet." This description fits very well with Hubbard's Navy and Veterans Administration records.

There are further contradictions in Hubbard's published Scientological works. At least twice Hubbard referred to an incident shortly before the end of the war, when, according to his other statements, he was supposedly incapacitated by his wounds. The first reference was made in a tape recorded lecture, given on July 23, 1951; the second in a bulletin published on November 15, 1957.[4] In both Hubbard claimed that he was on leave in Hollywood on July 25, 1945, when he was attacked by three petty officers, one with a broken bottle. Because of his knowledge of Judo, Hubbard was able to fight them off. An impossible feat for a blind cripple.

At the very time that he was supposed to have "recovered fully," in October 1947, Hubbard wrote to the Veterans Administration. In the letter, he claimed that after two years he was still unbalanced because of his wartime service. He was suffering from prolonged bouts of depression and frequently thought of taking his own life. He asked for psychiatric treatment.

Hubbard was examined again in December 1947, and a few dollars were added to his pension for the arthritic condition of his right hip, spine and ankles. Hubbard said he had sprained his left knee in the service, but the doctor did not allow this. His award was raised to a forty percent disability, which in 1947 amounted to $55.20 per month. In 1948, he applied for a Navy disability retirement, which at the time would have amounted to $181 per month, tax-free. His disabilities were not sufficient for such a retirement. Far from being "permanently disabled physically," Hubbard was twice refused a physical disability retirement from the Navy Reserve.

In his book *Dianetics: The Modern Science of Mental Health*, published in May 1950, Hubbard made many claims for the curative powers of his new therapy. They are very revealing in the light of the Veterans Administration documents. Dianetics would supposedly cure or alleviate arthritis, bursitis, poor eyesight, ulcers, and even the common cold. Hubbard suffered from all of these, and fifteen months after announcing his miracle cure to the world, he still privately claimed to be disabled and continued to collect his Veterans pension. On August 1, 1951, he was examined again. He said he had been suffering from stomach trouble since 1943. The examining physician noted:

> He states that he spent approximately thirteen months in hospitals during his navy service, and that a duodenal ulcer was demonstrated by x-ray on several occasions. . . . He says that he has been forced to follow a modified ulcer diet continuously since his initial gastro-intestinal disturbance in 1943. The spring and the fall of the year are the most troublesome times for him, and he states that he has exacerbations lasting usually about a week with rather severe distress during these months. . . . The patient states that he invariably has trouble with his stomach when he is working long hours and under nervous stress. He is a poor sleeper, and states that he has been unable to take the usual soporifics because they seem to upset his stomach. He smokes very little, and then only intermittently. He believes that smoking definitely aggravates his epigastric distress.

Under the heading "Impression," the doctor wrote: "duodenal ulcer, chronic." Under the heading "Diagnosis," he wrote: "Duodenal ulcer, not found on this examination."

This was one of two specialist examinations performed on Hubbard that day in 1951. The second was orthopedic. In that report, it is noted:

> He also gives a history of injuring his right shoulder, just how is not clear, and of developing numerous other things including duodenal ulcer, actinic conjunctivitis, and a highly nervous state. He has applied for retirement from the navy [from the Reserve list] which was eventually turned down. . . . He is a writer by profession and states he has some income from previous writing that helps take care of him. . . . This is a well nourished and muscled white adult who does not appear chronically ill. . . .
>
> He has a history of some injury to the right shoulder and will not elevate the arm above the shoulder level. However, on persuasion, it was determined at this time that the shoulder is freely movable and unrestricted. It is noted that he has had a previous diagnosis of BURSITIS WITH CALCIFICATION. X-rays will be repeated. It is not believed that this is of significant incapacity. . . . Records show a diagnosis of MULTIPLE ARTHRITIS. However, no clinical evidence of arthritis is found at this time.

Hubbard's Sea Org "Medical Officer," Kima Douglas, testified in court that while she attended him from 1975 to 1980, he suffered from arthritis, bursitis and coronary trouble, which Dianetics was also supposed to alleviate.[5] Hubbard wore glasses throughout his adult life, but only in private.

During the Armstrong case, a Hubbard letter to the Veterans Administration, dated April 2, 1958, was produced. Gerald Armstrong had this to say of it:

> In my mind there was a conflict between the fact that here he is asking to have his V.A. [Veterans Administration] checks sent to a particular address in 1958, and in all the publications about Mr. Hubbard he had claimed that he had been given a perfect score, perfect mental and physical score by 1950, and by 1947 had completely cured himself, and here he is still drawing a V.A. check for this disability. . . . It seems like there is at least a contradiction and possibly an unethical practice on his part.

During the case, a document was read into the record which clearly shows Hubbard's state of mind during the period when he was supposedly developing his science of mind. It is part of a collection of documents which Armstrong dubbed "The Affirmations," because they are a series of positive suggestions which Hubbard was instilling into himself through self-hypnosis. In ''The Affirmations'' Hubbard attributed each of his physical difficulties to some evasion on his part. His eyesight was poor because he had wanted to avoid school. His ulcer was an excuse to avoid discipline in the Navy. He admitted that he had never really had any trouble with his hip. He added, however, that through hypnotic command he would be able to convincingly pretend any of these and several other disabilities to obtain a pension, but would return to health an hour after any examination, amused by the stupidity of his examiners. He also commented that his lies would have no effect upon his true condition.[6]

CHAPTER SIX

His Magickal Career

The late Aleister Crowley, my very good friend—L. RON HUBBARD, *Conditions of Space/Time/Energy*, 1952, PDC lecture 18

Hubbard met Jack Parsons while on convalescent leave in Los Angeles, in August 1945. When Hubbard's terminal leave from the Navy began on December 6, 1945, he went straight to Parsons' Pasadena home. Jack Parsons was a science fiction fan, a rocket and explosives chemist, and a practitioner of ritual "magick." Hubbard and Parsons quickly formed a powerful bond, and over the following months engaged in variations on Aleister Crowley's "magick." Later, Hubbard was eager to make light of this involvement. After all, the world famous explorer, nuclear physicist, war hero and philosopher could not be known to have engaged in demonic sexual rites.

In 1969, the London *Sunday Times* exposed Hubbard's magickal connections. The Scientologists threatened legal action, and the *Sunday Times*, unsure of its legal position, paid a small out-of-court settlement. Without retracting their earlier article, they printed a statement submitted by the Scientologists:[1]

Hubbard broke up black magic in America: Dr. Jack Parsons of Pasadena, California, was America's Number One solid fuel rocket expert. He was involved with the infamous English black magician Aleister Crowley who called himself "The Beast 666." Crowley ran an organization called the Order of Templars Orientalis [sic, actually "Ordo Templi Orientis"] over the world which had savage and bestial rites. Dr. Parsons was head of the American branch located at 100 Orange Grove Avenue [actually 1003 South Orange Grove Avenue], Pasadena, California. This was a huge old house which had paying guests who were the U.S.A. nuclear physicists working at Cal. Tech. Certain agencies objected to nuclear physicists being housed under the same roof.

L. Ron Hubbard was still an officer of the U.S. Navy because [sic] he was well known as a writer and a philosopher and had friends amongst the physicists, he was sent in to handle the situation. He went to live at the house and investigated the black magic rites and the general situation and found them very bad.

Parsons wrote to Crowley in England about Hubbard. Crowley "the Beast 666" evidently detected an enemy and warned Parsons. This was all proven by the correspondence unearthed by the Sunday Times. Hubbard's mission was successful far beyond anyone's expectations. The house was torn down. Hubbard rescued a girl they were using. The black magic group was dispersed and destroyed and has never recovered. The physicists included many of the sixty-four top U.S. scientists who were later declared insecure and dismissed from government service with so much publicity.

During the Scientologists' case against Gerald Armstrong in 1984, the original of this peculiar statement was produced. It is in Hubbard's handwriting. The statement is mistaken on several points. Karl Germer, not Parsons, was in charge of Crowley's organization in America. Parsons, known as "Frater Belarion" or "Frater 210," was head of the single "Church of Thelema," or "Agape Lodge," in Pasadena. Hubbard's opening statement, the claim to have broken up black magic in America, is of course ridiculous. Hubbard did, however, contribute significantly to Jack Parsons' later financial difficulties. There is no evidence to support the claim that Hubbard was working for "Intelligence." Parsons' FBI file shows that he was routinely investigated from 1943 onwards, because of his peculiar lifestyle. There is no mention of Hubbard in the file, and despite investigations, Parsons retained his high security classification until shortly before his death in 1952.

However, the Scientology statement does admit Hubbard's involvement with Parsons. In a "Bulletin" written for Scientologists in 1957, Hubbard said this of the man whose black magic group he had "dispersed":

One chap by the way, gave us solid fuel rockets and assist take-offs for airplanes too heavily loaded, and all the rest of this rocketry panorama, and who [sic] formed Aerojet in California and so on. The late Jack Parsons . . . was not a chemist, the way we think of chemists. . . . He eventually became quite a man.[2]

Parsons was indeed "quite a man." He was one of the developers of Jet Assisted Take-Off (JATO) units, and an original member of Cal-Tech's rocket project, which became the Jet Propulsion Laboratory.

Hubbard also had something to say about Aleister Crowley, Parsons' mentor, and the most notorious practitioner of black magic of the 20th century. Crowley was a determined opponent of Christianity, who had proclaimed: "Do what thou wilt shall be the whole of the law." He was well known for his defiance of conventional morality. Crowley recorded his considerable abuse of drugs in *The Diary of a Drug Fiend*, and his bizarre sexual practices in numerous other works. He called himself the "Beast," after the "Beast" spoken of in the biblical Revelation of St. John the Divine.

In the Scientology "Philadelphia Doctorate Course" lectures, given by Hubbard in 1952, there are several references to Crowley.[3] Hubbard made it clear that he had read Crowley's pivotal *Book of the Law*. He also said: "The magic cults of the 8th, 9th, 10th, 11th, 12th centuries in the Middle East were fascinating. The only work that has anything to do with them is a trifle wild in spots, but it's fascinating work . . . written by Aleister Crowley, the late Aleister Crowley, my very good friend. . . . It's very interesting reading to get hold of a copy of a book, quite rare, but it can be obtained, *The Master Therion* . . . by Aleister Crowley. He signs himself 'The Beast', the mark of the Beast, six sixty-six."

In another Hubbard lecture we are told: "One fellow, Aleister Crowley, picked up a level of religious worship which is very interesting—oh boy! The Press played hockey with his head for his whole life-time. The Great Beast—666. He just had another level of religious worship. Yes, sir, you're free to worship everything under the Constitution so long as it's Christian."

Jack Parsons wrote to Crowley early in 1946:

About 3 months ago I met Capt L Ron Hubbard, a writer and explorer of whom I had known for some time. . . . [no omission] He is a gentleman, red hair, green eyes, honest and intelligent and we have become great friends. He moved in with me about two months ago, and although Betty and I are still friendly, she has transferred her sexual affections to him.

Although he has no formal training in Magick he has an extraordinary amount of experience and understanding in the field. From some of his experiences I deduce he is in direct touch with some higher intelligence, possibly his Guardian Angel. He is the most Thelemic person I have ever met and is in complete accord with our own principles. He is also interested in establishing the New Aeon, but for cogent reasons I have not introduced him to the Lodge.

We are pooling our resources in a partnership which will act as a parent company to control our business ventures. I think I have made a great gain, and as Betty and I are the best of friends, there is little loss. . . .

I need a magical partner. I have many experiments in mind. I hope my elemental gets off the dime [gets moving]—the next time I tie up with a woman it will be on [my] own terms.

"Betty" was both Parsons' sister-in-law (his wife's sister) and his mistress. Her full name was Sara Elizabeth Northrup, and there is no doubt that she was the girl Hubbard "rescued" from Parsons. She was later to play an important part in the creation of Dianetics.

Parsons' house was a meeting place for a group of California's eccentrics, so many people met Hubbard during his stay there. Science fiction fan Alva Rogers gave a detailed account of the comings and goings of the "Parsonage." He said the place was run as a "cooperative rooming house," so Parsons could afford to keep it up: "In the ads placed in the local paper Jack specified that only bohemians, artists, musicians, athiests, anarchists, or other exotic types need apply for rooms."

Rogers struck up a relationship with a girl who lived in the house, and came to know Parsons and Betty quite well. He gave this description of Parsons: "Jack was the antithesis of the common image of the Black Magician. . . . He bore little resemblance to his revered Master, Aleister Crowley, either in looks or in his personal conduct. He was a good looking man . . . urbane and sophisticated, and possessed a fine sense of humor. He never, as far as I saw, indulged in any of the public scatological crudities which characterized Crowley. . . . I always found Jack's insistence that he believed in and practiced magic hard to reconcile with his educational and cultural background."

Of Sara "Betty" Northrup, Rogers wrote: "She was young, blonde, very attractive, full of *joie de vivre*, thoughtful, humorous, generous, and all that. She assisted Jack in the O.T.O. and seemed to possess the same devotion to it and to Crowley as did Jack.''

Rogers' impression of Hubbard was favorable:

> I liked Ron from the first. He was of medium build, red headed, wore horn-rimmed glasses, and had a tremendously engaging personality. For several weeks he dominated the scene with his wit and inexhaustible fund of anecdotes. About the only thing he seemed to take seriously and be prideful of was his membership in the Explorers Club (of which he was the youngest member), which he claimed he had received after leading an expedition into the wilds of South America, or some such godforsaken place. Ron showed us scars on his body which he claimed were made by aboriginal arrows on this expedition. . . . Unfortunately, Ron's reputation of spinning tall tales (both off and on the printed page) made for a certain degree of skepticism in the minds of his audience. At any rate, he told one hell of a good story.

Alva Rogers had no involvement with Parson's attempt to conjure a "Moonchild." To Aleister Crowley the personification of female-kind was "Babalon," his capricious respelling of "Babylon." Chapter seventeen of St. John's Revelation tells of "Babylon the Great," the "Scarlet Woman":

> With whom the kings of the earth have committed fornication, and the inhabitants of the earth have been made drunk with the wine of her fornication. . . . I saw a woman sit upon a scarlet coloured beast, full of names of blasphemy, having seven heads and ten horns. And the woman was arrayed in purple and scarlet colour, and decked with gold and precious stones and pearls, having a golden cup in her hand full of abominations and filthiness of her fornication: And upon her forehead was a name written, Mystery, Babylon the Great, the Mother of Harlots and Abominations of the Earth. And I saw the woman drunken with the blood of the saints, and with the blood of the martyrs of Jesus.

Crowley's black magic centered upon Babalon, and he identified himself with the "Beast" upon which Babalon is to ride in her conquest of the Earth. In his novel, *The Moonchild*, Crowley described the creation of an "homunculus," elsewhere described by him as "a living being in form resembling man, and possessing those qualities of man which distinguish him from beasts, namely intellect and power of speech, but neither begotten and born in the manner of human generation, nor inhabited by a human soul." Crowley said this was "the great idea of magicians of all times: to obtain a Messiah by some adaptation of the sexual process.'' Crowley's ''Messiah'' was the Antichrist who would overthrow Christianity: Babalon the Great.

The secret rituals of Crowley's ''Ordo Templi Orientis'' were made public by Francis King in 1973.[4] They laid out the strict sequence of mystic rites and initiations that the adept is to follow as a series of ''degrees.'' Jack Parsons was intent upon conjuring Babalon as a ''Moonchild.'' He wanted to incarnate the ''Eternal Whore'' in human form using Crowley's Rituals. The ceremonies, which Parsons recorded, are known as ''The Babalon Working.'' Parsons' transcription was later typed and given very limited distribution as ''The Book of Babalon.''

In January 1946, Parsons performed the ''VIIIth degree'' of the OTO, with Hubbard's assistance. The ritual is called ''Concerning the Secret Marriages of Gods with Men,'' or the ''Magic Masturbation.''[5] After a lengthy preamble to the ritual we find the following, under the title ''Of Great Marriages'':

> On every occasion before sleep let the Adept figure his goddess before him, wooing her ardently in imagination and exalting himself with all intensity toward her.
>
> Therefore, with or without an assistant, let him purge himself freely and fully, at the end of restraint trained and ordered unto exhaustion, concentrating ever ardently upon the Body of the Great Goddess, and let the Offering be preserved in Her consecrated temple or in a talisman especially prepared for this practice. And let no desire for any other enter the heart. Then shall it be in the end that the Great Goddess will descend and clothe Her beauty in veils of flesh, surrendering her chaste fortress of Olympus to that assault of thee, O Titan, Son of Earth!

It does not take much imagination to understand what Hubbard was watching Parsons do. The ritual took place over twelve consecutive nights in January 1946. To the strains of a Prokofiev violin concerto, Parsons made a series of eleven invocations, including the ''Conjuration of Air,'' the ''Consecration of Air Dagger'' and the ''Invocation of Wand With Material Basis on Talisman.'' John Symonds, in his book *The Great Beast*, explains that ''wand'' is a Crowleyism for ''penis.''

Parsons wrote to Crowley ''nothing seems to have happened. One night, there was a power failure, but nothing more eventful, until January 14, when a candle was knocked from Hubbard's hand. Parsons said, "He [Hubbard] called me, and we observed a brownish yellow light about seven feet high in the kitchen. I banished with a magical sword, and it disappeared. His [Hubbard's] right arm was paralized [sic] for the rest of the night."

The next night, Hubbard saw a vision of one of Parsons' enemies. Parsons described this in a letter to Crowley, adding: "He attacked this figure and pinned it to the door with four throwing knives, with which he is expert." In the same letter, Parsons spoke of Hubbard's guardian angel again: "Ron appears to have some sort of highly developed astral vision. He described his angel as a beautiful winged woman with red hair, whom he calls the Empress, and who has guided him through his life and saved him many times. . . . Recently, he says, because of some danger, she has called the Archangel Michael to guard us. . . . Last night after invoking, I called him in, and he described Isis nude on the left, and a faint figure of past, partly mistaken operations on the right, and a rose wood box with a string of green beads, a string of pearls with a black cross suspended, and a rose."

Parsons performed rituals which led up to "an operation of symbolic birth." Then he settled down to wait. For four days he experienced "tension and unease. . . . Then, on January 18, at sunset, while the Scribe [Hubbard] and I were on the Mojave desert, the feeling of tension suddenly snapped. . . . I returned home, and found a young woman answering the requirements waiting for me."

The woman was Marjorie Cameron. Parsons wrote to Crowley: "I seem to have my elemental. She turned up one night after the conclusion of the operation and has been with me since. . . . She has red hair and slant green eyes as specified."

Parsons continued to invoke Babalon. On February 28, he went out to the Mojave on his own, and "was commanded to write" a "communication" from Babalon, supposedly the fourth chapter of the *Book of the Law*. This rambling "communication," similar in style to Crowley's "inspired" writings, describes Babalon, and the tribute she seeks to exact. Further, it describes the ritual which Parsons is to perform. Babalon is to provide a daughter, and Parsons is charged with a significant task:

> In My Name shall she have all power, and all men and excellent things, and kings and captains and the secret ones at her command. . . . My voice in thee shall judge nations. . . . All is in thy hands, all power, all hope, all future. . . . Thy tears, thy sweat, thy blood, thy semen, thy love, thy faith shall provide. Ah, I shall drain thee like the cup that is of

me, BABALON. . . . Let me behold thee naked and lusting after me, calling upon my name. . . . Let me receive all thy manhood within my Cup, climax upon climax, joy upon joy.

During the first two days of March 1946, Parsons prepared an altar and equipment according to the instructions he had just received. Hubbard has been away for a week, but: "On March 2 he returned, and described a vision he had that evening of a savage and beautiful women riding naked on a great cat like beast." Hubbard and Parsons set to work immediately. As Parsons described it, "He was robed in white, carrying the lamp, and I in black, hooded, with the cup and dagger. At his suggestion we played Rachmaninoff's 'Isle of the Dead' as background music, and set an automatic recorder to transcribe any audible occurrences. At approximately eight PM he began to dictate, I transcribing directly as I received."

Hubbard launched into a stream of suitably mystical outpourings, for example: "She is flame of life, power of darkness, she destroys with a glance, she may take thy soul. She feeds upon the death of men. Beautiful—Horrible."

Hubbard continued, instructing Parsons:

Display thyself to our lady; dedicate thy organs to Her, dedicate thy heart to Her, dedicate thy mind to her, dedicate thy soul to Her, for She shall absorb thee, and thou shalt become living flame before She incarnates. For it shall be through you alone, and no one else can help in this endeavour.

. . . Retire from human contact until noon tomorrow. Clear all profane documents on the morrow, before receiving further instructions. Consult no book but thine own mind. Thou art a god. Behave at this altar as one god before another . . .

Thou art the guardian and thou art the guide, thou art the worker and the mechanic. So conduct thyself. Discuss nothing of this matter until thou art certain that thine understanding embraces it all.

Using a mixture of his earlier desert inspiration, Hubbard's instructions, and a large helping of Crowley, Parsons began the rituals to incarnate the daughter of Babalon.

The next day, Hubbard once more acted as Babalon's medium, and gave instructions for the second and third rituals. During the second ritual, Parsons was to gaze into an empty black box for an hour when a "sacred design" would become apparent which he was to reproduce in wood. Then, robed in scarlet (''symbolic of birth'') with a black sash, Parsons was to invoke Babalon yet again.

The third ritual was to start four hours before dawn. Parsons was to wear black, and to ''lay out a white sheet.'' Hubbard's instructions continued:

> Place upon it blood of birth, since she is born of thy flesh, and by thy mortal power upon earth. . . . Envision thyself as a cloaked radiance desirable to the Goddess, beloved. Envision her approaching thee. Embrace her, cover her with kisses. Think upon the lewd lascivious things thou couldst do. All is good to Babalon. ALL. . . . Thou as a man and as a god hast strewn about the earth and in the heavens many loves, these recall, concentrate, consecrate each woman thou hast raped. Remember her, think upon her, move her into BABALON, bring her into BABALON, each, one by one until the flame of lust is high.
>
> Preserve the material basis. . . . The lust is hers, the passion yours. Consider thou the Beast raping.

A commentator has noted that the ''material basis'' was probably a mixture of semen and menstrual blood. On March 6, Parsons sent an excited letter to Crowley:

> I am under the command of extreme secrecy. I have had the most important—devastating experience of my life between February 2 and March 4. I believe it was the result of the 9th [degree] working with the girl who answered my elemental summons.
>
> I have been in direct touch with One who is most Holy and Beautiful mentioned in The Book of the Law. I cannot write the name at present.
>
> First instructions were received direct through Ron—the seer. I have followed them to the letter. There was a desire for incarnation. I was the agency chosen to assist the birth which is now accomplished. I do not yet know the vehicle, but it will come to me, bringing a secret sign I know. Forgetfulness was the price. I am to act as instructor guardian guide for nine months; then it will be loosed on the world. That is all I can say now. There must be extreme secrecy. I cannot tell you the depth of reality, the poignancy, terror and beauty I have known. Now I am back in the world weak with reaction. . . . It is not a question of keeping anything from you, it is a question of not dwelling or even thinking unduly on the matter until the time is right. Premature discussion or revelation would cause an abortion.

Parsons obviously thought Babalon was gestating in Marjorie Cameron's womb; it all smacks of horror tales like *The Omen* and *Rosemary's Baby*. Crowley thought so too, and said as much to Parsons: "You have me completely puzzled by your remarks about the elemental—the danger of discussing or copying anything. I thought I had the most morbid imagination, as good as any man's, but it seems I have not. I cannot form the slightest idea who you can possibly mean." A curious admission from the author of *The Moonchild*, and the "IXth degree magic," of which "Of the Homunculus" is a major part.

Crowley wrote to his deputy in New York: "Apparently he [Parsons] or Ron or somebody is producing a Moonchild. I get fairly frantic when I contemplate the idiocy of these louts."

Crowley's "IXth degree" ritual, which was performed by Parsons, Hubbard and Cameron, says this of the Homunculus: "Now then thou hast a being of perfect human form, with all powers and privileges of humanity, but with the essence of a particular chosen force, and with all the knowledge and might of its sphere; and this being is thy creation and dependent; to it thou art Sole God and Lord, and it must serve thee."[6]

None of the accounts of "The Babalon Working," performed by Parsons and Hubbard, fully explain the phrase "the essence of a particular chosen force." Crowley viewed the gods not as distinct individuals, but as representations of particular energies, which could be tapped. In his own words: "Gods are but names for the forces of Nature themselves."[7] The "IXth degree" magic is concerned with embodying such an energy or force.

In May, OTO member Louis T. Culling wrote to Crowley's deputy, Karl Germer, suggesting that Parsons should be "salvaged from the undue influence of another." He spoke of a partnership agreement signed by Parsons, Hubbard and Sara Northrup "whereby all money earned by the three, for life, is equally divided."

There was disquiet in the Ordo Templi Orientis. In a cable to his U.S. deputy, dated May 22, Crowley said, "Suspect Ron playing confidence trick, Jack evidently weak fool obvious victim prowling swindlers." On the 31st, he added, "It seems to me on the information of our Brethren in California that (if we may assume them to be accurate) Frater 210 [Parsons] has committed . . . errors. He has got a miraculous illumination which rhymes with nothing, and he has apparently lost all of his personal independence. From our brother's account he has given away both his girl and his money—apparently it is an ordinary confidence trick.''

Parsons and Hubbard had indeed agreed to pool their funds immediately after the original ceremonies. They set up Allied Enterprises to buy yachts in Florida and sell them in California. Parsons put up $20,970.80, and Hubbard $1,183.91. The third partner, Sara ''Betty'' Northrup, made no financial contribution. In May, Ron and Sara went to Florida and started buying yachts.

Parsons worried when Hubbard failed to give any account of the expenditure of Allied Enterprises. In June, Parsons travelled to Florida, writing to Crowley, ''Here I am in Miami pursueing [sic] the children of my folly. I have them well tied up: they cannot move without going to jail. However I am afraid that most of the money [in the joint account] has already been dissipated. I will be lucky to salvage 3,000–5,000 dollars. In the interim I have been flat broke.''

On July 1, 1946, Parsons filed suit against Hubbard. He charged that his partners had failed to present him with any accounting, and though using money from the company bank account, had paid nothing into it.

A receiver was appointed by the court to wind up Allied Enterprises, and a restraining order was placed on the boats involved, all of Hubbard and Sara's personal property, and any bank accounts in their names. Hubbard and Sara were also ordered to remain in Miami. On July 11, the partners signed an agreement dissolving Allied Enterprises. A settlement was approved by the court on July 16.

Parsons took two of the boats, a schooner, the *Blue Water II*, and the yacht *Diane*, and Hubbard a two-masted schooner called the *Harpoon*. Hubbard also gave Parsons a promissory note for $2,900 secured against the *Harpoon*, and paid half of Parsons' costs. The Parsons affair was over. Hubbard's affair with black magic was not.

Parsons and Hubbard went their separate ways after their legal settlement, in July 1946. In October 1948, Parsons repeated the ''Babalon Working,'' as it has come to be known, and in 1949 wrote *The Book of the Antichrist*, and proclaimed himself ''Belarion, Antichrist'' (''Belarion'' was his OTO name). In *The Book of the Antichrist*, Parsons alluded to his dealings with Hubbard:

Now it came to pass even as BABALON told me, for after receiving Her Book I fell away from Magick, and put away Her Book and all pertaining thereto. And I was stripped of my fortune (the sum of about $50,000) [sic] and my house, and all I Possessed.

Parsons was fatally injured by the blast of an explosion in his laboratory in 1952. Parsons has the distinction of being the only twentieth-century magician to have had a crater on the moon named after him (though for his contributions to rocketry). Appropriately, it is on the so-called dark side.

Hubbard continued the practice of Magick after leaving Parsons. During the Armstrong case, portions of Hubbard's "Affirmations" were read into the record, much to the protest of Mary Sue Hubbard's attorney, who said "this particular document is . . . far and away the most private and personal document probably that I have ever read by anybody." Armstrong's lawyer, Michael Flynn, tended to agree: "Most Scientologists . . . if they read these documents would leave the organization five minutes after they read them."

The "Affirmations" are voluminous. The introduction alone runs to thirty pages. They are in Ron Hubbard's own hand. Only a tiny portion was read into the court record, and the originals were held under court seal. In the "Affirmations" Hubbard hypnotized himself to believe that all of humanity and all discarnate beings were bound to him in slavery. Mary Sue Hubbard's attorney claimed these statements were part of Hubbard's "research."

Also under court seal was a document with the tantalizing title "The Blood Ritual." The title was Hubbard's own. This document was apparently so sensitive that no part of it was read into the record. The Scientology lawyer asserted that the deity invoked in "The Blood Ritual" is an Egyptian god of Love.

Parsons had mentioned Hubbard's *guardian angel*, "The Empress." Nibs Hubbard says his father also called his *guardian angel* Hathor, or Hathoor. Hathor is an Egyptian goddess, the daughter and mother of the great sun god Amon-Ra, the principal Egyptian deity. She was depicted as a winged and spotted cow feeding humanity; a goddess of Love and Beauty. But she had a second aspect, not always mentioned in texts on Egyptian mythology, that of the "avenging lioness," Sekmet, a destructive force. One authority has called her "the destroyer of man." This is the "God of Love" to whom "The Blood Ritual" ceremony was dedicated. Since doing my research I have seen a copy of "The Blood Ritual," and it is indeed addressed to Hathor. Nuit, Re, Mammon and Osiris are also invoked. The ceremony consisted of Ron and his then wife mingling their blood to become one.

Arthur Burks has left an account of a meeting with Hubbard before the Second War, where Hubbard said that his *guardian angel*, a "smiling woman," protected him when he was flying gliders.[8] One early Dianeticist asked Hubbard how he had managed to write *Dianetics: The Modern Science of Mental Health* in three weeks. Hubbard said it was produced through automatic writing, dictated by an entity called the "Empress." In Crowley's Tarot, the Empress card represents, among other things, debauchery, and Crowley also associated the card with Hathor.[9]

To Crowley, Babalon was a manifestation of the Hindu goddess Shakti, who in one of her aspects is also called the "destroyer of man." It seems that to Hubbard, Babalon, Hathor, and the Empress were synonymous, and he was trying to conjure his "Guardian Angel" in the form of a servile homunculus so he could control the "destroyer of Man."

There was also a correspondence between Diana and Isis to Crowley, and the Empress card represented not only Hathor, but Isis, in Crowley's system. Diana is the patroness of witchcraft. Hubbard later called one of his daughters Diana, and the name of the first Sea Org yacht was changed from *Enchanter* to *Diana*.[10]

Nibs has said he was initiated into Magickal rites by Hubbard, even after *Dianetics* was released, that his father never stopped practicing "Magick," and that Scientology came from "the Dark side of the Force."

After the settlement with Parsons, Hubbard left Florida for Chestertown, Maryland. On August 10, 1946, he married Sara Northrup, the girl he had "rescued" from Parsons' black magic group. The marriage was bigamous since Hubbard was still legally married to Polly.

The couple turned up next at Laguna Beach, California. By the end of 1947, Hubbard was living in Hollywood, and complaining to the Veterans Administration of his mental instability. He also mentioned that he was attending the "Geller Theater Workshop," presumably brushing up his acting skills. The VA was paying for this under the GI Bill.

In December, Hubbard's pension was increased (to about a third of a living wage), and his first wife's divorce from him became final, more than a year after his second marriage. Hubbard was not satisfied with the increase in his pension, and wrote to the Veterans Administration complaining about his poor physical condition, and saying that if he did not have to worry so much about money, he would be able to produce a novel which had been commissioned.

That novel, *The End Is Not Yet*, had already been published in *Astounding Science Fiction*, in August 1947. It is about a nuclear physicist who overthrows a dictatorial system with the creation of a new philosophy. It has been suggested that the novel had some bearing upon the creation of the Scientology movement.

Hubbard's writing and the VA pension combined apparently did not provide sufficient funds, and in August 1948 Hubbard was arrested in San Luis Obispo for check fraud. He was released on probation.[11]

By January 1949, the Hubbards were in Savannah, Georgia. In a letter written that month, Hubbard said that a manuscript he was working on had more potential for promotion and sales than anything he had ever encountered. Hubbard was referring to a therapy system he was working on. In April, he wrote to several professional organizations, offering "Dianetics" to them. None was interested, so Hubbard had to find another outlet for Dianetics, which he very promptly did.

PART THREE

THE BRIDGE TO TOTAL FREEDOM 1949–1966

Let us suppose that two plateaus exist, one higher than the other, with a canyon between them. An engineer sees that if the canyon could be crossed by traffic, the hitherto unused plateau, being much more fertile and pleasant, would become the scene of a new culture. He sets himself the task of building a bridge. —L. RON HUBBARD, *Dianetics: The Modern Science of Mental Health*

CHAPTER ONE

Building the Bridge

In December 1949, an announcement appeared in America's leading science fiction magazine:

> The item that most interests me at the moment is an article on the most important subject conceivable. This is *not* a hoax article. It is an article on the *science* of the human mind, of human thought. It is not an article on psychology—that isn't a science. It's not General Semantics. It is a totally new science, called *dianetics*, and it does precisely what a *science* of thought should do. Its power is almost unbelievable; following the sharply defined basic laws dianetics sets forth, physical ills such as ulcers, asthma and arthritis can be cured, as can all other psychosomatic ills. The articles are in preparation. It is, quite simply, impossible to exaggerate the importance of a true science of human thought.

On the facing page was a story by the originator of Dianetics, called "A Can of Vacuum." It is about an unschooled practical joker who makes remarkable scientific discoveries, for example that of "a quart of rudey rays." The magazine was *Astounding Science Fiction*, and editor John Campbell's article was the first mention in print of Dianetics.

The first Hubbard article on Dianetics was published in the Spring of 1950, in an unusual place for a "science of the mind," *The Explorers Club Journal*, under the title "Terra Incognita: The Mind." In the article Hubbard explained that Dianetics "was intended as a tool for the expedition commander and doctor who are faced with choosing personnel and maintaining that personnel in good health.''

Hubbard had arrived in Bay Head, New Jersey, in mid-1949, armed with the fundamentals of his new science. He was widely known in science fiction, having contributed to *Astounding Science Fiction* for over eleven years. John Campbell, the highly influential editor, had been converted to Dianetics by a counselling session which relieved his sinusitis, and became an eager recruiter. Soon, a small group of disciples gathered around Hubbard.

Among those brought into the Hubbard circle by Campbell was Joseph Winter, M.D., who had written medical articles for *Astounding*. Winter wanted to break down the mystique surrounding medicine. He specialized in endocrinology, and had tried to modify behavior with hormones, in experiments at the University of Illinois. Hubbard was later to claim that he had himself been involved in such experiments at Oak Knoll Hospital. An early letter to Winter, written in July 1949, shows Campbell's enthusiasm for the new subject:

> With cooperation from some institutions, some psychiatrists, he [Hubbard] has worked on all types of cases. Institutionalized schizophrenics, apathies, manics, depressives, perverts, stuttering, neuroses—in all nearly 1,000 cases. . . . He doesn't have proper statistics. . . . He has cured every patient he worked. He has cured ulcers, arthritis, asthma.

Winter wrote to Hubbard asking for more information about Dianetics. Hubbard replied that he was writing a technical paper and in the fall of 1949 sent a treatise on ''Abnormal Dianetics'' to Dr. Winter, who was so impressed that he gave copies to two colleagues in Chicago. Winter was disappointed when his colleagues pointed to the shortcomings of Dianetics without first trying it out.

Winter visited Hubbard in Bay Head in October 1949, later saying he ''became immersed in a life of Dianetics and very little else.'' By January 1950, Winter had closed his medical practice in Michigan and moved to New Jersey.

Winter, Campbell, Hubbard and Don Rogers, an electrical engineer, worked together refining techniques and coining a new language to voice Hubbard's ideas. Hubbard was probably the major contributor to these discussions, and certainly the final arbiter. Winter submitted papers to the Journals of the American Medical Association and the American Psychiatric Association. The papers were rejected, because of a lack of clinical experimentation, or indeed of any substantiation. The Bay Head group then decided to publish the therapy in *Astounding Science Fiction*, and by January 1950, Hubbard had prepared an article, a modified version of which later became the book *Dianetics: The Evolution of a Science*. Unbeknownst to his co-workers, while they were refining Hubbard's cure-all, he was still trying to obtain a naval disability retirement to augment his Veterans Administration award.

In 1950, *Astounding Science Fiction* had a circulation of approximately 150,000. Its most noteworthy subscriber was Albert Einstein. The letters pages often carried correspondence from research scientists and professors, disputing the feasibility of previous stories (including criticisms of the poor scientific understanding displayed in Hubbard's stories). Campbell continued to praise Dianetics in his editorials, generating considerable interest in the subject without giving away anything substantial concerning Dianetic methods.

Arthur Ceppos, the head of a medical and psychiatric textbook publishing company, joined the Bay Head circle, and commissioned a manual on Dianetics. In April 1950, the Hubbard Dianetic Research Foundation (HDRF) was incorporated to answer the many inquiries generated by Campbell's editorials. Hubbard, his wife Sara, Campbell, Winter, Ceppos, Don Rogers, and lawyer Parker C. Morgan made up the Board of Directors. The HDRF had its headquarters in Elizabeth, New Jersey, not far from New York City.

Hubbard's 400-page textbook was outlined and written in six weeks. He sometimes claimed it took him only three, and an eyewitness has confirmed this, saying the first three weeks were spent working out *how* to write the book.

The writing process was punctuated, on March 8, by the birth of a daughter to Sara Hubbard. The child, Alexis Valerie Hubbard, had her father's red hair, though he later denied paternity, suggesting she was Jack Parson's child![1] She was delivered by Joseph Winter.

The May 1950 edition of *Astounding* sold out at record rate. It was soon followed by the book *Dianetics: The Modern Science of Mental Health*, which became an immediate best-seller. The Hubbard Dianetic Research Foundation was inundated with inquiries and requests for therapy.

Dianetics was supposed to "Clear" people of irrational behavior. A "Clear," according to the book, would have no compulsions, repressions, or psychosomatic ills. A "Clear" would have full control of his imagination, and a near perfect memory. With Dianetic counselling, IQ would "soar" by as much as "fifty points," and the Clear would be "phenomenally intelligent." Dianetics would even rescue a broken marriage.

It was claimed that through Dianetics the individual would be freed of psychoses and neuroses. Among the "psychosomatic" conditions Dianetics claimed to cure were asthma, poor eyesight, color blindness, hearing deficiencies, stuttering, allergies, sinusitis, arthritis, high blood pressure, coronary trouble, dermatitis, ulcers, migraine, conjunctivitis, morning sickness, alcoholism and the common cold. Even tuberculosis would be alleviated. Dianetics would also have "a marked effect upon the extension of life." A Clear could do a computation which a "normal would do in half an hour, in ten or fifteen seconds."

Hubbard claimed to have examined and treated 273 people and, through this research, found the "single and sole source of aberration." The book claimed that Dianetics was effective on anyone who had not had "a large portion of his brain removed," or been "born with a grossly malformed nervous structure." Better yet, Dianetics could be practiced straight from the book with no training. Therapy would take anything from 30 to 1,200 hours, by which time the person would be Clear, and thus free of all irrationality, and every psychosomatic ailment.

The new therapy which prompted these incredible claims was basically a reworking of ideas abandoned by Freud in favor of the interpretation of dreams. Dianetics extended Freud's earlier techniques slightly, and allied them to a different theory. It was a form of abreaction in which the patient remembered and then acted out, or supposedly re-experienced, the memory of a traumatic incident. Freud had speculated that traumas with similar content join together in "chains," embedded in the "unconscious" mind, causing irrational responses in the individual. According to Freud a "chain" would be relieved by inducing the patient to remember the earliest trauma, "with an accompanying expression of emotion." Earlier traumas would only become available as later traumas were remembered and abreacted. Forty years before Dianetics, in the Clark lectures at Worcester, Massachusetts, Freud had explained this theory and methodology. The description is uncannily similar to Dianetics.

Freud would repeat one of the patient's common phrases to him. This would often induce a buried memory to surface. In Dianetics, the therapist asked the patient to repeat the phrases. Hubbard called this "repeater technique" and, in early Dianetics, it was the principal method for discovering traumatic incidents.

Hubbard renamed the "unconscious" the "Reactive Mind." He differentiated two principal types of trauma: "physical pain or unconsciousness," and "emotional loss." Before *Dianetics* was published, three words had been tried out to describe the first type of trauma: norn, impediment and comanome. Eventually, Dr. Winter suggested that a word already current would fit the bill. The word was "engram," defined in Dorland's 1936 Medical dictionary as "a lasting mark or trace. . . . In psychology it is the lasting trace left in the psyche by anything that has been experienced psychically; a latent memory picture." Hubbard limited the term to actual pain or unconsciousness, separating out emotional losses as "secondary engrams" or "secondaries," meaning they were only stored where an earlier, similar "engram" existed. Freud too had commented on trauma based on both physical pain and emotional loss.[2]

So, according to Hubbard, the "Reactive Mind" is composed of recordings of incidents of physical pain or unconsciousness called "engrams." The earliest engram (or "basic") is the foundation of a "chain" of engrams, and through re-experiencing it, the "chain" will dissipate. To make an earlier engram available it is necessary to "destimulate" more recent engrams by re-experiencing them.

Hubbard claimed it was possible to relieve all such engrams, thus "erasing" the Reactive (unconscious) Mind. A person without a Reactive Mind would be "Clear." To make a Clear, it would be necessary to erase the earliest engram by re-experiencing it. Hubbard asserted that the engram of birth was very important, and claimed it was possible, and necessary, to find the earliest engram, long before birth, perhaps as far back as conception, the "sperm dream."

A year before Hermitage House published *Dianetics: The Modern Science of Mental Health*, it published an extensive psychoanalytic study by Dr. Nandor Fodor, called *The Search for the Beloved*, subtitled "A clinical investigation into the trauma of birth and prenatal conditioning." Fodor credited Otto Rank, another Freudian, with original work on the trauma of birth.

Someone at the publishers must have noticed the similarities between the two books prior to the publication of *Dianetics*. Arthur Ceppos was both the head of Hermitage House and a director of the Hubbard Dianetic Research Foundation. It is highly unlikely that

Hubbard did not know about Fodor, even though his book was certainly not as popular as *Dianetics*. Fodor did publish first, and had been expressing his ideas on the trauma of birth in psychiatric journals for some years. The first edition of *Dianetics: The Modern Science of Mental Health* even carried an advertisement for Fodor's book on the dust-jacket, subtitle and all.

Fodor and Hubbard each argued that birth and the pre-natal period could be abreacted, or re-experienced, and were fundamental to later behavior. Scientologists mistakenly credit Hubbard with the discovery of the trauma of birth and the pre-natal period. Hubbard did nothing to disabuse them of this notion.

Although Fodor's patients supposedly relived their birth, his method differed from Hubbard's. Dianetics was closer to Freud's original approach. Fodor believed that very few people were able to re-experience their birth, whereas Hubbard claimed nearly everyone could.

Using hypnosis, Hubbard tried out some of Freud's ideas, and eventually came up with a "non-hypnotic" therapy, a few months before *Dianetics: The Modern Science of Mental Health* was published. Hypnosis, which already had a Hollywood Svengali image, was to be given an even more vicious, mind-bending image by Hubbard. To this day many people think that hypnosis refers only to a state of deep-trance. In that sense, Dianetics is not hypnosis, but Dr. Winter and others were later to argue that Dianetics creates a light trance, a highly suggestible condition.

In *Dianetics: The Modern Science of Mental Health*, Freudian ideas were presented in a new, elaborate language. Dianetics, a survivor of several abreactive therapies practiced in the 1940s, differed by approaching the general public directly, rather than through the psychiatric or psychological professions. Dianetics also completely avoided the libido theory, the interpretation of dreams, transference and complex Freudian evaluations. The early Dianeticist simply directed the individual in the exploration of his memory and, inevitably, his imagination, leaving the individual (or "Preclear") to make his own interpretations about the validity or significance of his memories.

According to *Dianetics: The Modern Science of Mental Health* ("DMSMH," as Scientologists call the book), an engram contains every "perceptic"—sight, smell, touch, taste, sound and so forth. It is a running, three-dimensional record of experiencing during moments of unconsciousness or pain which acts as a post-hypnotic suggestion on the recipient. He has no real idea why he reacts irrationally in certain circumstances, but rationalizes his responses.

In the book Hubbard described an engram and its effects:

> A woman is knocked down by a blow. She is rendered "unconscious." She is kicked and told she is a faker, that she is no good, that she is always changing her mind. A chair is overturned in the process. A faucet is running in the kitchen. A car is passing on the street outside. The engram contains a running record of all these perceptions . . . [and would contain] the whole statement made to her. . . . Any perception in the engram she received has some quality of *restimulation*. Running water from a faucet might not have affected her greatly. But running water from a faucet *plus* a passing car might have begun some slight reactivation of the engram, a vague discomfort in the areas where she was struck and kicked . . . add the sharp falling of a chair and she experiences a shock of mild proportion. Add now the smell and voice of the man who kicked her and the pain begins to grow. The mechanism [the Reactive Mind] is telling her she is in dangerous quarters, that she should leave . . . She stays. The pains in the areas where she was abused become a predisposition to illness or are chronic illness in themselves.

The experiential content of the engram is outside conscious recall except, of course, when probed by the Dianeticist. When enough elements of the environment match elements of an engram, then it, and all engrams similar to it (the "chain" to which it belongs), comes into force, or "key-in." The individual must either feel the pain of the engram, or "dramatize" (act out) the often inappropriate verbal content. An engram which contained the phrase "Get out!" might well create an escapist. The Reactive Mind is literal and puns crazily.

Hubbard called the sequential record of experience the "Timetrack." In Dianetics, he claimed that by finding the earliest engram on a chain the whole chain would refile in the "Analytical" (conscious) mind, losing its reactive power. So came the idea that finding the earliest engram ("basic-basic"), and thoroughly re-experiencing its content, will knock away the foundation of all later engrams, emptying the Reactive Mind, and creating a Clear.

A rather peculiar aspect of *Dianetics: The Modern Science of Mental Health* was Hubbard's emphasis on "attempted abortions." Hubbard claimed "it is a scientific fact that abortion attempts are the most important factor in aberration," and that "Attempted abortion is very common. . . . Twenty or thirty abortion attempts are not uncommon in the aberree." Hubbard asserted that ulcers were caused by attempted abortions. He had been suffering from a duodenal ulcer since 1943.

Going against popular belief, Hubbard insisted that life in the womb was fraught with pain and that the fetus is constantly receiving engrams. Hubbard gave a gruesome list, which he claimed was from a real case: Coitus chain, father fifty-seven incidents; Coitus chain, lover nineteen incidents; Constipation chain fifty-two incidents; Douche chain twenty-two incidents; Morning sickness chain twenty-three incidents; Fight chain thirty-eight incidents; Attempted abortion chain twenty-eight incidents; Accident chain eighteen incidents; Masturbation chain eighty-one incidents. This unfortunate individual had received over 300 engrams before coming into the world.

In *Scientology: The Now Religion*, author George Malko wrote that "Hubbard's extensive discussion of things sexual, his concern with abortions, beatings, coitus under duress, flatulence which causes pressure on the foetus, certain cloacal references, all suggest to me a fascination which borders on the obsessive, as if he possessed a deep-seated hatred of women. All of them are being beaten, most of them prove to be unfaithful, few babies are wanted."[3]

Dianetic counselling was called "auditing." Hubbard defined the verb "audit" as "to listen and compute," which he considered the basic functions of the therapist. So the Dianetic therapist was called the "Auditor."

In *Dianetics: The Modern Science of Mental Health*, Hubbard used the analogy of building a bridge. He had built a bridge to a better state for mankind, pleading with his readers "For God's sake, get busy and build a better bridge!" To Scientologists, the steps of Hubbard's therapy are still known as "The Bridge."

The original idea in Dianetics was that the Reactive Mind could be completely "erased," thus turning Homo sapiens into the new man, "Homo novis," the Clear. Otherwise the basic theory was not original, and the therapy a modification of earlier techniques. Dianetics was initially successful because it was so readily accessible, and because it was espoused by a brilliant publicist, John Campbell. All the reader needed was a copy of the book and a friend to "co-audit" with, and they could start erasing their engrams. Amateur Dianetic groups sprang up throughout the English-speaking world.

In June 1950, Hubbard gave the first full-time Auditor training course to ten students at the Elizabeth Foundation. Hubbard said students there were charged $500 to "hang around the office and watch what was going on'' for a month. August found him in California, where he lectured for a month to 300 students. The fee was still $500. Professional auditing was charged at $25 an hour. There were hundreds of thousands of dollars involved.[4]

Dianetics emerged against a backdrop of international tension and fear. Russia had added Czechoslovakia to its empire in 1948. The United States had reintroduced the draft. 1948 also saw the Soviet blockade of Berlin, and the U.S. airlift. In September 1949, the Soviets successfully tested an atomic bomb. The Communists came to power in China, under Mao Tse-tung, the following month. At the beginning of 1950, Senator Joseph McCarthy announced that he had a list of 205 card-carrying Communists in the employ of the U.S. State Department. The McCarthy Communist witch-hunt was to last four years. In June, the North Koreans, using Soviet arms and tanks, invaded the South, and the Korean war began. In *The New York Times*, Frederick Schuman's review of *Dianetics: The Modern Science of Mental Health* played to the fears of the United States of America: "History has become a race between Dianetics and catastrophe," echoing Hubbard's own sentiments.

In 1950, Dianetics was a craze. Campbell wrote that *Astounding* was receiving up to a thousand letters a week.[5] Within a year, the book had sold 150,000 copies. The Hollywood community eagerly embraced the new system. Aldous Huxley received auditing from Hubbard himself, and, although he did not complain about the therapy, he simply could not locate any engrams, even under Hubbard's direction.[6]

CHAPTER TWO

The Dianetic Foundations

Charlatanism is almost impossible where dianetics in any of its principles is being practiced.—L. RON HUBBARD, *Dianetics: The Modern Science of Mental Health*

By the end of 1950, five new Hubbard Dianetic Research Foundations had been added to the first at Elizabeth. They were in Chicago, Honolulu, New York, Washington and Los Angeles. The L.A. Foundation was headed by science fiction writer A.E. van Vogt. That year, much of the letters section of *Astounding Science Fiction* was devoted to Dianetics, where letters were answered by both Hubbard and Winter. *Dianetics: The Modern Science of Mental Health* was on the bestseller lists for several months. But despite the tremendous popularity of Dianetics, and the river of cash pouring into the Foundations, there was trouble on the horizon.

The first signs came in August 1950, when Hubbard exhibited a "Clear" at the Shrine Auditorium in Los Angeles. Despite claims of "perfect recall," and the fact that she was majoring in physics, the "Clear" was unable to remember a simple physics formula. When Hubbard turned his back, she could not even remember the color of his tie.

The Shrine Auditorium lecture has been published by the Scientologists as part of Hubbard's immense collected works. The girl is renamed "Ann Singer" in the Scientologists' version. The transcript has been edited, but the question about the tie remains, as does one about physics, with a vague answer. A Scientology account says Hubbard "spoke to a jammed house of over 6,000 enthusiastic people." According to author Martin Gardner, when Ann Singer could not remember the color of Hubbard's tie, "a large part of the audience got up and left." The incident had a marked effect on Hubbard's credibility, and he became cagey about declaring more Clears, avoiding public demonstrations of their supposed abilities from then on.[2]

In September, *The New York Times* published a statement by the American Psychological Association:

> While suspending judgement concerning the eventual validity of the claims made by the author of *Dianetics*, the association calls attention to the fact that these claims are not supported by the empirical evidence of the sort required for the establishment of scientific generalizations. In the public interest, the association, in the absence of such evidence, recommends to its members that the use of the techniques peculiar to Dianetics be limited to scientific investigations to test the validity of its claims.[3]

The following month, Dr. Joseph Winter and Arthur Ceppos, the publisher of *Dianetics*, resigned from the Board of Directors of the Hubbard Dianetic Research Foundation. Winter described his experiences in the first book critical of Hubbard, *A Doctor's Report on Dianetics*. Winter felt Dianetics could be dangerous in untrained hands, and asserted that repeated attempts to persuade Hubbard to adopt a minimum standard to test student applicants had failed. Winter felt Dianetics should be in the hands of people with *some* medical qualification. He had changed his mind since writing the introduction to *Dianetics* a year before. He had also begun to feel that "Clear" was unobtainable. In a year of close association with Hubbard, Winter had not seen anyone who had achieved the state described in the book.

Winter also said he saw no scientific research being performed at the "Research" Foundation. He was tired of Hubbard's disparagement of the medical and psychiatric professions, and alarmed by Hubbard's use of massive doses of a vitamin mixture called "Guk." Winter was even more alarmed by the auditing of "past lives," which he considered entirely fanciful. Winter wrote, "there was a difference between the ideals inherent within the dianetics hypothesis and the actions of the Foundation. . . . The ideals of dianetics, as I saw them, included non-authoritarianism and a flexibility of approach. . . . The ideals of dianetics continued to be given lip service, but I could see a definite disparity between ideals and actualities." Winter set up a psychotherapeutic practice in Manhattan, and soon drifted away from Dianetics.

In an article in *Newsweek*, entitled "The Poor Man's Psychoanalysis," American Medical Association representative Dr. Morris Fishbein labelled Dianetics a "mind-healing cult." Dianeticist Helen O'Brien has said that one member of the Elizabeth Foundation resigned because in a month when $90,000 income was received, only $20,000 could be accounted for. A Board member of the time denies this, but there are certainly questions about the disbursement of income. Later events suggest that much of it went into Hubbard's pocket. One early associate says Hubbard "spent money like water."

In November 1950, the Elizabeth Foundation set up a Board of Ethics to ensure that practitioners were using the "Standard Procedure" of Dianetic counselling approved by Hubbard. Innovators had been adding their own ideas to Dianetics, which was anathema to Hubbard who called techniques he had not approved "Black Dianetics," insisting they were dangerous.[4] This was in spite of his pronouncement in *Dianetics* that "if anyone wants a monopoly on dianetics, be assured that he wants it for reasons which have to do not with dianetics but with profit.'"[5] Hubbard obviously excluded himself from this pronouncement.

Hubbard moved to Palm Springs to work on his second book, *Science of Survival*. He was living with a girlfriend, and drinking heavily. He sniped at Foundation directors, trying to force their resignations. Distrust of his associates and subordinates manifested itself repeatedly throughout his life. Hubbard's paranoia had already shown itself in Elizabeth where he had assured a Foundation Director that American Medical Association spies made up a high proportion of the student applicants, the Preclears, and even the customers in the restaurant below the Foundation.

The Los Angeles Foundation cooperated with two university researchers, who tried to validate Dianetics by knocking a volunteer out with sodium pentathol, and reading him a passage from a physics textbook, while inflicting pain. In six months of "auditing" the subject failed to remember any of the passage. Hubbard dismissed the matter in *Science of Survival*, writing that "Psychotherapists with whom the Foundation has dealt have been eager to plant an engram in a patient and have the Foundation recover it. . . . The Foundation will accept no more experiments in this line. . . . A much more natural and valid validation [sic] of engrams can be done without the use of drugs.''[6]

For some time Sara Hubbard had been Ron's personal Auditor; now they were living apart, and her confidence in Dianetics had slipped so far that she urged the Elizabeth Foundation to obtain psychiatric treatment for her husband.

A few months later Hubbard wrote a secret missive to the FBI, giving his own account of his separation from Sara. He described himself as a nuclear physicist who had transferred his expertise into a study of psychology. He said that he had thought Sara was his legal wife, before realizing there was some confusion about a divorce. Sara was accused of destroying one of Hubbard's therapeutic organizations. She had supposedly forced him to make out a will, in October, 1950, bequeathing to her his copyrights and his share of the Foundations. Later that month, Hubbard claimed he had been attacked while sleeping, since which time he had been unable to recover his health. Hubbard blamed Sara for an incident in Los Angeles in which Alexis, their baby daughter, had been left unattended in their car, and for which Hubbard himself had been put on probation. In December, he was again supposedly attacked in his sleep.

Hubbard's letter went on to describe another assault, which supposedly took place in his apartment on February 23, between 2:00 and 3:00 a.m. Having been knocked unconscious, air was injected into his heart and he was given an electric shock, in an attempt, according to Hubbard, to induce a heart attack.

The night following this purported attack, Hubbard kidnapped baby Alexis, and deposited her with a nursing agency. To avoid detection, he called himself James Olsen. He claimed his wife was suffering from ill health. The same night, he also kidnapped Sara, with the help of two of his lieutenants. Hubbard wanted to have Sara examined by a psychiatrist, but failing to find one, they ended up in Yuma, Arizona, having driven through the night. After releasing Sara, Hubbard flew to Chicago. There Hubbard found a psychologist who was willing to write a favorable report about Hubbard's mental condition, refuting Sara's charge that he was a paranoid-schizophrenic.[7]

In March, Hubbard wrote to the FBI denouncing sixteen of his former associates as Communists, a serious charge during those days of the anti-Communist witch-hunts led by Senator McCarthy and the House Un-American Activities Committee. Hubbard even included in his accusations people who were still working at the Foundations. Two, Ross Lamereaux and Richard Halpern, continued to be his staunch supporters for years to come. Ironically, Hubbard's complaints about the executives running his organizations inevitably led to an investigation by the FBI of those very organizations.[8]

In the midst of these problems, Hubbard's first wife, Polly, demanded the forty-two months of support payments Hubbard had failed to make since their settlement forty-two months before. The bill, including interest and fees, came to $2,503.79. Hubbard had also failed to pay a debt to the National Bank of Commerce, taken out in 1940, which with interest now came to $889.55. Hubbard left a trail of unpaid bills, despite the fortune Dianetics had earned him. During the eventual collapse of the Los Angeles Foundation, one of its directors wrote, "I am being flooded with personal bills for L. Ron Hubbard, going back as far as 1948 and earlier."[9]

In his secret report to the FBI, Hubbard had said that Sara and her boyfriend, Miles Hollister, were Communists. He also said Sara was a drug addict. Hubbard offered a reward of $10,000 to anyone in Dianetics who could resolve Sara's difficulties by Clearing her. She was suspended as a trustee and officer of the California Foundation.[10]

Taking Alexis and his close supporter Richard de Mille with him, Hubbard flew to Florida, and from there to Cuba. He continued to drink heavily while finishing the dictation of *Science of Survival*. In a letter to his lieutenant in Los Angeles, Hubbard spoke of the enormous amount of money to be made by insisting that every Dianeticist buy a psycho-galvonometer. The mark-up would be sixty percent. There is no mention of any benefit to auditing from the use of the psycho-galvonometer or "E-meter," as it was later known.[11]

In her book, *Dianetics in Limbo*, Helen O'Brien wrote: "The tidal wave of popular interest was over in a few months, although a ground swell continued for a while. The book became unobtainable because of a legal tangle involving the publisher. People began to see that although dianetics worked, in the sense that individuals could cooperate in amateur explorations of buried memories, this resulted only occasionally in improved health and enhanced abilities, in spite of Hubbard's confident predictions."

By the end of 1950, Hubbard's world was collapsing, income had dropped dramatically and the Foundations were unable to meet their payrolls or their promotional expenditures. An attempt to start a new Foundation in Kansas City failed. In January 1951, Parker C. Morgan, a lawyer who had been a founding director of the Elizabeth Foundation, resigned. In March, John Campbell followed suit. He too complained of Hubbard's authoritarian attitude. Thus four of the seven original directors had resigned, and Sara had been suspended, leaving only Don Rogers and Hubbard.[12]

Campbell's resignation followed close on the heels of an investigation by the New Jersey Medical Association, which filed a case against the Elizabeth Foundation for teaching medicine without a license. Hubbard was not only claiming all sorts of cures, he was also experimenting on "Preclears" with drugs, especially benzedrine. In a lecture in June 1950, Hubbard had admitted to having been a phenobarbitol addict. He also spoke knowledgeably about the effects of sodium amytal, ACTH (a hor none), opium, marijuana and sodium pentathol.[13] New directors were appointed in Elizabeth and fought a losing battle to keep the Foundation solvent.

Sara, who despite her husband's reward was supposedly "Clear" already, brought a divorce suit in Los Angeles. She was desperate for the return of her one-year-old daughter. She alleged that Hubbard had subjected her to "scientific torture experiments," that her marriage was bigamous, that she had medical evidence that Hubbard was a "paranoid schizophrenic," and that he had kidnapped their daughter.

Sara Northrup Hubbard's original complaint against her husband has mysteriously disappeared from the microfilm records of the Los Angeles County Courthouse. Fortunately, copies are still in existence. Among the alleged torture experiments was this:

> Hubbard systematically prevented plaintiff from sleeping continuously for a period of over four days, and then in her agony, furnished her with a supply of sleeping pills, all resulting in a nearness to the shadow of death . . . plaintiff became numb and lost consciousness, and was thereafter taken by said Hubbard to the Hollywood Leland Hospital, where she was kept under a vigilant guard from friend and family, under an assumed name for five days.

Sara claimed that such "experiments" were frequent during the course of their marriage. She also claimed that Hubbard had many times physically abused her, once strangling her so violently that the eustachian tube of her left ear had ruptured, impairing her hearing. Hubbard had allegedly asked her to commit suicide "if she really loved him," because although he wanted to leave her, he feared a divorce would damage his reputation. Eventually, Hubbard decided

Sara was in league with his enemies—the American Medical and Psychiatric Associations, and the Communists. He quite usually levelled similar charges against anyone who criticized him.

In his May 14 letter to the FBI, Hubbard again attacked Sara as an agent of the Communist peril. He claimed he had discovered, and could undo, the techniques used by the Russians to obtain confessions. He said that whenever he made an overture to the Defense Department offering them his own techniques of psychological warfare, his organizations were harassed. He pleaded for the removal of the Communist elements who had obviously infiltrated even the Defense Department.

Hubbard went on to accuse Sara's father of being a criminal, and her half-sister of being insane. He said she was sexually promiscuous, and suggested that she had ruined Jack Parsons' life. Hubbard claimed that Sara had been on intimate terms with scientists working on the first atomic bomb, and suggested that she might yield under FBI questioning. What she might yield is unclear.

Despite remarkable income, the Foundations foundered. The Los Angeles HDRF went down with a retired rear admiral at the helm. In April 1951, Hubbard himself resigned from the Hubbard Dianetic Research Foundation.

Hubbard had risen from a penny-a-word science fiction writer to the leadership of the largest self-improvement group in the U.S. Now, after only a few months, the Foundations were more or less bankrupt, thousands of followers were disillusioned, and Hubbard's private life was splashed all over the newspapers. It was time to cut and run. For a less resourceful or a less fortunate man, this would have been the end. For Hubbard, it was just another of many new beginnings. The head of the Omega Oil Company, Don Purcell, an ardent Hubbard admirer who had been an early visitor to the Elizabeth Foundation, saved the day.

CHAPTER THREE

Wichita

Don Purcell was a self-made millionaire. He offered Hubbard funds and new premises in Wichita, Kansas. He also offered to pay the debts of the original Foundation, without realizing what he was letting himself in for. The paltry assets of the Elizabeth Foundation, some second-hand furniture and a lot of files, were moved to Wichita. The remaining Foundations were closed. Hubbard, who had been in Cuba for about a month, was in poor health, as his ulcer was flaring up. Purcell sent a plane and a nurse to bring Hubbard and Alexis back to the United States. They arrived in mid-April. The use of the name "Dianetics" was assigned to the new Wichita Foundation, and it was to retain the rights of Hubbard books it published. Purcell was the President, and Hubbard the Vice-President and Chairman of the Board. A few days after his return to the U.S. Sara, not knowing his whereabouts, filed for divorce.[1]

Hubbard felt so confident of his change of fortunes that he telegrammed a proposal of marriage to his Los Angeles girlfriend. Then in June he filed for divorce in Wichita, and negotiated a settlement with Sara. Alexis was returned to her mother, who had not seen her baby for over three months. In return, Sara dropped her Los Angeles suit, abandoned any claim to the million dollars that she said the Foundations had earned in its first year, instead accepting $200 per month for the support of Alexis. She also signed a retraction:

121

I, Sara Northrup Hubbard, do hereby state that the things I have said about L. Ron Hubbard in courts and the public prints have been grossly exaggerated or entirely false. I have not at any time believed otherwise than that L. Ron Hubbard was a fine and brilliant man.

I make this statement of my own free will for I have begun to realize that what I have done may have injured the science of Dianetics, which in my studied opinion may be the only hope of sanity in future generations. I was under enormous stress and my advisers insisted it was necessary for me to carry through as I have done.

There is no other reason for this statement than my own wish to make atonement for the damage I may have done. In the future I wish to lead a quiet and orderly existence with my little girl far away from the enturbulating influences which have ruined my marriage.

The retraction is clearly Hubbard's work (even containing his invented word "enturbulating"), which Sara has confirmed.[2] Sara remarried, and has largely evaded interviewers ever since. In 1972, she broke silence to write to author Paulette Cooper. In that letter, Sara described L. Ron Hubbard, the "fine and brilliant man," as a dangerous lunatic. She explained that her own life had been transformed when she left him, but that she was still frightened both of him and of his followers.

June 1951 brought a major change in Hubbard's fortunes. His divorce was made final, and his book *Science of Survival* was published by the new Wichita Hubbard Dianetic Foundation. The title was coined to appeal to readers of Korzybski's highly popular *Science and Sanity*. Korzybski was even acknowledged in Hubbard's new book. The size of the first edition, 1,250 copies, is evidence of Hubbard's decreasing popularity. He later blamed poor sales on Purcell.[3] The book elaborated the theories of *Dianetics: The Modern Science of Mental Health* in relation to Hubbard's "Tone Scale," gave variations on earlier Dianetics techniques, and made yet more claims for the miraculous properties of auditing.

In *Science of Survival*, Hubbard asserted that an individual's emotional condition, or "tone level," is the key to the interpretation of his personality. The purpose of Dianetics was to raise the individual's tone level to Enthusiasm. In *Dianetics: The Modern Science of Mental Health* the Tone Scale was divided into four numbered "zones": from Apathy to Fear, from Fear to Antagonism, from Antagonism to Conservatism, and on to Enthusiasm.

In *Science of Survival*, the Tone Scale was laid out in far more detail. Death was below Apathy at Tone 0; Grief at 0.5; Fear at 1.0; Covert Hostility at 1.1; Anger at 1.5; Antagonism at 2.0; Boredom at 2.5; Conservatism at 3.0; Cheerfulness at 3.5; and Enthusiasm at 4.0. The numbering was arbitrary, but Hubbard would continue to speak of an enthusiastic person as a "Tone 4," and the wolf in sheep's clothing, or covertly hostile individual, is still called a "1.1" (or "one-one") by Scientologists.

The new book was accompanied by a large fold-out "Hubbard Chart of Human Evaluation," with forty-three columns, each relating to a particular trait, from "Psychiatric range" to "Actual worth to Society," all related to "emotional tone level." By knowing some-one's emotional level, Hubbard claimed you would know their physi-ological condition, and be able to predict their behavior. An Enthusi-astic person will be "near accident-proof" and "nearly immune to bacteria." An Antagonistic person will suffer "severe sporadic ill-nesses," and a Frightened person will suffer from "endocrine and nervous illnesses." An Enthusiastic person will have a "high concept of truth," while a Bored person is "Insincere. Careless of facts," and an Angry person, engages in "blatant and destructive lying."

Hubbard also expounded upon the idea of A.R.C., which was to become central to Scientology. He asserted that Affinity, Reality and Communication are inextricably linked, and dubbed them the ARC triangle. The increase or decrease of one of the corners of this triangle would influence the other two by the same amount. Reality, according to Hubbard, was fundamentally agreement. In its eventual formulation, Affinity, Reality and Communication were said to equal understanding.

In *Science of Survival*, Hubbard referred to the exploration of "past lives." If the "pre-clear" offered a "past life incident," the Auditor should simply "run" him through it. Hubbard complained that Eliz-abeth Foundation Directors "sought to pass a resolution banning the entire subject" of "past lives." However, several Auditors trained at Elizabeth ran "past lives" on Preclears there and say it was Hubbard who was slow to adopt the idea. Eventually Hubbard adopted it with gusto and "past lives" became a focus of Scientology. Although reincarnation was a commonplace idea in the West by this time, Hubbard had undoubtedly met the notion in the works of Aleister Crowley, who also preferred the expression "past lives" to "reincar-nation."

In the new book Hubbard also advanced his "theta-MEST" theory. MEST stands for "Matter, Energy, Space and Time"—the *physical* world. By this time Hubbard asserted that "MEST" and that which animates it are two very different things. He used the Greek letter "theta" to categorize "thought, life force, elan vital, the spirit, the soul." Hubbard described the relationship between "theta" and "MEST":

> Consider that theta in its native state is pure reason or at least pure potential reason. Consider that MEST in its native state is simply the chaotic physical universe, its chemicals and energies active in space and time.
>
> The cycle of existence for theta consists of a disorganized and painful smash into MEST and then a withdrawal with a knowledge of some of the laws of MEST, to come back and smash into MEST again.
>
> MEST could be considered to be under onslaught by theta. Theta could be considered to have as one of its missions, and its only mission where MEST is concerned, the conquest of the physical universe.

The Dianetic movement in 1951 consisted mainly of small autonomous groups, many of which had rejected Hubbard's leadership after the collapse of the Elizabeth Foundation with the ensuing bad press. There were a number of newsletters in circulation, some openly hostile to Hubbard. There was an air of experimentation. Helen O'Brien, who attended, wrote "Audiences at Hubbard's lectures were always partly composed of oddly dynamic fringe characters who were known to us as 'squirrels'. . . . They practically never enrolled at a dianetic foundation, seeming to obey some unwritten law which prohibited them from supporting an organization acting in Hubbard's interest. Nevertheless, his ideas dominated their lives."

At the Wichita Foundation, Hubbard's only duties consisted of giving weekly lectures, and signing students' certificates which were awarded for time spent studying rather than as the result of any examination.

The price of the Dianetic Auditor course remained at $500, but there were far less takers than there had been in Los Angeles six months before. Only 112 people attended the first major conference held at Wichita. They were the remaining core of the Dianetic movement.

Small editions of new Hubbard books and pamphlets poured out of the Wichita Foundation: *Preventative Dianetics, Self Analysis, Education and the Auditor, A Synthesis of Processing Techniques, The Dianetics Axioms, Child Dianetics, Advanced Procedure and Axioms,*

Lectures on Effort Processing, Handbook for Preclears, and *Dianetics the Original Thesis* were all published in the last six months of 1951.

By October 1951, Hubbard attracted only fifty-one students to a brief series of lectures. In December, he held a convention for Dianeticists, and, according to O'Brien, felt betrayed when none of his old Elizabeth colleagues showed up. The men who had helped to make Dianetics a nationwide movement had deserted him. Winter, who had lent the air of medical authority; Morgan, the lawyer who had incorporated the first Foundation; Ceppos, the publisher who had unleashed *Dianetics: The Modern Science of Mental Health* on the world; and, most important, Campbell, Hubbard's first recruiter and greatest publicist, who had virtually created the Dianetics boom. Winter had even written a book which, although it defended Dianetics, attacked Hubbard. Ceppos had published Winter's book.

The first major challenge to Hubbard's leadership came in January 1952. A Minneapolis dianeticist, Ron Howes, was declared "Clear" by his Auditor, Perry Chapdelaine.[4] Remarkable claims were made for, and by, Howes including his statement that he was seeing if he could grow new teeth. To many dianeticists Howe seemed proof of Hubbard's claims. Unfortunately for Hubbard, Howes set up on his own, and attracted a following for his "Institute of Humanics."[5] More desertions from the Hubbard camp followed.

In an effort to raise money, Hubbard launched "Allied Scientists of the World," the name of the organization which had figured in his first post-war novel, *The End Is Not Yet*. From its headquarters in Denver, Colorado, Allied Scientists solicited donations from scientists. Some of the scientists approached were working on secret government projects, and the Justice Department took a keen interest in the approach. Long hours were demanded of the Foundation's lawyer to sort out the ensuing problems.[6]

Unsurprisingly, Hubbard and Purcell had a falling out. At Wichita, Hubbard had joined the "past lives" faction. This leap of attitude from a supposed precision study of the mind to a spiritual practice aggravated the conservative Purcell. Purcell had also initially failed to realize that the Wichita Foundation would be treated as the legal successor to the Elizabeth Foundation, and would therefore be forced to settle Elizabeth's extensive debts, which ran into hundreds of thousands of dollars. Purcell tried to persuade Hubbard to put the Wichita Foundation into voluntary bankruptcy. Hubbard refused, but in February, after creditors had threatened receivership, he resigned.

He sold his seventy percent holding to the Foundation for $1.00, and was granted permission to teach Dianetics. He opened the "Hubbard College" on the other side of town, leaving Purcell the complicated task of settling accounts. The Foundation filed for voluntary bankruptcy.[7]

On the same day, Hubbard sent a telegram to Purcell informing him that he was filing two suits against Purcell for a total of $1 million. Hubbard then published an attack on Purcell, accusing him of bad faith and incompetence. Despite this, the Foundation sent a moderate and matter-of-fact account of events to their members. No one was blamed. The report included a simple record of income and expenditure, showing that the Foundation had earned $141,821, of which $21,945 had been paid to Hubbard. The Foundation had overspent by $63,222 in less than a year of operation. Hubbard launched an out-and-out attack on the Foundation using its mailing lists, which he had misappropriated, and claiming Purcell had been paid $500,000 by the American Medical Association to wreck Dianetics.[8]

In March, a restraining order was put on Hubbard and his lieutenant, James Elliot, requiring that they return the mailing lists, the address plates, tapes of Hubbard's lectures, typewriters, sound-recorders, sound-transcribers and other equipment which had disappeared from the Wichita Foundation. Elliot admitted having "inadvertently" removed this immense haul from the Foundation. When they were eventually returned, in compliance with a court order, some of the master tapes of Hubbard lectures had been mutilated.[9]

The Court auctioned the Foundation's assets, freeing it from debt. Purcell bought the assets outright for $6,124; Hubbard had left the sinking ship a little too hastily. The battle between Hubbard and Purcell continued throughout 1952, with attacks and counterattacks being sent to everyone on the Wichita Foundation mailing list. Purcell distributed the record of the bankruptcy hearings. Hubbard sent out a statement insulting those who had chosen to remain with the official Foundation. He accused them of emotional inadequacy and intellectual shallowness, saying that they obviously preferred shams to the genuine article. Using the tone of a spoiled child in a tantrum, he grieved about his isolation, his unswerving devotion and his unselfishness. Yet again, he claimed to have new techniques which would solve the ills of mankind.[10]

Hubbard also sent out increasingly desperate pleas for funds. For the first time he introduced the ploy of steadily escalating prices. Would-be franchise holders could buy a package of tapes and books, along with the right to use and teach his methods, for $1,000. Soon the price would rise to $1,500, then $2,000 and finally $5,000 within three months. Hubbard outlined the goal of his new organization thus: "Bluntly, we are out to replace medicine in the next three years." He also promised "degrees" in Dianetics.[11]

When the fundraising efforts failed, Hubbard's chief lieutenant, James Elliot, sent out an impassioned plea to Dianeticists: "Dianetics and Mr. Hubbard have been dealt a blow from which they cannot recover. . . . Somehow Mr. Hubbard must get funds to keep Dianetics from being closed down everywhere. . . . He is penniless." Elliot went on to solicit funds for a "free school in Phoenix for the rehabilitation of auditors" and for "free schools across America," saying that Hubbard would "no longer commercialize Dianetics as organizations have made him do." Elliot asked for $25.00 per reader. Donors would be called the "Golds." A month after the announcement of the "free school," Hubbard was advertising counselling at $800 per twenty-five hours.[12]

For six weeks after deserting the Wichita Foundation, Hubbard tried to establish his rival Hubbard College. In this short time, Hubbard gave a series of lectures that changed the whole complexion of Dianetics. He demonstrated the "Electro-psychometer" (or "E-meter"), which later became an integral part of auditing. He talked openly about matters which in later years became the secret "OT" levels, and started to favor the word Scientology.

CHAPTER FOUR

Knowing How to Know

Scientology is used to increase spiritual freedom, intelligence, ability, and to produce immortality.—L. RON HUBBARD, *Dianetics and Scientology Technical Dictionary*

The word "scientology" was not original to Hubbard, having been coined by philologist Alan Upward in 1907. Upward used it to characterize and ridicule pseudoscientific theories. In 1934, the word "Scientologie" was used by a German advocate of Aryan racial theory, Dr. A. Nordenholz, who defined it as "The science of the constitution and usefulness of knowledge and knowing."

The "E-meter," adopted by Hubbard by the time of the 1952 Wichita lectures, has become an indispensable tool of Scientology. Electro-psychometers were not a new idea. Their origins trace back to the 19th century. Jung had enthused about "psychogalvanometers" before the First World War, and they were still in use in the 1940s. Some psychologists use them to this day, and they are standardly incorporated in polygraph lie detectors. None of these devices could have the mystique created around the E-meter by Hubbard.

A Preclear is connected to the meter by two hand held electrodes (soup cans), closing a circuit through which a small electric current is passed. Fluctuations in the current are shown on the E-meter dial. The E-meter used by Hubbard was designed and built by dianeticist Volney Mathieson. Its primary use was, and still is, to detect areas of emotional upset, or "charge." Hubbard once said that his E-meter compared to similar devices "as the electron microscope compares to looking through a quartz stone."[1] He was not given to understatement.

The greatest innovation of the Hubbard College Lectures of March 1952 was the introduction of a new cosmology: Hubbard's history of the universe. Dianeticists had sometimes audited "past lives," but Hubbard had published next to nothing on the subject. Now the "time-track" of the individual was extended long before the womb. The "Theta-MEST" theory (where Theta is "life," and MEST, "Matter, Energy, Space and Time") was expanded to include single "life-units" which Hubbard called "Theta-beings." According to Hubbard, the "Theta-being" is the individual himself, and is *trillions* of years old (he was later to increase even this, to "quadrillions"). In simple terms the "Theta-being" is the human spirit. Unfortunately, Theta-beings have to share human bodies with other lesser spirits, or entities, originally called "Theta bodies." The doctrine of the composite being emerged again in the mid-1960s, becoming the basis of the secret "Operating Thetan," or "OT," levels.

Hubbard claimed that "Theta-beings" had been "implanted" with ideas during the course of their incredibly long existence through the use of electrical shock and pain, combined with hypnotic suggestion; aversion therapy on a grand scale. Hubbard said it was necessary to recall these implants, and to separate out the different entities in an individual, and put them firmly under the command of the Theta-being. This was the direction of Hubbard's new auditing techniques.

Hubbard said he had been researching Theta - beings for over a year, but had not considered it timely to release his findings. He said he had originally called his subject "Scientology" as early as 1938, and was now reviving the name. Hubbard later said his third wife, whom he met in 1951, helped coin the word.[2] During 1952, he produced the basic substance from which Scientology was wrought. Hubbard also introduced the franchising of his techniques. Satellite organizations would pay a ten percent tithe to him, as well as paying for training in new methods created by Hubbard.[3]

In March 1952, Hubbard was married for the third and final time. Mary Sue Whipp had arrived at the Wichita Foundation in mid-1951, and worked on the staff there as an Auditor. By April, Ron and Mary Sue had left the short-lived Hubbard College in Wichita, and moved to Phoenix, Arizona, where they opened the new world headquarters of Hubbardian therapy. So it was that Scientology, which Hubbard defined as "knowing how to know" (close to Nordenholz's definition), was born.[4]

Despite Hubbard's assertions that Purcell was determined to wreck Dianetics, the latter continued to run the Wichita Foundation after buying it in bankruptcy court proceedings. Ron Howes' Humanics and other derivatives were flourishing, beyond Hubbard's control, and drifting away from his original ideas. Hubbard's former publicist, John Campbell, had accused him of increasing authoritarianism and dogmatism in an independent Dianetic newsletter, writing that "In a healthy and growing science, there are many men who are recognized as being competent in the field, and no one man dominates the work. . . . To the extent Dianetics is dependent on one man, it is a cult. To the extent it is built on many minds and many workers, it is a science."[5]

Hubbard had decided that psychology had forgotten that "psyche" meant "spirit," and with Scientology he was going to put this right. Therapy would now center upon the Theta-being, the spirit. By the final Wichita lectures, his audience had been down to around thirty. According to Helen O'Brien, the Hubbard College in Phoenix "languished with never more than a handful of students." Hubbard's image as a popular psychological scientist had deteriorated. To many he was a crank with a few impassioned devotees, all magnetized by his unflagging charisma.

Hubbard set up the Hubbard Association of Scientologists in Phoenix, and announced a new state of Clear. The Theta Clear was supposedly an individual "capable of dismissing illness and aberration from others at will" and "able to produce marked results at a distance."[6]

Hubbard's book *What to Audit*, was published in July, claiming in the foreword to be a "cold-blooded and factual account of your last sixty trillion years." As the book progresses, sixty million becomes seventy, and then seventy-four trillion years. With Scientology, we are told, "the blind again see, the lame walk, the ill recover, the insane become sane and the sane become saner."

In *Dianetics: The Modern Science of Mental Health* Hubbard insisted "Dianetics cures, and cures without failure."[7] In *What to Audit*, he said "in auditing the whole track [ie "past lives"], one can obtain excellent results . . . in auditing the current lifetime, one can obtain slow and mediocre results." In just two years, the allegedly miraculous techniques of *Dianetics* had become "slow and mediocre." When he left the Wichita Foundation, Hubbard also left the rights to his earlier books. He had to find something new and different if he was to retain any of his dwindling following.

What to Audit is the foundation of Scientology. It is still in print, minus one chapter, under the title *Scientology: A History of Man*. The material in the book is hardly encountered in contemporary auditing, but is still required reading for the second secret "OT" level of Scientology. A slim pretense at scientific method is blended with a strange amalgam of psychotherapy, mysticism and pure science fiction; mainly the latter. *What to Audit* is among the most bizarre of Hubbard's works, and deserves the cult status that some truly dreadful science fiction movies have achieved. The book leaves the strong suspicion that Hubbard had continued with his experiments into phenobarbitol, and into more powerful "mind-expanding" drugs, as his son Nibs later asserted.

Hubbard claimed to have absolute proof of past lives, though he made no attempt at verifiable case histories. He wrote that "Gravestones, ancient vital statistics, old diplomas and medals will verify in every detail the validity of 'many lifetimes.' " He was in fact relying on the E-meter which, if it works at all, can do no more than indicate the certainty with which a conviction is held.

The book contains the usual series of representations for the eradication of illnesses and physical disabilities, ranging from toothache to cancer. Scientologists' medical histories bear witness to the inadequacy of these remedies.

Hubbard was already equivocating about his discovery of the many "entities" compacted into the individual, and commented that these entities were probably just "compartments of the mind." Otherwise, his imagination ran on unchecked. The Theta-being, or "Thetan," governs the composite which we think of as the individual, but the body itself is governed by the "genetic entity," a sort of low grade soul, which passes to another body after death.

Hubbard claimed the Thetan could remodel his physical form, lose weight, enhance features, even add a little height and was readily capable of telepathy, telekinesis and remote viewing.

What to Audit lists a series of incarnations or a "time-track" from the beginnings of the universe to man: the evolution, or "genetic line," of the human body. According to Hubbard, the "time-track" runs back to a point where the individual seemed to be "an atom, complete with electronic rings." After which came the "cosmic impact," then the "photon converter," and then the first single-cell creature to reproduce by dividing, the "helper." Passing quickly through "seaweed," the evolutionary line moved on to "jellyfish" and then the "clam."

The description of the "clam" makes particularly fine reading. Hubbard was quite right when he warned that the reader may think that he, the author, has "slipped a cable or two in his wits." He warned his followers of dangers inherent in any discussion of "the clam":

> By the way, if you cannot take a warning, your discussion of these incidents with the uninitiated in Scientology can produce havoc. Should you describe "the clam" to some one [sic], you may restimulate it in him to the extent of causing severe jaw hinge pain. One such victim, after hearing about a clam death could not use his jaws for three days. Another "had to have" two molars extracted because of the resulting ache. . . . So do not be sadistic with your describing them [these incidents] to people—unless, of course, they belligerently claim that Man has no past memory for his evolution. In that event, describe away. It makes believers over and above enriching your friend the dentist who, indeed, could not exist without these errors and incidents on the evolutionary line!

The next stage in Hubbard's evolutionary theory was another shell-fish, the "Weeper" (also the "Boohoo," or as Hubbard jovially refers to it at one point, "the Grim Weeper"). This creature is the origin of human "belching, gasping, sobbing, choking, shuddering, trembling." Fear of falling has its origin with hapless Weepers which were dropped by predatory birds. After a few comments on "being eaten" (which allegedly explains diet fads and vegetarianism), Hubbard moves forward in evolution to the sloth. It seems that none of the incarnations between shellfish and the sloth was unpleasant enough to cause major psychological damage. From the sloth, Hubbard moves on to the "ape," and the Piltdown man (who had very large teeth, and a nasty habit of eating his spouse); then the caveman (who presumably had smaller teeth, and used to cripple his wife instead of eating her). From there, usually "via Greece and Rome," Hubbard's theory moves to modern times.

What to Audit was published in the year before complete proof discrediting the Piltdown man was announced. However, Hubbard's book has remained uncorrected. Quite typically, as Hubbard did not tend to revise or correct his earlier works.

However, this explanation of evolution relates only to the "genetic entity." The "Theta-being" only came to earth 35,000 years ago (presumably from outer space; Velikovsky's *Worlds in Collision* was on the best-seller lists with *Dianetics* in 1950), to transform the caveman into Homo sapiens. The Theta-being has been systematically "implanted" with a variety of control phrases. The earliest such implant was "facsimile one" (or "Fac one"), which originated a mere million years ago "in this Galaxy," but was only given out about ten or twenty thousand years ago in this particular neck of the galaxy.

Hubbard claimed that "Fac one" was inflicted with a black box, the "Coffee-grinder" which played a "push-pull wave" over the victim from side to side, "laying in a bone-deep somatic [pain]." After this the victim was "dumped in scalding water, then immediately in ice water," and finally whirled about in a chair. This was "an outright control mechanism" to prevent rebellion against the "Fourth Invader Force," and created "a nice, non-combative, religiously insane community."

Hubbard described many other implants in bizarre detail including the Halver, the Joiner, the Between-lives (administered in an "implant station" in the Pyrenees, or on Mars), the Emanator, the Jiggler, the Whirler, the Fly-trap, the Boxer, the Rocker, and so on, and so on.

In *What to Audit*, Hubbard also warned that the Earth was on the verge of psychic war. In a 1952 lecture called "The Role of Earth," he explained that the Fourth Invader Force still had outposts on Mars. These were the very individuals responsible for the "between lives implants." Hubbard made no comment on the later failure of planetary probes to discover any signs of the Invaders on Mars, nor of the Fifth Invader Force, who supposedly inhabit Venus.

After *What to Audit* was published, Hubbard went to England for three months, taking his pregnant wife with him. Mary Sue's first child, Diana Meredith DeWolf Hubbard, was born in London, in September some six months after their marriage. At the end of November, Ron was back in Philadelphia at the most successful of the Association centers, the Scientology organization run by Helen O'Brien and John Neugebauer (or "Noyga"). Helen O'Brien's book, *Dianetics in Limbo*, gives a vivid account of her close association with Hubbard.

In December 1952, Hubbard gave the Philadelphia Doctorate Course lectures to an audience of just thirty-eight.[8] The lectures were taped, all seventy-two hours of them. The tapes are still heavily promoted, and sold for a high price, as is a course including them all. The lectures were based on Hubbard's newest book, *Scientology 8.8008*. Here the cosmology of Scientology was further expanded. Hubbard took the symbol "8" for infinity (by turning the mathematicians' infinity symbol upright), and explained that the book's title meant the attainment of infinity (the first 8) by the reduction of the physical universe's command value to zero (the 80), and the increase of the individual's personal universe to an infinity (the last 08). In short, through the application of the techniques given in the lectures, the individual would become a god.

The Theta-being, or individual human spirit, acquired the name it retains in Scientology: the Thetan. The Thetan is the self, the "I," that which is "aware of being aware" in Man. Since its entry into the physical universe *trillions* of years ago the Thetan, originally all-knowing, has declined through a "dwindling spiral" of introversion into Matter, Energy, Space and Time. The Thetan can allegedly "exteriorize" from its physical body, and Hubbard gave auditing techniques which he claimed would achieve this result. The Thetan is immortal and capable of all sorts of remarkable feats. Scientologists call these "Operating Thetan" (or "OT") abilities. They include telekinesis, levitation, telepathy, recall of previous lives, "exterior" perception (or "remote viewing"), disembodied movement to any desired location, and the power to will events to occur: to transform, create or destroy Matter, Energy, Space and Time (or "MEST").

The main new auditing technique was Creative Processing. In Creative Processing, the Auditor asks the Preclear to make a "mental image picture" of something. During a demonstration Hubbard asked a female subject to "mock-up" a snake. She refused, because she was frightened of snakes. So Hubbard asked her to "mock it up" at a distance from her. He directed her to make it smaller, change its color, and so forth, until she had the confidence to let it touch her. Theoretically, this would allay the subject's fear of snakes.

In the seventy-two hours of the Philadelphia Doctorate Course, Hubbard expounded an *entire* cosmology. He talked about implants, the Tarot, a civilization called Arslycus (where we were all slaves for 10,000 life-times, largely spending our time polishing bricks in zero-gravity), how to sell people on Scientology, "anchor points" (which Thetans extend to mesh their *own* space with that of the physical universe), how to bring up children, and how to give up smoking (by smoking as much as you can)—about a hundred and one things. And he did it all with his usual mischievous charm.

Hubbard also defined his Axioms of Scientology at great length. We learn that "Life is basically static" without mass, motion, wavelength, or location in space or in time; that the physical universe is a reality only because we all *agree* it is a reality. (Robert Heinlein used this idea in *Stranger in a Strange Land*. Mahayana Buddhists have mulled it over for centuries.)

It was during the course of the Philadelphia Doctorate Course that Hubbard mentioned his "very good friend," Aleister Crowley, and in places his ideas do seem to be a science fictionalized extension of Crowley's black magic. Crowley too was an advocate of visualization techniques.

On the afternoon of December 16, the lectures were abruptly interrupted by the arrival of U.S. Marshals. A warrant had been issued against Hubbard for failing to return $9,000 withdrawn from the Wichita Foundation. There was something of a scuffle with the Marshals. Hubbard was arrested, but returned to finish the lecture that evening.[9] Almost immediately afterward, he left for England to complete the "Doctorate" series there. Hubbard had claimed to have no idea of his income from the Wichita Foundation, saying he had been denied access to the financial records.[10] Eventually, he settled by paying $1,000 and returning a car supplied by Purcell. Remarkably, this was the last time that Hubbard was apprehended by the law.

Hubbard kept his devotees apace of his ideas by issuing regular newsletters. He continued to make strenuous claims for his miraculous mental "technology," for example: "Leukaemia is evidently psychosomatic in origin and at least eight cases of leukaemia had been treated successfully with Dianetics after medicine had traditionally [sic] given up. The source of leukaemia has been reported to be an engram containing the phrase 'It turns my blood to water.' "[11]

In England in May 1953, Hubbard complained that he had just given "probably the most disastrous lecture in terms of attendance in the city of Birmingham." In the same month he explained that he was off to the Continent "to stir up some interest in Scientology. I will be stopping at various spas and have an idea of entering this little bomb of a racing car I have in a few of the all-outs in Europe. The car has a 2.5 litre souped-up Jaguar engine. It is built of hollow steel tubing and aluminium and weighs nothing. Its brakes sometimes work but its throttle never fails. I have also a British motorcycle which might do well in some of these scrambles. . . . I think by spreading a few miracles around the spas, I will be able to elicit considerable interest in Scientology.'' No report followed about the miracles performed or the races run. Hubbard seems instead to have taken a long holiday in Spain.[12]

Meanwhile, Helen O'Brien and her husband were managing the Scientology empire from Philadelphia. Under their direction, it started to prosper. The last Hubbard Congress they arranged was attended by about 300, and "each paid a substantial fee to attend.'' But in October, O'Brien and Noyga became disillusioned with Hubbard's attitude and actions:

> Beginning in 1953, the joy and frankness shifted to pontification. The fact filled "engineering approach" to the mind faded out of sight, to be replaced by a "Church of Scientology" . . . as soon as we became responsible for Hubbard's interests, a projection of hostility began, and he doubted and double-crossed us, and sniped at us without pause. We began to believe that the villains of dianetics-Scientology, had been created by its founder. . . . My parting words [to Hubbard] were inelegant but, I still think, apropos. "You are like a cow who gives a good bucket of milk, then kicks it over.''

Having entered the realm of the spirit, or Thetan, it was only natural that Scientology should shift its legal status from a psychotherapy to a religion. Religious belief is protected in the United States by the Constitution. So Hubbard could entice the public with claims of "spiritual" cures, and the U.S. government, the American Medical Association, and the American Psychiatric Association would be severely handicapped in any attempt to restrict him.

The Religion Angle

Dianetics and Scientology are more a crusade for sanity than they are a business.—L. RON HUBBARD, 1954

The things which have been happening . . . have removed Scientology entirely from any classification as a psychotherapy. . . . We can only exist in the field of religion.—L. RON HUBBARD, "The Hope of Man," 1955

In his autobiography *Over My Shoulder*, publisher Lloyd Arthur Eshbach remembered taking lunch with John Campbell and Ron Hubbard in 1949. Hubbard repeated a statement he had already made to several other people. He said he would like to start a religion, because that was where the money was.

In 1980, Hubbard issued a statement saying Scientologists had "insisted" their organization become a "Church," adding, "It is sometimes supposed that I founded the Church. This is not correct." Perhaps time had affected Hubbard's memory.

The Scientologists maintain that the Church of Scientology of California was their first Church. It was incorporated in California on February 18, 1954, by Burton Farber. In an explanatory letter of the following month, Hubbard said the new "Church" was contracted to the "Church of American Science," to which it paid a twenty percent tithe. Naturally, Hubbard was the President of the Church of American Science.[1]

In fact, both the Church of American Science and a Church of Scientology had been incorporated without fanfare by Hubbard in December 1953, in Camden, New Jersey, along with the "Church of Spiritual Engineering." The Church of American Science was represented as a Christian Church.[2]

Evidence of Hubbard's interest in moving Scientology into a religious position was given in the Armstrong case. On April 10, *1953*, Hubbard wrote from England to Helen O'Brien, who had just taken over the management of Scientology in the U.S., telling her that it was time to move from a medical to a religious image. His objectives were to eliminate all other psychotherapies, to salvage his ailing organization, and, Hubbard was quite candid, to make a great deal of money. Being a religion rather than a psychotherapy was a purely commercial matter, Hubbard said. He enthused about the thousands that could be milked out of preclears attracted by this new promotional approach.[3]

As usual, Hubbard was keeping all of the options open. In his explanatory letter to the membership about the new "Church," he also introduced the "Freudian Foundation of America." A variety of degrees were offered to students, including "Bachelor of Scientology," "Doctor of Scientology," "Freudian Psycho-analyst," and "Doctor of Divinity" to be issued by the "University of Sequoia," an American diploma mill (which was closed down by the California Department of Education in 1958). Hubbard had already received an "honorary doctorate" in philosophy from Sequoia.[4]

In New Zealand, the Auckland Scientology group also became a Church in February 1954. Gradually other centers followed suit, and "Churches of Scientology" came into being all over the world. These "Churches" were franchises paying a tithe to the "mother church." Scientology had become the McDonald's hamburger chain of religion, increasingly absorbing the mass-production and marketing aspects of North American commerce.

In 1954, Don Purcell, weary of the battle with L. Ron Hubbard, and unable to make his Dianetic organization self-sustaining, withdrew to join Art Coulter's "Synergetics," a derivative of Dianetics. Purcell dissolved the Wichita Dianetic Foundation, and gave its assets to Hubbard. These included the copyrights to several Hubbard books. The use of the word "Dianetics" and even the name "L. Ron Hubbard" had been in dispute. Hubbard had complete control of his original subject once again. He expressed his jubilation in a newsletter to Scientologists, in which he even forgave Purcell, if only for a short time. Purcell had given his own attitude succinctly earlier that year: "Ron's motive has always been to limit Dianetics to the Authority of his teachings. Anyone who has the affrontry [sic] to suggest that others besides Ron could contribute creatively to the work must be inhibited."[5]

Hubbard had learned from his mistakes. He employed a simple method of retaining complete control over his many Scientology and Dianetic corporations. He was not on the board of every corporation, so a check of records would not show his outright control. He did, however, collect signed, undated resignations from directors before their appointment. Hubbard also controlled the bank accounts.[6]

In May 1953, in a "Professional Auditor's Bulletin," Hubbard had written: "It is definitely none of my business how you apply these techniques. I am no policeman ready with boards of ethics and court warrants to come down on you with a crash simply because you are 'perverting Scientology.' If there is any policing to be done, it is by the techniques themselves, since they have in themselves a discipline brought about by their own power. All I can do is put into your hands a tool for your own use and then help you use it."

By 1955, Hubbard's attitude had changed markedly. In one of his most bizarre pieces, "The Scientologist: A Manual on the Dissemination of Material," Hubbard recommended legal action against those who set up as independent practitioners of Scientology, or "squirrels": "The purpose of the suit is to harass and discourage rather than to win. The law can be used very easily to harass, and enough harassment on somebody who is simply on the thin edge anyway, well knowing that he is not authorized, will generally be sufficient to cause his professional decease. If possible, of course, ruin him utterly."

Hubbard further urged that Scientologists employ private detectives to investigate critics of Scientology, adding: "we should be very alert to sue for slander at the slightest chance so as to discourage the public press from mentioning Scientology."

During the late 1950s, most of the independent groups either became "Churches," or went out of business. They had accepted Hubbard's direction, and were under contract to his "Hubbard Association of Scientologists International," but Hubbard wanted complete legal control. The franchised "Churches" were gradually absorbed into various organizations controlled directly by Hubbard.

Hubbard continued to write to the FBI's Department of Communist Activities. He asserted that the Russians had on three occasions tried to recruit him, and were upset by his patriotic refusal to work for them. By now, Hubbard felt that his organizations had been harassed from the outset not only by psychiatrists but also by Communist infiltrators. He claimed that the most recent approach was from an individual with a position in the U.S. government.[7]

A few months later, Hubbard again complained of Communist infiltration into Scientology organizations. He cited examples of Scientologists suddenly going insane, and attributed this to psychiatrists using LSD. He made no suggestion that Scientology itself might have had anything to do with these eruptions of insanity. He alleged that since offering his brainwashing techniques to the Defense Department, his organizations had been under constant attack.[8]

In September 1955, Hubbard published an issue entitled "Psychiatrists," calling Scientology "the only Anglo-Saxon development in the field of the mind and spirit," and insisting that Scientologists inform the authorities if they suspected that any of their clients had been given LSD surreptitiously by a psychiatrist.

The FBI tired of Hubbard's missives, and stopped acknowledging them. One agent wrote "appears mental" on a Hubbard letter. Hubbard later privately admitted to having taken LSD himself.[9]

At the end of 1955, the "Hubbard Communications Office" in Washington, DC, published a peculiar booklet entitled *Brainwashing*, which claimed to be a Russian textbook on "psychopolitics" written by the Soviet chief of the secret police, Beria. In an elaborate charade, Hubbard claimed the booklet had arrived anonymously, and mentioned a version in German, published in Berlin in 1947, and discovered in the Library of Congress. The Library has no record of the German booklet. The version published by the Scientologists cannot have been written before December 1953, as there are several references to the "Church of Scientology." In fact, the author of *Brainwashing* was none other than L. Ron Hubbard. There are two witnesses, and the literary style and the slant of the contents provide further evidence of Hubbard's authorship:[10]

> You must work until "religion" is synonymous with "insanity." You must work until the officials of city, county and state governments will not think twice before they pounce upon religious groups as public enemies. . . . Like the official the bona-fide medical healer also be-

lieves the worst if it [religion] can be shown to him as dangerous competition.

Hubbard was perfectly willing to cash in on the intense interest in brainwashing, a hot topic in the United States with the return of POWs from North Korea. He was also willing to infect his devotees with his paranoia, and the booklet highlighted the grand conspiracy supposedly directed against Hubbard and his organizations.

In 1956, Hubbard recommended that Scientologists recruit new people by placing the following advertisement in the newspapers: "Polio victims. A research foundation investigating polio, desires volunteers suffering from the effects of that illness to call for examination."

Hubbard said that the "research foundation" could also advertise for asthmatics or arthritics. Further: "Any auditor anywhere can constitute himself as a minister or an auditor, a research worker in the field of any illness. . . . It is best that a minister representing himself as a 'charitable organization' . . . do the research."

Hubbard also recommended that his followers engage in "Casualty Contact": "Every day in the daily papers one discovers people who have been victimized one way or the other by life. It does not much matter whether that victimizing is in the manner of mental or physical injury. . . . One takes every daily paper . . . and cuts from it every story whereby he might have a preclear. . . . As speedily as possible he makes a personal call on the bereaved or injured person. . . . He should represent himself to the person or the person's family as a minister whose compassion was compelled by the newspaper story."

This strategy underlines the cold-bloodedness which Scientology gradually inculcates in its adherents. Compassion becomes a tactical display rather than natural feeling. "Sympathy" is frowned upon as being emotionally "down-tone," and the word "victim" is a term of derision. The Scientologists even have a course which requires that students go into hospitals and, representing themselves as "volunteer ministers," use Scientology techniques on the patients, encouraging them to take up Scientology."

Hubbard was also making claims that his "technology" could deal with the effects of radioactive fallout. In 1956, he gave a lecture series in Washington, styled "The Anti-Radiation Congress Lectures." In April 1957, he held the "London Congress on Nuclear Radiation and Health Lectures" at the Royal Empire Society Hall. Three of these lectures were condensed, and became chapters in his book *All About*

Radiation, allegedly written by "a Nuclear Physicist and a Medical Doctor." The "Nuclear Physicist" was L. Ron Hubbard, the "Medical Doctor" hid behind the pseudonym "Medicus" (the Library of Congress lists him as Richard Farley, quite possibly a Hubbard pseudonym). In the section purportedly written by "Medicus" we are told that "some very recent work by L. Ron Hubbard and the Hubbard Scientology Organization, has indicated that a simple combination of vitamins in unusual doses can be of value. Alleviation of the remote effects and increased tolerance to radiation have been the apparent results."[12]

While it was possible to defend against prosecution in the United States for claims of miracle cures by invoking the First Amendment's freedom of belief, it was stupid of Hubbard to sell his vitamin mixture as a specific for radiation sickness. In 1958, the Food and Drug Administration (F.D.A.) seized a consignment of 21,000 "Dianazene" tablets, which were marketed by a Scientology company, the Distribution Center. The tablets were destroyed by the F.D.A. because their labeling claimed they were a preventative and treatment for radiation sickness.[13]

This was not the last time Hubbard tangled with the F.D.A. Nor was it the last time he claimed a cure for the effects of radiation. The Scientologists still advertise *All About Radiation* with a flier which claims that "L. Ron Hubbard has discovered a formula which can proof a person against radiation." Scientologists believe that enormous doses of Niacin, a form of vitamin B3, will protect them from the devastating effects of exposure to radiation in the event of nuclear war.

The Church encountered other legal problems in the United States. One of the possible advantages of dubbing an organization "religious" was the right to claim tax-exempt status. The Washington "Church" had obtained exempt status in 1956, and other "Churches" had followed suit. Then, in 1958, exemption was denied. The Washington Church appealed to the U.S. Court of Claims. The Tax Court ruled that exempt status was rightly withdrawn, because Hubbard and his wife were benefiting financially from the Church of Scientology beyond reasonable remuneration.

Between June 1955 and June 1959, Hubbard had been *given* $108,000 by the Scientology Church, along with the use of a car, all expenses paid. The Church maintained a private residence for him

through 1958 and 1959. His family, including his son Nibs and his daughter Catherine, had also withdrawn thousands of dollars. Mary Sue Hubbard derived over $10,000 income by renting property to the Church. On top of this, Hubbard received his tithes (ten percent, or more) from Scientology organizations throughout the world. Despite Hubbard's pronouncements, Scientology and Dianetics were very definitely a business, a profit-making organization, run by Hubbard for his personal enrichment.[14]

Through the 1950s, Scientology tried to develop a good public image. The therapy had become a religious practice, compared by Hubbard to the Christian confessional, and the therapists had become ministers. The trappings of religion were assembled, including ministerial garb complete with dog-collar, and wedding, naming and funeral rites. Hubbard's berserk outbursts were lost amid a welter of new auditing procedures. His paranoia was better contained, though Church leaders were told to cease communication with critics of Scientology whom Hubbard called "Merchants of Chaos," the beginnings of the doctrine of "disconnection."[15]

To the general public, Scientology was represented as a humanitarian, religious movement, intent upon benefiting all mankind. Its opponents were dangerous enemies of freedom, and were tarred with unfashionable epithets such as communist, homosexual, or drug addict. Opponents were portrayed as members of a deliberate conspiracy to silence Hubbard, and bring down the "shades of night" over the Earth.[16]

To its membership, Scientology was represented as a science, liberating man from all his disabilities, and freeing in him undreamt abilities. To the Church hierarchy, Scientology was the only hope of freedom for mankind, and must be protected at all costs. Hubbard was nothing short of a Messiah, whose wisdom and perception far outstripped that of any mere mortal. Hubbard's commandments might at times be unfathomable, but his word was law.

The Hubbard Communication Office *Manual of Justice* laid down the law for Scientology staff members. In it Hubbard wrote: "People attack Scientology; I never forget it, always even the score."

The *Manual of Justice* introduced a comprehensive "intelligence" system into Hubbard's organizations. Hubbard wrote: "Intelligence is mostly the collection of data on people which may add up to a summary of right or wrong actions on their part. . . . It is done all the time about everything and everybody. . . . When a push against Scientology starts somewhere, we go over the people involved and weed them out.''

If ''intelligence'' failed, then investigation was called for: ''When we need somebody haunted we investigate. . . . When we investigate we do so noisily always. And usually investigation damps out the trouble even when we discover no really pertinent facts. Remember that—*by investigation alone* we can curb pushes and crush wildcat people and unethical 'Dianetics and Scientology' organizations,'' and, ''intelligence we get with a whisper. Investigation we do with a yell. Always.''

Hubbard explained to staff members: ''Did you ever realize that any local viciousness against Scientology organizations is *started* by somebody for a purpose? Well, it is . . . rumours aren't 'natural'. When you run them down you find a Commie or a millionaire who wants us dead. . . . You find amongst all our decent people some low worm who has been promised high position and pay if we fail. . . . When you have found your culprit, go to the next step, Judgment and Punishment.''

Hubbard's instruction to use private detectives has certainly been followed by the Scientology Church over the ensuing years. The reader of the confidential *Manual* is told: ''Of twenty-one persons found attacking Dianetics and Scientology . . . eighteen of them under investigation were found to be members of the Communist Party or criminals, usually both. The smell of police or private detectives caused them to fly, to close down, to confess. Hire them and damn the cost when you need to.''

Magazine articles unfavorable to Scientology were to be met with a letter demanding retraction, followed by an investigation of the author for his ''criminal or Communist background'' by a private detective. The magazine would be threatened with legal action, and the author sent ''a very tantalizing letter . . . tell him we know something interesting about him,'' and invited to a meeting, ''chances are he won't arrive. But he'll sure shudder into silence.''

In the ''Judgment and Punishment'' section of his *Manual of Justice* Hubbard wrote:

> We may be the only people on Earth with a right to punish . . . never punish beyond our easy ability to remedy by auditing [a difficult point in an organization which believes it can mend the hurt of former lives and *deaths*] . . . . Our punishment is not as unlimited [sic] as you might

think. Dianetics and Scientology are self-protecting sciences. If one attacks them one attacks all the know-how of the mind . . . There are men dead because they attacked us—for instance Dr. Joe Winter. He simply realized what he did and died. There are men bankrupt because they attacked us—Purcell, Ridgway, Ceppos [Ridgway and Ceppos published *Dianetics* in England and the U.S. respectively].

In the *Manual*, Hubbard's suggested punishments were actually mild, consisting largely of the cancellation of any certificates awarded by his organizations. He suggested that an organization "shoot the offender for the public good and then patch him up quietly." A mood was being created in which staff members would become "deployable agents," as sociologist Roy Wallis called Hubbard's henchmen in his excellent study of Scientology. After all, Hubbard never gave any indication of the possibility that a complaint against him or against Scientology could be justifiable. The tactic of "noisy investigation" originated in the *Manual*, and came to mean harassment by defamation. Hubbard certainly did not mind if the defamation was grossly exaggerated, or even a total fabrication. If you throw enough mud, some will stick. The *Manual of Justice* clearly suggests outright blackmail.

The Scientology organizations grew steadily, and, in the spring of 1959, Hubbard purchased the Maharajah of Jaipur's English manor house and estate in the beautiful Sussex countryside, at Saint Hill village, a few miles from East Grinstead.

CHAPTER SIX

The Lord of the Manor

The least free person is the person who cannot reveal his own acts and who protests the revelation of the improper acts of others. On such people will be built a future political slavery.—L. RON HUBBARD, "Honest People Have Rights Too," 1960

Saint Hill, a sandstone, Georgian manor house, built in 1733, was an unlikely setting for the red-headed maverick from Montana. Upon his arrival, Hubbard set up the Scientology World-wide Management Control Center, though he told the East Grinstead newspapers he had retired to England to do horticultural experiments and to work in theoretical physics. He claimed to be treating plants with radioactivity. Hubbard became a regular contributor to *Garden News*, even demonstrating his horticultural findings on English television. His experiments consisted in part of using an E-meter to measure a plant's response to threats in its environment. There is an amusing newspaper picture which shows Hubbard gazing intently at a tomato, still on the vine, with two E-meter crocodile clips and a nail jabbed into it.[1]

With a typical lack of modesty Hubbard announced his horticultural innovations to Scientologists, claiming, in the third person, that "Ron has already created everbearing tomato plants and sweet corn plants sufficiently impressive to startle British Newspapers into front page stories about this new wizardry." How Hubbard knew the tomatoes were "everbearing" after only a few months is not known.

Hubbard's stated purpose for this project was "to reform the world food supply."[2]

At the end of the 1959 growing season, Hubbard introduced "Security Checking." The E-meter was now to be used to discover "overts" committed by Scientologists. An "overt" is basically a transgression against a moral code. In later times Security Checking was renamed "Integrity Processing" or "Confessional Auditing," linking the procedure to the Confessional of the Christian Church. Rather than a simple request to confess, the Preclear is asked a series of precise questions (often several hundred), and must describe very exactly any overt discovered during the process. The E-Meter is used throughout to try to ensure there are no evasions. The Auditor carefully notes the details of any overt he has "pulled" from the Preclear.[3]

In theory, Security Checking could be applied either as a Confessional, in which case the replies obtained were said to be confidential, or during the course of an investigation, in which case they were not. In practice, the Confessional has proved to be a double-edged procedure, sometimes giving genuine relief, but always harboring the potential future use of the material as blackmail. An enthusiastic convert is willing to expose even his most tortured secret. Should he become disillusioned by Church practices, he will keep quiet for fear that his confession will be disclosed.

Hubbard's oldest child, L. Ron Hubbard, Jr., or "Nibs," had been a leading light in Scientology since 1952, when, at the age of eighteen, he became Executive Director of the Washington Scientology Church. He was even one of the handful of people who had given "Advanced Clinical Courses" in Scientology. His father had described him as "one of the best auditors in the business." In November 1959, Hubbard senior ordered that the staffs of all Scientology Orgs be given an E-meter check. On November 23, Nibs left the Washington Org, and the Church of Scientology. Hubbard said his son was unable to "face an E-meter," and issued a Bulletin saying the cause of all "departures, sudden and relatively unexplained" was unconfessed overts.[4] According to Nibs, his departure from the Church was actually due to inadequate remuneration. Nibs later suggested that his father needed to confess *his* overts, and for many years Nibs was his father's most outspoken opponent. Hubbard senior disowned Nibs completely in 1983. Nibs accepted a financial settlement from the Scientologists after his father's death in 1986, agreeing not to make further comment.

The idea that unrevealed transgressions cause departures from the Church is now deeply embedded in Scientology theory. No one who leaves has a chance to explain his departure. Scientologists are sure that the person must have "overts" against Scientology, therefore nothing a former member says can be trusted, so it is not worth listening to them.

In March 1960, *Have You Lived Before This Life? A Scientific Survey* was published. The book is a jumble of Scientology auditing sessions, where Preclears related fragments of their "past life" experiences. No attempt was made to verify any of the incidents. Freudians would have a field day with the contents.

That month, in an internal memo to his press officer, Hubbard also commented on the public image he wished to create for himself. In every press release it was to be made clear that he was an atomic scientist, a researcher, rather than a spiritualist or a psychiatrist.[5]

Hubbard's major research at the time was into "Security Checking," and he was looking for applications for this new "technology." Hubbard saw potential political uses, and sent a Bulletin to all South African Auditors called "Interrogation (How to read an E-Meter on a silent subject)," which reads in part:

> When the subject placed on a meter will not talk but can be made to hold the cans (or can be held while the cans are strapped to the soles or placed under the armpit . . .) [sic], it is still possible to obtain full information from the subject.

This interrogation was recommended for tracing the true leaders of riots:

> The end product is the discovery of a terrorist, usually paid, usually a criminal, often trained abroad. Given a dozen people from a riot or strike, you can find the instigator. . . . Thousands are trained every year in Moscow in the ungentle art of making slave states. Don't be surprised if you wind up with a white.

In April 1960, the Bulletin "Concerning the Campaign for the Presidency" was published recommending that Richard M. Nixon "be prevented at all costs from becoming president." Hubbard blamed Nixon for a distinctly unfriendly visit to the Washington Scientology

Church by "two members of the United States Secret Service," which had upset Mary Sue Hubbard.

Scientologists were offered shares in the "Hubbard Association of Scientologists Limited," registered in England, for £25 each that June. When the HASI Ltd. failed to obtain nonprofit status in England, the shares were bought back, for a shilling each and a life-membership in Scientology, which was later cancelled.[6]

Also in June, the "Special Zone Plan—The Scientologists Role in Life" was promulgated by Hubbard. It recommended that Scientologists who were not on Church staff achieve influence in the society at large, by taking positions next to the high and mighty. "Don't bother to get elected. Get a job on the secretarial staff or the bodyguard," Hubbard advised.

The secretary or bodyguard would then use Scientology to transform the organization they had joined. These Scientologists would be part of a network, reporting back to the project's administrator; as Hubbard put it, "If we were revolutionaries this HCO Bulletin would be a *very* dangerous document."

The Special Zone Plan was absorbed into a new Church "Department of Government Affairs" within weeks of its inception. In the Policy Letter announcing this move Hubbard said, "The goal of the Department is to bring the government and hostile philosophies or societies into a state of complete compliance with the goals of Scientology. This is done by high level ability to control, and in its absence, by low level ability to overwhelm. Introvert such agencies. Control such agencies."

Hubbard not only defined the sinister and covert objective of the Department of Government Affairs, but also delineated the policy Scientology has rigorously followed to this day toward any perceived threat: "Only attacks resolve threats. . . . If attacked on some vulnerable point by anyone or anything or any organization, always find or manufacture enough threat against them to sue for peace. . . . Don't ever defend. Always attack."

During a visit in October 1960, Hubbard again gave his observations on the situation in South Africa: "There is no native problem. The native worker gets more than white workers do in England! . . . . The South African government is not a police state. It's easier on people than the United States government!"[7]

Scientology made the headlines in England when headmistress Sheila Hoad was accused of giving "Death Lessons" to her young pupils. For twenty minutes a day, her small prep school students were asked, among other things, to close their eyes and imagine they were dying, and then imagine they had turned to dust and ashes. After the story went to the press, Miss Hoad resigned.[8]

In the Spring of 1961, Hubbard expanded his Special Zone Plan, by introducing the Department of Official Affairs, "the equivalent of a Ministry of Propaganda and Security." The Department was to create "Heavy influence through our own and similarly minded groups on the public and official mind," and "A filed knowingness [sic] about the activities of friends and enemies."[9]

On March 24, Hubbard launched the Saint Hill Special Briefing Course (or, inevitably, "SHSBC"). Students arrived from all over the world to hear him lecture on new techniques in the Saint Hill chapel. One "technical breakthrough" followed another, and eventually the Briefing Course came to consist of over 300 taped lectures (most delivered during this period). All of Hubbard's recorded lectures, some 3,500 of them, have more recently been designated "religious scriptures" by his Church. Even the most dedicated of Scientologists can not have heard them all, but about 600 tapes are still used in courses.

Hubbard was a remarkable lecturer. A woman close to him in the 1950s, who thought he was fraud even then, says he was quite hypnotic. He raced from one idea to another, illustrating his talks with embroidered stories from his life (and sometimes his *previous* lives). He effused good humor, and spoke with apparent ease, usually without notes. There is nothing dry or academic about his lectures. He was an accomplished comedian, especially if you knew the "in" jokes, many about his pet hate, psychiatry.

On April 7, 1961, Hubbard published the "Johannesburg Security Check," which he described as the "roughest security check in Scientology." An amended form is still in use, and referred to by Scientologists as the "Jo'burg."

The security check began with a series of nonsense questions, such as, "Are you on the moon?" and "Am I an ostrich?" to ensure that the recipient's E-meter response was normal. Then there were a hundred questions. They covered sexual activities thoroughly, with questions such as:

Have you ever committed adultery?
Have you ever practiced Homosexuality?

Have you ever slept with a member of a race of another color?

Senator Joseph McCarthy and his House Un-American Activities Committee were long gone, but Hubbard was still inflamed with anti-Communist fervor, and the sec-check was interspersed with questions about Communism, such as:

What is Communism?
Do you feel Communism has some good points?

The "Jo'burg" covered all manner of wrongdoing, from simple theft to "illicit Diamond buying." It also asked, "Have you ever been a newspaper reporter?" A cardinal sin to Hubbard. At the end of the security check a series of fourteen questions designed to ensure the recipient's loyalty to Hubbard and his organization was asked, among them:

Have you ever injured Dianetics or Scientology?
Have you ever had unkind thoughts about LRH [Hubbard]?
Have you ever had unkind thoughts about Mary Sue [Hubbard]?
Do you know of any secret plans against Scientology?

Throughout 1961, additional Security Checks poured out of the church. There was even one for children. Hubbard ordered that *"All Security Check sheets of persons Security Checked should be forwarded to St. Hill.''*[10]

Hubbard was assembling a comprehensive set of intelligence files on Scientologists with their willing assistance, as well as on supposed enemies without their knowledge. The procedure has been refined, and remains to the present day. The Scientology Church keeps a file on everyone who has ever taken a course or even had a single hour of counseling. Scientologists are not allowed to see the contents of their own confessional files, so cannot correct any errors.

The most elaborate Sec Check was for the "Whole Track" (the whole "Time-Track," "past lives" included), and consisted of over 400 questions. It was written by a couple devoted to Hubbard, and was approved by the man himself. A few sample questions:

Have you ever warped an educational system?
Have you ever destroyed a culture?
Have you ever blanketed bodies for the sensation kick?

Have you ever bred bodies for degrading purposes?
Did you come to Earth for evil purposes?
Have you ever deliberately mocked up an unconfrontability?
Have you ever torn out somebody's tongue?
Have you ever been a professional critic?
Have you ever had sexual relations with an animal, or bird?
Have you ever given God a bad name?
Have you ever eaten a human body?
Have you ever zapped anyone?
Have you ever been a religious fanatic?
Have you ever failed to rescue your leader?[11]

Any wrongdoing discovered during the questioning would be traced back to "earlier similar incidents." It must have taken months to check and recheck all 400 questions. However, it was not very useful for intelligence gathering. You could hardly threaten to expose a person for "zapping" someone 20 trillion years ago. Security Checks were soon limited to "this lifetime."[12]

Hubbard even tried to extend Security Checking into the outside world, by advising Scientologists to set up a "Citizens' Purity League" in their area. The Scientologists would Sec Check local officials and the police. An attempt at this was made in Melbourne, Australia, which was soon to become a very dangerous place indeed for Scientology.[13]

On August 13, 1962, in between lectures at Saint Hill, Hubbard again offered Scientology to the American government. The FBI Communist Activities Department had ceased to exist, and Hubbard decided to go right to the top. He wrote to President Kennedy.[14]

The World's First Real Clear

On May 25, 1961, President Kennedy, in a momentous speech before the United States Congress, urged America to put a man on the moon before the decade was out. It took Hubbard a little while to jump on the bandwagon. His letter to President Kennedy began:

> In the early '40s a lonely letter wandered into the White House, uninvited, unannounced. It was brief. It was factual, and it gave America the deciding edge in arms superiority. Its subject was the atom bomb and its signature was Professor Albert Einstein. . . . This is another such letter.

Hubbard offered his mental "technology" to the President to assist in the Space Program. He repeated his usual tale about Russian interest in his work, saying he had been offered Pavlov's laboratory in 1938. He said Scientology "conditioning" would increase the IQ and "body skills" of astronauts, and that "the perception of a pilot or Astronaut can be increased far beyond normal human range and stamina and be brought to an astonishing level, not hitherto attainable in a human being."

The "conditioning" was to cost $25 per hour. Hubbard ended with an admonition to President Kennedy: "Such an office as yours receives a flood of letters from fakes, crackpots and would-be wonder-workers. This is not such a letter. . . . If that earlier letter from

Einstein had been filed away, we would have lost our all in the following twenty years. Is this such a letter?''

Hubbard did not receive a reply from the President. On January 4, 1963, however, the Food and Drug Administration raided the Washington Church, and Hubbard felt this constituted an indirect response.

The FDA seized a huge quantity of E-meters and books. As with ''Dianazene,'' the FDA charged mislabelling. The raid was precisely the sort of theater Hubbard could use to effect. The dour agents, and the scale of the raid, could only create public sympathy for Scientology. Such reactions by government agencies can do more good than harm to a cult, uniting it and feeding its public image. It makes wonderful press.

Eventually, the FDA won their case against the labelling of the E-Meter, and forced the Scientologists to label it ineffective in the diagnosis or treatment of disease. The Scientologists failed to thoroughly comply with the ordered wording, and took issue with the court's decision (never implemented) to destroy the confiscated books and meters, rather than returning them.

The U.S. government was not alone in its concern about Scientology. On November 27, 1963, the Governor of the Australian State of Victoria appointed a Board of Inquiry into Scientology. The board consisted of one man, Kevin Victor Anderson. He conducted his inquiry with considerable showmanship and ferocity, taking nearly two years to investigate and present his immense report.

While the Australian Inquiry was underway, Hubbard added to his mystique by telling the *Saturday Evening Post* he had been approached for the secrets of Scientology by Castro's Cuban government (the latest Communist threat).[1]

At Saint Hill, Hubbard released his ''Study Technology.'' He began with the premise that no one teaches people *how* to study. Korzybski had argued that it is crucial to fully understand every word in a text, and that there is a physiological response to misunderstood words. Hubbard adopted these ideas, without mention of their source. He dubbed the misunderstood word an ''m.u.'' (mis-understood).

Hubbard emphasized the necessity of studying ''on a gradient.'' It is important to base study on a completely understood idea, and to proceed from one fully comprehended idea to the next. A student should progress with no gaps in his understanding. In a school system, this process would mean that a child would need to do first year chemistry to a 100 percent pass, before moving on to second year chemistry.

Hubbard also asserted that much failure in study is due to an "absence of mass." Where possible the student should come to grips with what he is studying. So an engineer should have a good look at construction materials and real bridges, rather than spending all of his time studying books explaining the chemical makeup of materials, and structural mathematics. Abstractions should be represented by the student through drawing, or with plasticine models (called "clay demos"). Through these a sequence of actions could be demonstrated, and so more thoroughly grasped.

Typically, there has been no proper scientific evaluation of the effectiveness of Hubbard's Study Tech, but pupils of the several Scientology children's schools do not display astonishing aptitude; indeed they seem to perform below the educational average in some cases.

The Scientology world changed rapidly through the early 1960s. By 1965, Hubbard had released an entire organizational system with which Scientology "Orgs" had to comply, the Study Technology, the Ethics Technology, and the new "Bridge."

The approach to Preclears became more systematic. They would start with specific auditing processes or procedures at the bottom of the "Bridge," progressing through numbered grades of "release," at each of which a definite ability should be regained. These release grades deal with memory, communication, problems, "overts" and "withholds," upsets, and justifications for failure, from Grade 0 to IV.[2]

Perhaps the most drastic changes came with the Ethics Technology. Hubbard said that certain people are "antisocial," and are determined opponents of anything which can benefit humanity, especially Scientology. He labelled such people "Suppressive Persons" (or SPs), and asserted that SPs make up two and a half percent of the population. A further seventeen and a half percent are said to be influenced by SPs to such an extent that they are "Potential Trouble Sources" (or PTS). Hubbard decided that PTS people would have to "disconnect" (refuse any communication or contact) from SPs identified by the organization. The rigidity with which this rule has been applied over the years has varied, but marriages have been split up when someone had to disconnect from a spouse labelled "Suppressive."

With the new Ethics Technology came a department of the Org which would "keep ethics in." Hubbard determined that unethical people would not make gains in Scientology, so conversely anyone who did not make gains in Scientology was unethical ("out-ethics"). Where Scientology failed it was the fault of the recipient, never of Scientology. Ethics Officers came into being to deal with "out-ethics" people.

Hubbard introduced a system of reports, where any Scientologist seeing a supposed misapplication of the Technology, or any transgression against Scientology morality, would write a report, which was sent to the Ethics Office. A copy would be filed, and the original sent to the offender. When enough Knowledge Reports had stacked up in a person's folder, he would theoretically be hauled before a Committee of Evidence, and his behavior assessed against Hubbard's extensive list of "Crimes" and "High Crimes." If his "criminality" was sufficient, he would be given a Suppressive Person Declare, copies of which would be posted in Scientology Organizations. Suppressive Person Declares are still issued, and Scientologists could not, and cannot, associate with SPs, without themselves becoming the subject of a Declare.

John McMaster witnessed the introduction and intensification of Ethics first hand. He arrived at Saint Hill in 1963 to do the Briefing Course. His stepmother had pressured him into Scientology a few months earlier, in South Africa. McMaster had been a student of medicine, hoping to specialize in neurosurgery. His fascination for medicine came from direct experience—part of his stomach had been removed because it was cancerous. On his arrival at the Durban Scientology Center he had been in considerable pain for some years. McMaster claims that his first auditing session relieved the pain completely.[3]

By the time Hubbard introduced "SP Declares," in 1965, McMaster was overseeing the Saint Hill Special Briefing Course. Any interesting ideas generated by the students would be taken to Hubbard. The "Power Processes," or "Level V," came into being this way. They coincided with Hubbard's decision that he was the "Source" of Scientology. From this time on, Scientologists were assured that Hubbard had "developed" all of Scientology and Dianetics. To quote his own words, first published in February 1965, and still a part of every major Scientology course: "Willing as I was to accept suggestions and data, only a handful of suggestions (less than twenty) had long run value and *none* were major or basic."[4]

In the beginning, Hubbard tried to legitimize his ideas by acknowledging his debt to thinkers as diverse as Anaxagoras, Lao Tze, Newton and Freud. For a while, Hubbard had awarded the title "Fellow of Scientology" to major contributors. Time had convinced Hubbard that he alone was the fount of all wisdom.

Since its inception four years before, only Briefing Course students had received auditing at Saint Hill. However, with the advent of Power Processes, Saint Hill began to accept paying Preclears. A Hubbard Guidance Center came into being, initially consisting of one man, John McMaster. McMaster says huge amounts were charged to individuals for "Power" auditing, and adds, wryly, that he received none of the money. Despite the high price, Scientologists flocked to Saint Hill. The Hubbard Guidance Center rapidly increased in size.

Hubbard frequently released new "rundowns" or "levels" which attempted to justify the failure of earlier techniques. Each new rundown would be launched amid a fanfare of publicity, and claims of miraculous results. One critic has complained of "auditing junkies," forever waiting for the next "level" to resolve their chronic problems. The issue of a new "level," was invariably greeted with a rash of incredible Success Stories, written as soon as an individual finished the auditing in question. These were usually vague, and always enthusiastic. "This level cracked my case!" is a fair example of these often meaningless statements.

Power, or Level V, was more successful in attracting people than previous "rundowns," starting a financial boom at Saint Hill. Over the years, Hubbard asserted time and time again that he had achieved a routine way of "Clearing" people. Both the definition of Clear and the methods for its achievement changed periodically. After Power, he released Level VI, of which he said:

> A *clear* has no vicious Reactive Mind and operates at total mental capacity just like the first book (*Dianetics: The Modern Science of Mental Health*) said. In fact every early definition of CLEAR is found to be correct. . . . Level VI requires several months to audit through even with expert training. But at its end, MAGIC. *There's* the state of clear we've sought for all these years. It fits *all* definitions ever given for clear.[5]

Even this breakthrough proved ephemeral, and a few months later, Hubbard announced Level VII, which became the "Clearing Course." The Clearing Course was to prove the most durable method of Clearing, lasting until 1978, and is still occasionally used today.

The usual trickle of defecting members who set up their own Scientological groups continued through the 1960s. A splinter group called Compulsions Analysis came into being in London, in 1964, under the direction of a couple named Robert and Mary Ann Moor, who called themselves the "De Grimstons." They later renamed their organization "The Process," and later yet, "The Church of the Final Judgment." Mass murderer Charles Manson was an enthusiastic supporter both of The Process, and of Scientology. Author Maury Terry is convinced that David Berkowitz, the "Son of Sam" killer, was also involved with The Process.[6]

In 1965, Charles Berner, a leading Scientologist, left the fold, and founded "Abilitism." Berner later headed the "Anubhava School of Enlightenment," and was responsible for the "Enlightenment Intensive," which has achieved a certain respectability. Hubbard made Berner the target of considerable harassment.

A major challenge to Hubbard's leadership reared its head in 1964 in the shape of "Amprinistics." The founder of this new movement was Harry Thompson. He said Hubbard had refused his offer of a new and highly workable procedure in 1963, so he had spent two years researching it, and having proven its validity beyond doubt, wished to give it to the world. Unfortunately for Thompson, he chose to give it, or rather sell it, to Scientologists first. Thompson announced his discovery in a huge mailing to Scientologists. He asked that they simply try his method to see if it worked. Thompson also offered an escape from the Ethics Officers, and the increasing discipline of Hubbard's organization.

Jack Horner was one of the very few people who had stayed the course with Hubbard from his beginnings in Elizabeth, New Jersey. Horner took the first Dianetic course in June 1950. He was one of the first to try to convince Hubbard of the validity of "past lives" and the first "Doctor" of Scientology. Horner was one of the few people that Hubbard trusted to give Advanced Clinical Courses. In 1965, Horner had been promoted in *The Auditor* magazine as the first "Honors graduate" of the final section of the immense Saint Hill Special Briefing Course. Disillusioned with the increasing control which Hubbard was visiting upon Scientologists, Horner joined Amprinistics.[7]

Hubbard decided to designate certain materials "confidential" at this time, perhaps so that Scientology could offer something Amprinistics could not. Scientologists believe Hubbard's argument that confidentiality was introduced because the relevant materials are highly "restimulative" (upsetting) to people who are not ready for them. Whatever the reason, Power, Level VI and the Clearing Course were designated "confidential," and remain so to this day. The same is true of the later OT levels.

On September 27, 1965, Hubbard issued a "Hubbard Communications Office Executive Letter" dealing with Amprinistics and its members. Every member of the new group, whether they had entered it via Scientology or not, was labelled Fair Game. Their gatherings were to be broken up. Complaints were to be made to the police and any chance of litigation was to be taken. Scientologists were to attack the followers of Amprinistics in every way they could.

Hubbard forbade mention of the very word "Amprinistics." The "Executive Letter" disappeared from public circulation long ago, but despite these severe measures, Horner's "Eductivism," an offshoot of Amprinistics, exists to this day.

Level VI was "solo-audited," as was the Clearing Course. In solo-auditing the person holds both of the E-meter cans in one hand, while giving himself the "auditing commands." Level VI and the Clearing Course consist of similar material to OT2 (for which see the chapter "On to OT"). The auditing is likened by Hubbard to digging a ditch, because it is excruciatingly boring. The first Clearing Course Auditors spent at least six months solo-auditing for several hours daily.

In December 1965, while these pioneers were digging their respective ditches, the Australian State of Victoria introduced a Psychological Practices Act which completely outlawed Scientology. The Anderson Report, published in October, contains much sound, factual information and many perceptive remarks. However, it has been criticized even by some who are vocal in their opposition to Scientology. The report was 173 pages long and had nineteen appendices. The evidence of 151 witnesses was gathered into a supplement of 8,290 pages. In the report Anderson concluded:

> Scientology is evil; its techniques evil; its practice a serious threat to the community, medically, morally and socially; and its adherents sadly deluded and often mentally ill. . . . The Board has been unable to find any worthwhile redeeming feature in Scientology.

As with the earlier FDA raid in the United States, the ban in Australia probably did Scientology more good than harm. It provided free publicity, and because it had the trappings of a witch-hunt, made Scientology the underdog, gaining Hubbard much needed support.

Martyrdom is a valuable ingredient in the creation of mass movements. Further, it was impossible to ban Scientology. The followers in Victoria simply changed their name to the "Church of the New Faith," and carried on where they had left off.

In Britain on February 7, 1966, in the House of Commons, Lord Balniel asked Health Minister, Kenneth Robinson, for an Inquiry into Scientology. Within two days of Balniel's request Hubbard had published an "Executive Directive" in which he put forward his plan to "get a detective on that lord's past to unearth the tidbits. They're there . . . governments are SP [Suppressive People]."[8]

Soon after, Hubbard left England, travelling by stages to Rhodesia. Over the next few weeks he continued to react to Lord Balniel's demand for an official investigation. On February 14, Hubbard resigned his doctorate in a "Policy Letter" headed "Doctor Title Abolished": "The title of 'Mister', implying 'Master' I also abandon. I wish to be known solely by my name 'Ron' or Hubbard."

Another Policy Letter, "Attacks on Scientology," was issued the next day. If anyone started an investigation into Scientology the following actions should be taken:

1. Spot who is attacking us.
2. Start investigating them promptly for FELONIES or worse using own professionals, not outside agencies.
3. Double curve our reply by saying we welcome an investigation of them.
4. Start feeding lurid, blood sex crime [sic] actual evidence on the attackers to the press.[9]

On February 17, Hubbard created the "Public Investigation Section": "to help LRH investigate public matters and individuals which seem to impede human liberty so that such matters may be exposed and to furnish intelligence required in guiding the progress of Scientology."[10]

A month after these events, the story of a private investigator was carried in British newspapers. Vic Filson had been recruited to establish an investigation section. He lasted a week. The Scientologist who gave him his instructions at Saint Hill told him dossiers were to be made on "special subjects":

But the truth didn't dawn until I got a memorandum from Hubbard himself. It was horrifying. It was a set of instructions to investigate the activities of psychiatrists in Britain and to prepare a dossier on each. And I was told that the first victim was to be Lord Balniel.

Hubbard instructed Filson to find a skeleton in the cupboard of every psychiatrist practicing in England. Hubbard was looking for crimes such as assault, rape and homicide. His objective was to eliminate every single psychiatrist.[11]

The Hubbard Communications Office Policy Letter "Attacks on Scientology" was expanded on February 18, to include, "investigating noisily the attackers."

At the end of February, John McMaster, who had just flown to Los Angeles, was surprised to hear that he had become the "World's First Real Clear." Hubbard had sent out a promotional piece announcing this to Scientologists throughout the world. Only then was McMaster recalled to England, and given his "Clear Check," to set the record straight. After all, Scientologists needed a boost in morale.[12]

In March, Hubbard published "What Is Greatness?" which rounded off his statements of February: "The hardest task one can have is to continue to love one's fellows despite all reasons he should not. . . . A primary trap is to succumb to invitations to hate. There are those who appoint one their executioners. Sometimes for the sake of the safety of others, it is necessary to act, but it is not necessary also to hate them."

On March 1, the short-lived Public Investigations Section became the Guardian's Office (GO). "Noisy investigation," or rumor-mongering, was not their only talent, and the GO became a formidable force. After the false starts of the Department of Official Affairs and the Department of Government Affairs, Hubbard at last had his own private Intelligence Agency.

John McMaster became the ambassador of Scientology. He was Hubbard's deliberate choice for the "First Clear." McMaster is slight with naturally white hair, and is a remarkable public speaker with a compelling voice. He was Scientology's spokesman in television interviews throughout the English-speaking world, a personification, so it seemed, of gentleness and love. While his message was being beamed over the airwaves, and delivered personally to packed audiences the world over, the Scientology Organizations were becoming increasingly less gentle and loving in their treatment of both their members and their critics.

PART FOUR

THE SEA ORGANIZATION
1966–1976

CHAPTER ONE

Scientology at Sea

Scientology thrives on a climate of ignorance and indifference.—
KENNETH ROBINSON, British Minister for Health

The new Guardian took orders only from the Executive Director of
the Church of Scientology. L. Ron Hubbard was appointing a deputy.
He kept the new position in the family: Mary Sue Hubbard was the first
Guardian, later becoming the "Controller," a post created between the
Executive Director and the Guardian.[1]

Among the duties of the Guardian was the "LRH Heavy Hussars
Hat" (a misnomer, as Hussars were *light* cavalry). "Hat" was Hubbard's usual term for "job." The Guardian's Office (or "GO") would
deal with any "threat of great importance" to Scientology. The tenure
of executives in Scientology organizations is usually brief; the Guardian is one of the few exceptions. Jane Kember, Mary Sue's successor,
held the position for thirteen years. Mary Sue was her superior, as
Controller, throughout that time.

The Guardian's Office was responsible for responding to any attack
on Scientology. An "attack" might simply be a quizzical newspaper
article. The GO is well remembered in London, where the press is still
reticent about Scientology stories. The "Legal Bureau" of the GO
issued *hundreds* of court writs, itself losing count.[2] The GO dealt with
public relations, legal actions, and the gathering of "intelligence." It
conducted campaigns against psychiatry, Interpol, the Internal Reve-

165

nue Service, drug abuse, and government secrecy, largely under the heading "Social Coordination," or "SOCO."

The GO campaign against the tax authorities was not altogether altruistic. On April 30, 1966, the Hubbard Communications Office Ltd. filed its annual accounts with the Inland Revenue in Great Britain. Sir John Foster later commented in his government report: "According to the last set of accounts filed for HCO Ltd., that company seems to have been conducting an unsuccessful garage business [Hickstead Garage]. The auditor's [accountant's] certificate is heavily qualified: various documents could not be traced, vehicles had vanished, 'the sales figure in the trading account cannot be regarded as anywhere near accurate' [according to the Scientology accountant], and there had been litigation with a manager who went bankrupt. The company ended up owing Mr. Hubbard £1,356."

The man who was owed this sum was absent from Saint Hill for a large part of 1966. Most of that time was spent in Rhodesia. Hubbard quietly assured his lieutenants that he had been Cecil Rhodes in his last lifetime, so he saw his visit to Rhodesia as a homecoming.

Hubbard went into business in Rhodesia, putting up part of the purchase money for the Bumi Hills resort hotel on Lake Kariba. He also hob-nobbed with the social elite. He appeared on television, telling the audience he was no longer active in Scientology, and had become a permanent resident of Salisbury. He must have been dismayed when that permanence crumbled with the Rhodesian refusal to renew his visa. He put a brave face on it, returning to England in July, to be met at the airport by hundreds of cheering Scientologists.[3]

In Rhodesia, Hubbard had prepared the first two Operating Thetan levels. After attaining the state of Clear, Scientologists could now progress toward "total freedom" through the OT levels. Hubbard asserted that an Operating Thetan is capable of *operating*, of perceiving and causing events, while separate from his body. By doing the OT levels an individual would supposedly liberate latent psychic abilities. From 1952, Hubbard continually insisted that the latest techniques would bring about the state of "full OT."

The U.S. Internal Revenue Service was less interested in Hubbard's *spiritual* motivation than in the mounting evidence of his *financial* motivation. At the end of July, the IRS notified the Church of Scientology of California that its tax-exempt status was being withdrawn, giving three reasons: Scientology practitioners were making money from the "non-profit" Church; the Church's activities were commercial; and the Church was serving the private interests of L. Ron Hubbard.[4]

Hubbard's thoughts were elsewhere, and in a flight of fantasy, he proclaimed John McMaster the first "Pope" of Scientology in August 1966. The title did not endure.[5]

It seemed that McMaster was to be Hubbard's public successor. In fact, he was simply an emissary with little real power in the organization. Hubbard maintained the charade of handing over responsibility by resigning as President and Executive Director of the Church. His resignation was announced to Scientologists, but was not actually filed with the Registrar of companies in England for three years. It was yet another public relations gesture. Hubbard still controlled the bank accounts, and still held the undated resignations of the board members of his many corporations. He still wrote the Policy of the Church, and issued his orders via written Executive Directives. Indeed, the post of Executive Director remained vacant until 1981, when Hubbard finally appointed a replacement. Hubbard retained the day-to-day control of his empire of Orgs.[6]

Early in 1966, the LRH Finance Committee had been established to determine how much the Church owed Hubbard. In September, Hubbard told the press he had forgiven the Church a $13 million debt. The LRH Finance Committee had however failed to document the millions Hubbard had taken out of the Church. The Committee had appraised Saint Hill as having a business goodwill value of £2 million (the estate itself was valued at less than £100,000). The Committee also included such items as the purchase price of the yacht used by Hubbard for his Alaska trip in 1940. All part of the Hubbard's "research," from which the Church purportedly benefited.[7]

In August 1966, the Henslow case exploded into the British newspapers. Karen Henslow was a schizophrenic who had been institutionalized before her contact with Scientology. She had fallen in love with a Scientologist, who promised to marry her. Henslow had worked at Saint Hill, and taken a Scientology course. Then one night she was "Security-Checked" into the small hours, and deposited at her mother's house. She ran into the street in her nightclothes, and ended up at the police station at 3.00 a.m., in a highly distressed state.[8]

Hubbard responded to the Henslow scandal by approving a more thorough set of instructions for his tactic of "Noisy Investigation." A list was to be made of everyone associated with a perceived enemy. This was to include their dentist and doctor, along with their friends and neighbors. All of the people on the list were to be phoned and told that the perceived enemy was under investigation for the commission of crimes, having attacked the religious liberty of the caller. The person being called was to be told that alarming information had already been gathered. The primary purpose of this technique was not to collect information, but to spread suspicion about the perceived enemy.

This directive was followed by a Hubbard Bulletin called "The Anti-Social Personality, the Anti-Scientologist" (the two being one and the same). Hubbard restated his earlier theory that twenty percent of the population (the Suppressives and those under their influence, the Potential Trouble Sources, combined) "oppose violently any betterment activity or group." He asserted that "When we trace the cause of a failing business, we will inevitably discover somewhere in its ranks the antisocial personality hard at work."

In fact, the cause of all disaster at work or at home, according to Hubbard, lies with Suppressive Persons. They are characterized by a majority of the following traits and attributes. According to Hubbard, SPs speak in generalities ("everybody knows"); deal mainly in bad news; worsen communication they are relaying; fail to respond to psychotherapy (i.e. Scientology); are surrounded by "cowed or ill associates or friends"; habitually select the wrong target, or source; are unable to finish anything; willingly confess to alarming crimes, without any sense of responsibility for them; support only destructive groups; approve only destructive actions; detest help being given to others, and use "helping" as a pretext to destroy others; and believe that no one really owns anything.

These points are Hubbard's reworkings of the characteristics of the Antisocial Personality, or psychopath, given by Hervey Cleckley, M.D., in his 1950s book *The Mask of Sanity*.

Having failed to secure a "safe-point" in Rhodesia from which to resist the encroachments of the Suppressives, Hubbard planned to take to the High Seas. At the end of 1966, he incorporated the Hubbard Explorational Company Ltd. He titled himself the "expedition supervisor," holding ninety-seven of the 100 issued shares. The stated object of the HEC was to "explore oceans, seas, lakes, rivers and waters, land and buildings in any part of the world and to seek for, survey, examine and test properties of all kinds."[9]

Hubbard was still a member of the Explorers' Club of New York, and was authorized to fly their flag on his proposed Hubbard Geological Survey Expedition, which was going to make a geological survey of "a belt from Italy through Greece and Egypt and along the Gulf of Aden and the East Coast of Africa." The survey was intended to "draw a picture of an area which has been the scene of the earlier and basic civilizations of the planet and from which some conclusions may possibly be made relating to geological predispositions required for civilized growth."[10] The expedition never took place. Hubbard was good at promoting expeditions, even at inventing their details, but not so good at actually carrying them out.

Having given his last Saint Hill Briefing Course lecture, Hubbard left for North Africa at the end of 1966. On December 5, British Health Minister Kenneth Robinson denied that an Inquiry was necessary, but denounced Scientology as "potentially harmful," adding "I have no doubt that Scientology is totally valueless in promoting health." Hubbard responded in usual form with a twenty-page internal memo, asserting that the crimes of government would prove far more interesting to the newspapers than those of Scientology. Hubbard believed that events could be turned against the representatives of government, putting them into the courtroom rather than Scientology. He wanted nothing short of Kenneth Robinson and Lord Balniel's resignations. The emphases of the attack were to be religious persecution and psychiatric mayhem. Scientology's opponents were simply dismissed as fascists.[11]

Neither Robinson nor Balniel resigned their government positions, nor were any psychiatrists stampeded. However, on February 28, 1967, every Member of Parliament received a letter from the Hubbard College of Scientology. The letter spoke of the Karen Henslow case of a few months before: "This unhappy story gave the newspapers and others of a lurid turn of mind the opportunity to further their vehement attack against us with libel and slander. And so the pattern repeats itself, the well worn pattern."[12]

The letter went on to ask who was "behind this pattern of attack," and after discoursing on Scientologists' friendly relations with medicine in general, concluded with an attack on psychiatry in particular, adding, "Like the Russian authorities, we believe that brain surgery is an assault and rape of the individual personality."

The letter inevitably created an effect, but not necessarily that expected by its author. Hubbard's public relations "technology" only succeeded in bringing the boiling oil down upon Scientology. On March 6, 1967, Kenneth Robinson made a further statement about Scientology in the House of Commons:

I do not want to give the impression that there is anything illegal in the offering by unskilled people of processes intended in part to relieve or remove mental disturbance . . . provided that no claim is made of qualified medical skill. . . . What they do, however, is to direct themselves deliberately towards the weak, the unbalanced, the immature, the rootless and the mentally or emotionally unstable; to promise them remolded, mature personalities and to set about fulfilling the promise by means of untrained staff, ignorantly practicing quasi-psychological techniques, including hypnosis . . .

I am satisfied that the condition of mentally disturbed people who have taken scientology courses has, to say the least, not generally improved thereby. . . . My present decision on legislation may disappoint the honorable Members, but I would like to remind them that the harsh light of publicity can sometimes work almost as effectively. Scientology thrives on a climate of ignorance and indifference. . . .

What I have tried to do in this debate is to alert the public to the facts about scientology, to the potential dangers in which anyone considering taking it up may find himself, and to the utter hollowness of the claims made for the cult.

Meanwhile, Hubbard added "Degraded Beings" to Suppressives and Potential Trouble Sources. While the latter two groups comprised only one in five of the world's population, "Degraded Beings" outnumbered "Big Beings" by eighteen to one.[13] In Hubbard's eyes, Kenneth Robinson was undoubtedly not only a Suppressive Person, but also a Degraded Being.

Business was still fair, and the Scientology Church in Britain showed a total income of £457,277 for the year ending April 1967 (an average of almost £9,000 per week). Hubbard gave the following instructions to his subordinates a few months later:

The real stable datum in handling tax people is NEVER VOLUNTEER ANY INFORMATION. . . . The thing to do is to assign a significance to the figures before the government can. . . . I normally think of a better significance than the government can. I always put enough errors on a return to satisfy their bloodsucking appetite and STILL come out zero. The game of accounting is just a game of assigning significance to figures. The man with the most imagination wins.[14]

True to these maxims, the 1966–1967 accounts contained several creative designations for expenditure. Directors' fees stood at only £2,914, but £39,426 was justified as "provision for bad debts," and an astonishing £70,000 as "expenditure of United States Mailing List and Promotion." The previous year, £80,000 had been charged under this heading. In 1967–1968 the figure was again £70,000.

British action against Scientology was growing. The Ministry of Labour reported that a hundred American teachers of Scientology were to be banned from Britain. In a dramatic move, 500 Scientologists were interviewed by the police as they arrived at Saint Hill. This fiasco resulted in one American being fined £15 for failing to register as an alien, occasioning UFO cartoons in the newspapers.[15]

Hubbard had spent the last weeks of 1966 "researching" OT3 in North Africa. In a letter of the time, he admitted that he was taking drugs ("pinks and grays") to assist his research.[16] Early in 1967, Hubbard flew to Las Palmas, and Virginia Downsborough, who cared for him after his arrival, was astonished that he was existing almost totally on a diet of drugs. For three weeks Hubbard was bedridden, while Downsborough weaned him off this diet. According to her, he was obsessed with removing his "body-thetans."[17]

The *Enchanter*, a 50-foot Bermuda ketch, sailed to meet him in Las Palmas. Her dedicated Scientologist crew of nineteen were known as the Sea Project. Their formation and their departure from England were highly secretive. The Hubbard Explorational Company started to draw $15,000 per month from the Church of Scientology of California. The Church also paid $125,000 into one of Hubbard's Swiss accounts.[18]

From Las Palmas, having just forgiven Scientology $13 million, Hubbard issued orders that every Org set up an "LRH Good Will Repayment Account" at their local bank. Executives who failed to set up such an account would be dismissed as thieves. Hubbard also ordered the Church of Scientology to buy Saint Hill from him.[19]

As the British Health Minister had predicted, the "harsh light of publicity" had done its work, and Scientology had been propelled into the public eye. By August, Saint Hill was taking in as much as £40,000 a week, almost five times its income of the previous year.[20]

CHAPTER TWO

Heavy Ethics

In all the broad Universe there is no other hope for Man than ourselves.—L. RON HUBBARD, *Ron's Journal 1967*

"Ethics" were tightening up in the Scientology world. Since the mid-1960s, the Orgs have been managed on a strict system. Staff members add up points to measure their production. For an Auditor this is the number of "Well Done Auditing Hours"; for a Letter Registrar, letters in and out. Some jobs are less readily reduced to statistics: Even students doing Scientology courses keep "stats," where every word checked, every page read, every minute of tape heard, every "clay demo" and every "check-out" has a point value. The stats are graphed, from the income of an Organization, down to the number of toilets cleaned.

Staff members are assigned an "Ethics Condition" every week in accordance with their stats. A slight upward trend on the graph is called Normal, while a level graph, or a slight downtrend, is Emergency. From top to bottom the Conditions are Power, Affluence, Normal, Emergency, Danger, Non-Existence, Liability, Doubt, Enemy, Treason, Confusion. For each Ethics Condition, there is a "Formula," through the application of which the individual's stat is supposed to rise.

172

Hubbard insisted that his Ethics system should also be applied to "wogs" (non-Scientologists). At Saint Hill this quickly went from the vaguely to the utterly ridiculous. A local caterer who ran a mobile canteen was put into a condition of Liability in part for running out of apple pie. When he failed to apply the Liability Formula, he was declared Suppressive, which meant that Scientologists could not communicate with him, let alone buy his replenished stocks of apple pie.[1]

By autumn 1967, Hubbard was living in a villa on Las Palmas, adding the final touches to the OT3 Course, and putting the Sea Organization (as the Sea Project had become) through its paces. On Las Palmas he tested out his "Awards and Penalties" for Ethics Conditions on the Sea Org. The penalties for lower Conditions included deprivation of sleep for a set time (often several days), and the assignment of physical labor. Hubbard boasted in a September Policy Letter that penalties in the Sea Org were "much worse" than those for the other Scientology Orgs. The milder non-Sea Org penalty for Non-Existence required that an offender "Must wear old clothes. May not bathe. Women must not wear makeup or have hairdo's. Men may not shave. No lunch hour is given and such persons are expected not to leave the premises. Lowest pay with no bonuses."[2] Pay was pitiably low in Scientology Organizations anyway.

On September 20, Hubbard spoke of his new Sea Org, and the release of OT3, in a lecture taped in Las Palmas. Scientologists call this lecture "RJ 67" for "Ron's Journal 1967." Hubbard dubbed the third Operating Thetan level "the Wall of Fire." OT3 concerned an incident which he said occurred "on this planet, and on the other seventy-five planets which form this Confederacy, seventy-five million years ago." Hubbard claimed that exposure to OT3 is fatal to the uninitiated: "The material involved in this sector is so vicious that it is carefully arranged to kill anyone if he discovers the exact truth of it. . . . I am very sure that I was the first one that ever did live through any attempt to attain that material."

Hubbard claimed he had broken a knee, an arm, and his back during the course of his research. He attributed this to the tremendous increase in "OT power" he achieved doing OT3, making accidental damage to his body all too easy. While he was certainly accident prone at times (a characteristic of those surrounded by Suppressives, according to Hubbard), the cause was not necessarily paranormal. The evidence does not support any of his claims of injury.

In RJ 67, Hubbard spoke of an international conspiracy to destroy Scientology. From the early days Hubbard had felt that a group of "vested interests" was trying to keep both Dianetics and Scientology down. Hubbard's major targets had been the medical and the psychiatric professions.

According to RJ 67, the attack on Scientology had achieved epic proportions. It was vital for the Conspiracy which dominated the affairs of the world to crush Scientology. Hubbard claimed that his wife, the Guardian, had unearthed the highest level of the Conspiracy, the ten or dozen men who determined the fate of Earth: "They are members of the Bank of England, and other higher financial circles. They own and control newspaper chains, and they are all, oddly enough, directors in all the mental health groups in the world." Newspaper baron Cecil King was one of the ten (or twelve). Hubbard also claimed that the then Prime Minister of Britain, Harold Wilson, was controlled by these men, as were many other heads of state.

Hubbard ended RJ 67 with a message of hope: "From here on the world will change. But if it changes at all, and if it recovers, it will be because of the Scientologist, it will be because of the Organization. . . . In all the broad Universe there is no other hope for Man than ourselves."

A larger vessel had been purchased, and sailed with an inexperienced crew to meet Hubbard at Las Palmas. The *Avon River* was a 414-ton trawler. Her first voyage, from Hull, was reported in the British press after her non-Scientologist captain's return. Captain John Jones and the chief engineer were the only professional sailors aboard. Jones called it the strangest trip of his life:

My crew were sixteen men and four women Scientologists, who wouldn't know a trawler from a tramcar. But they intended to sail this tub 4,000 miles in accordance with the Org Book. I was instructed not to use any electrical equipment apart from the lights, radio and direction finder. We had radar and other advanced equipment which I was not allowed to use. I was told it was all in the Org Book, which was to be obeyed without question. We tried these methods. Getting out of Hull we bumped the dock. Then, using the Org Book navigation system based on radio beams from the BBC and other stations, we got down off Lowestoft before the navigator admitted he was lost. I stuck to my watch and sextant, so at least I knew where we were.[3]

Possibly this novel method of navigation, depending solely on radio, harked back to Hubbard's 1940 Alaska Radio Experimental Expedition.

On Las Palmas, the crew of the *Avon River* became guinea pigs for Hubbard's most advanced "research" into Ethics, or Heavy Ethics, as it came to be known. New lower Ethics Conditions were issued, each with a series of steps. The individual assigned a low Condition was expected to work through the Ethics Formulas progressing up through the Conditions. The poor woman who assisted Hubbard in his research into the Condition of Liability had to wear a dirty gray rag on her arm, to show her deficiency to her colleagues. In the Condition of Doubt, she walked around with a black mark on her cheek and a large, oily chain about her wrist.

The *Avon River*'s radio operator was ordered by Hubbard to remain awake until a new radio had arrived and been fitted on the bridge. The radio arrived after five days, the operator having complied with the "Commodore's" order. Hubbard seemed obsessed with sleep deprivation. It was one of the accusations made against him by Sara Northrup sixteen years before in her divorce complaint.

At about this time, one of the Sea Org crew suggested that their six-month contract be extended to a billion years. Hubbard adopted the suggestion with gusto, and Sea Org members still sign a billion-year contract, boasting the motto "We Come Back," life after life.

On October 6, new Formulas were issued for the Ethics Conditions. The Liability Formula contained the alarming order to "Deliver an effective blow to the enemies of the group one has been pretending to be part of despite personal danger." The invitation was obvious. The step remains a part of the Liability Formula, and any Scientologist assigned Liability (which happens frequently) must comply with it. The original Treason formula was shorter-lived, and included: "1. Deliver a paralyzing blow to the enemies of the group one has worked against and betrayed. 2. Perform a self-damaging act that furthers the purposes and or objectives of the group one has betrayed." This Formula was abandoned a year later.[4]

Twelve days later, Hubbard issued "Penalties for Lower Conditions" which included: "LIABILITY—Suspension of Pay and a dirty grey rag on left arm, and day and night confinement to org premises. TREASON— . . . a black mark on left cheek . . . ENEMY—SP Order. Fair Game. May be deprived of property or injured by any means by any Scientologist without any discipline of the Scientologist. May be tricked, sued or lied to or destroyed [punctuation sic]."⁵

In November, the Hubbard Explorational Company bought the *Royal Scotsman*, which for some years had been an Irish Channel cattle ferry, which weighed in at 3,280 tons, eight times the tonnage of the *Avon River*. The new owners requested permission from the Board of Trade to re-register the ship as a "pleasure yacht," with clearance for a voyage to Gibraltar. They were advised that considerable modifications would be necessary under the "Safety of Life at Sea Convention" (SOLAS) of 1960.⁶

A few days later, having docked the *Royal Scotsman* in Southampton, the owners requested registration as a "whaling ship." Permission was refused, and a detention order put on the vessel, preventing her from leaving port.

Reporters were given a handout which said Hubbard had already undertaken successful survey work in the English Channel, and was resuming this work. The earlier survey was allegedly for oil and gas on the sea floor. Yet another Hubbard expedition that failed to materialize.⁷

Seeing the failure of his subordinates to extricate the *Scotsman* from Southampton, Hubbard decided to take command, and flew from Las Palmas with a twenty-man crew. The *Royal Scotsman* was hastily re-registered under the flag of Sierra Leone. However, the name was misspelled, and the ship became the *Royal Scotman*.

Permission was requested for a single voyage to Brest, where the necessary repairs would be made. Permission was granted on November 28, and the *Royal Scotman* sailed. The ship followed in the tradition of the *Avon River*, and ran into fenders in the inner harbor. There were heavy storms in the English Channel, and the ship nearly foundered off Brest. Hubbard ordered her to sail to Gibraltar, where the *Avon River* was waiting. There was a heavy storm, and the hydraulic steering and the main compass were inoperative. One generator was out of action, and there were women and children aboard, but Gibraltar resolutely refused the *Scotman* entry. Eventually, emergency steering was rigged up, and the *Scotman* was steered from the aft docking bridge on directions from the main bridge via walkie-talkie. Finally the ship was allowed to dock at Ibiza, in the Spanish Balearic Islands.⁸

The ship travelled from port to port for several weeks before settling to overwinter at Valencia, in Spain. A non-Scientologist crew member said of Hubbard: "He called himself commodore and had four different types of peaked caps. . . . He told me he thought I was a reporter."

This "wog" started the voyage as ship's carpenter, but by being "upstat" ended it as Chief Officer. During the short voyage he had a brush with Ethics. He was put in a Condition of Doubt for "defying an order, encouraging desertion, tolerating mutinous meetings, and attempting to suborn the Chief Engineer." The boatswain was put into a Condition of Enemy for "undermining the Spanish crew, habitual drunkenness, holding nightly and morning meetings, and derogating Scientology."[9]

On New Year's Day 1968, Hubbard incorporated the "Operation and Transport Corporation Ltda." [sic] through the Panamanian consulate in Valencia. OTC took over from the Hubbard Explorational Company as Hubbard's principal channel for extracting money from Scientology. He owned ninety-eight of the 100 issued shares. Hubbard created a network of corporations the sheer complexity of which has daunted most tax investigators. The *Royal Scotman* was re-registered under the Panamanian flag, though she continued to sail under that of Sierra Leone.[10]

A glamorous picture of life at sea was presented to Scientologists the world over, and, when the stringent Scientology qualifications for Sea Org membership were abandoned, its ranks swelled. Largely with people completely unskilled in the nautical arts.

Sea Org members wore pseudo-naval uniforms, and were assigned naval ranks, from the lowly "Swamper" to Hubbard's own exalted "Commodore." The uniforms and ranks remain, in the largely land-bound Sea Org.

In January 1968, Hubbard released OT levels 4 to 6. OT 4 was supposed to proof the individual (or "Pre-OT") against future "implanting." Hubbard wheeled out the Clearing Course Implant list, and had his devotees "mock-up" and "erase" the implants yet again. OT 5 and 6 consisted of drills to be done "exterior from the body." Those who audited these levels usually admit later that their "exterior," or out-of-the-body, experience was entirely subjective. A few claim they could do exactly what the materials required, but do not even try to offer proof. Curiously, much of the highly secret material on levels 5 and 6 came from Hubbard's book *The Creation of Human Ability* first published in the mid-1950s.

The first Advanced Organization opened aboard the *Royal Scotman*, to deliver these OT levels on New Year's Day, 1968. It was soon transferred to shore in Alicante, and thence to Edinburgh. The Advanced Orgs (or AOs) were, and remain, the only Church Organizations to deliver the Operating Thetan levels. From the beginning, AOs were supposed to be run solely by Sea Org members.

Meanwhile, a Scientology magazine published an interview with an unlikely convert. William Burroughs, author of the controversial *Naked Lunch*, had trained as a Scientology Auditor, and was a Grade 5, or "Power," release. Burroughs said: "I am convinced that whatever anyone does, he will do it better after processing [auditing]." Burroughs later became Clear number 1163, of which he said: "It feels marvellous! Things you've had all your life, things you think nothing can be done about—suddenly they're not there any more! And you know that these disabilities cannot return."[11]

Burroughs' enthusiasm for Scientology did not last, and his later work is peppered with abstruse attacks on Scientology. He even wrote a book called *Naked Scientology*.

Scientology magazines were filled with news and photographs of smiling musicians, authors, models, dancers, doctors and scientists who espoused Scientology. Jazz composer Dave Brubeck's son went to Edinburgh to persuade a friend to leave the dreaded cult, and ended up joining the Sea Org. Actress Karen Black waxed lyrical about the benefits of auditing to other Hollywood stars. Bobby Richards, who orchestrated the music for *Goldfinger*, said "I always get much more out of Scientology than I expect." Scientologist Richard Grumm worked on the Mariner space program.[12]

In this climate, Hubbard decided to prove the validity of "past lives" by taking the *Avon River* on a tour of the haunts of his previous incarnations.

The "Whole Track Mission" was recorded in the book *Mission into Time*. Hubbard would make a plasticine model of an area before sending in a team to verify his predictions. They allegedly opened sealed caves, and found there what Hubbard had predicted. A variety of legends sprang out of the expedition. Among them that Hubbard was relocating caches of gold he had hidden in former lifetimes, especially as a Roman tax collector (it has been suggested that his earlier trip to Rhodesia was to recover the fortune buried in his supposed incarnation as Cecil Rhodes). Far more exciting, and less widely known, however, is the space ship legend.

During the "Mission," Hubbard showed the crew some notes about their next destination. It was a hidden "space-station" in northern

Corsica, "almost at the junction of the mainland and the northern peninsula and possibly slightly west of the island's meridian," according to one member of the "Mission," where a huge cavern, hidden among the rocks in mountainous terrain, housed an immense Mothership and a fleet of smaller spacecraft. The spaceships were made of a non-corrosive alloy, as yet undiscovered by earthlings. Only one palm print would cause a slab of rock to slide away, revealing these chariots of the gods. The owners of this machinery not only knew about reincarnation, they had even predicted Hubbard's palm print.

Tales about this discovery were rife among Sea Org members. Hubbard was going to use the Mothership to escape from Earth. The ship was protected by atomic warheads. It awaited the return of a great leader, and there were rumors about a "Space Org." On the day Hubbard was to be put to this final test, the Mission was abandoned because of the trouble the *Scotman* was generating with the port authorities in Valencia. Hubbard never returned to collect the Mothership.

The *Royal Scotman* had been asked several times to shift its berth. The ship's Port Captain steadfastly refused. What the Scientologists call a "flap" occurred, and the authorities, probably exacerbated by this quite usual display of Sea Org arrogance, had to be placated. A new captain was appointed, who did well for a short while, until the *Scotman* dragged anchor and nearly ran aground. Commodore Hubbard stayed aboard the *Avon River*, promoting his wife, Mary Sue, to the rank of Captain, and giving her command of the larger ship. The fleet moved to Burriana, a few miles along the Spanish coast, for repairs to the *Royal Scotman*. This time the *Royal Scotman* did run aground. The Commodore gravely assigned the *ship*, and all who sailed on her, the Ethics Condition of Liability.

For several weeks a peculiar spectacle could be seen travelling up and down the Spanish coast: a ship with filthy gray tarpaulins tied about its funnel. Every crew member wore a gray rag. It is rumored that even Mary Sue's corgi dog, Vixie, wore a gray rag about her neck. Mary Sue suffered the long hours, the poor diet and the exhausting labor with the rest of the crew. Finally, the *Royal Scotman* rejoined the *Avon River* in Marseilles. The crew paraded, sparkling in new uniforms, and the Commodore held a ceremony to upgrade the ship from Liability, so ending the "Liability Cruise." Soon after, Hubbard moved with his top Aides to the *Royal Scotman*, which became the Flagship of the Sea Org fleet. Scientologists called it simply "Flag."[13]

In 1968, Hubbard's Ethics was put into action with the chain-locker punishment. A chain-locker is "a dark hole where the anchor chains are stored; cold, wet and rats," to quote one ex-Sea Org officer. The lockers are below the steering in the bowels of the ship. A tiny manhole gives access, and they are unlit. When a crew member was in a low enough Ethics Condition, he or she would be put in a chain-locker for up to two weeks.

John McMaster says a small child, perhaps five years old, was once consigned to a chain-locker. He says she was a deaf mute, and that Hubbard had assigned her an Ethics condition for which the formula is "Find out who you really are." She was not to leave the chain locker until she completed the formula by writing her name. McMaster says Hubbard came to him late one night in some distress, and asked him to let the child out. He did, cursing Hubbard the while. Another witness claims that a three-year-old was once put in the locker.

Another Ethics Condition had the miscreant put into "old rusty tanks, way below the ship, with filthy bilge water, no air, and hardly sitting height . . . for anything from twenty-four hours to a week . . . getting their oxygen via tubes, and with Masters-at-Arms [Ethics Officers] checking outside to hear if the hammering continued. Food was occasionally given in buckets," according to a former Sea Org executive.

The miscreants were kept awake, often for days on end. They ate from the communal food bucket with their blistered and filthy hands. They chipped away at the rust unceasingly. As another witness has tactfully put it, "there were no bathroom facilities."

While these "penances" were being doled out, the first "overboard" occurred. The ships were docked in Melilla, Morocco, in May 1968. One of the ship's executives was ashore and noticed that the hawsers holding the *Scotman* and the *Avon River* were crossed. He undid a hawser, and found himself grappling with the full mass of an unrestrained ship as it drifted away from the dock.

Mary Sue Hubbard ordered that the officer be hurled from the deck. There was a tremendous crash as he hit the water. Ships have a "rubbing strake" beneath the waterline to keep other ships at bay in a collision. The overboarded officer had hit the steel rubbing strake! The crew peered anxiously over the side waiting for the corpse to float to the surface.

The bedraggled officer was surprised when he walked up the gangplank and found the crew still craning over the far side of the ship.

Fortunately for Mrs. Hubbard's conscience, and the failing public repute of Scientology, the officer concerned was not only a good swimmer, but also expert at Judo. Most fortunate of all, he had seen the rubbing strake, and the explosive crash was caused when he thrust himself away as he fell. For a short time, overboarding was abandoned.

It is difficult to comprehend the stoicism with which some Scientologists suffered the Ethics Conditions. It is remarkable even to many ex-Scientologists. It is even more remarkable that most Scientologists have probably never heard of the chain-locker, bilge tank or overboarding punishments. Scientologists were used to Hubbard's auditing techniques, where they did not question the reasoning behind a set of commands, but simply answered or carried them out. Many spent their time trying to keep out of trouble, or, when trouble unavoidably came, getting out of the Ethics Condition quickly by whatever means they could.

Most Sea Org members accepted these bizarre practices out of devotion to Hubbard. It is impossible to add to these stark details a convincing picture of Hubbard's charisma. The Sea Org saw themselves as the elite, the chosen few, who would return life after life to rejoin their leader in the conquest of suffering. Hubbard released religious and military fervors in his disciples.

Back on dry land in East Grinstead the farce of Scientology Ethics, and its applicability in dealing with non-Scientologists, continued with a letter to twenty-two local businesses:

> As a result of a recent survey of shops in the East Grinstead area, your shop together with a handful of others, has been declared out of bounds for Scientologists. . . . These shops have indicated that they do not wish Scientology to expand in East Grinstead and we are, therefore, relieving them of the painful experience of taking our money.[14]

The banned "shops" included a solicitor's firm. Another business was "highly commended" for displaying Scientology books, in the face of local criticism.

Hubbard's Public Relations and Ethics "technologies" rebounded in Britain. In July 1968, the British government finally made its move.

CHAPTER THREE

The Empire Strikes Back

I find it almost incredible that a Minister and his civil servants should be so reckless as to publish a White Paper and to seek mercilessly to expose the Scientologists. It will certainly advertise them even more widely and give them the fame they want.—RICHARD CROSSMAN, *The Diaries of a Cabinet Minister*, Volume 3

On July 25, 1968, Kenneth Robinson, the British Minister of Health, made a statement in Parliament about Scientology. Having called it a "pseudo-philosophical cult," he reminded the House of his earlier pronouncement:

Although this warning received a good deal of public notice at the time, the practice of scientology has continued, and indeed expanded, and Government Departments, Members of Parliament and local authorities have received numerous complaints about it.

The Government is satisfied . . . that scientology is socially harmful. It alienates members of families from each other and attributes squalid and disgraceful motives to all who oppose it; its authoritarian principles and practice are a potential menace to the personality and well-being of those so deluded as to become its followers; above all, its methods can be a serious danger to the health of those who submit to them. There is evidence that children are now being indoctrinated.

There is no power under existing law to prohibit the practice of scientology; but the Government has concluded that it is so objectionable that it would be right to take all steps within its power to curb its growth.

Scientology establishments in Britain were stripped of their educational status. Foreign nationals were prohibited from studying Scientology or working in Scientology Organizations, by invoking the "Aliens Act," through which the Home Secretary can deny entry to Britain. The Home Office banned Hubbard from Britain as an "undesirable alien." East Grinstead's Member of Parliament, Geoffrey Johnson Smith, repeated Robinson's earlier statement, originally made in Parliament, that Scientologists, "direct themselves towards the weak, the unbalanced, the immature, the rootless and the mentally or emotionally unstable." He made the statement on television, beyond the bounds of parliamentary privilege, so the Scientologists filed suit against him for defamation.[1]

At the end of July, a hundred foreign Scientologists were rounded up, and detained under guard in hotels, pending deportation. Scotland Yard began to investigate Scientology. The National Council for Civil Liberties objected to the use of the Aliens Act on the grounds that it was "objectionable in principle and dangerous in practice."[2]

The Scientologists sued four English newspapers, and sought injunctions to prevent further stories. The injunctions were denied. New telephone directories carried a large advertisement for Scientology, and an embarrassed General Post Office announced that no further ads would be accepted.[3]

There was a general feeling that although something should be done about Scientology the Aliens Act was not the way to do it. But the expression of public sympathy was restrained. A fortnight before the ban, the *Daily Mail* had reported the death of ex-Scientologist John Kennedy, in South Africa. Kennedy had left Scientology to set up his own Institute of Mental Health, taking a number of Scientologists with him. He allegedly shot himself accidently while cleaning his revolver, but the coroner returned an open verdict. Hubbard's *Auditor* magazine recorded the matter simply, and ominously:

> JOHN KENNEDY, SP [Suppressive Person], who messed up Rhodesia, shot dead in accident in South Africa.[4]

This was actually stale news, Kennedy died in 1966, but three days after the Aliens Act was introduced, another South African Scientologist died in mysterious circumstances. James Stewart had been a student at the Scientology Advanced Organization in Edinburgh. He was a thirty-five-year-old epileptic, whose body was found fifty feet beneath his hotel window. The newspapers missed vital information in their reports. A few days before his death, Stewart had completed an Ethics Condition wherein he stayed awake for *eighty* hours. One of his tasks during this period was to crawl about the carpets picking out bits of fluff. According to Robert Kaufman, in his firsthand account, a bulletin had been posted on the Advanced Org notice board:[5]

> James Stewart has been put in a Condition of Doubt for having [epileptic] seizures in public thus invalidating Scientology. If there is any reoccurrence of these either consciously or unconsciously on his part he will be placed in a Condition of Enemy.

Stewart's real crime, having had a severe seizure, was telling the hospital that he was a Scientologist, thus supposedly giving Scientology a bad name. He had injured his head, and wore a blood-stained bandage while performing his demeaning "amends project." He was possibly made to crawl across the steep and slippery slates of the Org roof, as a final part of his Doubt Formula. This bizarre practice was quite usual at the time.[6]

Shortly before his death, Stewart had been suspended from his course at the AO. On the day he read a funeral notice for Stewart, fellow student Robert Kaufman saw Stewart's widow, Thelma, giving an enthusiastic speech on her completion of OT2. In his book, *Inside Scientology*, Kaufman said Thelma "victoriously received the applause of AO members." A Scientology spokesman told the press, "Mrs. Stewart does not know how it happened, but she does know it had nothing to do with Scientology." The press was also told that Mrs. Stewart was a "more serious" student than her husband. In fact, Stewart, described in the newspapers as an encyclopedia salesman,[7] had been a founder of the Cape Town Scientology Org, and was a senior executive there. He was a Class VII Auditor, the highest level of training at the time, Clear number 153 (there were over 2,000 by then), and was on OT3 when he died. One of his Success Stories was published in the *Auditor* magazine at around the time of his death. It was headed, "How Scientology Training Has Helped Me In Life":

> I find that training and auditing experience helps me in innumerable ways—in driving a car (patiently, in heavy traffic), waking up in the morning, confronting anything unpleasant in life, keeping myself occu-

pied in leisure hours, in writing letters, making telephone calls, in chance conversations with strangers—In fact, training helps in every conceivable situation or experience anywhere, any place, anytime—Try it for yourself and see!

The Scientologists very readily disown embarrassing members, especially in death. Unfortunately, to them the repute of Scientology is invariably more important than the truth. In a curious twist, Stewart's name was given to the press by the police. In Scotland, the names of suicides were not given to the press. However, there is no evidence to suggest that Stewart was murdered.

This bizarre period of Scientology is recorded in stark detail in Robert Kaufman's *Inside Scientology*. Kaufman was the first who dared to publish details of the OT levels, and his book remains the best description of the Scientology experience.

The response to the British Aliens Act ban was fairly immediate. Hubbard announced that his work was finished, saying he had resigned his "Scientology directorships two or more years ago to explore and study the decline of ancient civilization," perpetuating the tale he had told to receive his Explorers' Club flag. Hubbard accused England of being a police state.[8] An Advanced Org was started in Los Angeles to serve Scientologists in the Western hemisphere. But the ban, although rigorously enforced at first, soon fell into disuse. By the early 1970s, most of the students and staff at Saint Hill were foreigners.

The London *Daily Mail* published details of Hubbard's private bank accounts in Switzerland, account numbers and all. It said Hubbard claimed to have $7 million. It also unearthed a prescription signed "L. Ron Hubbard Ph.D.," for the sedative Nembutal, "for horticultural purposes only." Abbott Laboratories, the manufacturers of Nembutal, said there was "no conceivable" way in which Nembutal could be used in horticulture. Perhaps it was for Hubbard's "ever-bearing" tomatoes.[9]

Hubbard was interviewed by the *Daily Mail*, aboard the *Royal Scotman*, in Bizerte, Tunisia: "He chain-smoked menthol cigarettes, fidgeted nervously. . . . He taped the conversation. . . . Outside Scientologists, some in uniform and some young children, stood rigidly to attention. . . . Hubbard's mood ranged from the boastful—'You'd be fascinated how many friends of mine there are in the British Government' to the menacing: 'I get intelligence reports from England. You'd be surprised at the dirty washing I have got.' "[10]

Hubbard insisted he was no longer connected with Scientology, and told the reporter that everything in the *Daily Mail*'s Scientology file was forged. He knew because he had seen it, through his "spies." Hubbard also gave a rare interview to British television, again looking nervous, and contradicted himself both on the number of his marriages, and whether or not he had a Swiss bank account. Despite his supposed discoveries about communication and public relations, Hubbard fell far short of winning over the press.[11]

At the end of August 1968 in New York, Jill Goodman became the world's youngest Clear. Her picture was featured in the *Auditor* magazine. She was ten years old, and she and her eight-year-old brother were already qualified Auditors.[12]

In mid-August, the *Royal Scotman* had slipped into Corfu harbor. At first all went well. According to one newspaper, the Sea Org enriched the Corfiot economy by about £1,000 per day. They were welcomed by the harbormaster, and the local press.[13]

In September, Hubbard announced the new Class VIII Auditor Course, in the *Auditor* magazine. The announcement was accompanied by a center spread of Hubbard's photographs. There is a shot of an Ethics Officer, carrying a heavy wooden baton, wearing dark glasses and full uniform, and scowling at a student who is smiling back, apprehensively. The caption reads: "No one can fool a Sea Org Ethics Officer. He knows who's ethics bait." Another shot shows a Sea Org member suspended in mid-air by two Ethics Officers, one wearing a broad grin. He is about to be thrown over the rail, into the sea. The caption reads: "Students are thrown overboard for gross out tech and bequeathed to the deep!" "Out tech" is a Hubbardism for "misapplication of Scientology auditing procedures." The editor of *Auditor* 41 thought the photos were a Hubbard joke. Hubbard was deadly serious.[14]

Every Scientology Org was ordered to send two Auditors to be trained as "Class VIIIs." As "VIIIs" their auditing would be "flubless." The course would take three weeks, so previous Ethics procedures were of little use—they took too long to administer. Rather than languishing in the chain-locker for a week, or doing three days without sleep on "amends projects," students were to be subject to "instant Ethics," or overboarding. There is no doubt that Hubbard ordered this (one ex-Sea Org officer says Hubbard even took out his home movie camera and filmed it once or twice).[15]

Scientologists who joined after 1970 are often unaware that over-boarding took place. Most who have heard of it, and those who were subjected to it, dismiss it as a passing phase; unpleasant, but no longer significant. People who experienced it often shrug it off, and even insist that it was "research." It can take persistence to extract an admission of the reality of overboarding. Students and crew were lined up on deck in the early hours every morning. They waited to hear whether they were on the day's list of miscreants. Those who knew they were would remove their shoes, jackets and wristwatches in anticipation. The drop was between fifteen and forty feet, depending upon which deck was used. Sometimes people were blindfolded first, and either their feet or hands loosely tied. Non-swimmers were tied to a rope. Being hurled such a distance, blindfolded and restrained, into cold sea water, must have been terrifying. Worst of all was the fear that you would hit the side of the ship as you fell, your flesh ripped open by the barnacles. Overboarding was a very traumatic experience.[16]

The course lectures too seem to have been a traumatic experience for many. Hubbard lectured from a spotlit dais, surrounded by the female Commodore's Staff Aides in flowing white gowns. The lectures were peppered with the old easygoing manner, but punctuated with table-banging and bouts of yelling. Later, some of Hubbard's tantrums were edited from the tapes of the lectures. The lectures were "confidential," and only fully indoctrinated Scientologists could attend.

Students wore green boiler-suits, and, after a certain point on the course, added a short noose of rope around their necks as a mark of honor. They had little time for sleep, and were inevitably extremely cautious in their auditing. If they made a mistake, it was "instant Ethics," and they were heaved over the side.[17]

Hubbard published the purpose of the Class VIII course: "It's up to the Auditor to become UNCOMPROMISINGLY STANDARD . . . an uncompromising zealot for Standard Tech." Sea Org "Missions" were dispatched from Corfu to all corners of the world to bully Org staffs into higher production. Hubbard pronounced that such "Missions" had "unlimited Ethics powers."[18]

Alex Mitchell of the London *Sunday Times* reported that a woman with two children had run screaming from the ship, only to be rounded up and returned by her fellow Scientologists. The journalist also said that eight-year-old children were being overboarded:

Discipline . . . is severe. Members of the crew can be officers one day and swabbing the decks the next. Status is conferred by Boy Scout like decoration; a white neck tie is for students, brown for petty officers, yellow for officers, and blue for Hubbard's personal staff. . . . Recently the crew decided to paint the water tanks. Unwilling to give the job to local contractors the Scientologists did it themselves—only to find that when they next used their taps the water was polluted with paint.[19]

Kenneth Urquhart joined the ship at Corfu. From Hubbard's butler he had risen to become a senior executive at Saint Hill. He had resolutely avoided joining the Sea Org, but was finally cajoled into travelling to Corfu. He was amazed at the change in Hubbard. At Saint Hill he had seen him every day. Although Hubbard occasionally lost his temper, Urquhart had only once seen him quivering with rage. Now screaming fits were a regular feature. OT 3 and the Sea Org had transformed Hubbard.

Amid the turmoil, and with the pressure of the UK ban, and swathes of bad press, Hubbard cancelled enforced Disconnection. The practice of *labelling* an individual Fair Game was also cancelled:[20]

FAIR GAME may not appear on any Ethics Order. It causes bad public relations. This Policy Letter does not cancel any policy on the treatment or handling of an SP [Suppressive Person].

Shortly after arriving in Corfu, Hubbard had issued a Bulletin to Scientologists abolishing Security Checks and the practice of writing down Preclears' misdeeds.[21] In point of fact the name of Security Checking was changed: first to Integrity Processing and then to Confessional Auditing. However, the Sec Check lists of questions written by Hubbard in the 1960s remained, and are still in use. A record of the Preclear's utterances during an auditing session is made by the Auditor, and kept by the Org he works for.

Many Corfiots seem to have accepted overboarding, and on November 16, Hubbard was a welcome guest at a reception at the Achillion Palace. With the notable exception of the Prefect, most of the island's worthies attended. The following day, with as much pomp as the Sea Org could muster, the *Royal Scotman* was renamed yet again, this time deliberately. Diana Hubbard, who had just celebrated her sixteenth birthday, and been awarded the rank of Lieutenant Commander, broke a bottle of champagne over the *Scotman*'s bow, and the ship became the *Apollo*. In the same ceremony, the *Avon River* was restyled the

Athena. The *Enchanter* had already been renamed the *Diana*, but was included in the ceremony nonetheless.

All was not well on the Scientology home front, in England. An application to local authorities for permission to expand Saint Hill castle had been denied. The Scientologists were ordered to pay the legal costs of three of the newspapers they were suing before they could proceed. The son of Scientology spokesman David Gaiman was refused a place at an East Grinstead school until Scientology had cleared its name. Foreign Scientologists posed as tourists to attend a Congress in Croydon, to evade enforcement of the Aliens Act. Gaiman said, "They disguised themselves as humans." It was fair comment.[22]

The English High Court refused to rule against the Home Office's use of the Aliens Act. The Scientologists fought back with more than forty court writs issued for slander or libel on a single day.

The Rhodesian government, which had refused to renew Hubbard's visa in 1966, introduced a ban on the importation of material which promoted, or even related to, the practice of Scientology. The states of Southern and Western Australia joined Victoria in banning Scientology totally. The Sea Org seemed to have put to sea just in time.

The Western Australian "Scientology Prohibition Act" was far more succinct than that of Victoria:

1. A person shall not practice Scientology.
2. A person shall not, directly or indirectly, demand or receive any fee, reward or benefit of any kind from any person for, or on account of, or in relation to the practice of Scientology.

   Penalty: for a first offence two hundred dollars and, for a subsequent offence, five hundred dollars or imprisonment for one year or both.

The Scientologists' response to the bans was in character:

The year of human rights draws to its close. The current English Government celebrated it by barring our foreign students, forbidding a religious leader to enter England, and beginning a steady campaign intended to wipe out every Church and Churchman in England. The hidden men behind the Government's policies are only using Scientology to see if the public will stand for the destruction of all churches and churchmen in England. . . . Callaghan, Crossman and Robinson follow the orders of a hidden foreign group that recently set itself up in England, which has as its purpose the seizure of any being whom they dislike or won't agree [sic], and permanently disabling or killing him.

To do this they believe they must first reduce all churches and finish Christianity. Scientology Organizations will shortly reveal the hidden men . . . [with] more than enough evidence to hang them in every Country in the West.

The public seemed perfectly willing to witness the destruction of Scientology. Neither the promised exposure of the "hidden men" nor the destruction of "all churches and churchmen" ensued. Instead, David Gaiman, head of the Public Relations Bureau of the Guardian's Office, issued a "Code of Reform." The severe puritanical and punitive approach was no longer necessary. The Church was going to become a moderate and liberal organization, which would continue its battle against the evils of psychiatry (spokesmen are trained to attack psychiatry as a response to any criticism of Scientology). Thirty-eight libel suits were dropped. And while the press and governments were being assured of this new liberal attitude, the new Class VIIIs were returning to their Orgs and instituting their own forms of overboarding.[23]

In the Edinburgh Advanced Org, the miscreant was thrown into a bath of hot, cold or dirty water. In Los Angeles, he or she would be hosed down fully clothed in the parking lot, though later a large water tank was used. John McMaster has said that in Hawaii the offender's head would be pushed into a toilet bowl, and the toilet flushed. The same technique was used in Copenhagen.

In the Advanced Orgs in Edinburgh and Los Angeles, staff were ordered to wear all-white uniforms, with silver boots, to mimic the Galactic Patrol of seventy-five million years before. According to Hubbard's Flag Order 652, mankind would accept regulation from that group which had last betrayed it. So the Sea Org were to ape the instigators of the OT3 incident. By the same token, all the book covers were revised to show scenes from the supposedly lethal incident.

"Captain" Bill Robertson, who introduced the uniforms to both Edinburgh and Los Angeles, also ordered a nightwatch in Los Angeles. The crew assembled on the roof every night to watch for the spaceships of Hubbard's enemies. "Captain" Bill has continued his crusade against the invading aliens, the "Markabians," into the 1990s.

In Britain, in January 1969, Sir John Foster was appointed to conduct an Inquiry into Scientology. In Perth, Australia, police raided the local Org, and fourteen individual Scientologists, and the Hubbard Association of Scientologists International, were prosecuted for "practising Scientology.'' In New Zealand in February, another Inquiry got underway.

Hubbard was still trying to ingratiate himself with the military junta which controlled Greece. He applauded them in a press interview saying "the present Constitution represents the most brilliant tradition of Greek democracy.'' To win favor, Hubbard announced the formation of the Help Greece Committee which issued a promotional piece for a "University of Philosophy in Corfu.'' He boasted that "Most professors of psychology and schools of psychology foresee as part of their lessons [the] subject of dianetics and scientology.''

The symbol of the Help Greece Committee was a Greek Orthodox cross set at the center of the thirteen-leaved laurels of the Sea Organization. This was not a tactful gesture; Bishop Polycarpos was already concerned about the spiritual influence of Scientology.

The British Vice-Consul, John Forte, was more concerned with the material influence of Scientology. He had been receiving complaints since the Scientologists arrived. He later published a booklet called *The Commodore and the Colonels* describing his experiences. Forte became interested in several defections from the *Apollo*, including that of William Deitch, who disappeared completely. Early in March 1969, a detachment of U.S. Marines arrived. Colin Craig met a group of them, and described life aboard a Scientology ship. The Marines insisted that he tell his story to the British Vice-Consul immediately.

Craig and another Belfast man, Jack Russell, had answered an advertisement for maintenance fitters. Arriving on Corfu, they were assigned to the *Apollo*'s fifteen-year-old Chief Engineer. Russell was attracted to Scientology, but Craig was so alarmed that he feigned illness and locked himself in his cabin. With Forte's assistance they were both repatriated.

While this was taking place, Hubbard announced that Scientology was "going in the direction of mild ethics and involvement with the Society. After nineteen years of attack by minions of vested interest, psychiatric front groups, we developed a tightly disciplined organizational structure . . . we will never need a harsh spartan discipline for ourselves.''[24]

The Greek government, concerned by the many complaints it had received, peremptorily ordered the two hundred or so Scientologists on Corfu to leave Greek territory. Protests were made that the *Apollo* was not seaworthy, so the ship was inspected, and declared fit for a voyage in the Mediterranean. The flagship *Apollo* was given twenty-four hours to leave Greek waters. She left on March 19, ostensibly for Venice.

Two days later a young Scientologist arrived, and introduced himself to Vice-Consul Forte. When asked why the *Apollo* had left, Forte simply handed him Hubbard's printed explanation. The departure was "due to unforeseen foreign exchange troubles and the unstable middle eastern situation." Forte discovered many years later that the Scientologist had subsequently burgled both his office and his villa looking for evidence of Forte's involvement with the Conspiracy.

Soon afterwards, an Inquiry started in South Africa. Hubbard turned his back on the "wog" world, and concentrated on introducing a new form of Dianetics, and integrating it into the Scientology "Bridge." He issued a bizarre order to the Sea Org, called "Zones of Action," which outlined his plans. Scientology was going to take over those areas controlled by Smersh (the evil organization fought by the fictional James Bond), rake in enormous amounts of cash, clean up psychotherapy, infiltrate and reorganize every minority group, and befriend the worst foes of the Western nations. Hubbard's stated intention was to undermine a supposed Fascist conspiracy to rule the world.

On June 30, 1969, the New Zealand Commission submitted its report. Their attitude to Scientology was sensible. Rather than banning, fining or imprisoning Scientologists, they recommended the cessation of disconnection and Suppressive Person declares against family members. Further, they recommended that no auditing or training be given to anyone under twenty-one, without the consent of both parents (including consent to the fee), and a reduction of the deluge of promotional literature and prompt discontinuance when requested.

The Commission recommended that no legislative action be taken. However, it found "clear proof of the activities, methods, and practices of Scientology in New Zealand contributing to estrangements in family relationships . . . the attitude of Scientology towards family relationships was cold, distant, and somewhat uninterested . . . the Commission received a letter from L. Ron Hubbard stating that the Board of Directors of the Church of Scientology had no intention of reintroducing the policy [of disconnection]. He also added that, for his part, he could see no reason why the policy should ever be reintroduced. . . . This undertaking does not go as far as the Commission had hoped . . . [it was seen that] the activities, methods, and practices of Scientology did result in persons being subjected to improper or unreasonable pressures." Nonetheless, the New Zealand Government did not outlaw the practice of Scientology. The tide appeared to be turning.

In July, the Church of Scientology scored a victory of sorts in their long-running battle with the Food and Drug Administration in the United States. In 1963, the FDA had raided the Washington Org, seizing E-meters and books. The whole affair had been in and out of the courts from that time. Now a Federal judge ruled that although the E-meter had been "mis-branded," and that its "secular" use should be banned, it might still be used for "religious" counselling, as long as it was carefully relabeled to indicate that it had no curative or diagnostic capabilities. To this day the Church of Scientology has never fully complied with the relabeling order, but E-meters do carry an abbreviated version of it. This was not the end of the FDA case, however.

Also in 1969, an Advanced Organization was opened in Copenhagen. Now the OT levels were available in England at Saint Hill (the Edinburg AO had moved there), in Los Angeles, in Copenhagen, and aboard the "flagship" *Apollo*.

Up until this time the "First Real Clear," John McMaster, had been the emissary of Scientology. He had braved the incisive questioning of television interviewers, and, overcoming much bad publicity, inspired many people to join Scientology. He had even been sent as a Scientology representative to the United Nations in New York by Hubbard, and managed to secure interviews with several important people. In November 1969, John McMaster resigned from the Church of Scientology. He felt that the "Technology" of Scientology was of tremendous value, but questioned the motives of those managing the Church, most especially Hubbard.

McMaster probably feared for his own safety. He had been overboarded several times, and the last time was left struggling in the water for three hours with a broken collarbone.

The last straw for McMaster had been the brutal murder of three teenagers in Los Angeles. Two had been Scientologists, the third was disfigured beyond identification. The mutilated bodies were left a hundred yards away from a house where Scientologists lived. McMaster felt that this was an act of retribution for Scientology's duplicity. A few weeks later, *The New York Times* revealed that Charles Manson had been involved in Scientology. Internal Scientology documents show that Manson had actually received about 150 hours of auditing while in prison. There was a cover-up by the Guardian's Office, which successfully concealed the extent of Manson's considerable involvement.

In 1970, the Ontario Committee on the "Healing Arts" pronounced: "With no other group in the healing arts did the Committee encounter the uncooperative attitude evinced by the Church of Scientology . . . the public authorities in Ontario . . . should keep the activities of Scientology under constant scrutiny." However, no recommendations were made for the proscription of Scientology.

In November that same year, the Scientologists' libel case against Geoffrey Johnson Smith, East Grinstead's Member of Parliament, finally came to court. The Church produced several impressive witnesses. William Benitez had spent most of his adult life in prison for drug offences by the time he encountered Scientology. His life had been transformed, he had overcome his drug habit, and set up Narconon to help others do the same. Sir Chandos Hoskyns-Abrahall, the retired Lieutenant Governor of Western Nigeria, said of his own involvement in Scientology: "I thought at first there might be something in it. I ended up convinced there was everything in it."

But the most startling witness was Kenneth Robinson's former parliamentary private secretary. William Hamling was the Member of Parliament for Woolwich West, and had decided to find out about Scientology for himself. He used the most direct method: going to Saint Hill and taking a Communication Course. In the witness box, Hamling called the course "first rate." He said the Scientologists he had met were normal, decent, intelligent people. He had received auditing, and, in fact, continued in Scientology after the court case.

Geoffrey Johnson Smith was on the witness stand for six days, and Kenneth Robinson also made an appearance. But the focal witness was Hilary Henslow, mother of the schizophrenic girl who had been abandoned by Scientology.

Instructing the jury Mr. Justice Browne said, "You may think that Mrs. Henslow picked up all the stones thrown at her in the witness box, and threw them back with equal force." He called the love-letters written by Karen Henslow to her Scientologist boyfriend "quite heartbreaking," and added: "You may think it absolutely disgraceful that these letters should have got into the hands of the scientologists, or been used in this case . . . you have to give those letters the weight that you feel right."

The case had lasted for thirty-two days when the jury showed exactly what weight they gave to the letters, and to the Scientologists.

They decided that Johnson Smith's statement—that Scientologists "direct themselves deliberately towards the weak, the unbalanced, the immature, the rootless, and the mentally or emotionally unstable"— was not defamatory; was published "in good faith and without malice"; and was "fair comment." The case had backfired completely on the Scientologists. Costs, which *The Times* newspaper estimated at £70,000, were awarded against them. Spokesman David Gaiman said there would be no appeal.

The decision seemed to have no effect on Hubbard, and two days later, he blithely issued Flag Order 2673 to the Sea Org. It was called "Stories Told," and explained that OTC, which ran the ships, was actually involved in training businessmen, and that is what Scientologists were to say if asked. The crew did tell this "shore" story, avoiding any mention of Scientology. It had become too controversial. So, another layer of deceit was built into Scientology's approach to the "wog" world.

But the Scientologists weren't the only people guilty of deceit. In the U.S., devious actions against Scientology were underway. President Nixon had put Scientology on his "Enemies List," and the Internal Revenue Service began to make life difficult for Scientologists. The CIA passed reports (some speculative and inaccurate) on Scientology through U.S. consulates to foreign governments. These underhand tactics all eventually backfired, making sensible measures curbing the Church of Scientology's abuses more difficult.[25]

After only three years' suspension, Scientology's hefty Ethics penalties were reintroduced in 1971, unnoticed by the media, or by the governments which had shortly before been so interested.[26] In December, Sir John Foster submitted his report to the British Government. In the introduction he said:

> Most of the Government measures of July 1968 were not justified: the mere fact that someone is a Scientologist is in my opinion no reason for excluding him from the United Kingdom, when there is nothing in our law to prevent those of his fellows who are citizens of this country from practicing Scientology here.

He further recommended that "psychotherapy . . . should be organized as a restricted profession open only to those who undergo an appropriate training and are willing to adhere to a proper code of ethics." Undoubtedly, the Scientology Ethics Conditions did not meet his criteria for a "proper code." The Foster report was a tour de force, patiently constructed, largely from Hubbard's own statements. However, the British Government did nothing. The use of the Aliens Act carried on, and foreign Scientologists continued to study and work for Scientology in Britain by the simple expedient of not declaring their philosophical persuasion when they arrived. The Guardian's Office gave advice and assistance to secure visas. One ex-Scientologist has joked that if the Home Office had checked they would have realized there were over 100 people living in his small apartment.

The treatment of crew aboard the ships did improve in the early 1970s, but only after several years of chain-locker punishments and overboarding. Nonetheless, the Sea Org still worked an exhausting schedule, and obeyed Hubbard's whims. At times he was patient, even tolerant, at other times a bellowing monster.

The kitchen staff were known as galley-slaves. They worked disgraceful hours in the heat and stench of the kitchens. In the summer of 1971, a tragic event befell one of those galley-slaves. It is shrouded in mystery to this day.

CHAPTER FOUR

The Death of Susan Meister

Susan Meister was introduced to Scientology in San Francisco in the autumn of 1970. By November, she was working at the San Francisco Org. She was an eager convert, and tried to persuade her parents to become Scientologists. She wanted to be close to the "Founder," and contribute to "Clearing the Planet," so in February 1971 she joined the Sea Org. By the end of the month she was aboard the "Flagship" *Apollo*. Her stay there was brief and tragic. On May 8, she wrote to her mother:

> Mother,
> Do you recall talking to me about WW III—and where it would start if it were to start—father and most everyone else maintained that it would start in either China or Russia vs. U.S. and you said—oh no—it would originate in Germany—that the Nazis hadn't given up yet—? Well babe, you were right—there is a new Nazi resurgence taking place in Germany—so now it's a race between the good guys in the white hats (Scientologists) [sic] and the Leipzig death camp (Nazis) [sic] the bad guys in the black hats—we'll win of course—but the game is exciting. Truth *is* stranger than fiction. As Alice [in Wonderland] says "Things get curiouser and curiouser!" Get into Scientology now. It's fantastic.
> Love, Susan

Four days later, Susan Meister wrote this letter:

Dear Family,
I just had a session or auditing session...
great! Great! GREAT!
and my life is EXPANDING
EXPANDING.
and it's All Hurry Up! Hurry, Hurry
SCIENTOLO
Be a friend to yourselves —
Get Into this Stuff NOW —
It's more precious than gold
it's the best thing that's
ever ever ever ever come
along. Love, Susan

Her last letter to her parents from the *Apollo* was dated June 15, 1971. In it she thanked them for a birthday card, and a variety of gifts, including a new dress. She continued, showing the effect upon a young and impressionable mind Hubbard's obsession with the "great conspiracy" against him:

> I can't tell you exactly where we are. We have enemies who are *profiting* from peoples' ignorance and lack of self-determinism and do not wish to see us succeed in restoring *freedom* and *self-determinism* to this planet's people. If these people were to find out where we are located—they would attempt to destroy us. Therefore, we are not allowed to say where this ship is located.

She once more urged her mother to read Hubbard's books, and take Scientology courses. Ten days after writing the letter, Susan was dead.

George Meister, Susan's father, was away from his Colorado home on a business trip when Guardian's Office Public Relations man Artie Maren phoned. George Meister met Maren the next day, and was presented with an unsigned "fact sheet" giving the Scientologists' account of events as a series of numbered statements.

Meister told Artie Maren that he wanted the body to be flown back to the U.S. for burial. Meister received a letter from Bob Thomas at the Church of Scientology in Los Angeles explaining that the "Panamanian" owners of the *Apollo* were not obliged to give information to the Church of Scientology. However, the *Apollo*'s captain, Norman Starkey, had offered to pay for a Christian burial in Morocco, but regretted that they would not pay for the body to be returned to the United States.

George Meister, dazed by the news, decided to go to Morocco to try and verify the circumstances of his daughter's death. He was told he would be able to see the body in the morgue in Safi. He left for Morocco on July 14.

Meister was met at the airport in Casablanca by Sea Org member Peter Warren, who escorted him to the Marhaba Hotel. Meister met the U.S. vice-consul, Jack Galbraith, and explained the purpose of his mission.

During this meeting with Galbraith, Warren phoned to say he would drive Meister the 120 miles to Safi. Warren said the *Apollo* was already past its scheduled departure date, but would wait a little longer, because of Meister's presence.

Meister arranged to leave the following morning at 6:00 a.m., accompanied by Galbraith, Warren and a Sea Org girl called Joni. Their first stop in Safi was the police station. Meister says the police official he spoke to genuinely tried to help. He showed Meister a photograph taken aboard the *Apollo*, showing the dead girl.

According to her father, Susan was "lying on a bunk, wearing the new dress her mother had made for her, her arms crossed with a long barreled revolver on her breast. A bullet hole was in the center of her forehead and blood was running out of the corners of her mouth. I began to wonder how Susan could possibly shoot herself in the center of her forehead with the long barreled revolver. She would have had to hold it with both hands at arms length. There were no powder burns on her forehead, which certainly would have been the case if the gun was against her forehead as it would have to be to shoot herself as the photograph appeared."

The police said the revolver was not available for inspection. Meister was shown the police report, but it was in French, which neither he nor Galbraith spoke. Meister was told that the police were unwilling to release copies of either the report or their photographs.

Meister and Galbraith went on to the hospital where Susan's body had been taken. During the autopsy her intestines and her brains had been removed. Meister says that Warren admitted that he had given permission, believing that Susan might have been on drugs. Meister asked to see the body, which he had been told was in a refrigerated morgue. To his amazement, he was told by a doctor that they did not know where the body was.

The next day, with Warren and Joni still in attendance, they had an audience with the Pasha of Safi. The Pasha told Meister he could not have copies of the police report, or the photographs. He said he had transferred the records to the provincial capital, Marrakesh. When Meister pressed him to find the whereabouts of Susan's body, the Pasha told him the interview was over.

Meister asked Warren if he could see Ron Hubbard. He knew that Hubbard's daughter, Diana, was about Susan's age. In Meister's own words:

> Passing the guarded gates into the port compound, we had our first look at Hubbard's ship, *Apollo*. It appeared to be old, and as we boarded it, the girls manning the deck gave us a hand salute. All were dressed in work type clothing of civilian origin. Most appeared to be young. Upon boarding we were shown the stern of the ship, which was used as a reading room, with several people sitting in chairs reading books. The mention of Susan seemed to meet disapproval from those on board. . . . We were shown where Susan's quarters were in the stern of the ship below decks where it appeared fifty or so people were sleeping on shelf type bunks. Susan's letter had mentioned she shared a cabin all the way forward with one other person. Next we were shown the cabin next to the pilot house on the bridge where the alleged suicide had taken place. It was a small cabin and appeared to be one where a duty officer might catch some sleep while underway. . . . We were not allowed to see any more of the ship. . . . I requested an interview with Hubbard as he was then on board. Warren said he would ask. . . . He returned in about a half hour and said Hubbard had declined to see me.

Meister and Galbraith returned to Casablanca. Meister found that the thirty or so films he had been carrying with him had disappeared, including the film he had shot of Safi and the *Apollo*.

> As I was preparing to leave the hotel [to take the flight home], the telephone in my room rang. It was Warren who said he had to see me at once on a matter of utmost urgency. I told him I would see him in the lobby. . . . Warren came into the lobby a very frightened man. His face was pale and he motioned me to a chair in the corner of the lobby . . . he told me he was sent to make a settlement with me in cash.

Meister was outraged by this suggestion, and told Warren to deal with his attorney. "At the airport, just prior to boarding, I was accosted by a large man in a pinstripe suit carrying a briefcase. He said, 'We are watching you and so are the CIA and the FBI.' "

After his return to the U.S., Meister found that his daughter had been buried in a Casablanca cemetery, wrapped in a burlap sack, before his visit to Morocco. He arranged to have the body exhumed and shipped to the U.S. in a sealed tin coffin. His local Health Authority, in Colorado, received an anonymous letter before the body was returned. It said in part:

> There has been a Cholera epidemic in Morocco . . . there have been a recorded two to three hundred deaths. And it's been brought to my attention that the daughter of one George Meister died in Morocco, either by accident or from cholera, probably the latter.

The Los Angeles Times picked up the story: "According to a Nov. 11, 1971, letter from Assistant Secretary of State David M. Abshire to the Senate Foreign Relations Committee—the *Apollo*'s Port Captain threatened in the presence of the American Vice Consul from Casablanca, William J. Galbraith, that he had enough material, including compromising photographs of Miss Meister, to smear Mr. Meister. . . . Meister is said to have left Morocco the day before the threat was made."

The Scientologists then launched a campaign against Galbraith, with little success; for example, telling newspaper men that he had threatened that the CIA would sink the *Apollo*!

Meister received anonymous letters saying that his daughter had made pornographic films, and that she had been a drug addict. Meister says he continued to be harassed for six years. The harassment stopped around the time of the FBI raids on the Guardian's Office, in the Summer of 1977.

If Susan Meister did commit suicide, several questions remain. She had been aboard the *Apollo* for four months. During that time, she sent consistently enthusiastic letters to her parents. To commit suicide, she must have undergone a very rapid mood change. She must also have lost her faith in the efficacy of Scientology. If this was so, what had caused this sudden shift of opinion, and why didn't she leave the *Apollo*?

Letters were censored before leaving the *Apollo*, and the passports of those aboard were held by the Ethics Office. So perhaps she was unable to write the truth of what she had discovered, and unable to leave the ship. Perhaps.

There is no concrete evidence to show that Susan Meister's death was not suicide. But the whole affair is compounded by the events which followed. By creating the Sea Org, and taking to the sea, Hubbard had successfully put himself beyond the law. There was no coroner's investigation into the death. It is likely that a verdict at least of foul play would have been returned if there had been such an investigation.

CHAPTER FIVE

Hubbard's Travels

Susan Meister's death had no effect upon the Sea Org's relationship with Morocco. The *Apollo* crew established a land base, called the Tours Reception Center, in Morocco in 1971. They were trying to get into the king's favor, and started training government officials, including Moroccan Intelligence agents, in Scientology techniques. Officials were put on the E-meter and Security-Checked by French-speaking Sea Org members. The Hubbards moved ashore.[1]

From his villa in Morocco, in March 1972, the Commodore explained his twelve point "Governing Policy" for finance. Points A and J were the same: "MAKE MONEY." Point K was "MAKE MORE MONEY." And the last point, L, was "MAKE OTHER PEOPLE PRODUCE SO AS TO MAKE MONEY." At last, an honest admission of this major plank of Hubbard's philosophy.[2]

Hubbard also introduced the "Primary Rundown," where a student would "word-clear" ten Hubbard lectures about study. That meant going through the definition of every word in the lectures in a non "dinky" dictionary (to use Hubbard's expression), and using the word in every defined context until it was thoroughly understood. It was a gargantuan task. The word "of," for instance, has fifteen definitions in the *World Book Dictionary*, favored by Hubbard at the time. At the end of this arduous procedure, the student allegedly became "super-literate."

202

The South African Commission of Enquiry submitted its report on Scientology in June 1972. It recommended that a Register for psychotherapists be established, as had the Foster Report in Britain. It also recommended that the practices of Disconnection, "public investigation" (i.e. *noisy* investigation), security checking, and the dissemination of "inaccurate, untruthful and harmful information in regard to psychiatry," should be legislated against. The report added: "No positive purpose will be served by the banning of Scientology as such." Neither this nor any other legislative action was actually taken.[3]

The *Apollo* sailed from Morocco to Portugal in October, for repairs. Hubbard and a contingent of Sea Org members stayed behind. Morocco was as close as Hubbard ever came to having the ear of a government, but relations broke down. In the Scientology world, there is a rumor that the upset had something to do with Moroccan Intelligence, which does lend a certain mystique. A secret Guardian's Office investigation revealed a more prosaic error, however. In 1971, Hubbard had reintroduced Heavy Ethics, and Scientologists continued to use the Ethics Conditions. For being persistently late for their Scientology courses, members of the Moroccan Post Office were assigned a condition of "Treason." To the Moroccans, "Treason," no matter how much it was word-cleared, meant only one thing: execution. The Post Office officials set themselves against the Scientologists, and won.[4] As a grim footnote, the Moroccan official who had negotiated with the Scientologists was later executed for treason. The contacts with Intelligence had actually been with a faction which was to fail in an attempted coup d'etat.

The panic, starting from Hubbard's typically exaggerated use of a simple word, ended with an order for the Scientologists to quit Morocco, in December 1972. Hubbard himself was given only twenty-four hours. He flew to Lisbon, and then secretly on to New York. The French had instituted proceedings against him for fraud, so he had to duck out of sight. He was being labeled undesirable by more and more governments.

Meanwhile, in Spain, eight Scientologists had been arrested for possession of chocolates laced with LSD. They were held in filthy cells for four days, and interviewed by a U.S. Drug Enforcement Administration agent. As it turned out the chocolates did not contain LSD.[6]

Two Sea Org members accompanied Hubbard to New York. The three stayed in hiding for nine months. Hubbard was in poor health:

Photographs taken at the time show an overweight, dishevelled man with a large growth on his forehead. Despite his supposed resignation from management in 1966, Hubbard had continued to control the affairs of his Church, usually on a daily basis. Now he had only a single telex machine. His prolific Scientological output ground almost to a halt. What little he wrote shows a preoccupation with his poor physical condition. In July, he published an exhaustive summary of approaches to ill health. He also initiated the "Snow White Program," directing his Guardian's Office to remove negative reports about Scientology from government files, and track down their source. He was convinced of the conspiracy against him, and had no qualms about breaking the law to achieve the "greatest good for the greatest number," meaning the greatest good for L. Ron Hubbard.[7]

While Hubbard was in New York, the Australian states began the process which eventually led to the repeal of their Scientology Prohibition Acts. The State of Victoria, which had started the Australian crackdown, even gave the Church of the New Faith (aka Scientology) tax-exemption.

In the U.S. the Food and Drug Administration was ordered to return all the materials seized eight years earlier, although the E-meters were still adjudged to be mislabelled, which had been the real issue at stake.

Another secret bank account was opened for Hubbard under the name United States Church of Scientology Trust. Hubbard was the sole trustee of this Swiss account, and it received large donations from Scientology organizations throughout the world.[8]

In one of the few Bulletins issued during his stay in New York, Hubbard wrote:

> The actual barrier in the society is the failure to practice truth. . . . Scientology is the road to truth and he who would follow it must take true steps.

Hubbard's hypocrisy knew no bounds. In an issue originally called "What Your Fees Buy" ("Fees" later became "Donations"), Hubbard continued to insist that he did not benefit financially from Scientology, and had donated $13½ million above and beyond the cost of his own research. He claimed that he had not been paid for his lectures and had not even collected author's royalties on his books. Scientologists could take Hubbard's word for it that none of the money they paid to the Church went to him.

In August 1973, yet another new corporation was formed, once again with the sole purpose of siphoning funds to Hubbard. Hubbard was to prove yet again that in matters of taxation, the man with the "most imagination" wins, and Hubbard had a very vivid imagination. The Religious Research Foundation was incorporated in Liberia. Non-U.S. students paid the RRF for their courses on the Flagship, so the corporation which ran the ship was not being paid, and the money was going straight into an account controlled by Hubbard. The Scientology Church was again billed retroactively for earlier services rendered. This was the second time the Church had paid Hubbard for these services: retroactive billing was the function of the "LRH Good Will Account" in the late 1960s. The Church paid for the third time in 1982. Millions of dollars paid in good faith by Scientologists for the further dissemination of their beliefs went straight into Hubbard's personal accounts, and were used to keep him in luxury, with a million dollar camera collection, silk shirts tailored in Savile Row, and a large personal retinue at his beck and call.[9]

Hubbard rejoined the *Apollo* at Lisbon in September 1973. He had complained about the dust aboard the flagship, so the crew spent three months crawling through the ventilation shafts of the ship cleaning them with toothbrushes, while the *Apollo* sailed between Portuguese and Spanish ports.[10]

In November, the *Apollo* was in Tenerife. Hubbard went for a joyride into the hills on one of his motorbikes. The bike skidded on a hairpin bend, hurling the Commodore onto the gravel. He was badly hurt, but somehow managed to walk back to the ship. He refused a doctor, and his medical orderly, Jim Dincalci, was surprised at his demands for painkillers. Hubbard turned on him, and said "You're trying to kill me." Kima Douglas took Dincalci's place. She thinks Hubbard had broken an arm and three ribs, but could not get close enough to find out. With Hubbard strapped into his chair, the *Apollo* put to sea, encountering a Force 5 gale. The Commodore screamed in agony, and the screaming did not stop for six weeks.[11]

In Douglas' words: "He was revolting to be with—a sick, crotchety, pissed-off old man, extremely antagonistic to everything and everyone. His wife was often in tears and he'd scream at her at the top of his lungs, 'Get out of here!' Nothing was right. He'd throw his food across the room with his good arm; I'd often see plates splat against the bulkhead. . . . He absolutely refused to see another doctor. He said they were all fools and would only make him worse. The truth was that he was terrified of doctors and that's why everyone had to be put through such hell."

While on the mend, Hubbard introduced his latest innovation in Ethics Technology: the "Rehabilitation Project Force." This became Scientology's equivalent to imprisonment, with more than a tinge of the Chinese Ideological Re-education Center. In theory the RPF deals with Sea Org members who consistently fail to make good. They are put on "MEST work," which is to say physical labor, and spend several hours each day confessing their overts (transgressions), and revealing their Evil Purposes.

Life in the Sea Org was already fairly gruelling, but the Rehabilitation Project Force went several steps further. Gerry Armstrong, who spent over two years on the RPF, has given this description:

> It was essentially a prison to which crew who were considered non-producers, security risks, or just wanted to leave the Sea Org, were assigned. Hubbard's RPF policies established the conditions. RPF members were segregated and not allowed to communicate to anyone else. They had their own spaces and were not allowed in normal crew areas of the ship. They ate after normal crew had eaten, and only whatever was left over from the crew meal. Their berthing was the worst on board, in a roach-infested, filthy and unventilated cargo hold. They wore black boilersuits, even in the hottest weather. They were required to run everywhere. Discipline was harsh and bizarre, with running laps of the ship assigned for the slightest infraction like failing to address a senior with "Sir." Work was hard and the schedule rigid with seven hours sleep time from lights out to lights on, short meal breaks, no liberties and no free time . . .
>
> When one young woman ordered into the RPF took the assignment too lightly, Hubbard created the RPF's RPF and assigned her to it, an even more degrading experience, cut off even from the RPF, kept under guard, forced to clean the ship's bilges, and allowed even less sleep.[12]

Others verify Armstrong's account. The RPF rapidly swelled to include anyone who had incurred Hubbard's disfavor. Soon about 150 people, almost a third of the *Apollo*'s complement, were being rehabilitated. This careful imitation of techniques long-used by the military to obtain unquestioning obedience and immediate compliance to orders, or more simply to break men's spirits, was all part of a ritual of humiliation for the Sea Org member.

Hubbard's railing against the "enemies of freedom" (i.e., the critics of Scientology) continued in a confidential issue: "It is my intention that by the use of professional PR tactics any opposition be not only dulled but permanently eradicated . . . If there will be a long-term threat, you are to immediately evaluate and originate a black PR campaign to destroy the person's repute and to discredit them so thoroughly that they will be ostracized."[13]

Elsewhere Hubbard had defined black PR as "spreading lies by hidden sources," and added "it inevitably results in injustices being done."[14] Most Scientologists remain ignorant of the confidential PR issue.

Despite Hubbard's research into the subject, public relations had not improved. In 1974, the *Apollo* was banned from several Spanish ports. In October, while she was moored in Funchal, Madeira, the ship's musicians, the "Apollo All Stars," held a rock festival. Something went terribly wrong, and the day ended with an angry crowd bombarding the *Apollo* with stones: a "rock" festival (the pun stuck and is generally used by those who were there). It started with a taxi arriving on the dock, from the trunk of which a small group of Medeirans unloaded stones. Bill Robertson, the *Apollo*'s captain at the time, ordered the fire hoses to be turned on this small group, and soon the dock was milling with jeering Madeirans. The rioters tried to set the *Apollo* adrift. They pitched motorcycles and cars belonging to the Scientologists off the dock. A Scientology story that a Portuguese army contingent stood by and watched is not confirmed by witnesses. They also failed to mention the response of the *Apollo* crew, some of whom returned the barrage of stones and bottles. The Commodore marched up and down in his battle fatigues yelling orders, and finally the *Apollo* moved away from the dock to anchor off shore. Ironically, the Madeirans seem to have thought the *Apollo* was a CIA spy ship. Scientologists attribute this to CIA black PR. Other observers attribute it to the intensely secretive behaviour of the *Apollo*, and the ongoing "shore stories" (lies) about her real function and activities.[15]

The Mediterranean had been effectively closed to the *Apollo* through Hubbard's paranoid secrecy and his inability to maintain friendly relations. Now the Spanish and Portuguese were set against her. Hubbard decided to head for the Americas, and it was announced that the *Apollo* was sailing for Buenos Aries. More subterfuge, as she was actually set for Charleston, South Carolina, by way of Bermuda.

The Scientologists have it that a spy aboard the *Apollo* alerted the U.S. government of her true destination. They do not mention the advance mission of the Apollo All Stars, who usually preceded the ship to create a friendly atmosphere with music and song. After their reception in Madeira, the All Stars should have realized it was time to change their image. Instead they went ahead to Charleston. According to the Scientologists, the welcoming party waiting there included agents from the Immigration Office, the Drug Enforcement Agency, U.S. Customs, and the Coast Guard, along with several U.S. Marshals who were to arrest Hubbard, and deliver a subpoena for him to appear in an Internal Revenue Service case.[16]

Just beyond the territorial limit, the *Apollo* caught wind of this reception committee, and, radioing that she was sailing for Nova Scotia, changed course for the West Indies. The *Apollo* then cruised the Caribbean. Initially relations were good, but soon, despite all the efforts of the Apollo All Stars, and Ron's new guise as a professional photographer (trailing his "photo-shoot org" behind him), the welcome wore thin.[17]

In Curaçao, in the summer of 1975, Hubbard had a heart attack. Despite his protests, Kima Douglas, his medical orderly, rushed him to hospital. While in the ambulance Hubbard suffered a pulmonary embolism (a blood clot in the artery to his lungs). He spent two days in intensive care, and three weeks in a private hospital. While there his food was carried ten miles from the ship. Three Messengers sat outside his room twenty-four hours a day (they had to make do with the hospital food). He did not return to the *Apollo* for another three months.[18]

While the Commodore was incapacitated, several of his U.S. churches recouped their tax-exempt status, and the Attorney General of Australia lifted the ridiculous ban on the word Scientology. An Appeal Court in Rhodesia also lifted a ban on the import of Scientology materials.

CHAPTER SIX

The Flag Land Base

In August 1975, the *Apollo* returned to Curaçao. The Scientologists allege that an Interpol agent had given the report of the 1965 Australian Enquiry (the Anderson Report) to local newspapers and officials, and that Henry Kissinger had sent an unfavourable memo to most of the United States embassies in the Caribbean. The Dutch Prime Minister demanded that the "ship of fools" be ejected from Curaçao. So in October the *Apollo* was once again ordered out of port.[1]

She sailed to the Bahamas. The crew was divided into three parties, and Scientology moved its headquarters back to shore, in the United States. Two groups established management outposts in New York and Washington, DC, and the third, including Hubbard, flew to Daytona, Florida. Hubbard lectured to a handpicked team of Sea Org members on his "New Vitality Rundown."[2] The *Apollo* lay at anchor in the Bahamas.

Maintaining its usual secrecy, the Church of Scientology started to buy property in Clearwater, Florida. The town's name was obviously too much of a temptation to Hubbard, and he personally directed the project through his Guardian's Office. In October, a front corporation, Southern Land Development and Leasing, agreed to purchase the 272-room Fort Harrison hotel for $2.3 million. The owners' attorney said it was one of the strangest transactions he had ever dealt with. He did not even have Southern Land Development's phone number.[3]

In November, Southern Land added the Bank of Clearwater building to its holdings for $550,000. A spokesman kept up the pretense, by announcing that the properties had been purchased for the United Churches of Florida. He pledged openness. No connection to Scientology was mentioned. The residents of Clearwater had no idea that their town was being systematically invaded. This organization which promised the world a "road to truth" was still treading its own back alley of duplicity and subterfuge.

The Guardian's Office was already preparing detailed reports on Clearwater, and its occupants and "opinion leaders." On November 26, Hubbard sent a secret order to the three principal officers of the Guardian's Office. It was called "Program LRH Security. Code Name: Power."

The entire Guardian's Office was put on alert, so that any hint of government or judicial action concerning Hubbard would be discovered early enough to spirit him away from potential subpoena or arrest. As Hubbard was staying near to Clearwater, security there was to be especially tight.

Despite contrary representations to Scientologists and the world at large, Hubbard was still very much in control of his Church. He said as much in an order to the head of the U.S. GO, complaining that he was not only having to direct the entire Church, but also the Guardian's Office. In the same order, Hubbard laid out strict security arrangements for his own proposed visits to the new Scientology properties in Clearwater. He explained that he wanted to become a celebrity in the area, as a photographer, and that his picture of the mayor would soon grace city hall.

GO Program Order 158, "Early Warning System," issued on December 5th, 1975, instituted Hubbard's orders regarding his personal security. Distribution of the Order was highly restricted. Security was to be maintained by placing agents in the Offices of the United States Attorney in Washington and Los Angeles, the International Operations department of the IRS, the American Medical Association in Chicago, and several government agencies in Florida. Agents were already in place in the Coast Guard, the Drug Enforcement Administration, and the IRS in both Washington and Los Angeles. This was not a matter of a small persecuted religion infiltrating government agencies to expose immoral actions committed by those agencies. In reality, it was a matter of protecting Hubbard from any inconvenience, let alone any litigation.[4]

The Guardian's Office was in full swing, especially its Intelligence section, B-1. On December 5, "Project Power" was issued. Its purpose was to make United Churches indispensable to the Clearwater community. The Guardian's Office was to investigate the opponents of community leaders, using a *minimum* of illegally obtained information. United Churches would give this information to the community leader in question, and offer to make further investigations on his or her behalf. GO Operations would be mounted against such opponents. The example given in the Guardian's Order concerned a fictitious child molester called Mr. Schultz. Having obtained the mayor's permission to see what might be done to enhance the local park, outraged officials of United Churches would catch Mr. Schultz in the act. A GO Operation would then ruin Schultz completely.

There was also an instruction to do a complete survey of the county to determine who was hostile to Scientology. There were to be dossiers on medical societies, clinics, hospitals, police departments, public relations agencies, drug firms, federal, state and local government agencies, the city council, banks, investment houses, Congressional representatives and Florida's two senators.

As part of his new image, Hubbard directed a radio show for United Churches. Amazingly, no-one seemed to realize that United Churches was a front for Scientology. Hubbard bustled around wearing a tam-o-shanter and a khaki uniform. Reverend Wicker, of the Calvary Temple of God, later said, "They introduced him to me as Mr. Hubbard, but that didn't mean anything to me—they said he was an engineer. . . . When I saw his picture in the paper, I felt like an idiot."[5]

The plans to win favor with the mayor of Clearwater did not materialize. Before Mr. Shultz could be caught molesting little girls in the park, Mayor Gabriel Cazares started asking questions. He made a public statement: "I am discomfited by the increasing visibility of security personnel, armed with billy clubs and Mace, employed by the United Churches of Florida. . . . I am unable to understand why this degree of security is required by a religious organization."

Cazares was added to the Enemies list. He was followed onto it by a journalist at the *Clearwater Sun*, who ran a story saying that the check paying for the Fort Harrison Hotel had been drawn on a Luxembourg bank. A day later the Guardian's Office put into effect a plan to destroy the career of journalist Bette Orsini of the *St. Petersburg Times*. She was closing in on the truth about the United Churches of Florida.[6]

The Scientologists actually managed to pre-empt Orsini's story by a matter of hours. On January 28, 1976, a spokesman announced that the purchasers of the Fort Harrison Hotel and the Bank of Clearwater building were none other than the Church of Scientology of California. He reassured local people that although half of the mysterious new occupants of the buildings were Scientologists, United Churches would not be used to convert people to Scientology. On the same day, June Phillips (aka Byrne), joined the staff of the *Clearwater Sun*. Although the *Sun* paid her salary, she filed daily reports with the Guardian's Office.

The next day, the Scientology spokesman said that if United Churches was not successful in its mission to bring harmony to the religious community (!), then the Fort Harrison Hotel would become a center for advanced Scientology studies. Then he made a series of allegations about the mayor, saying his "attack" was motivated by personal profit.

Clearwater was the site for the new "Flag," the "Flag Land Base." Even before the buildings had been occupied, a new American Land Base had been promoted to Scientologists throughout the world. United Churches was just another shore story. Suddenly the town was swamped with youths in sailor suits, and a new kind of tourist with a fixed stare.

The Hubbards and their retinue had moved into a block of apartments called King Arthur's Court, in Dunedin, about five miles north of Clearwater.[7] Hubbard decided to buy some new outfits. He did not follow his usual procedure, ordering the clothes from England via his personal secretary at Saint Hill. Instead he saw a local tailor, who turned out to be a great fan of Hubbard's science fiction, and promptly boasted about his meeting with the famous author. The newspapers soon followed the tailor's lead.

Hubbard was very shy of publicity by this time, perhaps because of his increasingly poor health and appearance. The superman revered by Scientologists could not be seen to be a grossly overweight chain-smoker, with a large pointed lump on his forehead. Worse yet, Hubbard was afraid he would be subpoenaed to appear in one of the many court cases involving Scientology. Taking only three devoted Sea Org members with him, Hubbard fled Dunedin. His photo-portrait of the mayor of Clearwater never did hang in City Hall.[8]

Hubbard had continued to direct the Guardian's Office, including the attack on Mayor Gabe Cazares. He personally ordered that Cazares' school records be obtained, perhaps believing that everyone lies about their academic qualifications.

In February 1976, the Guardian's Office in Clearwater was a hive of activity. The *St. Petersburg Times* was threatened with a libel suit. Cazares was more than threatened: A million dollar suit was filed against him for libel, slander and violation of civil rights. As Hubbard had said in the 1950s, "The purpose of the suit is to harass and discourage rather than to win. . . . The law can be used very easily to harass."[9] Scientologists went to Alpine, Texas, and pored over records concerning the Cazares family at the county clerk's office, the police department, the office of the Border Patrol, and the local Roman Catholic church. They talked with doctors, long-term residents, even the midwife who had delivered Gabe Cazares. The Cazares' headstones in the graveyard were checked. The GO decided that the Gabriel Cazares who had been born in Alpine, Texas, could not possibly be their man. Obviously the accounts did not accord with their image of a Suppressive enemy of Scientology.

A GO official assured his seniors that a handling of the Clearwater Chamber of Commerce was also underway (a Scientology agent had already joined). A Scientologist had applied for a job at the *St. Petersburg Times*. A dossier had been prepared on the Clearwater City Attorney, and data collections had been made on three reporters perceived to be enemies.

A radio announcer who had been making broadcasts unfavorable to Scientology was fired after threat of legal action. He was rehired only after promising not to discuss Scientology on his program.

These actions were bound to provoke some response. The Guardian's Office probably did not realize that their "enemies" would fight fire with fire. The *St. Petersburg Times* filed suit, charging that Hubbard and the Scientologists had conspired to "harass, intimidate, frighten, prosecute, slander, defame" *Times* employees. They sought an injunction against further harassment.

Gabe Cazares filed an $8 million suit. He alleged that the Scientologists were attempting to intimidate him and prevent him from doing his job. February had been a very busy month. As we shall see in the next chapter, 1976 proved to be a very busy year.

In October, Hubbard suffered a tragic blow. Back in 1959 his son Nibs had left Scientology. From that time, Hubbard had pinned his dynastic dream upon Quentin, his oldest son by Mary Sue. He had frequently announced that Quentin would succeed him as the leader of

Scientology. At the end of October 1976, Quentin was found, co-matose, in a parked car in Las Vegas with the engine still running. Quentin was rushed to a hospital where he died two weeks later, without regaining consciousness. He was not identified until several days after his death. Although no precise cause of death was deter-mined, Quentin had certainly suffered from carbon monoxide poison-ing. He was twenty-two years old.[10]

Quentin had tried to measure up to his father's expectations—he was one of the few top-grade Class Twelve Auditors—but he did not share his father's temperament. By all accounts he was far too gentle to govern Scientology, or indeed to govern anything. All he wanted was to fly airplanes, and he often pleaded with his father to allow him to leave the Sea Org and do just that. He had disappeared several times in an attempt to escape. There was also an aspect of his nature which could never be reconciled with his father's philosophy: Quentin was a homosexual. There is little doubt that his death was self-inflicted, as he had attempted suicide before.[11]

Mary Sue broke down and wailed when she heard the news. She later tried to persuade friends that her son had died from encephalitis. Quentin's father's response was cold-blooded, he was furious that his son had let him down. There was an immediate cover-up. Documents were stolen from the coroner's office and taken to Hubbard. In accor-dance with Hubbard's policy regarding bad news, Scientologists were not told about Quentin's death. Some who found out were told he had been murdered.

In hiding in Washington, Hubbard busied himself trying to discover the secrets of the Soldiers of Light and the Soldiers of Darkness. He thoroughly agreed with the old gnostic belief that we are all born belonging firmly to one band or the other.

PART FIVE

THE GUARDIAN'S OFFICE
1974–1980

"We had to establish a militant and protective organization that could shield the church so that it could proceed peacefully with its principal aims and functions, without becoming embroiled in the constant skirmishing with those who wanted to annihilate us," a top ranking church official told me.—OMAR GARRISON, *Playing Dirty*

CHAPTER ONE

The Guardian Unguarded

There is no more ethical group on this planet than ourselves.—L. RON HUBBARD in "Keeping Scientology Working," 1965

The Office of the Guardian was created by Hubbard in a Policy Letter of March 1, 1966. He gave this as the Guardian's purpose:

TO HELP LRH ENFORCE AND ISSUE POLICY, TO SAFEGUARD SCIENTOL-OGY ORGS, SCIENTOLOGISTS AND SCIENTOLOGY AND TO ENGAGE IN LONG TERM PROMOTION.[1]

In the Policy Letter, Hubbard spoke of the Guardian's role in the collection of information, so "one can predict which way cats are going to jump." The eventual downfall of the Guardian came through her use of methods which showed precisely where certain cats planned to jump.

Hubbard kept the job in the family by appointing his wife, Mary Sue, as the first Guardian. After Hubbard took to the seas, Mary Sue joined him, and in January 1969, a new Guardian, Jane Kember, was appointed. However, Mary Sue retained control of the Guardian's Office with the creation of the Controller's Committee, which served as an interface between Hubbard and the GO. Mary Sue Hubbard was appointed as the Controller "for life" by her husband.[2]

The headquarters of the Guardian's Office were at Saint Hill in England. This was GO World Wide, or GOWW. In Hubbard's management system, the continents differ from those of the geographers': along with many of its occupants, Hubbard conceived the United Kingdom as a continent, quite distinct from Europe. America was divided in two, not at the isthmus of Panama, nor even along the Mason-Dixon line, but approximately at the Mississippi River. The Continental offices were: U.K., East U.S., West U.S., Europe, Australia and New Zealand, and Africa ("Latam" has been added since). The GO had Continental offices in each, run by a Deputy Guardian. These in turn had deputies in every Scientology Org, called Assistant Guardians. The Guardian's Office had six Bureaus: Legal, Public Relations, Information (initially called Intelligence), Social Coordination, Service (for GO staff training and auditing), and Finance. At GO World Wide there was a Deputy Guardian dealing with each of these functions.

The Guardian's Office was administratively autonomous, taking orders only from Hubbard or from the Controller, who in turn took orders only from her husband. Usually GO staff did not belong to the Sea Org, and signed five-year rather than billion-year contracts. Hubbard generated a powerful rivalry between the Sea Org and the Guardian's Office.

The Guardian's Office image within the Church was of an efficient, devoted group which dealt with threats to Scientology. They would counter bad press articles (often by suing for libel), defend against government enquiries, and promote Scientology through its good works. These good works were monitored by the Social Coordination Bureau (SOCO). They included "Narconon," a drug rehabilitation program; the Effective Education Association, Apple and Delphi Schools; and various anti-psychiatry campaigns.

Because Hubbard insisted there was a conspiracy against Scientology, the GO investigated and attacked the "conspirators" tirelessly. By the 1970s, the GO had lined itself up against its "enemies," principally the entire psychiatric profession and civil governments. They produced a newsletter called "Freedom," reminiscent of Fascist and Communist propaganda in its overblown language.

On a day-to-day basis the Finance Bureau of the GO oversaw the management of money within the Church. Each Org was supposed to have an Assistant Guardian for Finance who would scrupulously monitor all payments to and from the Org. Local Assistant Guardians would deal with bad press, and make sure no one who had received psychiatric treatment, or had a criminal record, found their way onto Scientology courses without first doing lengthy "eligibility programs." These usually consisted of reading several Hubbard books over a six-month period, and writing testimonials to show that they had applied Hubbard's teachings to their lives. Such people would also have to waive the right to refunds of any type from Scientology.

Most Church members knew little or nothing about Branch One of the GO Bureau of Information commonly referred to as "B-1." They gathered information about Hubbard's "enemies." The Information Bureau's Collections Department had two sections: Overt and Covert data collection. B-1 also housed an Operations section, which should more properly have been called the Dirty Tricks Department. B-1 was so self-contained that only the top executives in the other Guardian's Office Bureaus were privy to their activities. B-1 was Hubbard's private CIA, keeping tab on friend and foe alike. They also maintained comprehensive files on *all* Scientologists, compiled from the supposedly confidential records of confessional sessions. At times Hubbard maintained daily, and even hourly, contact with B-1, sending and receiving double-coded telex messages.[3]

The Guardian's Office was the most powerful group within the Church. Following Hubbard's rigid Policy, they could not believe in defense: "The DEFENSE of anything is UNTENABLE. The only way to defend anything is to ATTACK." The GO attacked ruthlessly and relentlessly.[4]

During 1968, while they were filing suits against all and sundry for libel, one of the major targets in England was the National Association of Mental Health (NAMH). Several trails crossed there. Lord Balniel, who first raised the question of Scientology in Parliament, and Kenneth Robinson, the Health Minister who invoked the Aliens Act, were both highly involved with the NAMH. Further, the NAMH was a public body which had an influence upon the practice of psychiatry. So through their campaign against the NAMH the GO thought they could kill several birds with one stone.

In November 1968, Hubbard issued a peculiar Executive Directive called "The War" where he triumphantly announced: "You may not realize it . . . but there is only one small group that has hammered Dianetics and Scientology for eighteen years. The press attacks, the public upsets you receive . . . were generated by this one group. . . . Last year we isolated a dozen men at the top. This year we found the organization these used and all its connections over the world. . . . Psychiatry and 'Mental Health' was chosen as a vehicle to undermine and destroy the West! And we stood in their way.''[5]

The Church of Scientology dropped thirty-eight complaints in Britain, and told the press this was ''in celebration of the fact that we now know who is behind the attacks on Scientology in Australia, New Zealand, South Africa, and Britain.'' It was an ''international group'' that had just moved its headquarters to Britain.[6]

In December, a group calling itself the Executive Committee of the Church of Scientology went to the National Association of Mental Health's offices in London, and demanded a meeting with the Board of Directors. Being told that the NAMH was governed by a Council of Management, none of whom was in the building, the Scientologists deposited a list of questions, and departed.

Many of the questions were loaded. For instance: ''Why do your directors want to ban an American writer from England?'' and ''Besides the human rights of English Scientologists, who else's human rights were you attempting to restrict or abolish?''

The ''American writer'' was presumably not unconnected with the Scientology Church; Hubbard had been labelled an undesirable alien and denied re-entry to Britain only a few months before. The Council must have been perplexed by the tenor of the questions. What on earth were the Scientologists suggesting? But then, the Council had not seen LRH Executive Directive 55, ''The War,'' and they probably did not know that they were perhaps the most important channel for the ''World Bank Conspiracy,'' as Hubbard had dubbed it.

In February 1969, shortly after Hubbard's announcement that Scientologists were to develop their image as ''the people who are cleaning up the field of mental healing,'' the NAMH was offered a settlement in a pending suit. A few days later, the Scientologists started a series of demonstrations outside the NAMH's offices. They marched with catchy slogans such as ''Psychiatrists Make Good Butchers'' on their banners.[7]

Then came Hubbard's bizarre secret directive ''Zones of Action,''[8] instructing the takeover of Smersh and psychiatry. After a pause of several months, the Guardian's Office took heed of Hubbard's order, and orchestrated the takeover of the National Association of Mental Health. The plan was simple, as NAMH membership was open to the public. The NAMH was governed by a Council, elected each year at the Annual General Meeting. Time was a little tight, but five weeks before the meeting, Scientologists started joining the Association in droves. The plan was a little *too* simple. The NAMH noticed the sudden explosion of applications, from ten or so a month to over two hundred. They also noticed that many of the Postal Orders paying the subscription bore the stamp either of the East Grinstead or London's Tottenham Court Road Post Office, the locations of the two principal English Scientology Orgs.

Five days before the election, the new Scientologist members nominated eight of their number for the Council of Management, among them a Deputy Guardian. Just two days before the vote, the NAMH demanded the resignation of 302 new members.

The Guardian's Office responded by seeking an injunction to prevent the Annual General Meeting. After elaborate proceedings, Justice Megarry eventually ruled against the Scientologists. C.H. Rolph, in his well researched book about the attempted takeover, *Believe What You Like*, described a later tactic. In November, 1970, the Scientologists offered a deed of covenant to the NAMH of £20,000 a year for seven years, if the NAMH would discontinue its support for shock therapy, resign its membership of the World Federation of Mental Health, and support a Scientology Bill of Rights for mental patients. The NAMH was to "make no public announcement of any sort" if it accepted the covenant. The offer was rejected. Soon afterwards the NAMH received a copy of an article detailing nineteen of its alleged shortcomings. To take up the story from Rolph: "among the latter being the sad story of a house for mentally confused old ladies in which the luckless residents were punished for misbehavior by being made to scrub floors. The grounds of this sinister place were patrolled . . . by men with shotguns; though it did not say specifically that their task was to shoot down any of the aged occupants caught running away."

Mary Sue Hubbard's deputy, Guardian Jane Kember, was a fanatical Scientologist. It is worth quoting one of her Scientology Success Stories. It was written in 1966, before the GO really gathered steam.

Before Scientology I couldn't have a baby, having miscarriage after miscarriage. I have recently had twin boys, after training and processing in Scientology. Before Scientology I had kidney trouble. I have no kidney trouble now. Before Scientology I had skin trouble, chronic indigestion, was very nervous, very unhappy, highly critical of all around me, felt inferior, inadequate and unable to cope with life. Now the skin troubles have gone and the chronic indigestion. I am no longer nervous, feel happy, have lost my inferiority complex and feel no need to criticize others.[9]

No wonder Kember later ran the Guardian's Office with steely and unswerving devotion.

In 1971, Alexis, Ron's twenty-one-year-old daughter by his second marriage, attempted to find him. Ron sent instructions to Jane Kember to deal with what he saw as a potential embarrassment. Alexis is undoubtedly Hubbard's daughter, but he had lost all paternal feeling for her, and had dropped contact with her after his divorce from her mother in 1951.

On Hubbard's instructions, two GO agents visited Alexis, and read a letter to her. Kember had followed her orders exactly. The letter had been typed on a "non-general-use" typewriter, which is to say the typewriter was used solely for this letter and then ditched.[10]

The letter that Hubbard sent to Kember for her to relay to Alexis came to light in the Armstrong case. Hubbard's description of events, as given in the letter, is manifestly different from the facts. He claimed that Sara had been his secretary in Georgia, at the end of 1948. In July 1949, she had arrived in New Jersey, where Hubbard was supposedly working on a filmscript, flat broke and pregnant. Hubbard referred to Sara's involvement with Jack Parsons, and claimed to be unsure who she had lived with in Pasadena. He further claimed that Sara had tried to take the Los Angeles Dianetic Foundation as part of a divorce settlement. Hubbard said that Sara could not obtain such a settlement, because legally they had not been married.[11]

The wording is crucial. Hubbard did not deny his marriage to Sara, simply its legality. He was technically correct, the marriage, being bigamous was illegal, but that was hardly the fault of either Alexis or Sara.

Under Jane Kember's direction, the Guardian's Office ran scores of operations, many illegal, many more simply immoral. She irrefutably received her orders from the Hubbards. Written orders survive.

In 1976, the GO was determined to silence all opposition in the City of Clearwater. Mayor Cazares was its chief target. A GO agent, posing as a reporter, interviewed the mayor when he was on a visit to Washington, DC. The "reporter" introduced Cazares to Sharon Thomas, another GO agent. She offered to show Cazares the sights of Washington. While they were driving, they ran into a pedestrian.

Sharon Thomas drove on. The mayor did not know that the "victim" of the accident was yet another GO agent, Michael Meisner.[12]

The GO was sure that it could use Cazares' failure to report the accident to its advantage. The next day an internal dispatch gloated that Cazares' political career was finished. That same day, Hubbard sent a dispatch asking whether the Miami Cubans could be persuaded that Cazares supported Castro.[13]

The GO initiated "Operation Italian Fog" which was to bribe officials to put forged documents into Mexican records showing that Cazares had been married twenty-five years before. The Scientologists could then accuse him of bigamy.

To gain information for an inside story, an editor at the *Clearwater Sun* enrolled on the Communication Course in the Tampa Org. The staff at the *Sun* did not know that their every move was being leaked to the GO by agent June Phillips. The Scientologists saw the editor's move as "infiltration" and Phillips reported that the editor was traumatized when a suit was filed against him and the *Sun* for a quarter of a million dollars. The Scientologists charged that he had caused their members "extreme mental anguish, suffering and humiliation."

"Op Yellow," launched in April 1976, was to consist of sending an anonymous letter to Clearwater businesses congratulating the mayor for his Christian hostility to Scientology, and for keeping the Miami Jews out and the Clearwater negroes where they belonged.

After the publication of her book *The Scandal of Scientology*, in 1971, Paulette Cooper became a major target for harassment. Distribution of her book was severely restricted through a series of court actions in different states, and even different countries. Cooper simply did not have the legal or financial resources to defend against all of these actions. As a result of a GO Op she was indicted for making a bomb threat against the Church of Scientology. The GO wanted to finish her off for good. Operation Freakout was intended to put Cooper either into prison or into a mental hospital.

A U.S. Court Sentencing Memorandum gave this description of Operation Freakout:

> In its initial form Operation Freakout had three different plans. The first required a woman to imitate Paulette Cooper's voice and make telephone threats to Arab Consulates in New York. The second scheme involved mailing a threatening letter to an Arab Consulate in such a fashion that it would appear to have been done by Paulette Cooper. Finally, a Scientology field staff member was to impersonate Paulette

Cooper at a laundry and threaten the President and the then Secretary of State, Henry Kissinger. A second Scientologist would thereafter advise the FBI of the threat.

Two additional plans to Operation Freakout were added on April 13, 1976. The fourth plan called for Scientology field staff members who had ingratiated themselves with Cooper to gather information from Cooper, so that Scientology could assess the success of the first three plans. The fifth plan was for a Scientologist to warn an Arab Consulate by telephone that Paulette Cooper had been talking about bombing them.

The sixth and final part of Operation Freakout called for Scientologists to obtain Paulette Cooper's fingerprints on a blank piece of paper, type a threatening letter to Kissinger on that paper, and mail it.[14]

GO operations were burgeoning. Operation Devil's Wop was an attack on an Arizona senator who had supported anti-cult groups. The Clearwater Chamber of Commerce had been infiltrated. Agents had been inside the American Psychiatric Association for several years. The GO had penetrated anti-cult groups and newspapers, and was beginning to move into U.S. government agencies, including the Coast Guard.

However, the vehement application of Fair Game, and the use of the law to harass were making trouble for Hubbard. Those on the receiving end wanted Hubbard himself to testify in court, which had to be avoided at all costs. Elaborate precautions were taken to prevent process servers from reaching Hubbard. His location was kept secret, and his retinue was ready to whisk him away at a moments notice. In May 1976, Hubbard fled, shrouded in secrecy, from Washington, DC, to Culver City, a suburb of Los Angeles. With him were only his wife and a few dedicated Sea Org staff. His new location was codenamed Astra, and it maintained contact with, and control of, Scientology through telex links to Church management in Clearwater, and to the Guardian's Office in Los Angeles.

In June 1976, the GO received the first blow against its elaborate and highly successful Intelligence machine. A GO agent who had infiltrated the IRS was arrested. For a month the GO carried on with their Ops, confidently believing that the agent's connections would never be traced.

Mayor Cazares was running as a congressional candidate. As a part of "Op Keller" his opponent was offered supposedly damaging information about Cazares. When the opponent declined the offer, a letter signed "Sharon T" was mailed to politicians and newspapers in Florida. It sought to implicate Cazares in the fake hit-and-run "accident" staged in Washington. To cover the exits, an anonymous letter was sent to Cazares' opponent, Bill Young, saying the "Sharon T" letter was Cazares' work, and that he would claim it had been a dirty trick on Young's part! Young turned the letter over to the FBI.

In July, the GO instituted "Operation Bulldozer Leak" which was supposed to convince the press and governments that Hubbard was no longer involved in the management of the Church.

Hubbard moved to a hacienda in La Quinta, near Palm Springs in California. The hacienda was codenamed Rifle. About him he assembled the Controller's staff (Mary Sue's assistants), a few chosen teenage Commodore's Messengers, and his Household Unit. For a while, they took a vacation from Scientology, fulfilling the pretense of Hubbard's lack of control. There were no Scientology books at the hacienda, and the speaking of Scientologese was briefly forbidden. While the Commodore fiddled, the Guardian's Office was beginning to burn.

Hubbard had been in such a rush to leave Florida that he had left part of his gun collection behind. Shortly after "Op Bulldozer Leak" the Assistant Guardian for Flag [Clearwater] reported that the Bureau of Alcohol, Tobacco and Firearms had discovered some of Hubbard's guns, which had been mislaid in the flight from Dunedin.

One of the guns was a Mauser machine-pistol, which should have been registered. Somehow the GO managed to avert prosecution. But on the day the report on Hubbard's guns was made, the FBI issued a warrant for the arrest of one Michael Meisner. The FBI was beginning to make the necessary connections.

CHAPTER TWO

Infiltration

Michael Meisner took his first Scientology course in 1970. He was so impressed that he left college before taking his finals, and became a full-time staff Scientologist. In May 1973, he was recruited by the Guardian's Office, and assigned to the Intelligence Bureau, shortly to be renamed the Information Bureau.

From July to October 1973, Meisner was in Los Angeles learning the complicated internal procedures followed in all Scientology organizations, and other procedures peculiar to the Guardian's Office. He was indoctrinated in Information Bureau techniques. He was taught how to conduct covert investigations, how to recruit undercover agents and place them in ''enemy'' organizations, as well as techniques of surveillance.

This was nothing new. The GO had been placing ''plants'' in organizations perceived to be hostile for some years. From 1969 the GO had infiltrated the Better Business Bureau and various mental health organizations including, in 1972, the American Medical Association. The pattern was well established.

In November, Meisner became Director of Branch 2 (B-2) in Washington, DC. Branch 2 dealt with internal security. It monitored Scientology itself, looking for infiltrators, and weeding out anyone who was a ''potential trouble source.'' Independent, or ''Squirrel'' Scientology groups were also the province of B-2, which would do anything in its power to destroy such groups. At about the time Meisner was posted, Guardian Jane Kember wrote to tell Henning Heldt, her deputy in the

United States, that the GO had illegally obtained documents relating to Interpol. She now ordered Heldt to acquire Ron Hubbard's file from the Interpol Bureau in Washington.

Meisner rose quickly through the ranks. In January 1974, he was promoted by Kember to Assistant Guardian for Information in Washington, DC. From this position he oversaw both Branch 1 and Branch 2.

In her letter to Heldt, the Guardian had said the GO Legal Bureau had made Freedom of Information Act requests for certain documents, but because the legal approach took too long, B-1 should obtain them anyway. Meisner was given the job. Some Scientologists claim he was a government agent provocateur, who instigated the use of illegal tactics. As we've seen, infiltration and the theft of files was well underway before Meisner began his incredibly successful career. Meisner's orders came from the Guardian, and the theft of government files was an extension of the program written by Hubbard himself in New York in 1973. He had called it Operation Snow White. In 1974, Kenneth Urquhart, who was ''L. Ron Hubbard Personal Communicator'' at the time, overheard a conversation between Ron and Mary Sue about an agent working in the IRS in Washington.[1]

Meisner initiated a ''project'' to obtain all Interpol files relating to Hubbard and Scientology which called for the Interpol National Bureau to be infiltrated by a Guardian's Office agent. The project was approved by Meisner's direct senior, Duke Snider, and Meisner assigned it to his B-1 Director, Mitchell Hermann. No immediate action was taken.

In the late summer of 1974, Cindy Raymond, who was the GO Collections Officer U.S., ordered Meisner to recruit a Scientologist to infiltrate the Internal Revenue Service. Prospective candidates were interviewed, but no one with the right psychological makeup was found. In September, Raymond sent her own choice, Gerald Wolfe, to Washington.

It took Wolfe, codenamed Silver, a while to find a job as there was an employment freeze at the IRS. He started work as a clerk-typist on November 18, 1974.

Shortly before Silver started his job, GO agent Don Alverzo flew to Washington from Los Angeles. On the afternoon of October 30, following a briefing by Alverzo, Meisner and Hermann walked into the main IRS building looking for the Chief Counsel's Office. The Scientologists had heard from their lawyers that there would be a meeting to discuss Scientology litigation there on November 1.

On the appointed day, Alverzo and Hermann went into the Chief Counsel's Office before the meeting, and installed an electronic bug. They taped the proceedings via a car FM receiver. Then Hermann went back into the office (on the fourth floor), and retrieved the bug.

At first, Silver did not do well on his IRS mission. In fact, he did not do anything. After a month, Meisner decided to coax him by showing just how easy it was. Meisner and Hermann went into the IRS building on a week day at four in the afternoon. They waited for the building to empty out, and then at about seven went into the offices of the Exempt Organization Division of the IRS, and stole a file on Scientology. The file was photocopied and Hermann returned it the next day.

At the end of December, three weeks after Meisner's little mission, the Silver lode opened up. He was asked to steal and photocopy files from the office of IRS official Barbara Bird. Meisner reviewed the copies, and sent an edited version to his superiors.

In January 1975, Meisner was also supervising an agent in the U.S. Coast Guard, Sharon Thomas, and another in the Drug Enforcement Administration, Nancy Douglas. Thomas was placed in the Coast Guard in compliance with Kember's Guardian's Order 1344. Later, Thomas and Meisner also performed the fake hit-and-run accident for Mayor Cazares.

In May 1975, Meisner received a copy of Project Horn from its author, Gregory Willardson. Willardson was B-1 Director U.S. "Project Horn" was meant to create a cover story whereby stolen documents could be publicly released, without revealing the identity of the thieves. Meisner's team was to steal documents which did not relate to Scientology. They were also to steal IRS stationery, so that a fictitious disgruntled ex-employee of the IRS could release these documents to the organizations and individuals they concerned.

The Church of Scientology would also ostensibly receive letters from this "former IRS employee," along with a wealth of documents, which would help in their fight against the immoral steps the IRS had taken against them.

Having banished his initial hesitance completely, Silver stole, copied and replaced a *ten-foot stack* of documents from the IRS by May 1975. About 30,000 pages.

Jane Kember's Guardian's Order 1361 ordered the theft of documents from the Tax Division of the United States Justice Department. Meisner set to work in April 1975.

The Guardian's Office Legal Bureau told Meisner that attorneys Harold Larsen and Stanley Krysa had represented the government in litigation against Scientology in both Hawaii and Florida. Meisner ordered Silver to go into their offices, in the Tax Division of the Department of Justice, and steal all files relating to Scientology.

On three successive Saturdays in May 1975, Silver went into the Star Building, to the offices of the Tax Division. He used his IRS identification card. He stole and copied twelve files relating to litigation against the Church. He passed the copies to Meisner at their usual rendezvous, Lums restaurant in Arlington, Virginia. As usual, Meisner wrote a synopsis of the material, and sent this to his seniors. The Controller, Mary Sue Hubbard, was among those informed of the thefts from the IRS. A letter in her hand approving the strategy was later used in evidence against her.

On June 11, 1975, Meisner wrote "Project Beetle Clean-up," the purpose of which was to obtain copies of all the Washington IRS files on the Hubbards and Scientology. This included files held in both the Intelligence Division and the Internal Revenue Service's Office of International Operations. The project was approved by Meisner's senior, Willardson.

Silver set to work immediately. The IRS was about to begin a major audit of the Church of Scientology of California—the then "mother church." During this audit, between two and three million pages of material would be reviewed. Heading the audit was Lewis Hubbard of the IRS Chief Counsel's Office. So Silver broke into Hubbard's office and made copies of everything he could find, even his daily jottings. Now the Guardian's Office knew the IRS strategy, and which of the Church's many weaknesses it would have to defend.

In July, Cindy Raymond told Meisner that the Church had brought a Freedom of Information Act suit against the Internal Revenue Service, charging that the IRS had failed to give proper access to files on Scientology. Meisner was ordered to obtain documents from the office of Charles Zuravin, the IRS attorney who would be defending the Freedom of Information case.

The Church created a pattern, bringing suits against agencies, then penetrating their attorneys' offices to see how the agencies proposed to defend themselves. In the Freedom of Information Act (FOIA) suits, these attorneys had access to the very files which the Scientologists were suing to obtain. Eventually, the Scientologists stole far more material than they were ostensibly trying to gain through legal action.

Silver added Zuravin's office to those he was monitoring. Zuravin was amassing documents relating to Scientology from IRS offices throughout the United States, so he could prepare an FOIA index. These documents represented the dealings of the IRS with the Church over twenty years. Zuravin's task was awesome. He had to prepare a Vaughn Index (listing every document potentially subject to an FOIA request). Zuravin also had to explain IRS reasons for non-disclosure for each document the IRS had refused to release.

The IRS was doing the GO's work for it. All Silver had to do was copy the documents as they came in, and the GO would have every scrap of information from the IRS files, indexed at IRS expense, with the added bonus of the list of IRS reasons for non-disclosure.

In September 1975, Guardian Jane Kember issued "commendations" (yet another military term used in Scientology) to those who had worked on Guardian's Order 1361; those who had committed the criminal acts of burglary and theft for the good of the cause.

In October, attorney Zuravin completed his index. Every document was numbered, giving the GO an excellent reference work. The index was handed over to Scientology attorneys. Within days it had been edited, so Silver would only steal the "exempted" documents, not wasting his time on those already obtained through FOIA requests.

Silver went to Zuravin's office, and in a single weekend stole some 3,000 pages of documents. Even this haul did not net all of the denied documents. At the end of November 1975, before Silver had completed his work, Zuravin's office, and that of Lewis Hubbard, were placed within a "red seal," or high security area, inside the main IRS building. From this point the doors were locked at all times. Zuravin's papers were moved into a locked file room.

At the beginning of December, Meisner flew to Los Angeles for a conference with his superiors. He was shown the newly issued "Guardian's Program Order 158—Early Warning System," which the Guardian had approved. This program had come into being as a direct result of a Hubbard order. Its purpose was to keep Hubbard out of the hands of the courts. The GO were to anticipate any law suit against or subpoena on the Hubbards.

The Order directed that an agent be placed in the U.S. Attorney's Office in Washington, DC. Any Federal agency which was in litigation with the Church, or was planning litigation, would report to the U.S. Attorney's Office. An agent was also to be placed in the U.S. Attorney's Office in Los Angeles. Another agent was to be infiltrated into the IRS Office of International Operations (OIO), because they were preparing a tax case against Hubbard. This last agent was to steal any files on either of the Hubbards, and to report any developments. Close liaison was to be maintained with the agents already in place in the Coast Guard, the Drug Enforcement Administration in Washington, DC, and the IRS in Los Angeles and Washington, DC.

Back in Washington, Meisner started his compliance with the Order. The internal procedures of the GO required that all major actions be "okayed" in writing by a senior. These Orders, and Meisner's responses to them, were reported step by step through the hierarchy to Mary Sue Hubbard, the Controller. Mary Sue Hubbard was living with her husband at this time, and no doubt kept him informed of Meisner's spectacular offensive against the United States government.

Meisner and Silver performed a series of burglaries on the Justice Department. They stole documents from the offices of Paul Figley and Jeffrey Axelrad in the Civil Division's Information and Privacy Unit. Figley had been assigned to the defense of the Freedom of Information Act suits brought against government agencies by the Church of Scientology.

Meisner and Silver went into the Justice Department library using Silver's IRS identification card. They waited until after office hours, and went into Figley's office. As ever, they used the nearest photocopier. On two occasions they stayed in the building until 10:00 p.m., copying files on Scientology, and every Interpol document they could find. Further burglaries of Figley's office were committed by Silver, with GO agents Joseph Alesi and Richard Kimmel.

On Saturday, January 17, 1976, Don Alverzo again flew to Washington. The next evening, accompanied by Silver and Meisner, he entered the main IRS building, using Silver's IRS identification. They went up to the third floor where Lewis Hubbard's office and Zuravin's file office were. Silver stood guard while Alverzo tried to pick the lock on Hubbard's door. Meisner worked on Zuravin's door. Their GO training, the "Breaking and Entering Hat," did not serve them well. After about an hour and a half, the exasperated Meisner forced Zuravin's door. The three went into the office, stole the remaining "exempt" documents from Zuravin's index, and took them to a photocopier on another floor. After a while, Meisner and Alverzo left Silver to the copying and returned to Hubbard's office. Eventually, Alverzo managed to force the latch with a strip of cardboard. They took all the files which had not previously been copied. The party left at two in the morning with a one foot stack of documents. Alverzo returned to Los Angeles the next day.

At the beginning of February, Meisner again flew to Los Angeles for a conference. There were representatives from the Guardian's Office Legal and Finance Bureaus at the meeting, as well as Church accountant Martin Greenberg. The meeting discussed IRS strategy with regard to the Scientology audit, as revealed in the stolen documents. Meisner was instructed to look out for any documents dealing with the Religious Research Foundation, a front through which Scientology monies were paid to Hubbard. Mary Sue's Office was informed.

In Washington, Meisner relayed his instructions to Silver. The offices of the Exempt Organizations Division were to be monitored for files. The GO wanted advance warning in case there was an adverse ruling on Scientology's current attempt to regain tax-exempt status. They wanted to know before it was finalized, so they could prepare their next line of defense.

Meisner had ordered Sharon Thomas to leave the U.S. Coast Guard, and find a job at the Department of Justice. After initial difficulties, she finally managed to do this, and started work there on February 29, 1976.

Silver had to be slightly more inventive than usual to get into Joseph Tedesco's suite of offices. During the day, Silver removed the knob from a door which led into the suite, and disabled the lock. The door was not normally in use, so the ploy went unnoticed. That night Silver returned and carried out his usual procedure.

Silver also stole files relating to the American Medical Association's tax-exemption, as ammunition for Scientology's long standing battle against the AMA.

At the beginning of March, Meisner decided to refine the GO operation. He and Silver went into the main IRS building, again using Silver's legitimate card, in his real name, Gerald Wolfe. They went to the IRS Identification Room on the first floor, and forced the door. While Meisner read the instruction booklet for the photo equipment, Silver typed two fictitious names for himself, and two for Meisner, onto cards. They then used the photo equipment to put their faces to the names. Meisner selected numbers from the log of previously issued cards. During the next few months, false identification cards were made for four other GO agents.

In March 1976, Mary Sue Hubbard approved a Program written by Cindy Raymond, for the collection of what were termed "non-FOI data"—i.e. documents not available through the Freedom of Information Act. Raymond, who was the GO Collections Officer U.S., planned to infiltrate no less than 136 government agencies! She also ordered Meisner to obtain material relating to proposed amendments of the Freedom of Information Act.

In April, Meisner and Silver returned to the Justice Department. Meisner used an identification card made out to "John M. Foster," while Silver used his own genuine IRS card, which later proved to be a crucial mistake. They burgled the office of Deputy Attorney General of the United States, Harold Tyler, and copied memoranda which the Justice Department was about to send to Congress outlining its position on proposed amendments to the FOIA. The office door was forced to gain entry.

A few days later, Cindy Raymond wrote to Meisner explaining that the Justice Department had just conducted an investigation of the Drug Enforcement Administration (DEA). The distribution of the "DeFeo Report" was designated "severely limited." The Church had just lost an FOIA case against the DEA. Raymond told Meisner to steal the DeFeo Report. Meisner knew where to go, having noticed the Report during his last raid.

Meisner put "Operation Chaos Leak" into action. The DeFeo Report was highly critical of the DEA, so leaking it would create adverse press. The GO believed a scandal might help to color the judge's view in their appeal against the DEA decision. Half of the DeFeo Report was given to the *Village Voice* in New York by Meisner, who pretended to be a disaffected Justice Department employee.

Meisner had been ordered to obtain all files relating to Ron and Mary Sue Hubbard from the Office of International Operations of the IRS (OIO). Silver and Meisner, the latter using his "Foster" identification, entered the OIO building, and went to the tenth floor to burgle the office of Thomas Crate. The door was locked. One of the cleaning ladies told a security guard there were two suspicious characters on the tenth floor. Silver and Meisner fobbed the guard off with their IRS identification cards. The cleaning lady then opened Crate's office for them. By this time, Meisner had nerves of steel.

They found more documents in a locked cabinet belonging to Crate's superior, Howard Rosen. They could not find a photocopying machine in the OIO building, so took the files to the main IRS building, and copied them there.

During the next few months, Sharon Thomas stole files from the Information and Privacy Unit of the Department of Justice relating to pending Scientology initiated FOIA suits. Files relating to the Church's FOIA suit against the Energy Research and Development Administration were also stolen. The Interpol Liaison Office was raided, and the safe broken into. The material stolen included Interpol files on *terrorism*. Meisner had been instructed to take all and any Interpol files, so that material obtained could be used to show Interpol's "criminality." Several thousand pages of Interpol documents were taken.

In a chambers hearing of a Scientology FOIA case, Judge Hart asked Justice Department attorney Nathan Dodell whether he had considered taking L. Ron Hubbard's deposition. The Scientologists' attorney, Walter Birkell, reported back. In the panic, Meisner was ordered to check Dodell's office to see what he was planning. He was also ordered to find information which could be used to remove Judge Hart from the case. Safeguarding Hubbard, even from an appearance, was the GO's top priority.

Early in May, Silver and Meisner reconnoitered the United States Courthouse building. They went first to the Bar Association library, on the same floor as Dodell's office. They found the nearest photocopy machines, and then went to Dodell's office. The door was locked, and the tool they usually used failed to lift the latch. For once, they left a mission incomplete.

A few days later, Silver phoned Meisner from Dodell's office. No doubt in hushed tones, he excitedly told his superior that a secretary had left her keys on the desk. Silver and Meisner found a locksmith, who made copies of the keys for them. Once again GO operatives had waltzed through the security system of a U.S. government agency.

On the evening of May 21, Silver and Meisner presented themselves at the U.S. Courthouse, showing the security guard their fake IRS credentials. They were given permission to do legal research in the Bar Association Library. They went up to the third floor and signed the log. Putting a few books out on a table at the back of the library, they left through the back door, which led into the hallway outside Dodell's office. Using the duplicate keys they entered the office. With a flashlight they peered at the files on Scientology. After copying about 1,000 pages, they returned the originals, and went back to the library, leaving at about 11:00 p.m. The documents were the Interpol files which had been withheld from Scientology by the National Bureau of Interpol.

A week later, Silver and Meisner again went to do ''research'' in the Bar Association Library. They had signed in as ''John Foster,'' and ''W. Haake'' (perhaps an elaborate joke since Sir John Foster and F.W. Haack were both critics of Scientology), and copied about 2,000 pages of documents relating to Scientology, most from Washington, DC, police files, and Food and Drug Administration files. All were taken from Dodell's office.

They were replacing the originals, when librarian Charles Johnson stopped them. He asked if they had signed in, and told them not to come back without the permission of a chief librarian. Having braved this challenge, they had to sneak back to Dodell's office and replace the stolen originals.

Operation Meisner

Why should a man certain of immortality think of his life at all?—
JOSEPH CONRAD, *Under Western Eyes*

Early in June 1976, the GO issued "Project: Target Dodell." Dodell
was too successful in the defense against the Scientology FOIA legal
suits. Meisner was ordered to steal files from Dodell's office which
could be used to formulate an operation to remove him as an Assistant
U.S. Attorney. By this time Meisner had requested and received
written permission to use the Bar Association Library.

At seven o'clock on the evening of June 11, Meisner and Wolfe
(Silver) signed in. This time Wolfe was using a card in the name of
"Thomas Blake." Meisner showed librarian Johnson the written per-
mission he had obtained. They followed their usual route through the
back of the library, but found that cleaners were still at work in
Dodell's office.

While Meisner and Wolfe were waiting at the back of the library,
two FBI agents approached them. Librarian Charles Johnson had
reported their earlier visit to the U.S. Attorney's Office. Little was
made of it at the time, but Johnson was instructed to call the FBI if the
two suspicious IRS men returned. Meisner presented his false IRS
credentials, and said he had since resigned from the IRS. One of the

agents stayed with Meisner and Wolfe, while the other went to find an Assistant U.S. Attorney.

Meisner said they were doing legal research, and had been using the photocopier to copy legal texts. He gave an address, a few doors from his own, to FBI agent Christine Hansen. After about fifteen minutes of questioning, Meisner asked if they were under arrest. When he was told they were not, he said they were leaving. The other agent, Dan Hodges, saw them on his way back to the Library. Meisner called to him to say Hansen had given them permission to leave. Once again Meisner had faked out the enemy.

They walked for several blocks to make sure they were not being followed, and then took a taxi to Martin's Tavern restaurant. Meisner phoned his superior, Mitchell Hermann, in Los Angeles, and in a roundabout way told him they had been stopped. Hermann told him to call him back at a public telephone. In the subsequent conversation, Hermann told Meisner to wait at the restaurant, and phone back an hour later, so Hermann could contact the Deputy Guardian for Information U.S., Richard Weigand.

Meisner's incredible luck had finally turned. The GO operation in Washington was finished. A "Church" had penetrated U.S. government agencies willy-nilly. They had come and gone undetected for eighteen months, copying tens of thousands of pages of government files, including very sensitive and restricted material. It is little wonder that when the FBI raid against the Church of Scientology finally came, a year later, it was a show of strength. Few people would understand the reason for such a show. It was intended for those in the Guardian's Office, who would understand only too well.

The GO ordered Wolfe to turn himself in, as part of the operation to conceal their involvement. He was arrested at his desk at the IRS before he had a chance to surrender. The FBI had simply checked every record where "John M. Foster" had signed into official buildings. Then they had checked the identifications given by the man with him. "W. Haake" and "Thomas Blake" had not turned up anything, but sometimes Wolfe had used his real IRS credentials. He was arrested for using false credentials the other times. The FBI proved that the monolithic U.S. government agencies were not quite as stupid as the GO had come to believe.

Wolfe told the FBI he had been doing legal research under his own steam, and said he had never known the other man as anything other than "Foster." The story was manufactured in the GO, and Wolfe was drilled on it. He maintained it through a grand jury hearing, adding perjury and conspiracy to obstruct justice to his other crimes.

Two months later, at the end of August 1976, an FBI agent arrived at the Church of Scientology in Washington with a warrant for the arrest of Michael Meisner. In the Courthouse library, he had given an address a few doors from his own. The FBI had traced him by talking to his neighbors.

Instead of turning Meisner in, the GO added harboring a fugitive to its growing list of crimes. The GO was in a state of panic, and suggestions of how best to handle the situation multiplied. The first plan was to fly Meisner to Europe to wait it out. His appearance was immediately changed. He was to look like a middle-aged man trying to be fashionable. He was to shave his head, wear contact lenses, have a tooth capped, lose or gain weight, and wear "earth shoes" to change his posture. He went through a rapid succession of identities, becoming first "Jeff Burns," then "Jeff Marks," and then "Jeff Murphy." Controller Mary Sue Hubbard wrote to one of her juniors that it would be safest for Meisner to disappear in a big city.

Mary Sue Hubbard also acknowledged receipt of a copy of Meisner's arrest warrant, and continued to discuss various concocted alibis for Meisner with Guardian Jane Kember and other GO officials. The FBI discovered these exchanges in their 1977 raid.

Lieutenant Warren Young, a Scientologist in the San Diego police, checked the National Crime Information Center computer records to see how the hunt for Meisner was progressing. The FBI questioned Young, who claimed he had arrested Meisner for a pedestrian violation.

The GO in Washington supplied false samples of Meisner's handwriting to the FBI. These were to be compared to the signatures in the logs of various government buildings. Mary Sue Hubbard requested a list of buildings illegally entered by Meisner. It was impressive, eleven were listed in the the reply: the Department of Justice, the Internal Revenue Service, the Office of International Operations, the Post Office, the Labor Department's National Office, the Federal Trade Commission, the Department of the Treasury, U.S. Customs, the Drug Enforcement Administration, the offices of the American Medical Association's attorneys, and the offices of the St. Petersburg Times' attorneys in Washington.

One of Meisner's seniors even toyed with the idea of creating a cover for Meisner whereby he would claim to have been researching the poor security of government buildings.

By the end of October, Meisner, in hiding in Los Angeles, was expressing concern at the vacillations of his superiors. He was assured that Mary Sue Hubbard was working on his case personally. Indeed she was, and a few days later she suggested that Meisner turn himself in, saying the whole affair had arisen out of his jealousy of his wife's consistently superior performance in the Guardian's Office. To outdo her, he had organized the burglaries of government offices, unbeknown to any of his GO colleagues.

Then it was suggested that Meisner turn himself in, plead guilty, and take the Fifth Amendment (refuse to answer questions because they might incriminate him) if asked about his superiors. Meisner was willing to be the scapegoat, and willing to go to prison, such was his devotion to the cause: but the sooner the "shore story" was settled the better. Otherwise the FBI might hit paydirt. He was fearful of the consequences for Scientology, and aware that his own fate could only be worsened by delay.

While in hiding, Meisner continued to work for the Guardian's Office, and to receive Scientology auditing. His pleas for a swift resolution were repeatedly rejected, and he threatened to leave, for either Washington or Canada, if decisive action was not taken. This was the situation in April 1977, ten months after the Courthouse library incident. He had been a fugitive for eight months. The GO responded to Meisner's threat by transforming his "case officer," Brian Andrus, into his jailer.

Andrus and three heavies, accompanied by two high officials of the Guardian's Office, visited Meisner. He was told that from now on he would have to follow orders. His apartment was searched, and anything which might conceivably connect Meisner to Scientology removed. As usual, Mary Sue Hubbard was informed.

A month later, Andrus visited Meisner and told him he was going to be moved to another apartment. He refused to leave, and the "two guards handcuffed him behind his back, gagged him and dragged him out of the building. Outside, they forced him onto the floor in the back of a waiting car. In the car, one of the guards held Meisner down with his feet." This account comes from the Stipulation of Evidence signed by Mary Sue Hubbard and eight senior GO officials, as do all of the principal details of this chapter. There is no conjecture. There are reams of uncontested documents.

Meisner gradually persuaded his captors that he was willing to cooperate, and by the end of May he was down to a single guard. One day, Meisner broke away and leapt into a taxi. He went to a bus station, and from there to Las Vegas. Despite everything, Meisner was still devoted to Scientology. He felt his captors had failed to take the proper course for the good of Scientology, and wanted time to think the situation through.

The next day, Meisner phoned the GO and told them he was in Las Vegas. They had already worked out a new angle or "shore story" in case Meisner had gone over to the "enemy." Cindy Raymond suggested that the FBI be told that Meisner was trying to blackmail the Church, by threatening to pretend that it had harbored him after the warrant for his arrest was issued.

Meisner agreed to meet one of his former guards, Jim Douglas, in Las Vegas. At the meeting, Meisner refused to return to Los Angeles. It was too late, the GO had found out where he was staying, and another official met him there, and persuaded him that everything had changed with the removal of a senior GO executive.

The Scientologists constantly excuse reprehensible acts by blaming them on a Suppressive who has subsequently been removed. Hubbard had first used this scapegoat approach as early as 1952 with his outlandish attack on Don Purcell. This is what comes from believing in the evil influence of Suppressives, and their magical power for disruption. Most Scientologists accept the excuse every time it is trotted out. Meisner did, and he returned to Los Angeles.

In fact, Andrus had ordered that a new apartment be found for Meisner. Meisner was to be put in a room either with a window too small for him to escape through, or no window at all. He was to have no further contact with the outside world. Meisner was installed in the apartment immediately upon his return to Los Angeles.

In June 1977, in Washington, DC, Gerald "Silver" Wolfe was sentenced to probation and community sevice, having pleaded guilty to the forgery of credentials. On the day he was sentenced, Wolfe was subpoenaed to appear the same afternoon before a grand jury, which had been investigating the entries into the U.S. Courthouse. The FBI was hot on the trail.

Wolfe paraded his carefully drilled story, claiming he had gone to the courthouse library to educate himself in legal research, so he would be able to get a better job. He said his accomplice was only known to him as "John Foster." After his appearance, Wolfe was meticulously debriefed by the GO.

Meisner managed to ingratiate himself with his captors again. From June 17, 1977, he was no longer guarded at night. Three days later, he collected a few clothes and left the apartment. He watched his back carefully to make sure he was not being followed, and changed buses twice en route to a bowling alley. From there he made a collect call to an Assistant U.S. Attorney in Washington, pretending to be Gerald Wolfe, just in case the GO had an operative in the Attorney's office. Two hours later, Meisner surrendered himself to the FBI.

While the GO was concocting a story about Meisner having tried to blackmail them after setting up the Washington operations on his own initiative, the FBI, with Meisner to help them, was moving at full speed. Meisner contacted the GO to say he was thinking things over. They were put off guard. In fact, Meisner had at last thought things over, and concluded that there was something very wrong with an organization which resorted to the criminal tactics of the Church of Scientology. He had broken out of the Kafkaesque nightmare, and made his confession, this time not to a Scientology Auditor, but to the FBI. On July 7, 1977, the FBI carried out one of the largest raids in its history: on the Guardian's Office of the Church of Scientology, simultaneously in both Los Angeles and Washington, DC.

As a result eleven GO officials, including Guardian Jane Kember and Controller Mary Sue Hubbard, were eventually imprisoned.

PART SIX

THE COMMODORE'S
MESSENGERS
1977–1982

When you move off a point of power, pay all your obligations on the nail, empower all your friends completely and move off with your pockets full of artillery, potential blackmail on every erstwhile rival, unlimited funds in your private account and the addresses of experienced assassins and go live in Bulgravia [sic] and bribe the police.— L. RON HUBBARD, HCO Policy Letter, "The Responsibilities of Leaders," February 12, 1967

CHAPTER ONE

Making Movies

In the late 1960s aboard the *Apollo*, Hubbard used the children of Scientologists to run messages. He set them up with their own "Org," and their own child Ethics Officers, one of whom was only eight years old. Eventually they came to be known as the Commodore's Messenger Org, or CMO. They grew up around Hubbard, usually separated from their parents.

Several former members of the CMO have given full and shocking accounts of their time with Hubbard. In addition to carrying messages, Messengers looked after all the Commodore's personal needs. Teenage girls wearing white hot pants would put out his clothes for him, prepare his shower, dress him, change the music on his tape recorder, light his cigarettes, even catch the ash as it fell. The CMO Household Unit would rinse Hubbard's washing seven and later as many as seventeen times to rid it of the vaguest hint of the smell of soap. There was a Messenger on "watch" twenty-four hours a day to attend to his slightest whim.

The story of Messenger Tonja Burden is compelling. Her parents were enthusiastic Scientologists, and encouraged their daughter to join the Sea Org in March 1973, when she was only thirteen. A few months later, she was separated from them and sent to the *Apollo*. In September, her parents left the Sea Organization, and Scientology. Tonja remained in the custody of the Sea Org. Legally she was beyond their reach, on a Panamanian vessel far from U.S. waters. She was told that her father had been declared Suppressive. Nonetheless, she wanted to go home, and tried to persuade her seniors that she could convince her parents to rejoin Scientology. She says she was told to Disconnect, which "meant no more communication with my parents. They told me that my parents would not make it in the world, but that I would make it in the world."

She was assigned to "Training Routines" to teach her the duties of a Commodore's Messenger:

> During the Training Routines, myself and two others practiced carrying messages to LRH. We had to listen to a message, repeat it in the same tone, and practice salutes.
>
> "Ghosting" was on the job training where I learned how to serve LRH. I followed another messenger around and observed her carry his hat, light his cigarettes, carry his ashtray, and prepare his toiletries. Eventually, I performed those duties.
>
> As his servant, I would sit outside his room and help him out of bed when he called "messenger." I responded by assisting him out of bed, lighting his cigarette, running his shower, preparing his toiletries and helping him dress. After that I ran to the office to check it, hoping it passed "white-glove" inspection [if their was the slightest mark on a white glove run over a surface, the whole area would have to be re-cleaned]. He frequently exploded if he found dust or dirt or smelled soap in his clothes. That is why we used 13 buckets to rinse. . . .
>
> While on the *Apollo*, I observed numerous punishments meted out for many minor infractions or mistakes made in connection with Hubbard's very strict and bizarre policies. On a number of occasions, I saw people placed in the "chain lockers" of the boat on direct orders of Hubbard. These lockers were small, smelly holes, covered by grates, where the chain for the anchor was stored. I saw one boy held in there for thirty nights, crying and begging to be released. He was only allowed out to clean the bilges where the sewer and refuse of the ship collected. I believe his "crimes" were taking or using a musical instrument, I believe a flute, of someone else [sic] without permission.

This is how Tonja summed up her days in the CMO: "I was in Scientology from the age of thirteen to the age of eighteen. I received at some times $2.50 per week pay, and at other times approximately $17.20 a week. I received no education."

Tonja Burden remained in the Commodores Messenger Org until November 1977, when, aged eighteen, she made her escape from Scientology. In 1986, the Scientologists paid her an out of court settlement to abandon a suit she had brought for kidnapping.

In October 1975, when the *Apollo* finally ran out of ports in which to berth, Hubbard flew ashore with a small CMO unit. When he fled to Washington, DC, in 1976, he was again accompanied by a small CMO unit. The CMO became Hubbard's eyes and ears in the new Flag Land Base, from whence the Scientology Church was controlled. They were known as CMO CW for Commodore's Messenger Organization, Clearwater.

Hubbard was at "Winter Headquarters," codenamed Rifle, his hacienda in La Quinta, from October 1976 until July 1977. In one of the few Scientology "technical bulletins" written while there, he took a characteristic swipe at the medical profession: "Doctors are often careless and incompetent, psychiatrists are simply outright murderers. The solution is not to pick up the pieces for them but to demand medical doctors become competent, and to abolish psychiatry and psychiatrists as well as psychologists and other famous Nazi criminal outgrowths."[1] This was the view of the outside world which Hubbard implanted into his naive, adolescent Messengers.

Commodore's Messenger Anne Rosenblum joined Hubbard's retinue at La Quinta in the late Spring of 1977. His appearance surprised her: "He had long reddish-grayish hair down past his shoulders, rotting teeth, a really fat gut, and I believe at that time he had a full beard for 'disguise.' He didn't look anything like his pictures."[2]

In July, with the FBI raids of the Guardian's Offices in Los Angeles and Washington, Hubbard went into even deeper seclusion. One of his two controlling lines into Scientology had been through the GO in Los Angeles. He fled with three of his Messengers. It was obvious to Hubbard that for the GO to have been caught it must be riddled with Suppressives. Communication to the GO was therefore dangerous, and the CMO became his only remaining link with the Church. The young Messengers had not suffered the corruption of the outside (or "wog") world. They were the children of Scientologists, often indoctrinated since birth, and many had spent their formative years in the company of the Commodore. Now the key Messengers, nearly all girls, were in their late teens, and ferociously dedicated to their Commodore. From this point, Hubbard would increasingly place his trust in them.

Hubbard, with three Messengers, left for Sparks, Nevada, in the dead of night, in Hubbard's station-wagon, *Beauty*. They drove away from the hacienda with their lights off, so pursuit could be readily detected. Hubbard had stomach trouble throughout the trip. Perhaps his old "wound," the ulcer which still provided him with a veteran's pension, was acting up? A scheme went into effect almost immediately to camouflage Hubbard, and keep him hidden from the world. The two older Messengers were married, under assumed names. The marriage was bigamous for both of them, but legal considerations rarely stopped close devotees from serving Hubbard. The bigamists then claimed that Hubbard was their elderly grand-uncle, and the third Messenger a cousin, and set up house together.

Hubbard stayed in seclusion for almost six months, maintaining control of the Scientology Church through his Messengers. He used the time to outline thirty-three Scientology training films, writing the scripts for fifteen. He also wrote a peculiar screenplay called *Revolt in the Stars*. Despite his admonitions that OT3 was lethal to the uninitiated, *Revolt in the Stars* centered on the supposed incidents of seventy-five million years ago, providing many new details. The evil prince Xenu, perpetrator of the massacre of millions, was apparently assisted in his malicious deeds by the Galactic Minister of Police, Chi, and the Executive President of the Galactic Interplanetary Bank, Chu. Along with Chi and Chu, we find Mish, one of the few "Loyal Officers" to survive the catastrophe, the Lady Min, and the heroic Rawl, whom one suspects is the Hubbard character.

By December 1977, Hubbard could no longer resist the temptation to turn his scripts to celluloid. The would-be spectacular *Revolt in the Stars* was too ambitious, and would require the skills and budget of the movie *Star Wars*, but he could make a start with Scientology promotional and Tech films. The Tech films were to be demonstrations of good auditing practice. Hubbard moved back to winter HQ at La Quinta.

Two properties were purchased in Indio, California. A ten-acre ranch, codenamed Monroe, became a barracks for the CMO crew who made the Tech films. The 140-acre ranch where shooting actually took place was called Silver, a popular codename, it seems. In the grapefruit orchards of Silver, a huge barn was built, camouflaging Hubbard's film studio.

A recruitment drive was launched in the Scientology world for professionals experienced in music or film. At the age of fifteen, Ver-Dawn Hartwell left school to join the Commodore's Messenger Organization. Her older sister had been involved in Scientology for several years. Their parents were accomplished dancers, and had just finished the introductory Communication Course when they were approached by recruiters for the "CMO Cine Org." They were lured out to the desert with glib promises of excellent pay, exciting work and a beautiful location. They were even shown photographs of the resort hotel they would be staying in—in Clearwater. Instead they ended up in the desert in the squalor of Monroe, with the rest of the Cine Org.

Adell and Ernie Hartwell had given their family and friends the address of their supposed destination. They were surprised when the Scientologist who met them in Los Angeles checked to see if the car was bugged, and drove down sidestreets to make sure they were not being followed. He explained that the precautions were because Hubbard's whereabouts were top secret.

Ernie was startled when they arrived: "I was absolutely shocked to see everybody running around in shorts, ragged clothes, dirty, and unkempt. . . . They put us in a . . . little three-room shack on the edge of the ranch. . . . We go inside and what a mess . . . the place was totally overrun with bugs, insects. . . . The facilities consisted of a mattress on the floor . . . when somebody turned the lights on, of course, it stirred up all the bugs and everything began to fly all over the place."

The Hartwells set to work, initially on a schedule starting at seven in the morning and finishing at eleven or twelve at night. In spite of their protests, they were given no free time, even on weekends. They were told the recruiter who had lied to them about the wonderful pay and working conditions was being disciplined. The same old Scientology excuse, "he's been removed." It did not help.

Adell Hartwell was confused by the set up:

> The main thing that I disliked . . . before we could see the place, we had to be programmed on the lies that we had to tell. If we ran into one of our friends, we had to tell a lie to them and tell them we were just there for a vacation. We had the man's name and everything to give. We had to go twenty-five miles to use the telephone, and . . . usually there was somebody with us . . . There was [sic] no papers . . .
>
> We were schooled on how to get away from process servers, FBI agents, any government official or any policeman who wanted anything to do with Hubbard. . . . There was [sic] four different ways that they trained us to handle them, even if . . . [we] had to use . . . physical force. And that went on for days, that training. One of us would be the FBI agent and the other one would be who we are . . . until we had it down pat.
>
> . . . We were just like we had been cut off from the world. We were behind closed—locked doors with curtains always pulled. . . . We were to hide anything pertaining to the word "Scientology" in books or

anything that would disclose that it was the Church of Scientology. . . . Anytime we left from one building to another, everything that we carried had to be in sacks. There was nothing that could be visible that had "Scientology" on it. . . . Fred Roth was put in the RPF [Rehabilitation Project Force] because he said the word "Scientology" on the golf course.

All outgoing mail was censored, and all incoming mail came via Clearwater. Ernie Hartwell was a Navy veteran, so Adell had not led a sheltered life, even so she was startled by Hubbard's turns of phrase:

I was in the shed one day, the wardrobe, working . . . I hadn't met Hubbard at this time. And I heard this terrible screaming filthy language like I had never heard before. I had something in my hand and it fell to the floor and my mouth flew open. I said, "Who in the world is that?" And they said it was the Boss, because we weren't allowed to use the word "Hubbard" for security reasons. And I said, "You mean the leader of the Church speaks like that?" And they said, "Yes. He doesn't believe in keeping anything back."

Ernie confirmed this: "He was a screaming maniac. . . . He'd tell you to do one thing and turn around two minutes later and tell you not to do it." Many people who were once close to Hubbard have remarked on his screaming fits.

In her five month stay, Dell never saw Hubbard vary his wardrobe: "He's a big man with a big stomach. His hair was long and shabby—gray, with reddish spots, and he always wore pants that were way too big with one suspender, and he always had a bandana and a cowboy hat."[3]

In keeping with Hubbard's dust phobia, the set had to be washed down, with special odor-free soap, before he arrived each day, and rinsed four times over with clean water. A "white glove inspection" would take place. This could be problematical when sets had just been painted. The crew would desperately use anything at hand to dry the paint, after a lookout atop a pole sighted Hubbard's car in the distance. Sets which would have taken Hollywood weeks to prepare had to be built in a single day. Filming was usually done at night.

People with a fever would be "quarantined" in a ten by twelve foot room. Adell Hartwell says that at one time there were thirteen teenagers crammed in, all running fevers, and all still smoking (cancer being the result of engrams or body thetans or whatever, supposedly granting Scientologists immunity).

Hubbard would arrive at eight in the evening, and the crew would slavishly follow his screamed instructions until seven the next morning with a single half-hour break, but nothing to eat or drink.

As a makeup assistant, Adell Hartwell helped Hubbard to satisfy one of his obsessions. Gallons of imitation blood were prepared:

> Did he ever like those films to be bloody. . . . We'd be shooting a scene and all of a sudden he'd yell "Stop! Make it more gory, make it more gory." We'd go running out on the set with all this Karo syrup and food coloring and we'd just dump it all over the actors. Then we'd film some more and he'd stop it again and say "it's not gory enough." And we'd throw some more blood on them.
>
> . . . We were doing a scene where they were bombing the FBI office . . . and we had so much blood on those actors . . . we couldn't even get enough on them to suit Hubbard. We had guys' legs off, there were hands off, arms—I mean, it was a mess from the word go. We had so much blood on those actors that they had to take their clothes and all and soak in the shower before they could undress. This is what Hubbard wanted.

This film about the FBI was shown to U.S. Scientologists through the time leading up to the trial of Mary Sue Hubbard and other Guardian's Office staff. On one occasion, Hubbard ordered so much gore that two actors had to be cut out of their clothes which had stuck fast.

The Commodore would explode into furious tantrums. According to Adell, "I actually saw him take his hat off one day and stomp on it and cry like a baby. I have seen him just take his arm . . . and throw it wild and hit girls in the face. . . . One girl would follow him with a chair. If he sat down, that chair had to be right where he was going to sit. One girl missed by a few inches; he fell off of it, and she was put in the RPF."

The crew was kept under intense and constant pressure. Even Hubbard's cook would work from six in the morning to ten at night simply to prepare three meals to the Commodore's satisfaction. Hubbard frequently complained that the crew was overspending. At one time they had to use pages from phone directories for toilet paper, because of the supposed extravagance. Conditions were dreadful even for the crew who were in "good standing," but for those on the

Rehabilitation Project Force conditions were well nigh impossible. RPFers kept their few clothes in boxes, and slept on mattresses thrown out in the open through the few daylight hours alloted to them.

Adell's teenage daughter was put on the RPF, and Adell was traumatized when she was not even allowed to talk to her: "I would see her dragging her mattress from one shade tree to another. I said, 'Why are you doing this?' And she was ill and she couldn't be in with the others, and so she was hunting shade . . . it's 117 degrees."

Ernie Hartwell takes up the story: "We were not programmed into Scientology; we were not brainwashed. We were not following a great guiding light or any great pull that L. Ron Hubbard had. . . . All the other people . . . accepted those conditions. . . . They didn't mind the bugs and the snakes . . . the lousy food, the lousy living conditions, all the dirt."

The Hartwells decided they were not going to take any more, and were told they would have to appear in front of a "Board" before they could leave. They were kept waiting for two weeks. Throughout this time the Scientologists worked on Adell, and on the day they were due to go, she told Ernie she was staying behind. They had been married for nearly fifteen years. She was ill, and both of them felt that Scientology auditing would help her. Ernie resolved to go back to Las Vegas, and find a job to help pay for any medical treatment that Adell needed to supplement her auditing. Ver-Dawn was determined to stay close to Hubbard.

Ernie said, "It seems like they do everything they can to destroy families and happiness. For me . . . it was the hardest thing I ever had to do in my life, leaving them there in the condition that they were in and leaving them with a man that was totally insane."

Back in Las Vegas, Ernie found work. About six weeks after he left the CMO Cine Org, he was visited by a Scientologist "chaplain," who accused him of disclosing Hubbard's whereabouts. Having done this, the Scientologist produced the Hartwells' marriage license, and said Adell wanted a divorce. Ernie was speechless. Then he was asked if Adell and Ver-Dawn could use his address for passport applications, as they were leaving the United States.

Adell had been told that because Ernie had given away Hubbard's location, the whole crew would have to go overseas. She was told that her marriage license would be needed to obtain a passport. She knew nothing about any divorce.

The recruiters had promised that Adell Hartwell would be given special auditing and proper medical care for her illness. No treatment was given, and her condition was growing progressively worse. One day she worked without eating. It was 102 degrees in the shade:

> By five-thirty I just got deathly ill, and I told them I had to leave. And I staggered quite a ways. . . . I fell in the ditch; it was like I was drunk. . . . They came in and woke me up and said it was seven o'clock I had to go down because Hubbard was going to be on the set. And I wouldn't do it. And I was written up [reported to Ethics].
> . . . Another time I complained I had to go home because I wasn't being treated. I was thin and bleeding and in quite severe pain, and they took me right in and put me on the Meter. . . . The next night they had us scrubbing the barn; we started at six o'clock and we scrubbed that barn until four o'clock in the morning . . . anybody that ran a fever was immediately put out of commission. But anybody that was ill and not running a fever, they were made fun of and ridiculed.

Nearly three months after their separation, Adell Hartwell left the film crew, and rejoined her husband. Their next shock was receiving a "Freeloader Bill" for the auditing and training Adell had received during her five month stay in the desert. The bill was for $5,500. When Ernie complained to the Las Vegas Guardian's Office, he was told that they had neglected to bill him the $5,000 *he* owed, bringing the total to $10,500.

A few days later, Ernie Hartwell was asked to sign a bond for $30,000, payable if he said anything bad about Scientology. Infuriated, Ernie pointed out that he had kept his part of every bargain, while the Scientologists had kept to nothing. He demanded a letter from *them*, saying they would leave him alone. After half a dozen futile meetings, the Scientologists raised their demands. Ernie was to sign a statement saying he had been an alcoholic all his life, had abused his children, had been a poor father and provider, had murdered his father, and owed Scientology $60,000. The threats and harassment continued for several months. Even the FBI raids had failed to halt the excesses of the Guardian's Office.

Eventually, worn down and scared half out of his wits, Ernie felt compelled to do exactly what the GO was trying to prevent. To protect Adell and himself, he went to the police and told them everything.

Somehow the GO persuaded a newspaper to run a story saying Ernie

Hartwell had tried to extort money from Scientology. Television picked it up. Ernie was one man against a powerful organization. Eddie Walters, who was working for the Las Vegas GO at the time, has since confirmed the Hartwells' claims of harassment. Another witness has testified that Hubbard himself ordered that Ernie Hartwell's confessional folders be "culled" for anything reprehensible.[4]

Indeed, there are many witnesses to the systematic "culling" of confessional folders throughout Scientology over a period of many years, with the purpose of finding material to blackmail individuals into conformity with Church objectives. Mary Sue Hubbard wrote an order in 1969 for the GO to use this information gathering tactic. During the making of the Tech films, most of the crew's folders were similarly culled for potentially useful information.

Most of the energy put into the films was wasted anyway, as Adell has said: "Funny thing about those movies is that they never get shown to anyone. Hubbard would always blame somebody for screwing it up and order the movie shelved."[5]

In 1986, the Church of Scientology paid $150,000 to Adell Hartwell in a secret settlement of her litigation against it.

While pursuing his directorial dreams and bloodlust through the Tech films, Hubbard once more revised Dianetics. It became New Era Dianetics, or "NED." Hubbard had also been railing against LSD, and devised the "Sweat Program." Hubbard was convinced that LSD "sticks around in the body," a questionable hypothesis, as LSD is both unstable and water-soluble. Hubbard's program was supposed to "flush" traces of LSD from the body. Anyone who had taken LSD was to take a mega-dose of vitamins, and a teaspoon of salt a day. The diet was restricted to fruit, fruit juice and "predigested liquid protein." The victim was then to jog in a rubberized nylon sweat suit, for at least an hour a day.[6] Some unfortunates spent months on this program, until it was eventually replaced with the "Purification Rundown." There is no doubt that this bizarre program severely damaged some people's health.

Hubbard did not undertake the Sweat Program himself, but he did have a great deal of New Era Dianetic auditing. It did nothing for his temper tantrums. The Tech film project ground to a halt shortly before Adell Hartwell left. Hubbard was in a very bad way.

CHAPTER TWO

The Rise of the Messengers

Hubbard's health had deteriorated over the years. He continued to suffer from heavy colds, and chain-smoked three to four packs of cigarettes a day. In 1965, he was bedridden and thought he was going to die.[1] This feeling recurred almost annually. Early in 1967 he was again bedridden, this time because of drug abuse. In 1972, he went into hiding in New York for almost a year, again very ill for much of this period. Shortly after his return to the ship at the end of 1973, he hurt himself badly in a motorcycle accident. He had suffered a heart attack in 1975, and the attendant embolism had forced him to take anticoagulant drugs for a year. His bursitis had never ceased to plague him, and he was usually grossly overweight.

David Mayo had been involved in Scientology since the late 1950s. He had joined the Sea Org soon after its inception, becoming one of the few Class 12 Auditors. By the time the Flag Land Base was established in Florida, in 1975, Mayo had become the Senior Case Supervisor Flag. He was the top dog in the world of Scientology "Tech."

In September 1978, a confidential telex ordered Mayo to quit Florida immediately for Los Angeles. A Commodore's Messenger met him at the airport. As they drove down the freeway to Palm Springs, the Messenger apologized to Mayo, but asked him to put on a pair of dark glasses. It was the middle of the night, but Mayo humored his escort. The glasses had been painted over. Top security was being maintained. Mayo dozed, until the driver braked hard because he had nearly overshot the freeway exit. The glasses flew off and Mayo had to reassure the driver that he had not seen the Indio exit sign.

Mayo was told that Hubbard was very ill, and was given Hubbard's "case folders" to study. Mayo was to determine what auditing errors Hubbard's current condition stemmed from. He was taken to see the Commodore: "I must admit I got quite a shock, because the last time I'd seen him he'd been full of energy and active and it was a surprise to see him lying on his back. . . . He was lying there almost in a coma, although he had his eyes open, and when I went in the room and said hello to him his eyes flickered and he gave me a little smile."

Hubbard had suffered another pulmonary embolism, a blood clot in the artery to the lungs. Kima Douglas had once again saved his life. This time she was unable to overrule his refusal to go to hospital, so, imitating the doctors at Curaçao, she fed him a huge dose of his pills. He drifted into a coma. Douglas stripped an electric wire, with the desperate idea that he could be shocked back to life. She stayed by him for forty-eight hours. Scientologist medical doctor Eugene Denk was rushed from Los Angeles, blindfolded, to relieve her.[2]

While Kima Douglas and Dr. Denk ministered to Hubbard's physical needs, Mayo devised an auditing program and set to work. He concluded that the New Era Dianetic auditing had been to blame, and it was decided that Dianetics should not be given Clears, because of its deleterious effect upon them. This was not heartening to the thousands of Clears who had paid huge amounts for hundreds of hours of Dianetics.

The procedures brought into being by Mayo and Hubbard became known as New Era Dianetics for Operating Thetans, ("NED for OTs," or, most simply, "NOTs"). Mayo says that what they actually concentrated upon during the auditing were misconceptions; somehow the emphasis changed to Body Thetans when Hubbard helped Mayo rework his notes. Still, Mayo was made Senior Case Supervisor International, an entirely new position, as a mark of Hubbard's gratitude.

While recovering, Hubbard approved the purchase of the Massacre Canyon Inn resort complex at Gilman Hot Springs. There were several buildings, including a motel and a hotel, set in 520 acres and including a twenty-seven-hole golf course. The property was about forty miles from La Quinta, near the small town of Hemet. The purchase price was $2.7 million.

At the end of 1978, the CMO Rehabilitation Project Force started to prepare Gilman. The CMO Special Unit, the channel through which Hubbard managed Scientology, moved there the following February. Mayo continued to audit Hubbard, and had to move in with the CMO.

Hubbard went even deeper into hiding for a few weeks in March 1979, travelling with a CMO escort to nearby Lake Elsinore. In April, he moved to an apartment in Hemet, where he lived with about ten Messengers. The security around him was extremely tight. Very few people knew his whereabouts; by this time he was even hiding from the Guardian's Office.

In February, Hubbard, at last recovering from his illness, had turned his attention back to the worldwide Scientology scene. The CMO did a statistical analysis for him. How many people were receiving auditing and training? How much money was being made? How many new people were coming into Scientology? Hubbard did not like what he saw. The number of active Scientologists was diminishing, as was the amount of money being made. Students were abandoning their courses and demanding refunds. The obvious reasons were the twenty-fold increase in prices since November 1976, and revelations in the media about the Guardian's Office. Hubbard ignored the obvious however, and issued the "Change the Civilization Eval[uation]."[3] The Guardian's Office had let him down, and so had Sea Org management. The Commodore's Messenger Organization had been concerned with Hubbard's personal welfare, and with his personal projects (the films, for instance). Now they seemed to him to be the remaining loyal unit of his private army, and they were to enforce his will upon the renegades. Hubbard reprimanded the CMO for issuing orders under their own title. Hubbard must not be seen to be managing Scientology under any circumstances. The pretence of his resignation from Church management in 1966 had to be rigorously maintained. Otherwise he would be wide open to the extensive litigation against Scientology. Worst of all he was implicated in the case against his wife, and her cohorts in the Guardian's Office, and he too might be indicted. He had already been named (along with twenty-nine others) as an as yet unindicted co-conspirator.

The CMO were a latter-day Praetorian Guard, at first protecting and serving the whims of their Emperor, but gradually becoming the most powerful element in the hierarchy of command. Long the interface between Hubbard and the rest of the Church, part of the CMO became the senior management body: the Commodore's Messenger Organization International, or CMO Int. But as the Commodore's Messenger Organization was quite obviously connected to the Commodore, they had to find a new title. So the Watchdog Committee (WDC) came into being, in April 1979. It consisted solely of the senior executives of CMO Int.

The function of WDC was to "put senior management back on post." They did this by absorbing all top management posts. The members of the Watchdog Committee remained anonymous, and many Scientologists thought Hubbard was in fact the mysterious Chairman WDC.

In July 1979, a member of CMO issued a directive seeking to explain the rather contradictory notion that although CMO was in no way involved in management, it could give orders to any of Scientology's International Management bodies. Early in 1978, Hubbard had reinforced their position by approving an order which made them answerable only to him, and urging the compliance of all other Sea Org units with CMO orders. The rule was basically obey first, ask questions later, if at all.[4]

Hubbard's orders grew progressively more wild. Gerald Armstrong was in the CMO at Gilman: "In the summer of 1979, on the orders of Hubbard . . . I became involved in a project to build Mr. Hubbard a completely new house near Hemet. I was personally involved with the architectural plans for this property and saw an order from Mr. Hubbard to have built around the property a high block wall with openings for gun implacements."

Amongst Hubbard's requirements were that the house be "in a non-black area, dust-free, defensible, with no surrounding higher areas, and built on bedrock."

To maintain security, Hubbard even stopped seeing his wife, shortly before she changed her plea to an admission of guilt. They last saw each other at Gilman in August 1979. Despite her years of faithful service, and her willingness to take the rap for him, Hubbard cast her off. Nonetheless, she retained control of the still powerful Guardian's Office, and was able to remove the Deputy Commanding Officer of the CMO for meddling in GO affairs.[5]

In September 1979, nine of the indicted GO executives and staff, led by Mary Sue Hubbard, signed a stipulation admitting their involvement in the break ins, burglaries, thefts and buggings. By their admissions they stopped further investigation into their numerous other misdeeds. They also avoided a drawn out trial with the inevitable adverse publicity. The 282 page stipulation revealed the story of the infiltration of government agencies, in startling detail. In December, the GO nine were sentenced. Agent Sharon Thomas received the shortest prison term—six months. The others, including Mary Sue Hubbard, were sentenced to four and five year terms. They managed to stall the day by appealing the sentences.

With the pressure building, Hubbard issued an ominous warning from his secret headquarters, "The Purification Rundown and Atomic War." The faithful were summoned to meetings in Orgs the world over to hear Hubbard's terrible message. Executives in full dress Sea Org uniform spoke to groups of frightened Scientologists. The Bulletin began: "I want Scientologists to live through World War III."[6]

Hubbard went on to make it perfectly clear that he held out very little hope for the world. There was going to be a nuclear war very, very soon. He confidently asserted that "those who have a full and complete Purification Rundown will survive where others not so fortunate won't. And *that* poses the interesting probability that only Scientologists will be functioning in areas experiencing heavy fallout in an Atomic War."

In fact, Hubbard's "Personal Communicator" visited several principal Sea Org executives and told them that if they did not raise Scientology's stats by 540 percent in six months, then the world would end. They did not, and it did not, and in later reissues the phrase quoted above was changed to "those who have had a full and complete Purification Rundown *could fare better than* others not so fortunate. And that poses the interesting probability that only Scientologists will *have had the spiritual gain that would enable them to function* in areas experiencing heavy fallout in an Atomic War."

At about the time that the "Purification Rundown and Atomic War" was invoked in an effort to galvanize Scientologists into action, the GO predicted an FBI raid on the Gilman complex. It seemed likely that Hubbard would be indicted either by a New York grand jury investigating Scientology harassment of author Paulette Cooper, or a Florida grand jury investigating Scientology's dealings in Clearwater.

There was a panic at Gilman Hot Springs to remove any material demonstrating Hubbard's management of Scientology. A massive document shredder was moved to Gilman Hot Springs. The crew affectionately called it "Jaws." Anything which connected Hubbard to the La Quinta or Gilman properties, or to the Guardian's Office; any order, or anything even resembling an order from Hubbard had to go, and accordingly tens of thousands of documents were shredded. The Messenger logs, which were the painstaking record of *every* verbal order given by the Commodore to his Messengers, were buried for safe keeping.[7] These logs have never come under public scrutiny.

Gerald Armstrong was the head of the Household Unit, which was preparing a house on the Gilman property for Hubbard's occupation. One of Armstrong's juniors was perplexed when she found a cache of boxes containing faded Hubbard letters and the like. She asked Armstrong if this material should be shredded. Armstrong was amazed and delighted to find twenty boxes packed with old letters, diaries, photographs, even some of Hubbard's baby clothes.[8]

At last an accurate and fully documented account of the remarkable exploits of the Founder would be possible. The fabrications of conspiring government agencies could be disproved once and for all. Armstrong sent a request to Hubbard asking permission to establish an archive with this material at its core. Hubbard granted the request. The process eventually discredited Hubbard's fictional autobiography for good.

Shortly thereafter in February or March 1980, Hubbard hightailed it out of his apartment in Hemet, with the two Messengers who were "on Watch," Pat and Annie Broeker.[9] The Broekers had been in Scientology for a long time. Annie had been a Messenger on the ship. Hubbard disappeared without trace. He probably left because of the strong possibility that he would be subpoenaed by the Paulette Cooper grand jury in New York.

Armstrong was busy with a series of projects, including the Nobel Peace Prize Project which was intended to win the Prize for Hubbard's development of the Purification Rundown. Increasingly stringent measures were taken to conceal Hubbard's control of Scientology. Armstrong was also assigned to "Mission Corporate Category Sort-Out" (MCCS). Members of the Guardian's Office Legal Bureau and of the L. Ron Hubbard Personal Office met with Hubbard's attorney to discuss strategy. They were trying to cover the tracks of the Religious Research Foundation, and other dubious or downright illegal schemes, which had poured Church of Scientology money into Hubbard's private accounts.[10]

MCCS started an eddy which would become a tidal wave, sweeping away the majority of veteran Scientologists. The entire corporate structure was to be changed in a desperate attempt to avoid the consequences of Guardian's Office activities, and the ensuing concerted legal action against the corporate entity of which it was part, the Church of Scientology of California, the corporate heads of which were GO executives

Hubbard dabbled with a follow-up to the Purification Rundown, called the Survival Rundown, but most of the work was done by his Technical Compilations Unit at Gilman Hot Springs. After lengthy surveys, the new Rundown was released with illustrations of an American Indian paddling a canoe, or loosing an arrow at a buffalo. Unfortunate choices as examples of survival. The "Purif" had been advertised with a waterfall, unintentionally suggesting an ad for menthol cigarettes.

During the summer, Armstrong's growing collection of documents relating to the life and times of L. Ron Hubbard was appraised by a Scientologist collector, who valued it at around $5 million. MCCS were toying with the idea of creating a Trust to legitimize some of the immense payments being made to Hubbard.[11]

On July 16, 1980, the GO, which had precious little to celebrate, was able to rejoice with the news that the British government's use of the Aliens Act against Scientology was finally over. After twelve years, foreign Scientologists could once more enter Britain legally. However, the restrictions on Hubbard's re-entry were not lifted.

Hubbard was beginning to let slip clues to the terrible truth of the OT levels. He issued a Bulletin called "The Nature of a Being" in which he quite publicly, yet mystifyingly, declared that "a human being . . . is not a single unit being."[12] Plans were underway to film *Revolt in the Stars*, volcanic eruptions and all. Hubbard itched to make OT 3 public.

Hubbard continued railing against psychiatry: "Almost every modern horror crime was committed by a known criminal who had been in and out of the hands of psychiatrists and psychologists often many times. . . . Spawned by an insanely militaristic government, psychiatry and psychology find avid support from oppressive and domineering governments. . . . The credence and power of psychiatry and psychology are waning. It hit its zenith about 1960: then it seemed their word was law and that they could harm, injure, and kill patients without restraint." Hubbard assured his readers that his own work had been a major reason for a purported decline of psychiatry and psychology. He added, "At one time they were on their way to turning every baby into a future robot for the manipulation of the state and every society into a madhouse of crime and immorality."[13]

In October 1980, the Chairman WDC caused much rejoicing by making the enormous price cuts mentioned earlier. Scientology was still not cheap, but it was a great deal cheaper, and the monthly price rises had stopped. It looked as if the Scientology world was finally going to right itself. Many thought that "LRH" was "back on the lines." In fact, quite the opposite was true.

Omar Garrison, who had already written two books favorable to Scientology, was now contracted to write Hubbard's biography, using the enormous collection of material discovered and gathered by Gerald Armstrong. The contract negotiations were elaborate, with Mary Sue Hubbard representing both her husband to the publisher, and the publisher to Garrison. The publisher was to be Scientology Publications, Denmark, a subsidiary of the Church of Scientology, though its executives knew nothing of the negotiations made by Mary Sue on their behalf.

Garrison was firm in his approach, as he later said: "I wasn't prepared to write a eulogy for Mr. Hubbard . . . it would be like trying to write a biography of Christ for a very fanatical Christian organization . . . they agreed that I can [sic] write it without any restriction."[14]

The day after the contract was signed, on October 31, 1980, the Internal Revenue Service placed a lien on the Cedars of Lebanon complex, the huge old hospital which by then housed Scientology's Los Angeles operation. Within a fortnight, the Scientologists' appeal against the IRS tax assessment for the years 1970–1972 went to court.

Hubbard's written Scientology output for 1980 was small. A few already lengthy Confessional lists were extended on his instruction, and there were various pronouncements about drugs. He kept busy with other matters. The first was an attempt at writing the longest science fiction novel of all time. He later boasted to A.E. van Vogt that it had taken him only six weeks to write.[15] It is rumored that Hubbard did not even read the proofs, leaving this to his close confidant, Messenger Pat Broeker. But how could a Messenger alter the words of the great OT? Perhaps *Battlefield Earth* is the longest science fiction novel ever written. Certainly, some reviewers found it among the most boring, and possibly the most turgid. One headed his review, succinctly, "Brain Death." In his history of science fiction, *Trillion Year Spree*, Brian Aldiss gave a good synopsis of the novel:

The Psychlos, thousand pound alien monsters with "cruelty" fuses in their solid bone skulls and a penchant for shooting the legs off horses one at a time, have taken over Earth. The Psychlos are materialists, miners and manipulators . . . they are baddies, there to be shot and killed in the cause of freedom. Fighting for humankind is Johnnie Goodboy Tyler, a young, well-muscled hero, supported by a bunch of mad Scots and Russians, brave fighters and dreadful caricatures to the last man. In the course of the story, Johnnie gets the girl . . . frees the Earth, wreaks vengeance on the Psychlos' home planet, and eventually gets to own the Galaxy. Just a simple boy-makes-good story. A bit like Rambo.

When Scientology's Bridge Publications printed the paperback issue, the over-muscled figure of Johnnie on the cover was topped by a very Hubbard-like head.

Hubbard's second work of 1980 was somewhat shorter. Hubbard had decided that society lacked a moral code, and wrote *The Way to Happiness*, for public distribution. The lack of mention of Scientology or Dianetics is striking, and a publishing front was even developed so that the booklet would not be seen to emanate from the Scientology Church. The booklet lays out a series of twenty-one maxims from "Take Care of Yourself" to "Flourish and Prosper," each with a page or two of explanation. It includes the unoriginal and awkwardly phrased "Try Not to Do Things to Others That You Would Not Like Them to Do to You." Most of the advice is sensible if obvious, and much of it Hubbard had ignored throughout his life. The maxim about lying is carefully worded: "Do not tell harmful lies." At the end of each explanation is a summating phrase. "Do Not Murder" is followed by "The way to happiness does not include murdering your friends, your family, or yourself being murdered." The booklet is sugary, but harmless enough. It certainly does not reflect the morality Hubbard instilled into his followers, least of all in B-1, the Intelligence section of the Guardian's Office. Just after the completion of *The Way to Happiness*, Guardian Jane Kember and Deputy Guardian for Information World Wide, Mo Budlong, were sentenced to two to six years for "burglary, aiding and abetting." By following Hubbard's instructions they had violated point nine of *The Way to Happiness*: "Don't Do anything Illegal."

CHAPTER THREE

The Young Rulers

In December 1980, the long-dormant post of Executive Director International was resurrected. It had remained vacant since Hubbard's supposed resignation in 1966. Scientologists the world over were aware that Hubbard, the Founder, Commodore and Source, was the real head of their Church, but under the new corporate strategy, it was necessary to conceal Hubbard's control. The new Executive Director International was Bill Franks, and he was to be "ED Int for life." It turned out to be a very short life. Scientologists the world over assumed that Franks was Hubbard's immediate junior, and was being groomed to succeed the Commodore.

Hubbard's legal situation was worsening. Early in 1981, the All Clear Unit was set up at the Commodore's Messenger Organization International ("CMO Int") reporting directly to the Commanding Officer CMO, who was also chairwoman of the Watchdog Committee. The unit's purpose was to make it "All Clear" for Hubbard to come out of hiding.

David Miscavige was a cameraman with the CMO Cine Org in 1977, at the age of seventeen, and had gained a reputation for bulldozing through any resistance. Miscavige could get things done, and had even been known to stand his ground before Hubbard. His parents were Scientologists, and his older brother, Ronnie, was also in the CMO. David Miscavige had trained as an Auditor at Saint Hill at the age of fourteen. He was not a long-term Messenger, but his dogged determination led to rapid promotion.

One of Miscavige's former superiors had this to say of "DM" as he is usually known: "When he's under control . . . he's a very dynamite character. . . . He is willing to take on and confront anything."And this despite Miscavige's touchiness about being little over five feet tall and asthmatic.

The Guardian's Office had failed Hubbard. Mary Sue, the Controller, never saw him again after their meeting a few months before his disappearance early in 1980. According to Hubbard, mistakes do not just happen, somebody causes them, always. Mistakes and accidents are the result of deliberate Suppression. A catastrophe as big as the government case against the GO was obviously the result of a very heavyweight Suppressive. Hubbard could not admit that the GO had merely been following his orders, so rather than reforming his views, he set out to reform the GO.

In 1979, Hubbard had issued a so-called "Advice" (an internal directive with limited distribution) stating that when situations really foul-up there is more than one Suppressive Person at work. Further, those who have submitted to the SPs, the SP's "connections," also have to be rooted out. The GO, and all of the "connections" within and around it, had to be purged. Ironically, the GO had finally persuaded Hubbard that his hand must not be seen in the management of Scientology, so the All Clear Unit became Hubbard's instrument. The Suppressive-riddled GO had to be removed completely; but it had to be removed with dexterity, because it was the most powerful force in Scientology. Everyone concerned had to be sure that the orders were coming from Hubbard, but there must be no tangible evidence.

If the GO had believed there was a palace revolution in progress they would have been perfectly capable of destroying the tiny CMO. There were 1,100 GO staff, most of them seasoned, their leaders well-known in the Scientology world. There were a score of Messengers at CMO Int, and despite their newly acquired role in management, they were virtually unknown to the vast majority of Scientologists.

The CMO's first task was to remove the Controller. In May 1981, David Miscavige, by now twenty-one, met with Mary Sue Hubbard. He told her that as a convicted criminal her position in the Church was an embarrassment. The attorneys had suggested that as long as she remained in an administrative position her husband was implicated in all Scientology affairs, including the burglaries. Miscavige doubtless reminded her that the appeal of her prison sentence would probably be lost, and that when it was lost the Church's public position would be far better if the Church was seen to have disciplined her. Mary Sue screamed and raged, but Miscavige kept his bulldog grip on the situation. He was immune to tirades, and probably smiled as he dodged the ashtray she hurled at him. For her husband's good, the Controller finally stepped down. Afterwards she decided she had been tricked, and sent letters of complaint to her husband. There was no reply. She thought that her letters to her husband were being censored. They were, but on her husband's order.

Gordon Cook became the new Controller, and the Controller's Aides were replaced. The head of CMO, Diane "DeDe" Voegeding, considered Mary Sue Hubbard her friend. Having spent her teenage years on the ship without her parents, Mary Sue must have seemed almost a mother to her. Voegeding protested and was removed from her position, ostensibly for divulging Hubbard's whereabouts to the Guardian's Office.

Laurel Sullivan had been Hubbard's Personal Public Relations Officer (Pers PRO) for years. She was part of the small Personal Office, and was Armstrong's immediate superior on the biography project, as well as head of the huge financial reorganization, Mission Corporate Category Sort-out (MCCS). Sullivan too was a close friend of Mary Sue Hubbard. MCCS was closed, and Laurel Sullivan was removed from her post. Voegeding and Sullivan were both consigned to the Rehabilitation Project Force. They were the first of hundreds of "connections" to be purged.[2]

The CMO were responding to the belief, fostered by Hubbard, that the U.S. government was working to smash Scientology. Through the collection of unpaid taxes, the Internal Revenue Service was capable of destroying the parent Church of Scientology of California. There was also a distinct danger that all the subsidiary corporations would be sucked under with it. The Scientology Publications Organization U.S. was re-incorporated as a for-profit corporation, called Bridge Publications. The Publications Organization in Denmark became New Era Publications. A new Legal office was established distinct from, and eventually controlling, the GO Legal Bureau. It was the beginning of a proliferation of allegedly distinct and separate Scientology corporations.

The All Clear Unit (ACU) had to all intents become autonomous under the control of David Miscavige. It was not subject to the CMO, the Watchdog Committee, or any other Scientology entity. Miscavige took his orders only from Pat Broeker, who in turn took his orders only from Hubbard.

In July 1981, ED Int. Bill Franks and a small group of Messengers arrived at the headquarters of the U.S. Guardian's Office in Los Angeles. All GO staff were ordered to join the Sea Org, and a Criminal Handling Unit was established. Franks and his cohorts were there to remove the last real obstacle to CMO control of the Guardian's Office, Jane Kember, the Guardian. Kember had received a prison sentence for her part in the Washington burglaries, but was on bail pending an appeal. Upon hearing of Franks' moves, Mary Sue Hubbard reappointed herself Controller, and rescinded her previous permission for the CMO to investigate the GO. Franks and his team were physically ejected from GO headquarters in Los Angeles. The locks were changed. Mary Sue appointed Jane Kember Temporary Controller.

Franks, as Executive Director International, maintained his occupation of the Controller's office itself, and Kember visited him there with a group of GO heavies. Franks launched into an attack on Mary Sue Hubbard, among other things accusing her of being a ''squirrel'' who practiced astrology. Ignoring Franks' threats, Kember's crew removed the Controller's files, leaving Franks in an empty office.

The GO took over an office in the former Cedars of Lebanon complex, the home of most of the Scientology Orgs in Los Angeles. There the Controller's files were guarded day and night. Mary Sue made a desperate bid to find her husband, so that he could quash the CMO. For three days the screaming match continued, with David Miscavige and other high-ranking Messengers joining in. They played on Kember's fear of a schism in the Church. Eventually, she was shown an undated Hubbard dispatch which suggested that the GO should be put under the CMO when its senior executives went to prison. Jane Kember and Mary Sue Hubbard admitted defeat.

At the end of July, the new leaders of the Guardian's Office issued ''Cracking the Conspiracy'' which assured Scientologists, ''The GO is now working around the clock to crack the conspiracy in the next six weeks. This is not 'PR' or a 'gimmick.' It is the truth.'' Ironically, the conspiracy against Scientology seemed to have emanated from the Guardian's Office itself.

The last vestige of resistance to the CMO takeover would come from Guardian's Office headquarters, GO World Wide, at Saint Hill in England. A CMO ''Observation Mission'' travelled to England, and on August 5 convened a "Committee of Evidence" against leading members of the Guardian's Office. The Committee was made up solely of Messengers, and chaired by Miscavige. The members were found guilty. A CMO unit was established at Saint Hill, and Bill Franks, the Executive Director International, issued a directive explaining that as Hubbard's management successor he was senior in authority to the Guardian's Office.

The Findings and Recommendations of the Committee of Evidence were not published. Senior GO officials were shipped to Gilman Hot Springs where they underwent a "rehabilitation program." Messengers called them "the crims," for criminals. These middle-aged Church executives were made to dig ditches, and wait table for the young rulers. They were awakened in the middle of the night and subjected to a new type of "Confessional." The privacy of the auditing session was abandoned, along with the polite manner of the auditor. A group of Messengers would fire questions, and while the recipient fumbled for an answer, yell accusations at him. Answers were belittled, and the Messengers all yelled at once. The exhausted GO official would be threatened with eternal expulsion from Scientology. The questions were also new. The CMO was convinced that the GO had been infiltrated by "enemy" agencies, so the "crims" were asked, "Who's paying you?" over and over again, and accused of working for the FBI, the AMA or the CIA. This brutal form of interrogation came to be known as "gang sec-checking." It was in total violation of the publicized tenets of Scientology. GO staff began to crack under the pressure. Most of these hardened executives eventually left Gilman willing to do the bidding of their new masters.

The Watchdog Committee assigned one of their number to the control of the Guardian's Office. David Gaiman, the former head of GO Public Relations, became the new Guardian upon his return from Gilman Hot Springs.

The great GO machine was grinding to a halt. Members of the Legal Bureau, who understood the weak position of Scientology in many of the increasing number of suits, wanted to settle out of court wherever possible, but were overruled in favor of a fight to the death policy. The stalwarts of the Legal Bureau were dismissed, and their place taken by expensive private law firms. Most of these suits were eventually settled for far larger amounts than GO Legal had negotiated. The CMO was in control of the entire administrative structure of Scientology.

Although still in hiding, Hubbard made himself available for comment, but only on matters of Scientology "Tech," in September 1981.[3]

While taking over the GO, the CMO had been establishing yet another corporation called Author Services Incorporated (ASI). It was incorporated in California in October 1981 as a for-profit company, and represented the literary interests of L. Ron Hubbard. ASI was not activated for several months. A few final adjustments had to be made to the Scientology corporate structure.

In November, Hubbard ordered the CMO to send him information outlining the entire international position of Scientology. He wanted to know all the "stats." It took two weeks to collect the information, and then it had to be presented in a way which would demonstrate the efficacy of Hubbard's orders to the CMO to take over Church management. Hubbard had trained Messengers to censor information going to him to shield him from upsetting news. After the huge ritual of information gathering, the CMO remained in power, so Hubbard was obviously happy with what he received.

The various parts of the Organization continued to function, largely unaware of the drastic changes that were taking place at the top. During Hubbard's absence from direct management in 1980, the prices had been cut, and moves were underway to reconcile estranged Scientologists. These measures were still penetrating to the membership, as the new regime brought in stringent changes at the top. It was in this setting, in November 1981, that Scientology Missions International, which monitored the progress of the supposedly independent Mission, or "Franchise," network, called a meeting to try and resolve some of the ongoing conflicts between Mission Holders and the Church.

During the 1970s, several major Mission Holders had been declared Suppressive, and their Franchises given to others. Most had exhausted Scientology's internal justice procedures in an attempt to be reinstated and to retrieve their Missions. A Mission Holder sometimes found himself in the peculiar position of having invested most of his assets into his Mission, but after being declared Suppressive was forced to surrender control to the Church's Mission Office, who would place the mission under new management. The Mission Holder would have no access to his assets, which often amounted to hundreds of thousands of dollars, and found it impossible to work his way back into the good graces of Scientology. Several ousted Mission Holders had initiated civil litigation against the Church.

Hubbard's published policy states that an individual can be declared Suppressive for suing the Church. It was a Catch 22 situation. The November 1981 meeting attempted to resolve this impasse by "open two-way communication." Both the Mission Holders and the Sea Org's Scientology Missions International staff felt progress had been made at the meeting. Both groups had failed to comprehend what was happening at the very top of the Church.

Ray Kemp, a very early supporter of Hubbard and at one time a close confederate, had been declared Suppressive in the mid-1970s, and his California Mission taken from him. Shortly before Kemp and his wife were "declared," a Church of Scientology publication had carried an article boasting about the Kemp Mission in California which said the Mission consisted of five modern buildings in two acres, with a parking lot for 200 cars. Kemp had even managed to persuade the town council to rename the site of his Mission "L. Ron Hubbard Plaza."

Kemp had tried every recourse within the Church to retrieve his Mission, but his efforts were to no avail. Eventually Kemp reluctantly started civil legal proceedings against the Church, but only after alleged physical abuse by members of the Guardian's Office. As a result of the first Mission Holders' meeting, Kemp and his wife were restored to "good standing." A Board of Review was established to investigate similar cases. Another meeting was scheduled to take place a few weeks later.

Peter Greene, who had been a Mission Holder, made a tape in 1982 describing the events of these meetings, and the background to them. The Guardian's Office had grown increasingly worried that a series of moves by U.S. government agencies might put the Church out of business. The FBI had acquired a huge quantity of incriminating material, and the IRS suits might eventually bankrupt Scientology. Greene alleges that since the mid-1970s there had been a Guardian's Office Program to take over the Missions, which were separate corporations, if the worst happened. The leading Mission Holders had been expelled, and replaced with new people who would be less willing to resist the GO.

Shortly after the first Mission Holders' meeting, yet another corporation came into being: the Church of Scientology International. It was to become the "Mother Church," replacing the Church of Scientology of California. The old lines of command had to be obscured by giving new titles to departments; for example, Hubbard's Personal Office became the Product Development Office International.[4]

The second Mission Holders' meeting was held at the Flag Land Base in Florida in December 1981, in the Scientology owned Sand-castle Hotel. The meeting was scheduled to last for two days, and fifty people arrived for the first day. The swell of excitement took hold, the meeting continued for five days, and by the time it was broken up, about two hundred people had attended.[5]

The meeting was chaired by Mission Holder Dean Stokes. Most of the Holders of larger Missions, and some of those deprived of their Missions, were in attendance. Quite a few GO staff were also there, and the meeting turned into a mass confessional, as those present gradually admitted the plans and actions taken secretly in the past. Greene described the exhilaration as the Mission Holders, the Guardian's Office, and Mission Office staff came back into touch with one another.

One executive was noticeably absent: Bill Franks, the Executive Director International, who had called the meeting. The Mission Holders had heard by now that the anonymous Watchdog Committee were Franks' superiors, despite the Hubbard Policy Letter saying Franks was head of the Church. They demanded Franks' presence. He arrived accompanied by a CMO missionaire.

One of the Mission Holders, Brown McKee, said he was assigning the lowest of Hubbard's Ethics Conditions, "Confusion," to the Watchdog Committee. The formula for completion of this Condition is simple: "Find out where you are." The *confusion* was that WDC was ostensibly running the Church, in contradiction to the Executive Director International Policy Letter, and without any apparent authority. The Watchdog Committee was seen by the Mission Holders as part of a mutinous takeover. Paradoxically, this was exactly how the Watchdog Committee saw the Mission Holders.

The Mission Holders demanded the presence of the Watchdog Committee. Mission Holder Bent Corydon, whose Riverside Mission had just been returned to him, has joked that the Mission Holders were quite ready to fly out to Gilman Hot Springs, and explain matters to the WDC "with baseball bats." Before this could happen, representatives of the WDC arrived to quell the "Mutiny."[6]

Senior Case Supervisor International David Mayo was there, and rather lamely started giving a pep talk on new "Technical" research. Mayo did not get very far. Norman Starkey, who had arrived with the WDC, and was actually in charge of the Church's new non-GO legal bureau, tried to read a Hubbard article about tolerance and forgiveness called "What Is Greatness?" He did not get very far either. David Miscavige looked on, as the meeting broke up into smaller groups, with the Mission Holders trying to explain their actions to the WDC representatives. Their attempts were unsuccessful.

Unbeknownst to most of those at the meeting, there really was a plan to wrest control from the Watchdog Committee. A small group of Scientologists, including a few Mission Holders and veteran Sea Org members, took part in this plot. It fell apart when one of their number reported their secret discussions.

Hubbard was given the CMO account of events, and started to send dispatches to senior executives at Gilman describing the Mission Holders' "mutiny," and an infiltration by enemy agents. Hubbard raged about Don Purcell and the early days, when "vested interests" had tried to prize Dianetics from his control.[7]

Swift action was taken to counter the "mutiny." On December 23, 1981, a Policy Letter was issued entitled "International Watchdog Committee." Perhaps only a few people noticed that it was not signed by L. Ron Hubbard, but by the International Watchdog Committee. It stated, quite simply: "The International Watchdog Committee is the most senior body for management in the Church of Scientology International."

Four days later, Executive Director International "for life" Bill Franks was replaced. The coup was very nearly complete. In the midst of this frantic activity, a redefinition of the revered state of Clear was issued over Hubbard's name. All earlier definitions involving perfect recall, a complete absence of psychosomatic ailments and the like, although true were no longer valid. The new definition was a wonderful piece of circular reasoning, beautifully self-perpetuating in its illogic: "A Clear is a being who no longer has his own reactive mind."[8]

If one accepts the hypothesis of the reactive mind, then a Clear does not have it. The definition does, however, imply that he could have the reactive minds of others (Body Thetans?), and be as incapable as ever. No scientific experiment could defeat this new definition. Dianetics would continue to pretend itself a science, but remain beyond verification. It could neither be proven nor disproven, having been moved squarely into the realm of faith.

CHAPTER FOUR

The Clearwater Hearings

In 1979, attorney Michael Flynn was approached by a former Scientologist who wanted her money back. She told him that if he took the case, he would receive a letter giving unsavory details of her past. He did not believe her, but sure enough the letter arrived. Flynn became interested in the Church of Scientology, and his interest increased markedly when someone put water in the gas tank of his plane. He and his son had a fortunate escape. Flynn suspected Scientology, and took on more and more clients with litigation against Scientology.[1]

The town of Clearwater, Florida was increasingly worried by the Scientology presence. The *St. Petersburg Times* had won a Pulitzer Prize for its coverage of Guardian's Office dirty tricks. The courts had made the documentation used in the GO case available; the *St. Petersburg Times*, and Clearwater's own *Sun* newspaper, had publicized several Guardian's Office operations. The Clearwater City Commissioners, headed by a new mayor, approached Michael Flynn, by now an expert on Scientology, to help them in their investigation of Scientology.

Public Hearings were held in Clearwater in May 1982. Flynn was to present witnesses and evidence regarding Scientology for a week, and then the Church would be given the same time for its reply. Religious issues were not in question. The City Commissioner James Berfield opened the Hearings with a statement of intent:

273

The purpose of these public hearings is to investigate alleged violation of criminal and civil laws, and the alleged violation of fundamental rights by the Church of Scientology, an organization which now conducts extensive activities within our city. The purpose of the investigation is to determine whether there is a need for legislation to correct the alleged violations. It is not our purpose to interfere with any of the beliefs, doctrines, tenets, or activities of Scientology which arguably fall within the ambit of religious belief or activity in the broadest legal interpretation. It is not our purpose to conduct a witch hunt and receive testimony, documents, or any other type of evidence which is not reasonably related to significant, vital areas of municipal concern.

The Clearwater Hearings were locally televised. Scientologists were warned not to watch them. Eddie Walters, who had been a Class VIII Auditor and Case Supervisor, and a member of the Las Vegas GO, set the stage with a broad account of Scientology and its underhanded dealings. Then Hubbard's estranged son, Nibs, took the stand. He painted his father as a complete con-man, a sinister black magician whose philosophy resulted from horrendous drug abuse.

Lori Taverna spoke of some of her experiences. She had joined Scientology in 1965, completed all of the available OT levels, and become a Class VIII Auditor. She abandoned her business and her family when "NOTs" was released in 1978, to become a Sea Org NOTs Auditor. A year at Flag, in Clearwater, slowly disabused her of the world-saving mission of Scientology. She returned to Los Angeles ill and confused, and after sixteen years of involvement, gradually drifted out of the Scientology fold. She described the last scene of her withdrawal:

A particular friend came over to the house—she had just received her NOTs auditing—and she came in and she said how wonderful she was feeling, that she went to a restaurant, she was eating a hamburger, and all of a sudden the hamburger started screaming at her, and then the walls started screaming. And then she said tears came out of her eyes because she felt so sorry for the other people in the restaurant because they didn't know what she knew.

Casey Kelly had been Director of Income at the Flag Land Base. He testified that income there had averaged $400–500,000 per week. In a good week they could take $1 million. The highest income Kelly remembered was $2.3 millon.

Kelly spoke of a time when Church staff were forbidden to have children because there was insufficient room in the Flag Land Base nursery. Former Messengers have said that children were completely prohibited at Gilman Hot Springs as well. Abortions were common.[2]

Kelly complained about the CMO unit at Flag, the youngest of whom were ten-year-olds. He described them as a "small army": "most of the younger ones don't have positions of vast authority, but if one of them had told me what to do, I would have said, Yes, sir.' " When asked what happened if someone annoyed one of these child Messengers, Kelly said: "You'll find yourself in a blue tee shirt scrubbing a garage usually." In other words on the Rehabilitation Project Force, living in the garage at Flag.

Rose Pace was introduced to Scientology by her sister, Lori Taverna, when she was thirteen. She joined the Church, and her formal education ended. The Board of Education accepted representations made by the Scientologists that Pace needed counselling. At fourteen, Pace became an Auditor, and began a career which culminated in her working at the Flag Land Base, in Clearwater, as a NOTs Auditor. After sixteen years in Scientology she said of its curative claims: "I have never seen someone be cured of an illness."

David Ray was at the Flag Land Base cleaning the rooms of paying public: "Well, if your statistics are up, every two weeks you're supposed to have twenty-four hours off, called liberty. . . . I would keep asking them for time off because I was working, oh, anywhere from eighteen to twenty hours a day. . . . And they wouldn't give it to me."

Ray went on to express his profound resentment at the treatment he had received: "The thing that really kills me about this whole . . . operation is . . . by the questions they ask and the things they do, they open you up to your innermost personal self . . . you're extremely vulnerable. . . . They pick you up and they'll raise you so high you feel like you're on top of the world and, then, they'll drop you and they'll let you feel like a bottomless pit. . . . And those are the kinds of terror and searing emotions that go through a person's mind when they're there. . . . They want to leave; they want to help themselves. You get physically tired. Sometimes you don't even have time to take a shower. Ninety percent of the people that walk around there just— they stink."

Ray inevitably ended up on the Rehabilitation Project Force. His account of it is horrifying. The RPF lived on a diet of leftovers including wilted lettuce which was beginning to rot, and cheese with mold all over it. One day, they were given french fries, and while eating them Ray discovered that one of the potatoes was in fact a fried palmetto bug. From that point on, he used his weekly pay of $9.60 to buy cookies from a health food store. It was all he could afford.

The Hartwells talked about their bizarre experiences making movies with Hubbard in the California desert. George Meister told of the tragic death of his daughter aboard the *Apollo* in 1971, and the disgraceful treatment he received thereafter.

Lavenda van Schaik, Flynn's first Scientology litigant, claimed that her Confessional folders had been "culled," and a list of her deepest secrets sent to the press. She was persistently harassed by the Guardian's Office, whose Op against her was codenamed "Shake and Bake." Before leaving Scientology, she had been to the Flag Land Base, and found a serious outbreak of hepatitis there, which was not reported to the authorities. An affidavit by one of the victims of this outbreak was read into the record.

Janie Peterson, who had belonged to the Guardian's Office, testified about her departure from Scientology: "I was terrified to even discuss the possibility of leaving Scientology with my own husband. I was afraid that he would stay in Scientology. I was afraid that he would write me up to the Guardian's Office and that they would then come and take me away somewhere because I had so much information."

Scientology had driven such a wedge between Peterson and her husband that she did not realize that he was also contemplating leaving. Neither dared tell the other. After leaving, she received a series of phone calls in which the caller would hang up when the phone was answered. Then she found a note in her car saying simply, "Watch it." Then a note in her mailbox saying, "Die." In the middle of the night, she would hear a knock on her door, and open it to find no one there.

Scott Mayer was on Scientology staff for twelve years. He had held many posts in that time, from Quentin Hubbard's bodyguard, when Quentin was trying to escape or to kill himself, to being manager of the *Apollo* just prior to its abandonment. In his time Mayer had seen Orgs throughout the world.

Mayer left Scientology in 1976. Two years later, he was still a GO target, staying more or less in hiding. He eventually decided to find out just how serious the GO was. Mayer let it be known that he was staying at a certain address, and left his car parked outside. It was

Christmas Eve, 1978. The car was blown up. Although he could not substantiate anything about the attack, he decided the Guardian's Office meant business, and stayed in hiding. Mayer's resolve to act was strengthened, and he became a consultant to the IRS in their ongoing litigation against Scientology.

Mayer had worked on confidential operations for Scientology, among them an elaborate smuggling system which used a series of five fictitious companies to courier money out of America. Couriers were carefully trained, told exactly what to say if apprehended, and sent out with double-wrapped packages. The inner wrapper was labelled with the true destination. He also talked about blackmailing a potential defector into silence, using information from the person's Scientology Confessional auditing. He put a photocopy of an order to "cull" auditing folders into evidence.

Probably Mayer's most heartbreaking assignment was the maintenance of a ranch for Sea Org children in Mexico. They were called the "Cadet Org": "Children were routinely transported from Los Angeles to the Mexican base and berthed and housed there . . . so that their mothers and fathers could get on with their business within the Church."

It was cheaper to ship the kids to Mexico than to provide acceptable housing in L.A. The ranch was not a safe environment for children: "Bandits were coming in at night and they were stealing grain and they were stealing saddles and whatever wasn't tied down." Mayer was ordered to set up a rifle with an infrared sniper scope to deal with the marauding bandits. As it turned out the project was never fulfilled, because the woman running the ranch shot one of the bandits before Mayer arrived, and they did not return.

Bandits were not the only problem the children faced in Mexico. There were scorpions, snakes and poisonous spiders. The brush grew right up to the house, and neither money nor personnel were available to clear it away. Because the Sea Org is run on a shoestring budget, it took Mayer some time to resolve this intolerable situation. He did so not by appealing to his superior's compassion, but by pointing out what bad public relations a death would cause. He took a jar of scorpions with him to emphasize his point.

Scientologists believe that "Considerations" govern "Matter, Energy, Space and Time." Which is to say, they believe in mind over matter. "Clearing the Planet" is far more important than any individual's physical well-being. Self-sacrifice is a common trait of the True

Believer. Life in the Sea Org is a peculiar mixture of "making it go right" (to use Hubbard's phrase), and an often child-like belief in the miraculous power of Scientology. According to Mayer: "Staff members were always ill-fed, ill-clothed. . . . I had an abscess in my tooth and I was being audited for it. I'm ready to go to the dentist, and I was being audited for it. I spent about a week, week-and-a-half, doing . . . what they call touch assists—to get rid of the pain. . . . And, finally . . . I was just delirious and—well, there wasn't any money for medical is what it boiled down to. . . . I went to the dentist . . . he told me I'd just made it . . . if it had been another day or so, I wouldn't be here to talk to you."

Before journalist Paulette Cooper took the stand, a former Scientology agent who had stolen Cooper's medical records testified. He also talked about another agent placed in a cleaning company so he could steal files from a Boston attorney's office. He gave this picture of the B-1 cell he worked in:

> We used code names and our reports were written in code names. . . . The letters that were written in the smear campaigns—the typewriters were stolen and usually used just for a short time. . . . Everything was done with plastic gloves so that there wouldn't be any fingerprints.

He was a case officer for Scientology agents who had infiltrated the Attorney General's Office, the Department of Consumer Affairs and the Better Business Bureau. "Each week these people would file reports . . . it was very difficult for a public person in Boston to make a complaint about the Church and have it go anywhere. We had all the bases covered."

Paulette Cooper then testified about the effects of being on the receiving end of the Church's harrassive tactics. The Scientologists had just filed their *eighteenth* law suit against her:

> I am being sued now repeatedly by individual Scientologists, who, in some cases, I don't even know, suits for distributing literature at functions I didn't even attend. Part of the purpose in harassing people with law suits is to keep deposing them and preventing you from writing or making a living and making you show up at legal depositions. I've

been deposed for nineteen days total since this started, with four more coming up in a couple of weeks.

There has also been some other harassment in the past six months or so: continued calls to me, calls to my family. The Scientologists find out what the person's "buttons" [sensitive spots] are, as they put it, and the way to get to them. And they know that a way to get to me is to harass my parents . . .

They've put out libelous publications about me; they've sent letters saying that I was soon to be imprisoned . . . attempts have been made to put me in prison. They've sent false reports about me to the Justice Department, the District Attorney's Office, the IRS. As you know, government agencies have to investigate any complaints that they get. So, then, Scientology sends out press releases that I am under investigation by the Attorney General's Office, I am under investigation by the DA, and so on.

They have put detectives on me; they have put spies on me. A few months ago, they put an attempted spy on my mother to try to get information about me from her and to fix me up with the woman's son. . . . Somebody cancelled my plane to Florida about a month ago, and that is the third time that happened to me this year . . . I'd like to say that this was a very good year compared to the previous years.

Cooper went on to describe her one-woman battle against Scientology, which began in 1968. She commented wryly that she had been alone in this battle for five years, and that she was glad that more people were finally speaking out.

After her first article on Scientology, in 1968, Cooper received a flood of death threats and smear letters; her phone was bugged; lawsuits were filed against her; attempts were made to break into her apartment; and she was framed for a bomb threat.

At one point Cooper moved, and her cousin Joy, of rather similar appearance, took over her old apartment. Soon afterwards, before the cousin had even changed the name plate on the door, someone called with flowers:

When Joy opened the door to get these flowers, he unwrapped the gun . . . he took the gun and he put it at Joy's temple and he cocked the gun, and we don't know whether it misfired, whether it was a scare technique . . . somehow the gun did not go off . . . he started choking her, and she was able to break away and she started to scream. And the person ran away.

Many of the 300 tenants in the new apartment building were sent copies of a smear letter, saying that Paulette Cooper had venereal disease and sexually molested children.

To answer the bomb threat charges brought falsely by Scientology, Cooper had to find a $5,000 advance to retain an attorney. She appeared before the grand jury, and truthfully denied the allegations throughout. She was indicted not only for making the threats, but also for perjury! She faced the possibility of a fifteen-year jail sentence.

Her career as a free-lance journalist was in jeopardy: "What editor is ever going to give an assignment to someone who's been indicted or convicted for sending bomb threats to someone they've opposed? I was very concerned about the indictment and the trial coming out in the newspapers. The public does not know the difference between indict and convict . . . where there's smoke there's fire."

Cooper developed insomnia, sleeping for only two to four hours a night, and wandered around in a daze of exhaustion. The lawyers' bills for the preparation of her case came to $19,000. She could not write. She lost her appetite and stopped eating properly. The Scientologists were merciless; having stolen her medical records, they knew very well that she was recovering from surgery when they began their attack. Her boyfriend of five years left her. The Scientologists had pressed her to the edge of extinction.

At this point, she met Jerry Levin, who took pity on her terrible situation. She helped Levin to find an apartment in her building. He did everything he could to help, even doing some of her shopping. At last she had a friend and confidant who would listen to everything. And having listened, she later discovered, Levin would file his report with the Guardian's Office. After the GO trial in 1979, Levin's reports were made public. Jerry Levin was also known as Don Alverzo, one of the Washington burglars. Paulette Cooper was Fair Game; in Hubbard's words she could be "tricked, sued or lied to or destroyed."[3]

It took over two years for the bomb threat charges against Cooper to be dropped. She was completely exonerated after the FBI found the GO Orders for the Ops against her. By that time her book, *The Scandal of Scientology*, had long been out of print. The Guardian's Office had even imported small quantities into foreign countries, so they could obtain injunctions against its distribution. Copies were stolen from libraries and bought up from used book shops, then destroyed.

Cooper's final point to the Clearwater Commission was the insistence that Scientology incessantly claims to have reformed itself, to have expelled the bad elements. She had heard such claims in 1968. We are still hearing them now. They have never been true. The Scientologists expel another scapegoat ("put a head on a pike" in Hubbard's terms), make a great show that the culprit has been removed, and then replace him with someone who will repeat the offending behavior.

Dr. John Clark, a noted psychiatrist who has been a persistent observer and critic of cults, also took the stand and gave his opinion of the intrusive nature of Scientology techniques. He explained the incredible pressure brought to bear upon him by the Scientologists in their attempt to discredit him. He spoke at some length about the conversion experience: the sudden change of personality which members of Cults often undergo.

Flynn's last witness was former Mission Holder Brown McKee, who a few months earlier had been a major voice at the Flag Mission Holders' conference. After twenty-four years of membership, having trained to a high level as an Auditor, and having done the vaunted OT levels, Brown McKee took a surprisingly short time to put Scientology in perspective:

> After this meeting in December [1981], we went back to Connecticut with the firm conviction that there was no interest within this Church for reform. The dirty tricks, the Guardian's Office operations, and that type of thing, which they had told us were all a matter of the past, we found out were not a matter of the past. . . . I've been a minister of the Church for some sixteen years, and I really took it seriously. I've married people, I've buried them, and to me it was a duty and an honor. And to find out what my Church had been doing—it's a little hard on me.

McKee described his most traumatic experience while in Scientology. His wife, Julie, who was a highly trained Auditor, had started to feel tired:

> You must realize both of us were totally persuaded that the source of all illness was mental, except for, say, a broken leg, and the way of curing it is with auditing . . .
>
> So, during the summer, Julie lost more and more of her energy and had some swelling and some small chest pains . . . and began to lose

her voice. So, I thought, "Well, Flag has the best Auditors in the world and should be able to help her out." So, I sent her down here to Clearwater in, I guess it was, October of 1978. We never even really thought about going to see a doctor . . . the Scientologist doesn't think about that.

Well, they sent her back a week later sicker and . . . she couldn't even whisper any more. She'd write notes. So, I tapped her on the back, because she was complaining about her chest, and on one side I could hear . . . the hollow sound that you hear when you tap, and the other side, it wasn't hollow. And so, I knew that there wasn't any air on that side.

So, we went to see a doctor, and he had her in the hospital very quickly. She was there two days when we were given the report. And what it was was adenocarcinoma, which was a cancer of the lymph glands of the lungs, and her right lung had totally collapsed . . . this cancer had totally infiltrated her throat and paralyzed her vocal cords. And it had progressed to the point where it was totally hopeless. I mean, they didn't even suggest chemotherapy. And they sent her home, and I cared for her for ten days. And she died in my arms.

Hubbard mocks medical doctors, and most Scientologists believe that all physical maladies have a mental or spiritual cause, and can be relieved through auditing. OTs believe that by ridding themselves of Body Thetans they will also rid themselves of disease. They avoid seeking proper medical advice, which means they are often too late. Hubbard made specific claims that his techniques had cured both cancer and leukemia.[4]

On May 10, 1982, the Scientologists were scheduled to start presenting witnesses to rebut the earlier testimony to the Clearwater City Commission. Instead their lawyer questioned the legality of the proceedings, and, quite typically, tried to impugn Flynn's character. He criticized the dramatic way in which witnesses had given evidence, as if people whose lives had been ruined should retain their composure at all costs. He complained that he had not been allowed to cross-examine witnesses, though he failed to note that the questions had been asked by the Commission itself, and not by Michael Flynn.

It was an empty show. The Scientologists were too late. The evidence of their appalling past had been broadcast on local TV. No argument regarding legal technicalities would erase from the viewers' minds the heartrending accounts given by the witnesses.

Even so, the Commission was not established to pronounce judgment, simply to investigate and make recommendations for possible future action. Despite the blaze of publicity in Florida, Scientology's young rulers were faced with other, more urgent problems.

CHAPTER FIVE

The Religious Technology Center and the International Finance Police

As the Organization rapidly expands so will it be a growing temptation for anti-survival elements to gain entry and infiltrate, and attempts to plant will be made.—L. RON HUBBARD, Policy Letter "Security Risks & Infiltration," October 30, 1962

The organizational restructuring of Scientology continued apace through 1982. On January 1, the Religious Technology Center (RTC) was incorporated. RTC took over the trademarks of Dianetics and Scientology. David Mayo's signature is on the incorporation papers, but he claims that the terms were altered after he signed. David Miscavige was another of the seven signatories. Through the control of the trademarks RTC could control Scientology, withdrawing the right of any intransigent group to use such words as "Scientology" or "OT" in advertising, and suing if the group continued to use them. There were hundreds of registered trademarks, including the word "Happiness," the phrase "The friendliest place in the whole world," and tens of Dianetic and Scientology symbols. The new rulers were seeking to use laws relating to business to effect a total monopoly for their supposed religion.

International Church management had been taken from the Flag Bureau by the Commodore's Messengers Organization in 1979. The Guardian's Office had been defeated and absorbed by the CMO without bloodshed in 1981. Author Services Incorporated was waiting in the wings to license Hubbard's copyrights to Bridge Publications and New Era Publications, which had separated from the Church, at least on paper. The Church of Scientology International had come into being to assume the management of the Orgs. By 1982 Scientology in the U.K. was already registered as the Religious Education College Incorporated, with its headquarters in Australia. Continental offices each had their own incorporation. It was a hasty attempt to divide the sinking ship of the Church of Scientology of California into watertight compartments.

The CMO, acting on Hubbard's instructions, attacked the mutinous Mission Holders. Those readmitted during the 1981 conferences were once again declared Suppressive, and others were added to the list. Several previously untouched Mission Holders were also declared Suppressive, Brown McKee among them. McKee had broken one of the great taboos by making his complaints against Scientology public, speaking to the press and to the Clearwater Commissioners.

Hubbard was in the habit of issuing a "Ron's Journal" to the faithful at New Year and on his birthday. On March 13, 1982, Scientologists who were attending birthday parties at Orgs and Missions the world over heard Ron's Journal 34. It was called "The Future of Scientology," and concentrated on supposed religious persecution:

> Time and again since 1950, the vested interests which pretend to run the world (for their own appetites and profit) have mounted full-scale attacks. With a running dog press and slavish government agencies the forces of evil have launched their lies and sought, by whatever twisted means, to check and destroy Scientology. What is being decided in this arena is whether mankind has a chance to go free or be smashed and tortured as an abject subject of the power elite.

Hubbard claimed that attacks upon Scientology were doomed to fail because its opponents are "mad monkeys." Hubbard gave Scientologists a new maxim: "If the papers say it, it isn't true." The issue also hinted at some current catastrophe, saying "The last enemy attack is winding down.'' It was Hubbard's way of expressing approval for the small group of new rulers.

Having taken over the Guardian's Office, and consigned ''mutinous'' Mission Holders to the outer darkness, the CMO began an internal purge. Long-term Messengers were ''off-loaded.'' So savage was the purge that CMO Int's own staff dwindled to less than twenty.

Author Services Incorporated is ostensibly a non-Church organization set up to manage Hubbard's affairs as a writer. It was activated in the spring of 1982. *Battlefield Earth* had been published by this time, and Hubbard had written numerous film scripts intended for Hollywood movies, including the OT3 story, *Revolt in the Stars*. ASI also collected the author's royalties from the books produced by the two Scientology Publications organizations.

David Miscavige resigned from the Sea Organization to become Chairman of the Board at Author Services Incorporated. The directors of a large share of Hubbard's ballooning personal fortune could not be seen to be members of the very organization which would continue to enlarge that fortune. However, Miscavige maintained his tight control of the Church. ASI was staffed solely with top Sea Org staff who had been allowed to resign their billion-year contracts to join. Only those at Gilman knew that ASI was actually the controlling group. This superiority was demonstrated when ASI staff arrived and started issuing orders even to the Watchdog Committee.

Five of the seven incorporators of the non-profit Religious Technology Center became ASI staff. ASI is a for-profit corporation, which derives most of its income from the Scientology organizations controlled by the RTC.

In April 1982, David Mayo received a long dispatch from Hubbard, copies of which were circulated to CMO executives. Stating that he anticipated his own demise within the next five years, Hubbard gave the ''Tech hats'' to Mayo for twenty to twenty-five years. This would give Hubbard time to ''find a new body,'' grow up and resume his Scientological responsibilities. Giving Mayo the ''Tech hats'' meant that Mayo would decide what was ''Standard'' Scientology, and what was ''non-Standard'' or ''squirrel'' Scientology. Mayo would be the final arbiter of Hubbard's ''Technology'' of the human mind and spirit. This appeared to be a position of tremendous power, because Mayo could not be removed. Others could ostensibly control the assets of Scientology, but Mayo could adjudge people ''out-Tech,'' and have them cast out of the Church itself. On Hubbard's orders, Mayo set about creating yet another corporation for his Office of the Senior Case Supervisor International. His twenty to twenty-five year posting was shorter even than Executive Director Bill Franks' posting "for life." Mayo had only a few months left.

In June, yet another Commanding Officer of the CMO fell. John Nelson was replaced by Miscavige's nineteen-year-old protégé, Marc Yaeger. Yaeger looks old for his years, in part because he is prematurely balding. While still a teenager he became the senior officer in the management structure of Scientology, at least in name.

Yaeger had risen far from his start as video-machine operator on the Tech films. "Video-machine operator" is a rather grandiose title for someone who pushes the button to start and stop the recorder. Yaeger joined the Sea Org when he was fifteen, so has minimal formal education. The same holds for most CMO staff. Indeed, most of the original Messengers were even younger when they were taken away from their schooling.

Ex-CO CMO John Nelson was assigned to physical labor. Rumor had it that Miscavige's All Clear Unit would quash the legal threats against Hubbard by the end of 1982, so preparations were made at Gilman Hot Springs for Hubbard's return. The Founder's love of the sea is well attested, so to welcome him the CMO decided to construct a replica of the top and interior of a full-scale, three-masted clipper ship, some fifty miles inland. The materials for the ship cost about half a million dollars, but Sea Org labor was cheap at less than $20 a week for a 100-hour week. Miscavige was ostensibly in control of Hubbard's royalties, Hubbard's Church, the Guardian's Office, and, until the Commodore's triumphant return, was the master of a landlocked clipper ship, the *Star of California.*

John Nelson has described his cloak and dagger meetings with Pat Broeker, who delivered orders from Hubbard to Gilman. These orders came in the form of tapes from Hubbard, which would be transcribed as "Advices." This was designed to perpetuate the fiction that Hubbard was not the head of the Church. In theory, the Church could take or leave his "Advices." In practice, these Hubbard *orders* were carried out to the letter.

In June 1982, Wendell Reynolds became the first International Finance Dictator, and was sent to Florida, where he recruited staff for the International Finance Police. The titles reflect the mood of the time.

A peculiar Hubbard Bulletin called "Pain and Sex" was released in August. In the Bulletin the seventy-one-year-old Commodore released his newest discovery: "Pain and sex were the INVENTED tools of degradation." (Emphasis in original.)[1]

Hubbard alleged that psychiatrist, "who have been on the [time] track a long time and are the sole cause of decline in this universe" had invented sex as a means of entrapment eons ago. As a result of Hubbard's diatribe, some Scientologists stopped having sexual intercourse with their spouses.

At the end of August, David Mayo and his entire staff were removed from their positions, and put under guard at Gilman. The next month, Franks' successor as Executive Director International, Kerry Gleeson, was removed, and replaced by the head of Scientology's operations in continental Europe, Guillaume Lesevre. In October several other well known, long-term Sea Org members were rounded up and taken to Gilman Hot Springs. One of these, Jay Hurwitz, described the experience in some detail:

> The first day I arrived at INT [International HQ, Gilman] I had a Nazi style "Interrogation" sec check which was done by the highest authorities of Scientology. There were four interrogators present in the room firing questions at me while I was on a meter.
>
> They were: David Miscavige, one of the three highest execs running Scientology today; Steve Marlowe, Executive Director of RTC; Marc Yaeger, CO CMO INT; Vicky Aznaran, Deputy Inspector General.
>
> Their first question to me was "Who is paying you?" . . . I was then subjected to enormous duress with statements like "we will stay here all night until you tell us who is running you" (in other words I was a plant, an enemy agent). Miscavige said he would declare me [Suppressive] on the spot if I didn't tell him who my operations man was. . . .
>
> For the first five days I was at INT I was kept locked up under guard with three other people (females) . . . for the first two days, we were kept in an office. . . . For the next three days, we were kept confined in a toilet, under guard. . . . We used the same toilet facilities in the presence of one another.[2]

Hurwitz accused Miscavige of physically assaulting three people during the course of his investigation. A Committee of Evidence was convened and lasted for several weeks. Hurwitz was one of those who left before the Findings and Recommendations of that "Comm Ev" were published in January 1983.

While so many former top executives of Scientology were confined at Gilman Hot Springs, the new management took its final strike at the power of the Mission Holders.

Howard "Homer" Schomer, who was the Treasury Secretary of Author Services Incorporated, has testified that money was being channeled frantically into Hubbard's bank accounts during 1982. Schomer was in a position to know since he made the transfers. He has said that during his six months at ASI, about $34 million was paid into Hubbard's accounts. Schomer says this money came mostly from the Church, rather than from book royalties. Yet again Scientology was billed retroactively by Hubbard. Orgs were charged for their past *use* of taped lectures. They were charged for their past *use* of Hubbard courses. Schomer says there was a target figure of $85 million by the end of 1982. If this figure was achieved, there would be fat bonuses for ASI staff. Probably acting on Hubbard's orders, the new management called the Mission Holders to a conference at the San Francisco Hilton Hotel on October 17, 1982. At this fateful meeting, any degree of independence the Mission Holders retained was torn away from them. The meeting was also part of the desperate attempt to raise the targeted $85 million.

PART SEVEN

THE INDEPENDENTS
1982–1984

CHAPTER ONE

The Mission Holders' Conference

From the early 1950s, Hubbard had been trying out various franchise schemes. In return for a substantial licensing fee, the purchase of a large quantity of books, E-meters and Hubbard tapes, and the payment of ten percent of their gross income, new Scientology Centers would be franchised. From 1953, when the Philadelphia Center was taken over, successful Centers were periodically absorbed as assets by Hubbard.

In the 1960s, Hubbard created a new scheme. The same rules applied, including the tithe, and in return the Franchises (also called Centers or Missions) had the right to give introductory courses and auditing, eventually constituting about the first third of Hubbard's "Bridge." They would have to send their graduates on to the Orgs for higher level services. They were to adhere to the Policies and the Technology of Scientology, but were not as tightly controlled as the Orgs. Having paid their dues, the Mission Holders could keep the remaining profits. Some of them created very lucrative businesses.

During 1982, Scientology Missions International, which oversaw the activities of Missions, issued new contracts to Mission Holders. In the words of Mission Holder Bent Corydon, "we were quickly confronted with new articles to sign, which would essentially take away all our legal autonomy as a separate corporation. All our corporate

293

books were removed. . . . About a month after most of us had signed these articles we were called to the Mission Holders' Conference."[1]

The CMO, using their new corporate guises, were going to put the mutineers in their place. The Guardian's Office had quietly intimidated individuals in private, but the CMO were going to confront a whole group of Scientologists in a noisy showdown. Putting aside the mask of friendliness, they would show their true faces. The iron fist was on public display with no pretense at a kid glove. The Mission Holders were summoned to the San Francisco Hilton on October 17, 1982.

Before the meeting began, Mission Holder Gary Smith, who was sitting at the back with his wife and four-year-old daughter, was ordered to move to the unoccupied front row. He refused and was declared Suppressive on the spot.

During 1981, Kingsley Wimbush and his Missions had become the talk of the Scientology world. The major Mission, Steven's Creek Boulevard, in San Jose, was making so much money Wimbush did not know what to do with it. It could take in over $100,000 in a week, outperforming the combined incomes of most of the other eighty or so Missions. Before the 1982 Conference, Wimbush had been declared Suppressive, allegedly for being the author of a "squirrel" counselling procedure, "de-dinging." This "squirrel" procedure had in fact been enthusiastically distributed around the world by the Church itself. Wimbush had been doing everything within his power to appease the new rulers and regain his former status. So, on the morning of October 17, when a Sea Org member rolled up on his doorstep and told him he had a few minutes to ready himself for the journey to San Francisco, he had jumped at the chance. He thought he would be exonerated at last. He had no idea that he was being taken to San Francisco just to be part of a degrading spectacle.[2]

The aisles were lined with unsmiling Sea Org Ethics Officers watching the audience closely, and carrying clipboards to take note of the least sign of dissent. The Master of Ceremonies was twenty-two-year-old David Miscavige, a Sea Org "Commander," and, unbeknownst to the attendees, Chairman of the Board of Author Services Incorporated. At the beginning of the harangue, the Mission Holders were told that the trademarks were now in the hands of the Religious Technology Center (RTC). Larry Heller, who was introduced as the Church's Attorney, had this to say:

RTC has a right to send a mission directly to the individual Mission Holders to determine whether the trademarks are being properly used by you. This mission may review your books, your records, and interview your personnel. . . .

RTC . . . has the right to immediately suspend any utilization by the individual Missions of those trademarks. The word "immediate" is the key word here. There need not be a hearing in order for there to be a suspension. RTC will order that you no longer use the trademarks and you must stop or be subject to civil penalties and ultimately criminal prosecution.

Attorney Heller was the only speaker not dripping with braid and campaign ribbons. The new leaders had strutted onto the podium, puffed up with the self-importance of their paramilitary titles, and looking like the new rulers of a tin-pot dictatorship. But the comic elements were lost in all the shouting. Of the new Mission articles "Warrant Officer" Lyman Spurlock, the Corporate Affairs Director of the Church of Scientology, said the following:

From now on all Missions will be corporations. There's [sic] very good reasons for this. A lot of you may know that you just recently received new corporate papers, let's see some nods, okay. These new corporate papers are designed to make the whole structure impregnable, especially as regards to the IRS [Internal Revenue Service]. . . . RTC is a very formidable group of Sea Org members who have the toughness to see that the Tech is standardly applied.

"Commander" David Miscavige, the Master of Ceremonies, gave a fervent, if bizarre, guarantee: "The [new] corporate structure assures Scientology being around for eternity."

"Commander" Steve Marlowe, the Inspector General of the Religious Technology Center, was next in line to browbeat the Mission Holders: "We are a religion and this religion is what is going to save mankind. Get the idea? Thirty years from now, someone squirrels Scientology and starts calling it Scientology because there's a lot of money to be made. . . . Suddenly you have factions, schisms, all kinds of very horrible things—they will never occur to this Church, *never* . . . you have a new breed of management in the Church. They're tough, they're ruthless. . . . They don't get muscled around by the IRS or by crazy loonies . . . you're playing with the winning team.'' (''The IRS'' was edited from the CMO's published transcript of the meeting.)

Ironically, the Conference itself precipitated a schism. The Inspector General next accused the Mission Holders of ''ripping-off'' public from the Orgs, the major theme of the meeting:

> This management means business. There are ecclesiastical concerns, there are secular concerns. Violations will be prosecuted *without a doubt* [emphasis in transcript]. And we're just not here to threaten you or whatever. This is your salvation too. You just take a look at the viewpoint that someone would have behind bars looking out at the rest of Scientology. Not too sweet. We're not going to get stepped on. . . . The Inspector General Network exists within RTC. They have tremendous information lines. They have resources that enable them to get down to the very lowest echelon of the field. And quite frankly, things will get found out about.

''Commander'' Norman Starkey, one of only two veteran Sea Org members to be accepted into the CMO, then took his place at the rostrum and announced that the legal battles of both the Commodore and the Church were almost over. This was far from the truth. Starkey went on to berate the Scientology Church's most effective critic, attorney Michael Flynn, at great length. Starkey asserted that former Mission Holder Brown McKee, who had spoken at the Clearwater Hearings, was in Flynn's hire. Of McKee, he said:

> He will never, ever, ever and I promise you, for any life time, ever again get on any E-meter [changed to ''auditing'' in transcript] or ever have a chance to get out of his trap. And those who are on OT3 knows [sic] what that means! That means dying and dying and dying and dying again. Forever, for eternity.

If he had bothered to check, Starkey would have found that McKee had completed his OT3 years before. However, it gives a glimpse of the weight Scientologists attach to their saviour Hubbard's ''Tech.''

''Captain'' Guillaume Lesevre had flown over from Europe to become the new Executive Director International only days before the Conference. He complained that although Missions were sending their public to the relatively plush Flag Land Base, in Clearwater, they were not sending them into their local Orgs. He found the practice unreasonable. Simply because an Org was ''dirty'' was not reason enough not to send well-heeled new public to it. Lesevre accused those who had written books about Scientology, on sale throughout the Church, of "trying to make money out of the [sic] L. Ron Hubbard's technology,' although most of these books were copyrighted in Hubbard's name, and published by his own Scientology Publications Organizations.

Then Lesevre issued a quota to each Mission. The U.S. Missions were to send a total of 348 people to Orgs during the following *week*. There was a real threat that if they failed to meet these quotas, which were very high, something unpleasant would happen to them. Furthermore, the quotas would be increased each week.

But all of this was just a warm up. The International Finance Dictator took the stage, and came right to the heart of the matter. He did not mince words:

> All right now, collectively you guys are in some weird lower [Ethics] condition. By association, if no other reason, you have allowed the Missions to go squirrel and I mean squirrel . . . right now you guys are CI [Counter Intention] on my lines, maybe one exception in this room, but I doubt it, because you guys are sitting on public, you're ripping off the Orgs, you're doing all manner of crazy things. . . .
>
> Now some of the guys you see standing around here are International Finance Police and their job is to go out and find this stuff [crimes against the Church] and if you guys are guilty of it, you've just had it. . . .
>
> The old routine here was you got Scientology justice procedures applied to you when you did something wrong. Well you guys are a separate corporation from the Church and when you rip-off or steal from the Org, or bribe people it's a corporate crime and you can be real sure that you're going to all end up in the slammer.

The International Finance Dictator then told the Mission Holders they were going to pay $75 a head for the privilege of having been shouted at, and ordered them to donate five percent of their net income to a campaign to promote *Dianetics: The Modern Science of Mental Health*. He added: "If I hear one person in this room who is not coughing up five percent minimum you've got an investigation coming your way because you've got other crimes."

The Dictator then explained how his International Finance Police were going to raise money. He did not tell the Mission Holders why vast sums were needed, and perhaps he did not know.

Do you have any idea about the penalties for taking public off the Orgs' lines—it's $10,000 a head per policy. If you rip-off a staff member or have a staff member working in your Mission at the same time he's employed by an Org you pay for the entirety of his training/processing [counselling] plus a $2,000 fine . . .

If we will pull this thing together and get these nuts off the line and actually do Dianetics and Scientology, you can go anyplace you want to go. Right now there is so much criminality floating through this mission network I don't want to hear about it. If you come clean we'll work out some reparations for all the rip-offs that you've done in the past and straighten the record. If you don't want to come clean, forget it. If you've done stuff in the past and you come clean now we'll give you the benefit of the doubt. . . . You don't come clean tonight and I find out something after this, man, you've had it.

The Mission Holders were ordered to write up their "overts" (transgressions), not an unusual procedure for staff in Scientology Orgs. They were then subjected to the largest multiple Security Check ever witnessed in Scientology. The interrogators sat behind their E-meters at a row of tables, and the Mission Holders sat in rows facing them, confessing their "crimes."

Although the International Finance Dictator gave assurances that if they "came clean" it would be easier for them, it is hard to see how it could have been made more difficult. After the Sec-Check, Dictator Reynolds took the platform again, and gave examples of the "reparations" the Church demanded. The best established Mission chain, the Church of Scientology Mission of Davis, or COSMOD, was to pay "millions of dollars." Wimbush's former Mission had been assessed for a quarter of a million dollars for the last few months alone. The Missions in these two chains were to be visited first, followed by every other Scientology Mission in the world.

Missions were allowed to train people only to a certain level. Beyond that level, trainee Auditors would have to go to a Church Org. It was alleged that Missions had taken to "delivering" some of these prohibited courses, thus invading the exclusive domain of the Orgs.

Missions were only allowed to audit people on the levels below Clear. Then they had to go to an Org, and on to one of the four Advanced Orgs. The Missions were not allowed to audit Clears. It was alleged that they had. And they were to be fined $10,000 for each and every Clear they had audited.

It was a peculiar situation. As Commander Lesevre observed, the Church Orgs were often rather scruffy. Their operating funds were low, and their staff pay very poor, usually well below the poverty level, as members of religious organizations are not protected by minimum wage laws. Of course, the lion's share of the income was going to Hubbard. The Mission Holders were willing to invest profits back into their Missions, and were not subject to a constant round of Sea Org missionaires, so their operation was far more efficient. The Missions were almost invariably more attractive environments, and more of their income went to the staff. Consequently, the Missions attracted the best qualified Scientologists as staff. It was not unusual to find Class 8 Auditors in the Missions. They had received the equivalent of two years' full-time training in Scientology counselling procedures, everything up to and including OT3. Orgs would often struggle along with a single Class 4 Auditor, who had received only a few months' training. The Missions were generally far more financially successful than the Church's Orgs, but they were restricted in the services they could deliver, because the Sea Org controlled the levels beyond Clear.

Finance Dictator Reynolds, having informed the Mission Holders of the fines, told them that the International Finance Police would be sending out "verification missions," at a cost of $15,000 per day, payable by the Mission Holder at the start of each new day.

It is difficult to convey the force with which these tirades were delivered. A tape does exist, and, gloating over their achievement, the young rulers even published a carefully censored and reworded transcript. They wanted Scientologists to make no mistake about how "tough and ruthless," their new masters were. This transcript was crucial in my decision to leave the Church. Further, I used it very successfully to persuade others to leave.

CHAPTER TWO

The Scientology War

Over the years the Mission Holders had learned to be wary of the Sea Org. They had watched the pageant of faces alternately screaming and smiling; seen the little tyrants rise and fall. In the past, Hubbard had stepped in and put a few "heads on pikes." The Mission Holders also knew that expulsion from the Church of Scientology would effectively ruin their Missions, so all they could do was knuckle under and wait. Lambasted by the leaders of the new order, surrounded by scowling members of the International Finance Police, the Mission Holders tried to stay cool. This time, however, waiting it out would not work. The situation did not blow over, and the usual horrified Hubbard edict denying all knowledge did not appear either.

Martin Samuels was a legend among Scientologists. He ran a chain of five Missions. The Church's magazine *Center*, devoted to the Mission network, was always heavy with praise for Samuels. A 1975 issue says that in a single year *3,000* new people started the Communication Course in Samuels' Missions. His Missions usually came out at the top in the quarterly Mission statistics, even taken individually. In *Center* 23, Martin Samuels was "Particularly COMMENDED" for his "brilliant application." Out of the fifty listed, his Sacramento, Portland and Davis Missions were the top three in the *Center* "Award of Merit" contest for that quarter.

In early 1970s, Samuels started the Delphian Project. It began as a center for research into Alternative Energy, but a school, the Delphian Foundation, was established for the children of Project staff. The school used Hubbard's "Study Technology." It soon generated interest from other Scientologists, so the school became Delphi's main activity. By the time of the Mission Holders' Conference Samuels had twelve schools, with over 600 pupils.

Scientology Missions report various performance statistics to the Church every week. The Mission income figures are listed and distributed to Mission Holders to show which are most successful. For the first week of September 1982, just before the Conference, the total income of the eighty or so Missions throughout the world was $808,435. For the U.S. Missions it was $643,737, and Samuels' Missions made up $172,825 of that. Which is to say they represented over a quarter of the U.S. Missions income, and over a fifth of the worldwide income. Incidently, Kingsley Wimbush's major Mission made $154,101 that week. So between them Samuels and Wimbush accounted for more than half of the U.S. Missions income. Ten percent of this was paid straight to the Church.

But at the end of the Mission Holders' Conference Samuels spoke out. On top of their normal ten percent tithe to the Scientology Church, the Mission Holders had been ordered to pay five percent for a promotional campaign to Bridge Publications. Samuels explained that he could not pay the additional tithe. His Missions were non-profit, tax-exempt corporations, and Bridge had been separated from the Church and made into a for-profit corporation, and such donations would be illegal. Samuels was taken into a side room by eight members of the International Finance Police, and given a "Gang Sec-check." He was threatened with a "Suppressive declare" if he did not make "personal payments to L. Ron Hubbard." So he handed over $20,000 and a $10,000 wrist watch to a Finance Policeman.

Samuels' access to his Missions' bank accounts was frozen. His wife was warned that she would have to "disconnect" from him if he was declared Suppressive. He was ordered to Flag, in Florida, to undergo more Security Checks, for which he had to pay $300 an hour.

Within a month Martin Samuels had paid $40,000 to the Scientology Church. This still was not enough, and he was ordered to the International Finance Police Ethics Officer at Flag. At the meeting, Samuels was told he had been declared Suppressive, and shown the confession of a Scientology executive who had admitted to being a transvestite with homosexual tendencies. Samuels claims that he was ordered to *publicly* confess to "acts that were similarly degrading." Otherwise the Church would file both civil and criminal prosecutions against him that would keep him "tied up in court forever." He was also warned that he would be watched and the Church would "keep tabs on him forever."

Samuels refused to demean himself by signing a fictitious confession, even though his Missions were now in the hands of the Church, and he had surrendered control of his personal accounts. The Scientologists now launched their campaign in earnest. Samuels' wife, family, business associates and friends were told he had stolen funds from his Missions, and that he was "insane" and an enemy of the Church of Scientology.

The Suppressive declare was published, and Samuels' wife left him, taking the children with her. She "disconnected" and started divorce proceedings. His children were told he was a "criminal and would probably be going to jail in the near future." Scientologist business associates and friends were ordered to disconnect from him or be declared Suppressive themselves. Even Samuels' stockbroker, who was a Scientologist, was ordered to disconnect, and refused to take instructions to sell stock. As he had been declared, Samuels was told he must leave his sister's house, where he was staying, or she too would be declared Suppressive.

In a few weeks, Samuels had lost the business he had built up over thirteen years, with an annual turnover of millions of dollars. His seventeen year marriage was destroyed, and he was deprived of his possessions. Samuels felt like a college kid again, rolling up penniless on his parents' doorstep. He responded by filing a lawsuit against Hubbard in 1983, claiming damages of $72 million. A jury awarded $30 million, and the Scientologists appealed the decision. The case was finally settled in 1986 with an out of court payment of $500,000 to Samuels.

There were very few of the big Mission Holders left. Among them was Bent Corydon, who held the franchise for Riverside, in southern California. Soon after the Conference, in October 1982, the Finance Police arrived. They demanded, and were paid, $15,000 for their first day. They demanded, and were paid, $15,000 for their second day. At this point Corydon ran out of ready money.

Corydon wanted to stay in the Church. He had built the Mission up from nothing, lost it in the 1970s, and finally fought his way back, only to discover that the reserves of nearly a million dollars that he had built up were gone. He could not face losing the Riverside Mission again. In desperation he took his attorney's advice to put the valuable

Mission building into a trust before it was seized in lieu of some trumped up "fine."

Corydon's wife was a Class 8 Auditor. The retaliation to the "can't pay" claim was rapid. Mary Corydon's Auditor certificates were cancelled. Corydon wrote:

> Without Mary's certificates, we were no longer in a position to operate at all, according to laid-down policy. The Church would have to come to our "rescue." I soon got the call to come down to Los Angeles to the Scientology Missions International Ethics Officer. This could mean only one thing. They would propose that we be turned into an Organization. Orgs are under total domination of management, and they own no property. . . . This in other words would be the final and total takeover of our Mission.

Corydon had heard that both the Kansas City Org and the Omaha Mission had splintered from the Church. He talked to these "squirrels," and decided that to continue delivering Scientology he too would have to splinter. At the end of 1982 he did just that.

The International Finance Dictator fulfilled a part of his promise, and all of the wealthier Missions were "verified," handing over an undoubtedly enormous sum for the privilege. A year after the Mission Holders' Conference, the Scientology Missions International statistic sheet for the week ending September 29, 1983, shows a sad decline. From $808,435 worldwide in a week, in September 1982, down to $171,356; a seventy-nine percent reduction, and actually less than the earlier combined income of Samuels' five Missions.

After the Mission Holders' Conference another corporate instrument of the new management appeared: The International Hubbard Ecclesiastical League of Pastors (or "I HELP"). Rather than working for Orgs or Missions, some Scientologists simply give individual counselling. They are known as "Field Auditors." The more successful Field Auditors made very good money. In December 1982, I HELP called a meeting in Los Angeles. Several hundred field Auditors attended and were ordered to join this new body. Membership would cost $100 a year, and ten percent of their gross income. The Field Auditors would also have to fill in weekly reports. None of this was too worrying; however, to join they had to waive all previous agreements with the Church, and sign a contract binding them to the decisions of I HELP. Many shied away from signing. The tone of the meeting reflected that of the earlier Mission Holders' Conference, news of which had inevitably travelled to the Scientology "field." Of the hundreds who attended, perhaps a dozen signed contracts that night. Then the bullying began.[1]

For many years, Valerie Stansfield ran her own auditing practice. She had been in Scientology for twenty years, and as a Class 9 Auditor was very highly trained. In March 1983, she was telephoned by a Finance Policeman and given half an hour to come to his office. She politely refused, and after a harangue agreed to an appointment that evening. When she and her husband Manfred arrived, she was told that her nutritional counselling was "squirrel." Then the Finance Policeman read a list of accusations, and demanded that she hand over the counselling folders of all her clients immediately. Valerie reluctantly agreed to give the Finance Police the folders, but urged that they wait for a more opportune time to pick them up, as there were clients at her house.[2]

Then International Finance Police Ethics Officer Don Larson walked in and started berating Valerie. He screamed abuse at her, and ordered his underlings to remove Manfred Stansfield, who refused to leave. Larson accused them both of "squirreling," and told Manfred he was Suppressive. Manfred returned the insult, to which Larson replied "You're a fucking SP [Suppressive]. Get out."

Shocked by this aggressive treatment, the Stanfields wrote to their friends. The letter was one of the first public statements about the tactics of the new management; it was recopied and distributed to an increasingly bewildered Scientology field.

Outlandish fines were imposed on some of the new members of I HELP. One Field Auditor was fined for introducing two of his Preclears who subsequently did business together. This was somehow construed as a breach of ethics.[3]

In the 1970s, the "World Institute of Scientology Enterprises" (WISE) came into being to cash in on successful businessmen who were also Scientologists. Ostensibly it existed to offer consultancy services, provide the most up-to-date Hubbard Policy Letters on administration, and train the staff of Scientology businesses in the immense Hubbard Administrative Technology. Practically, WISE gave very little to its members for their tithes. Now the Scientology business community in Los Angeles was invaded by the Finance Dictator's henchmen, and fines were levied for alleged abuses of privilege. Intransigent businessmen were threatened with Suppressive declare. Those who depended upon other Scientologists for the bulk of their business had no choice but to pay up. At least one sizeable business had to send its entire staff to Flag, in Clearwater, to do the Keeping Scientology Working Course, at a cost of tens of thousands of dollars. Employees who complained were given Security Checks, at their own expense. The man who had created the business was ostracized for his "squirrel Tech."[4]

WISE also altered its contracts with businesses managed by public Scientologists, which now had to pay a $250 annual membership, in addition to a percentage of their income.

The Religious Technology Center, and its International Finance Police, had effectively wrecked the network which had provided Scientology's interface with the public at large. They had also started a massive schism, especially in California where most of these events took place. Whether Hubbard's $85 million Christmas present was delivered we do not know, but Miscavige and company did their damnedest.

The purge of the so-called Executive Strata of the Sea Org had continued. David Mayo and his staff had been removed in August 1982. By the time of the San Francisco Mission Holders' Conference in October, there were seventeen key executives at Gilman awaiting a Committee of Evidence. Among them were the former Executive Director International and his Deputy; the Commanding Officer Canada; the Commanding Officer of Scientology Missions International and his superior, the Church Management Executive over Missions; the Commanding Officer Eastern U.S.; four members of the International Management Organization; the Commanding Officer of the CMO film unit; the two senior Field Executives (whose boss, Hubbard's daughter Diana, had left shortly before); and former Chairman of the Watchdog Committee and Commanding Officer CMO International, John Nelson.[5]

Hubbard had organized Scientology in a series of compartments, and with the detention of these executives the CMO had removed all potential major opposition from each compartment of the Organization.

The detainees were moved to a place dubbed "Happy Valley," a remote camp inside an Indian reservation not far from Gilman. Although they were not prevented from leaving, the former Sea Org executives were watched by security guards. They were, however, told that if they left they would be declared Suppressive for all eternity, and never readmitted to the Scientology congregation. It was a dreadful threat to committed Scientologists who had devoted most of their adult lives to the Tech.

The group were subjected to a Committee of Evidence: a Scientology trial, where the Committee act as prosecutors, judges and jury rolled into one. They were charged with thirty-six offences, ranging from somehow employing Scientology to receive sexual favors to being in the pay of the enemies of Scientology. David Mayo was found guilty of "committing" a problem. The Findings and Recommendations of the Committee came to a total of over ninety pages. The major thread of the Findings was the purported plot to overthrow the CMO. It was asserted that Deputy Executive Director International Allen Buchanan, one of the defendants, had been "brainwashed" by former ED Int, Bill Franks. Franks had brought Buchanan to believe that he must protect the Church from senior management. There were very few specifics amongst the bombast.

Although the Findings would usually remain an internal document, there are translations of the Scientologese throughout. This suggests that it was composed in part for the benefit of attorneys, should litigation ensue.

The Committee recommended that earlier threats of perpetual excommunication be carried out. Most of the recommended sentences include the assertion that the defendant will never in any lifetime be allowed Scientology services. It also included a perpetual writ of disconnection, forbidding all Scientologists to assist or communicate with the defendants. It further recommended that the Church should look into the possibility of filing criminal charges against the defendants. The investigation was to take into account a list of charges including sabotage and industrial espionage.

The Inspector General of the Religious Technology Center approved the recommendations for seven of the defendants, one of whom was the only party to be exonerated (she had been seized by mistake); the other six had already left Happy Valley in disgust. The ten who remained were informed that the Committee's recommendations would not be carried out if the defendants recanted. Nonetheless, all of their Scientology certificates were cancelled. David Mayo and his wife Merrill were both Class 12s, the highest Auditor class, attained by only a handful of Scientologists. It would have taken at least four years of full-time training for them to regain this status.

Each of the defendants would have to publish a witnessed statement confessing their evil motives. The Inspector General ended his statement by speaking about the benevolence of his decisions.

The Happy Valley story was not over. During the summer of 1982, Hubbard had tested out a new idea with Mayo's help. Executives were becoming exhausted, so rather than shortening their eighteen-hour day, Hubbard had issued the Running Program. Executives were to run around a fixed point for about an hour a day, and take huge quantities of mineral supplements. For the Happy Valley detainees the time was extended. They were to run, in desert heat, for five hours a day, round and round a tree.

Perhaps because of his especially potent contaminating effect, Mayo was separated from the rest of the group, given a pole to run around (and even ordered to paint it red). The runners took the affair as lightly as possible. Only one guard was assigned to them, so Mayo and those at the tree would take turns to sit down, and the guard would have to trek between them to goad them back into action.[6]

The Running Program took its toll. Mayo, a slight man, lost twenty-five pounds. Whether through the program, or the general lack of medical care within the Sea Org, Mayo's teeth and gums also suffered badly. In February 1983, convinced that he could do nothing to change the attitude of management, he accepted his Suppressive Person declare and left.

CHAPTER THREE

Splintering

To in any way encroach upon the Church or to distract one from moving up the Bridge to Total Freedom is the ultimate crime.—Religious Technology Center Information Letter 1

The core group of Commodore's Messengers had completed their task. When they were first appointed to management at the end of 1979, with the creation of the Watchdog Committee, there were two power groups, linked only through Hubbard. The CMO had to take over both the Guardian's Office and the Sea Org without being allowed to show any evidence that they were following Hubbard's direction.

The Watchdog Committee had gradually asserted control over the everyday management of Scientology Churches. By May 1981, it was strong enough to successfully challenge Mary Sue Hubbard. The GO was in its control by August. Hubbard's Personal Office was absorbed in 1981, with the creation of the Product Development Office International. A purge of long-term Messengers also took place in 1981, with the removal in June of Diane Voegeding, then Commanding Officer of CMO. Her sister, Gale Irwin, replaced her, only to be ousted at the end of the year. After removing Executive Director International, Bill Franks, that December, John Nelson, the next Commanding Officer of the CMO, lasted six months. By the end of 1981, the Missions had been placed under the control of the new Scientology Missions International. A purge of Mission Holders began early in 1982 culminating in the San Francisco Mission Holders' Conference that October, where leading Mission Holder Dean Stokes was added to the growing list of excommunicants. Mayo and his staff had been removed in August. By the end of 1982, most of the Sea Org veterans who had held high positions had been declared Suppressive.

The whole restructuring had to be engineered without a single appearance by Hubbard. The CMO had to persuade the management organizations of the Church that they were acting with Hubbard's authority, but with no signed orders from him, nor even orders issued over his name. At the same time, a new management structure had been created through an elaborate series of supposedly separate corporations. Author Services Incorporated looked after Hubbard's finances, in reality causing millions to be transferred from the Church into his personal accounts. The Religious Technology Center controlled the use of the trademarks. The International Finance Police, part of the new Church of Scientology International, monitored income.

To add insult to injury, the CMO announced monthly price rises starting in January 1983, and distributed a newsletter with extracts from the San Francisco Mission Holders' Conference. Photographs of the uniformed and beribboned speakers glared out ferociously. Most Scientologists had conceived themselves part of a crusade to bring sanity to the world. The savage rhetoric, the aggressive attitude and the perplexing new corporate titles, especially the International Finance Police and their Dictator, did not fit easily into that concept of sanity.

The problems were not just with the faithful. In March 1983, there was a huge raid on Scientology premises in Toronto. The warrant ran to 158 pages, and described the earlier theft of files from an Ontario hospital, the Committee on Healing Arts, the *Toronto Sun* and the Ontario government.

A few days before the raid, on March 2, the Religious Technology Center began to publish Information Letters. The first Letter claimed that Hubbard "saw in this group [RTC] the willingness and ability to do whatever is necessary, no matter how unpleasant or unsocial it may seem." After quoting Hubbard liberally, the Information Letter continued, "The importance of the white taped road out for man can in no way be underrated. To in any way encroach upon the Church or to distract one from moving up the Bridge to Total Freedom is the ultimate crime." This first Information Letter ended with the rather confusing statement:

To be very blunt, if not for LRH, the Religious Technology Center and the Church of Scientology, one could never obtain Scientology Technology. There is no one else. Think about it.

They lay the very Bridge we all must travel upwards. There is no "second chance." Don't allow anyone to wreck the chance you do have. Travel up that Bridge with our best wishes. We will be happy to know you are doing so and you can be assured of the Standard Technology by which to do so. As with that, we all win—many times over.

The second RTC Information Letter contained an attack upon "squirrels":

You may have heard of some such fellows (now removed from the Church). They hoped to create considerable damage to the Church and internal discord so they could then "valiantly emerge" upon the scene to "save Scientology technology" (from the damage they themselves created). Intent upon achieving some sort of "notoriety," false status, and some fast bucks these squirrels denigrated Standard Tech and the Church and encouraged others to join them in the establishment of their own "way" against the long existing structure of the Church. Their plans never bore fruit however, and they were easily nixed.

It is longstanding Scientology Policy that any Suppressive Person declare order should detail the offenses of the alleged Suppressive. Although the CMO usually ignored an accused's supposed right to a Committee of Evidence prior to Suppressive declare, they did issue written orders. These made puzzling, and often bizarre, reading, as an order concerning a former senior Sea Org executive clearly shows. This hapless individual was accused of the whole gamut of criminality prior to his involvement in Scientology. According to the Scientology order, he had been a pimp, a drug dealer, a thief, a smuggler, an automobile thief, an arsonist, an embezzler, and a forger. He had also committed armed robbery, been a hired thug, helped to perform illegal abortions, seduced minors, and been involved in illegal gambling.[1]

In reality, the Scientologist who was the subject of the order had actually had his first auditing at the age of eight, working at Saint Hill before joining the Sea Org when he was eighteen. He has never been convicted of a crime, and spent no time in juvenile institutions for this remarkable display of criminality, all purportedly undertaken before his eighth birthday.

In January 1983, the Scientology Church published a list of 611 individuals who had been declared Suppressive.[2] The CMO had overplayed their "ruthless" efficiency. Too many people had been expelled in too short a period of time. It was inevitable that groups of these Suppressives would form an independent Scientology movement. The new snarling face of management, the price rises and Hubbard's conspicuous absence from public view created a climate in which members questioned the authority of the new Church management, and moved towards splinter groups. The sheer quantity of Suppressive Declares could only assist such a movement. Perhaps a few individuals had been attacking the Church from within, but hundreds of long-term and popular Church members, many of whom had worked with Hubbard for years? It was too much to believe. Many of the new Suppressives had good reputations among Scientologists, not readily destroyed by the vague Declare Orders.

In 1983, a loose independent Scientology network came into being. Letters describing the bizarre events within the Church were written anonymously, or under pen names. Sympathizers would redistribute them. Some Church members receiving such letters would either destroy them, or send them to the Ethics Officer at their local Org, often unread. It was a strange response, bearing in mind the oft-repeated Hubbard maxim "more communication, not less, is the answer." It seemed that many Scientologists had been so conditioned to accept the authority of Church publications that they chose to ignore even the most obvious abuses.

There were also tapes. In the summer of 1983, John and Jeanny Hansen visited Gilman Hot Springs, and were startled by its military atmosphere. The Hansens interviewed various key figures of the CMO takeover who had since been excommunicated. A Los Angeles Field Auditor, Jon Zegel, produced a series of tapes at six-month intervals, explaining the events behind the purge. He released his first tape in August 1983. His excellent sources, grasp of the situation, and persuasive delivery made the tapes important in convincing many Scientologists of the trouble within their Church. The tapes were distributed, copied and recopied almost to the point of inaudibility.

By design, there was very little to connect Hubbard with the new regime, as written communications were signed by the Watchdog Committee or the Religious Technology Center. The speeches had been made by Messengers largely unknown outside top management circles. The familiar faces were gone. Paradoxically, Scientologists' loyalty to Hubbard was a main force in the mass exodus from the Church. Many Scientologists resigned believing that Hubbard was either dead or a captive of the CMO. They were sure the Church had been infiltrated by hostile forces, and that the Tech was being used to intimidate, harass and possibly even brainwash members. Hundreds resigned, and, with great fervor, set about creating a new Scientology movement beyond the confines of the Church. It was to be a Scientology without "gang sec-checks," without enforced "disconnection" and without mass Suppressive Person declares. It would also be far more affordable.

The CMO was quick to respond to the threat. One of the first splinter groups, the Church of Scio-Logos in Omaha, Nebraska, was soon struggling against a suit brought by the RTC. The group in Kansas City had disappeared without trace. Bent Corydon had managed to keep his Center afloat, despite the defection of most of his staff back to the Church after his decision to splinter in November 1982. For a short while, Corydon was an apostle of the new movement, travelling from his Center in Riverside to Denmark and to England. Many members simply retreated from the Church and quietly set up counselling practices, without advertising. If there was to be a movement, it would have to find a focal point. By issuing a torrent of abuse against David Mayo, the Church created such a focal point.

David Mayo had been involved in Scientology since 1957. He had devoted his life to L. Ron Hubbard's Tech, working in the Auckland Org in New Zealand, and joining the Sea Org in January 1968, shortly after its inception. For over ten years, Mayo had held increasingly senior positions in the Church. When he left the Happy Valley Running Program, in February 1983, he was penniless, homeless, without a job, and ostracized by most of the people he had known and worked with. He wanted to forget Scientology for a while and recover his health. He joined forces with John Nelson, who had been the first to leave Happy Valley, and they started a tiling business. One of their customers was another of Hubbard's former Personal Staff, Harvey Haber. They inevitably discussed Scientology. Julie Gillespie, Mayo's former assistant, also participated in these long and painful discussions which led to the decision to form a splinter group. In July 1983, the Advanced Ability Center (AAC) of Santa Barbara came into being.

They worked out of Haber's house at first. In the Church, personal auditing from David Mayo would have cost at least $1,000 an hour. After all, he had been Hubbard's own Auditor. The AAC's first client

cut the grass in exchange for counselling. To promote their endeavor
the group mailed a letter in which Mayo explained his background in
Scientology. They had all been in the Sea Org, and claimed that
between them they could only muster the names and addresses of
twenty-five Scientologists who might be interested in counselling. To
their amazement, the letter was picked up and redistributed throughout
the world. They began to receive requests for counselling from as far
away as South Africa, Britain and Japan. Soon they had their own
center, thronged with Independent Scientologists either taking services
or demanding an explanation for the perplexing events in Scientology.

The Scientology Church responded swiftly: Ray Mithoff, Mayo's
replacement as Senior Case Supervisor International, wrote his seven-
teen-page attack "The Story of a Squirrel: David Mayo," which
quoted extensively from Hubbard dispatches, and was distributed to
the Church's full mailing list. It was this issue, the transcript of the San
Francisco Mission Holders' Conference, and a harangue from the Saint
Hill Ethics Officer which drove me out of the Church.

By now the reader is familiar with the term "squirrel." Inside the
Church, the term has almost demonic connotations. David Mayo had
become Scientology's Lucifer. To quote from "Story of a Squirrel":

> Betrayals like this are not new. Groups and organizations have had to
> contend with covert attacks such as this since ancient times. And over
> the past thirty-three years our group has weathered its share of those
> who sought to infiltrate and sabotage our activities, gaining positions
> within the Church through deception in order to halt the expansion of
> Scientology or disrupt its organizational structure.

Quoting from Hubbard, the Directive continued: "Mayo was the
boy they were relying on. He is a very clever fellow in that he could lie
to me consistently, convincingly report, this, that or the other thing.
. . . He directly lied, and was found to be squirreling the simplest
process there ever was." Hubbard went on to call Mayo "that Mr. SP
[Suppressive Person] Mayo, the darling of the psych[iatrist]s," a
"criminal" and "a dramatizing megalomaniac."

Without explanation, Mithoff accused Mayo of "sexually perverted
conduct." Mayo had worked with Hubbard for several years on the as
yet unreleased Operating Thetan levels above OT7. In a clumsy attempt
to discredit any use by Mayo of these materials, Mithoff said: "He
knows that there are many OT levels above Solo NOTs [OT7] which

have been fully researched, and knows that he does NOT have any of the data on these, nor has he ever seen them.''

There was also a simple message for Scientologists thinking of receiving counselling from Mayo: ''The actions of Mayo and the little group he has joined amount to *not only* an attempt to lure some people off the Bridge, but an attempt to deny that Bridge to them for eternity (because once they become involved with this squirrel practice they will thereafter be denied access to the upper levels) [sic] . . . those few who might fall for his PR should be forewarned.''

Foreseeing that Scientologists would question Hubbard's failure during their long association to notice that Mayo was Suppressive (after all, Hubbard had ''discovered'' the characteristics of the Suppressive, and if he couldn't spot one, who could?), Mithoff continued: ''It is a testimony to LRH's refinement of the tech and streamlining of the Bridge, with Scientologists becoming more aware and more perceptive in less time, that we're discovering bird dogs such as this faster now than ever before.''

''Story of a Squirrel'' did nothing to contain the move towards independence. Soon after the independent Santa Barbara Center opened, former Mission Holder Eddie Mace set up the first independent Australian Center, and others followed in Denmark and England. The English group's first public meeting was held in October 1983, with ''Captain'' Bill Robertson as the main speaker. Robertson was a former Sea Org Captain, who had been a Hubbard aide at various times since the 1960s. Captain Bill, as he was commonly known, had been declared Suppressive in 1982. Since that time he had been preaching his own elaboration of Hubbard's conspiracy theory.

Along with Hubbard, Robertson was sure that U.S. government agencies had infiltrated Scientology. Robertson further believed that Hubbard was dead, and that the government agencies, using Miscavige as their dupe, had succeeded in their takeover of the Church. Robertson also believed that Hubbard was the embodiment of one ''Elron Elray,'' and had returned to the Mothership of the Galactic Patrol, from whence he was sending telepathic directives to Robertson about the Markabian invasion of the Earth. At the meeting Robertson made no mention of these peculiar notions, and was successful in galvanizing British Independents into action.

Soon there were independent centers in Switzerland, New Zealand, Germany and Italy. In fact, they sprang up wherever there were Scientology Orgs. Along with this came an increasing availability of information about Hubbard and his organizations, as former Hubbard aides spoke out.

The first direct contact between Mayo's group and European Independents came at a meeting in Spain, in November 1983. Harvey Haber arrived late, having been detained and thoroughly searched by Spanish Customs. Someone had told them he was a narcotics dealer. After the meeting, Harvey flew on to England.

Haber had been a senior Hubbard aide, and had many startling experiences to relate. He and Donna, his wife, joined staff at the Flag Land Base, in Clearwater. Donna carelessly left a packet of tampons leaning against a small light in their bathroom. The packet was smouldering when someone discovered it. An executive decided that Donna was a "security risk." She was immediately assigned to the Rehabilitation Project Force. Harvey was told he would never be given a bed as long as he was in the Sea Org (for a billion years, presumably). That evening, as he prepared to sleep in the garage, he heard his wife's laughter drifting toward him. On investigation, he found that she was trampling down the contents of a huge garbage bin, looking for pieces of wood, having been ordered quite literally to make her own bed. At that moment Harvey grasped the surreal essence of the Sea Organization, and started laughing too.

CHAPTER FOUR

Stamp Out the Squirrels!

A squirrel is doing something entirely different. He doesn't understand any of the principles so he makes up a bunch of them to fulfill his ignorance and voices them off on a pc [Preclear] and gets no place.— L. RON HUBBARD, *Dianetics and Scientology Technical Dictionary*

The major obstacle to the continuance of Scientology outside the Church was that the Independents did not have all of the so-called "confidential" materials. They had the OT levels up to NOTs (which was listed as "new OT5"), but not NOTs itself. The NOTs issues are held by the Advanced Organizations of the Church of Scientology. That is to say there were copies at Saint Hill in England; at Los Angeles; at Clearwater, in Florida; and at Copenhagen, in Denmark.

Former Sea Org executive Robin Scott saw the increasing autocracy of the Church, and made grand plans to save Scientology. While most Independent Centers were run from front rooms on a shoestring, Scott purchased a baronial mansion near Aberdeen, Scotland, the breathtaking Candacraig House set in over twenty acres with two lakes. It came to be known as "the castle."

Scott attempted to acquire the NOTs materials through a Saint Hill staff member, but failed miserably. His attempt only served to alert Saint Hill, and tighten up their security. So Scott met with Morag Bellmaine and Ron Lawley of the East Grinstead Independent Center, and in December 1983, they mounted their own commando operation.

They did not know that David Mayo, who had written the original NOTs materials with Hubbard, was already producing a new version. They could have saved themselves, and many others, a great deal of trouble.

The trio travelled to Denmark. During the afternoon Scott went into the Advanced Org in Copenhagen to see if anyone was there who knew either of his partners. Scott pretended to be interested in paying a great deal of money for NOTs auditing, so was treated like royalty, and given a guided tour. He memorized the layout of the building, saw no one he knew, and returned to brief Ron and Morag.

Late that evening, dressed to the gills in Sea Org uniform (and with Bellmaine wearing the wrong cap-badge for her supposed rank), Lawley and Bellmaine walked into the Copenhagen Advanced Organization. They had carefully drilled the dismissive attitude of Sea Org missionaires, and demanded to see the Commanding Officer. He arrived, quivering. Lawley said they were "on mission" from the Religious Technology Center, and had come to investigate serious "out-tech." Here they had taken a chance as there might have been an RTC mission there already. To their surprise the CO readily admitted to "gross out-tech," but said he had sent his Senior Case Supervisor to Florida for retraining, and what more could he do? The bullying missionaires told him what more. He could show them a NOTs pack, because they were sure there was something wrong with the materials, so poor were Copenhagen's results.

The Commanding Officer did not hesitate, rounding up every available NOTs pack, and apologizing that two of his Auditors were still in session with theirs. Lawley and Bellmaine found themselves in a private room, with over thirty NOTs packs. They loaded two into a brief case, and their feet didn't touch the ground until they had left Denmark.

George Orwell's fated 1984 began for Scientologists with a taped message from Ron Hubbard, the first in a year. It was called "Today and Tomorrow: The Proof," and retailed to Church members at $22 per cassette. Hundreds were sent free of charge to Independents (paid for by "donations" from Church members, in fact). The tape was a departure from the usual Hubbard procedure. The talk was scripted, and there were interruptions throughout, where Hubbard was asked questions, given answers, even corrected on some slight underestimation of a statistic, or assured of the enthusiasm generated by his recent bland issues. The statistics were very good, taken at face value, but when Independent Jon Zegel cross-checked them, for his third taped talk, he discovered several major inconsistencies. The talk was the longest eulogy ever delivered by Hubbard about management:

> The Church had some hard times a few years ago. For a very long while, as you know, I have not been connected with active management of the Church. . . . It took quite a while, I'm told, for the Church to sort itself out. . . . Scientology Churches are very vast and influential global organizations, and there were people around whose claws itched to take them over, and in a perverted form exploit them for their own profit. . . . Certain people infiltrated the Legal department, the old Guardian's Office, and set it up to lose left and right, and get people in trouble. They also infiltrated top management. Being off lines I was not involved with any of this. . . . At last a small hardcore group of founding members, devoted on-Policy, in-Tech Scientologists who suddenly understood what was happening, used their power as trustees and just as it looked like the Churches were finished and about to fall into hostile hands, they suddenly isolated the infiltrators and threw them out.

Hubbard showed none of his usual loud humor on the tape. He sounded cheerful, but somehow the power was gone, if indeed it was Hubbard's voice. By this time the Messengers had very sophisticated sound equipment, and some Independents insisted that a Fairlight synthesizer had been used to generate a voice similar to Hubbard's. The solution was probably far simpler: the tape was processed with Hubbard's "Clearsound," a rather primitive filtering system, which would have reduced the impingement of Hubbard's gasping breathing, giving the voice its slightly artificial feel. At the beginning of 1984, proof positive of Hubbard's support of the CMO might have induced many resignees to return. The tape simply was not enough.

The Advanced Ability Center East Grinstead came into being in January 1984, in a loose alliance with Mayo's group in Santa Barbara. In February, Robin Scott opened Candacraig House, in Scotland, and it became the third AAC. Independent Centers were springing up throughout the U.S. and Europe.

In February, Independents received the first mailings from the anonymous "Stamp Out the Squirrels Committee," postmarked Los Angeles. The letters were headed with the design of a badge distributed within the Church, depicting a gleeful cartoon squirrel, rubbing its paws together, in a red circle, with a red bar across it. The anonymous letters carried this logo, with the legend "Trademark Religious Technology Center" printed beneath it.

The principal target of these scandal sheets was David Mayo. Mayo and his staff were attacked in fifteen newletters dated from February to April 1984. Of the suggestion that Mayo might be able to release the long awaited Operating Thetan levels above OT7, the second letter said this: "Obviously he doesn't care about people's spiritual freedom, so what is his motivation in making this false promise—money?" Mayo's group were charging about a fifth of Church prices.

Mayo and his staff were pilloried unrelentingly. Of course, this character assassination convinced many members that the Church really had gone crazy. Most of the letters were couched in such elaborate Scientologese that they are difficult to comprehend without a sizeable glossary.

The first letter said, "Rumor in the field has it that the clientele now frequenting the Mayo Clinic [i.e., the AAC] has regressed from the 'colorful' to the 'bizarre.' " From the second letter: "The numbers of disillusioned's [sic] who have failed to find the 'Holy Grail' at Mayo's are growing in alarming numbers. Many are now saying they wished they'd listened to and duplicated [understood] 'The Story of a Squirrel.' The more fortunate one's [sic] are applying Ron's tech and are on the road to getting their cases unsnarled."

The attack on the AAC did not stop at venomous libels. The AAC's offices were watched constantly by private investigators. Mayo was followed day and night. Listening devices were quite openly aimed at the windows of counselling rooms. A Religious Technology Center "mission" was permanently posted to observe and interfere with the AAC.

In England, in January 1984, four health professionals, three of them medical doctors, resigned from the Church and mailed their joint resignation broadly to Scientologists. A copy found its way to the national *Daily Mail* newspaper. There had been a tacit agreement between the Church and the Independents that Scientology's dirty linen was best kept out of the public view. Journalist Peter Sheridan, broke through that agreement. Sheridan interviewed a father whose three teenage children had "disconnected" from him. The children's mother, who had remarried, was a Sea Org member. The youngest child, aged thirteen, had written a disconnection letter to his father. Sheridan had also spoken to an Independent whose children had been expelled from Greenfields, the East Grinstead school run on Scientology principles. On February 11, the *Daily Mail* carried a full-page article titled "We disconnect you!" or in its northern issue, "The Disconnection Terror."

The Office of Special Affairs had retained not only many of the old Guardian's Office staff, but many of the old tricks too. Robin Scott, who had helped extract the NOTs materials from the Advanced Org in Denmark, was phoned by a prospective customer inviting him to Sweden. His air fare would be paid. Scott boarded a plane which stopped at Copenhagen on March 13, Hubbard's birthday. He was apprehended at Copenhagen airport. Sea Org members accompanied the arresting officers, and took photographs of the whole affair.

During the course of Scott's incarceration, an opinion was sought on the authenticity of Hubbard's signature on the documents transferring his Scientology trademarks to the Religious Technology Center. These had been examined by an American expert at Michael Flynn's request in May 1983. The expert had stated that the signatures "were not written by the individual represented" in the specimen signatures provided. A signed letter dating from the 1950s, definitely written by Hubbard, was given to a Scandinavian expert, who said there was "a probability amounting almost to certainty" that the RTC signatures were *not* Hubbard's. She added that this is the most definite statement given by handwriting experts.

Diane Voegeding, who had formerly been the Commanding Officer of the CMO, came to Scott's aid by giving an affidavit that questioned the Religious Technology Center's right to the trademarks. Voegeding said that David Miscavige was in fact the Notary Public responsible for Hubbard's legal documents, and that Miscavige illicitly kept a book of undated Hubbard signatures.

On March 23, 1984, the English High Court issued a Summons on behalf of the. "Church of Scientology Advanced Organization Saint Hill Europe and Africa" requesting an injunction against Robin Scott, Morag Bellmaine and Ron Lawley to restrain them from the use, distribution or copying of the stolen NOTs packs. A temporary injunction was issued, pending the response of the defendants. The surveillance by private detectives continued. A similar order was issued in Scotland a few days later, again naming Scott, and adding several of the staff at Candacraig.

The East Grinstead newspapers carried an article announcing that the Church was offering a £120,000 reward for information "leading to the recovery of what are said to be scriptures stolen from its

European headquarters.'' The use of the word "scriptures," first introduced at the Mission Holders' Conference in 1982, still came as a surprise. Despite Scientology's alleged religious nature, very few Scientologists thought of Hubbard's writings as scriptures. After all, Hubbard claimed that they were scientific research.

After nearly five weeks in jail, the theft charge against Robin Scott was thrown out by the Danish judge, but he was found guilty of a mixture of industrial espionage and trespass. He was given a four-month sentence, the remainder of which was suspended. The Church issued a triumphant account in their "Keeping Scientology Working News." In the newsletter, Scott is called an "apostate," and there are three photographs taken at the time of his arrest, all giving a good view of the back of Scott's head.

In March 1984, Hubbard reinforced his alibi for failures of the Tech. Such failures could be attributed to insufficient Security Checking, "evil purposes," communication with Suppressives, or paying heed to any criticism of Scientology. Many Independents had received tens, even hundreds of hours of such counselling while in the Church. In fact, this obsession with the evil that men do was a major reason for the disintegration of the Church.[1]

Solo NOTs, or "New OT7," had been released to Scientologists in 1979. After five years, usually of daily "solo-auditing," no one in the Church had finished the level. With some relief, Independents were at last allowed to attest their completion. Realizing the situation, the "Captain" of Flag, in Clearwater, sent out a letter to Church members on this highest level, saying how alarmed he was that no one had finished. A flood of Church completions started three months later.

In the United States, Religious Technology Center member Kurt Weiland had moved into an apartment above the AAC in Santa Barbara. While there Weiland did everything possible to upset those below, including haranguing and snapping photographs of arriving clients, and playing deafening music. Eventually, an injunction was issued protecting Mayo and his staff and clients from this childish but extremely disturbing behavior.

Such harassment of Independents was widespread. An Independent was picked up by Swedish police, again accompanied by Sea Org members. It took three days for the police to realize that they could not charge the man, and he was released. A girl was picked up in Munich, again based on trumped up charges. She was released, but the aftermath was a little more serious: At the end of May, German officials raided both the Scientology Org and the Mission in Munich, and carted away reams of documents.

Shortly before the German raid, Scottish Independent Fred Smithers called me. He explained that his stepson, Gulliver, was a member of CMO U.K. at Saint Hill. Gulliver had just phoned him to say he wanted to leave the Church. Fred asked if I could give Gulliver a room for the night. He arrived that Sunday evening while we were having dinner with friends. It came as a shock when he realized his stepfather had sent him into the lair of an infamous Suppressive, but he soon recovered and sustained a two-hour interview. The incredulity of his audience increased by the minute.

For six months, Gulliver had been a top executive in the Commodore's Messenger Organization U.K. which controlled all other Scientology organizations in Britain. He rated himself one of the top four executives in CMO U.K. He was *fourteen* years old. He explained that there were several others his age, and some "kids" in the CMO.

The Watchdog Committee was now bypassing the whole elaborate management structure of the Church. WDC was sending telexes down to individual Orgs on a daily basis, often hourly, demanding "compliance."

A CMO newsletter had claimed that the CMO "Continental" units (including the U.K.) are "the OBSERVATION, EXECUTION and POLICE ARM of WDC" (emphasis in original).[2] Gulliver's job was to enforce Watchdog Committee orders. He had been in charge of seasoned Sea Org veterans, OTs who had received a great deal of auditing, and were highly trained counsellors well versed in Scientology administration, having done the "Organization Executive Course," and sometimes even the "Flag Executive Briefing Course." They had had months of training, and years of on the job experience. Gulliver had neither.

In a Scientology Organization everything is meant to be done per Policy (in accordance with the thousands of Policy Letters written almost exclusively by Hubbard). Policy is very elaborate, but hinges on certain basic ideas. Among these are the supposed right to question an order, and the right to demand that an order be put in writing. A CMO teenager would frequently issue a verbal order, and threaten the recipient with the Rehabilitation Project Force (RPF) if the order was questioned. Again the staff member theoretically has a right to demand a Committee of Evidence prior to assignment of the RPF, which is reasonable as an RPF can take anything up to two years to complete. These rights were all denied.

Gulliver said that all of the U.K. Organizations were losing money. He also said that the majority of the money they did make was sent to the U.S., so periodically the Watchdog Committee would have to pay even the lighting and heating bills, following a complex Purchase Order system. Nearly all of the U.K. Orgs had their telephones disconnected at some point during 1984, because of the delay in receiving funds.

The Sea Org crew at Saint Hill had been living on a diet of rice and beans throughout Gulliver's six months there. The high point of their week would be a baked potato with cheese, or soup. This diet, and the deprivation of sleep which is usual for Sea Org members, can tell dramatically. Sea Org members have for years collected hundreds of millions of dollars, in return for bare subsistence and pitiful "wages." Gulliver was paid £1.25 for his last week's work, (less than $2 U.S.), and this as a senior executive. Sea Org pay is usually less than £4 a week, and often measured in pence. With this pittance, most buy chocolate, tobacco, or a junk meal on their weekly morning off.

Most alarming of all, the fourteen-year-old Gulliver talked about the last Watchdog Committee program he had worked on, the "Non-SO spouse program" ("SO" being Sea Org). Sea Org members whose spouses were not in the Sea Org were either to persuade them to join up, or to divorce them. When I wrote my article about the meeting (inevitably called "Gulliver's Travels") for the Independent newsletter, *Reconnection*, I felt compelled to draw a parallel to the chapter in Lewis Carroll's *Alice in Wonderland* called "The Queen's Croquet Ground," where the players use live hedgehogs for balls, and flamingos for mallets. The Church had entered the realms of the utterly surreal.

PART EIGHT

JUDGMENTS

All that Ethics is for . . . is simply that additional tool necessary to make it possible to apply the technology of Scientology. Man does not have that purpose for his law or his justice. He wants to squash people who are giving him trouble.—L. RON HUBBARD, *Introduction to Scientology Ethics*

CHAPTER ONE

Scientology at Law

The law can be used very easily to harass, and enough harassment on somebody who is simply on the thin edge anyway . . . will generally be sufficient to cause his professional decease. If possible, of course, ruin him utterly.—RON HUBBARD, *The Scientologist*, March 1955

The litigious nature of the Church of Scientology is well-known. It has waged a twenty-year battle against the Internal Revenue Service in the United States. The IRS insists that the profits of Scientology have accrued to the benefit of a private individual, namely L. Ron Hubbard. There was a ten-year battle against the Food and Drug Administration. The Courts upheld the FDA's assertion that the E-meter was improperly labeled. But the Church did manage to overturn a ruling that material seized from them be destroyed. So the Church claims victory. In the 1970s in France, Hubbard was sentenced in absentia to a prison term for fraud.

In the 1970s, the Church fought to prevent the sale of books critical of Scientology. They failed in this attempt, but caused authors George Malko, Paulette Cooper, Cyril Vosper and Robert Kaufman considerable difficulty (not only from the law suits: Roy Wallis, in his *Salvation and Protest*, described the harassment he received after writing about Scientology). In 1982, Paulette Cooper, author of *The Scandal of Scientology* testified that the Church had brought *eighteen* suits against her. More recently Russell Miller has defended against attempts to prevent distribution of his *Bare-Faced Messiah* in England, Canada, Australia and the United States.

In 1983, the Legal office of the Church admitted that it did not know how many suits were outstanding in England alone. So many writs had been issued for libel it had lost track. In 1968, *thirty-eight* libel suits were dropped by the Church in England. Cases which continued were uniformly lost by the Church.

Boston attorney Michael Flynn won fourteen of the sixteen complaints brought against him by the Church, the remaining two being withdrawn. The Church has from time to time filed suits against the FBI, the IRS, the Justice Department, Interpol and even against Henry Kissinger (for $800 million).

Scientology has filed hundreds of cases over the years. Most have been withdrawn before trial, but in Britain suits against a former Police Commissioner and against Member of Parliament Geoffrey Johnson-Smith were both lost by the Church. In return, there have been hundreds of suits filed against Scientology. The Church was forced to pay substantial damages to former Health Minister, Kenneth Robinson, and withdraw their allegations that he had instigated "death camps," likened by the Church to Belsen and Auschwitz.[1]

Also in the legal arena are the reports of the many Commissions of Inquiry, and of several U.S. grand jury investigations. These run to tens of thousands of pages. Two books have been written about the attempt made by the Guardian's Office to take over the National Association of Mental Health in the U.K. in the late 1960s, which also ended in a ruling against Scientology in the English High Court.

Of all the court cases, two stand out. Their verdicts came down within a month of each other: one in Los Angeles, the other in London. The first, and perhaps the most revealing to date, was the case brought by the Scientologists against Gerald Armstrong.

Armstrong had joined the Sea Org in 1971. Over the years he held various positions close to Hubbard. During the trial he gave detailed testimony of these periods, and of his time in the Rehabilitation Project Force. His accounts highlighted the extreme duress of life in the Sea Org.

Armstrong saved over twenty boxes of Hubbard letters, diaries and photographs from the shredder at Gilman Hot Springs. On January 8, 1980, he wrote to Hubbard asking permission to collect material for a biography. A few years earlier Hubbard had lamented that no biography could be written because his personal documents had been stolen, and the great Conspiracy against him would by now have altered all public records.

Far from being stolen by the Russians in the early 1950s, as Hubbard had claimed, his personal archive had quite remarkably been preserved. When the Hubbards left Washington for Saint Hill, in spring 1959, the boxes had been put into storage, where they stayed until the late 1970s. Somehow they had been shipped to La Quinta, and thence to Gilman. Armstrong was excited by the discovery, as it would no longer be necessary to rely on the supposedly corrupted government records, with Hubbard's personal documents in hand.

Hubbard approved Armstrong's request only days before he went into deep hiding. Armstrong was titled "L. Ron Hubbard Personal Public Relations Office Researcher," and he collected over half-a-million pages of material by the end of 1981.

Omar Garrison, who had already written two books favorable to Scientology, was contracted to write the biography in October 1980, and the Archives were made available to him. Armstrong became Garrison's research assistant, copying tens of thousands of the most relevant documents for Garrison's use.

In his judgment in the Scientologists' case against Armstrong, Judge Breckenridge explained the gradual erosion of Armstrong's faith in Hubbard:

> During 1980 Defendant Armstrong remained convinced of Hubbard's honesty and integrity and believed that the representations he had made about himself in various publications were truthful. Defendant Armstrong was devoted to Hubbard and was convinced that any information which he discovered to be unflattering of Hubbard or contradictory to what Hubbard has said about himself, was a lie being spread by Hubbard's enemies. Even when Defendant Armstrong located documents in Hubbard's Archives which indicated that representations made by Hubbard and the Organization were untrue, Defendant Armstrong would find some means to "explain away" the contradictory information.
>
> Slowly, however, throughout 1981, Defendant Armstrong began to see that Hubbard and the Organization had continuously lied about Hubbard's past, his credentials, and his accomplishments.

Armstrong began a campaign to correct the numerous misrepresentations, but met with considerable resistance. In November 1981, he was ordered back to Gilman from Los Angeles. He was told by senior

Church official Norman Starkey that he was to be Security-checked. There was no desire to correct Hubbard's biography. To this day, Scientology Orgs sell books which contain the very biographies which Armstrong had proved false; Hubbard's *Mission into Time* is the worst example of many.

On November 25, 1981, Armstrong wrote to Commodore's Messenger Cirrus Slevin:

> If we present inaccuracies, hyperbole or downright lies as fact or truth, it doesn't matter what slant we give them, if disproved the man will look, to outsiders at least, like a charlatan. This is what I'm trying to prevent and what I've been working on the past year and a half.

A few weeks later, Armstrong decided to leave the Church. Before leaving, he worked desperately hard to ensure that Omar Garrison had all of the documents necessary for an honest biography. After leaving, he maintained contact with the Biography Project, even helping to find documents in the Archives when the new Archivist was unable to do so, for two months following his departure. Judge Breckenridge's opinion continues:

> On February 18, 1982, the Church of Scientology International issued a "Suppressive Person Declare Gerry Armstrong," which is an official Scientology document issued against individuals who are considered enemies of the Organization . . .
>
> Defendant Armstrong was unaware of said Suppressive Person Declare until April of 1982. At that time a revised Declare was issued on April 22, 1982. Said Declare charged Defendant Armstrong with eighteen different "Crimes and High Crimes and Suppressive Acts Against the Church." The charges included theft, juggling accounts, obtaining loans on [sic] money under false pretenses, promulgating false information about the Church, its founder, and members, and other untruthful allegations designed to make Defendant Armstrong an appropriate subject of the Scientology "Fair Game Doctrine." Said Doctrine allows any suppressive person to be "tricked, cheated, lied to, sued, or destroyed."
>
> . . . from his extensive knowledge of the covert and intelligence operations carried out by the Church of Scientology of California against its enemies (suppressive persons), Defendant Armstrong became terrified and feared that his life and the life of his wife were in danger, and he also feared he would be the target of costly and harassing lawsuits. In addition, Mr. Garrison became afraid for the security of the

documents and believed that the intelligence network of the Church of Scientology would break and enter his home to retrieve them. Thus Defendant Armstrong made copies of certain documents for Mr. Garrison and maintained them in a separate location.

Armstrong, with Garrison's permission, made copies of about 10,000 pages of these documents, and deposited them with attorneys for safe keeping. Michael Flynn was one of these attorneys.

On August 2, 1982, the Church of Scientology of California filed suit against Gerald Armstrong for Conversion (a form of theft); breach of fiduciary duty (breach of trust); and breach of confidence. Mary Sue Hubbard joined the suit against Armstrong as an "intervenor," and added a charge of "Invasion of Privacy" to the suit. Judge Breckenridge's opinion continues:

> After the within suit was filed . . . Defendant Armstrong was the subject of harassment, including being followed and surveilled by individuals who admitted employment by Plaintiff; being assaulted by one of these individuals; being struck bodily by a car driven by one of these individuals; having two attempts made by said individuals apparently to involve Defendant Armstrong in a freeway automobile accident; having said individuals come onto Defendant Armstrong's property, spy in his windows, create disturbances, and upset his neighbors. During trial when it appeared that Howard Schomer (a former Scientologist) might be called as a defense witness, the Church engaged in a somewhat sophisticated effort to suppress his testimony.

After hearing four weeks of testimony, and deliberating for two weeks, Judge Breckenridge ruled that Gerald Armstrong was entitled to judgment and costs. The preceding quotations come from a fifteen-page appendix to the opinion. The main body of the decision is one of the most forceful statements ever made against the Church of Scientology. Of the Founder and his Church, Judge Breckenridge wrote:

> In addition to violating and abusing its own members' civil rights, the organization over the years with its "Fair Game" doctrine has harassed and abused those persons not in the Church whom it perceives as enemies. The organization clearly is schizophrenic and paranoid, and this bizarre combination seems to be a reflection of its founder LRH. The evidence portrays a man who has been virtually a pathological liar when it comes to his history, background, and achievements. The writings and documents in evidence additionally reflect his egoism,

greed, avarice, lust for power, and vindictiveness and aggressiveness against persons perceived by him to be disloyal or hostile. At the same time it appears that he is charismatic and highly capable of motivating, organizing, controlling, manipulating, and inspiring his adherents. He has been referred to during the trial as a "genius," a "revered person," a man who was "viewed by his followers in awe." Obviously, he is and has been a very complex person, and that complexity is further reflected in his alter ego, the Church of Scientology. Notwithstanding protestations to the contrary, this court is satisfied that LRH runs the Church in all ways through the Sea Organization, his role of Commodore, and the Commodore's Messengers. He has, of course, chosen to go into "seclusion," but he maintains contact and control through the top messengers. Seclusion has its light and dark side too. It adds to his mystique, and yet shields him from accountability and subpoena or service of summons.

LRH's wife, Mary Sue Hubbard is also a plaintiff herein. On the one hand she certainly appeared to be a pathetic individual. She was forced from her post as Controller, convicted and imprisoned as a felon, and deserted by her husband. On the other hand her credibility leaves much to be desired. She struck the familiar pose of not seeing, hearing, or knowing any evil. Yet she was the head of the Guardian Office for years and among other things, authored the infamous order "GO [Guardian's Order] 121669" which directed culling of supposedly confidential P.C. [Preclear] files/folders for the purposes of internal security. In her testimony she expressed the feelings that defendant by delivering the documents, writings, letters to his attorneys, subjected her to mental rape. . . . The court is satisfied that he [Armstrong] did not unreasonably intrude upon Mrs. Hubbard's privacy under the circumstances. . . . It is, of course, rather ironic that the person who authorized G.O. order 121669 should complain about an invasion of privacy. The practice of culling supposedly confidential "P.C. folders or files" to obtain information for purposes of intimidation and/or harassment is repugnant and outrageous. The Guardian's Office, which plaintiff headed, was no respector of anyone's civil rights, particularly that of privacy.

The documents involved in the case were extensive. They included copies of letters from Hubbard to his father, to his first two wives, and to the children of his first marriage. They also included Hubbard's teenage diaries, his Boy Scout records, poems, and the manuscript of an unpublished book called *Positive Mental Therapy*. Also included were Hubbard's letters to Mary Sue Hubbard over the years, where he said exactly what he was doing while researching the "Technology" of Scientology. For example, there are letters sent from North Africa in late 1966, to Mary Sue at Saint Hill, which give details of the drugs

Hubbard was taking to "research" the most secret of Scientology's levels, OT3.

During the course of the trial, the judge heard testimony from Armstrong; his wife Jocelyn; Laurel Sullivan, who had been Armstrong's senior on the Biography Project; the proposed author Omar Garrison; Hubbard's nurse Kima Douglas (who left Hubbard in January 1980); and former Author Services Incorporated Treasury Secretary Howard Schomer.

Omar Garrison, who had been commissioned to write the biography, had this to say of the documentation Armstrong provided:

> The inconsistencies were implicit in various documents which Mr. Armstrong provided me with respect to Mr. Hubbard's curriculum vitae, with respect to his Navy career, with respect to almost every aspect of his life. These undeniable and documented facts did not coincide with the official published biography that the church had promulgated.

Garrison intended to complete the biography, and continued with this work through 1982. In June 1983, he agreed to a settlement with the Church. The Church wanted to be absolutely sure that the manuscript wasn't made public. Garrison reluctantly agreed. He too had been followed by private detectives, "bumper to bumper." However, Garrison retained copies of documents from the Hubbard archives to ensure the church's good behavior.

Jocelyn Armstrong testified that she had worked on a project where Mission Holders were to sign backdated contracts, Board minutes and resignations.

Kima Douglas was Hubbard's personal Medical Officer from 1975 until her departure on January 16, 1980. From 1977, she was with Hubbard on a daily basis. She was also the head of no less than *fourteen* Scientology corporations, and had written undated resignations from each. Among these was the Religious Research Foundation, which was used to channel monies from the Flagship, and later the Flag Land Base, into non-Church accounts controlled by Hubbard.

Douglas testified that she was with Hubbard when he approved Armstrong's request to collect material for a biography. She had also been present when Hubbard had ordered that supposedly confidential counselling folders should be "culled" for admissions of crimes, and anti-social or immoral actions, for future use. Douglas admitted that she had seen Hubbard display "irrational and abusive" behavior, to the extent of striking someone. She also revealed the extent of Hubbard's ill health throughout the years she served him.

The myth of L. Ron Hubbard was badly fractured. It seemed that his mesmeric hold over Scientologists, whether Church members or Independents, was slipping. The trance could only be maintained through a stubborn refusal to consider the material now available.

The Judgment in the Armstrong case was filed on June 22, 1984, just as Justice Latey was preparing to hear a child custody case in London.

CHAPTER TWO

The Child Custody Case

What can we do to refute what is stated in Scientology's own documents?—Counsel for the Scientologist father in the custody case

In Spring 1984, I learned of a child custody case in which Scientology was at issue. The father, a Church Scientologist, was seeking to retain custody of his two young children. The mother and stepfather had left Scientology.

Prior to the hearing, the stepfather called me. He launched into a speech, saying he did not want to blacken Scientology, only to gain custody of the children. His caution was unnecessary, I had no desire to conceal the facts about either Hubbard or Scientology. Although prepared to help the Independents defend themselves, I was no longer a Scientologist. We began to work together on a daily basis.

The stepfather already had an enormous amount of material, much of which he could not use in court. His solicitor felt, for example, that the 1,500 page transcript of the Clearwater Hearings was inadmissible in an English court. The father, a convinced Scientologist, had insisted that he did not practice Disconnection. I was given three letters he had written to his business partner in 1983, Disconnecting from him, and suggesting that a screen be put in their office to avoid even visual contact with his Suppressive partner.

The head of the Scientology school in East Grinstead was being called as a witness. She denied that a twelve-year-old girl had received a "withhold pulling session" at the hands of three of the school's staff. To "pull withholds" is Scientologese for making someone confess to their transgressions. Minutes of the school's board meetings had to be publicly available, yet the filed copy made no reference to the "withhold-pulling" session. I obtained an *unedited* copy of the school's board minutes, which not only proved the headmistress's sworn statement untrue, but showed the school's attempt at concealment.

Then there were Hubbard's own published statements. I found references to Fair Game, a passage where Hubbard called non-Scientologists "raw meat," and much more.

Of course, Church members are forbidden by Policy from making any public criticism of either Hubbard or Scientology. The strength of this taboo is shown by the criticism I received from some Independents for my wholehearted involvement in the case. The future of the children, and their future happiness, was less important to them than maintaining a Public Relations shield for Hubbard and Scientology. This attitude stems from the belief that the Tech is a world-saving force, and that if anything is awry it will not help to broadcast it. It has to be emphasized that public admissions of wrongdoing, apologies, and steps to prevent repetition are foreign to the mentality instilled into Hubbard's converts.

The case concerned the custody of a ten-year-old boy, and an eight-year-old girl. To quote from the judgment:

> At the heart of the mother's case is the contention that if the children remain in the care of the father they will be brought up as Scientologists and will be seriously damaged . . .
>
> It is important, indeed essential, to stress from the start that this is neither an action against Scientology nor a prosecution of it. But willy-nilly Scientology is at the center of the dispute of what is best for the children. The father and his counsel have stressed that they are not here to defend Scientology. That is true in the strict sense that the "Church" of Scientology is not a party to the proceedings. But they have known from the start what the mother's case is. . . . The father's solicitor is a Scientologist. He has been in communication with the solicitors who act for Scientology. There has been ample time and opportunity to assemble and adduce documents and evidence in refutation of the mother's allegations. None has been adduced. Why? Because the mother's case is based largely on Scientology's own documents and as the father's

counsel . . . candidly albeit plaintively said "what can we do to refute what is stated in Scientology's own documents?"

. . . The parents were married in 1973 and late that year B [the son] was born. G [the daughter] was born in December, 1975. The parents separated in November, 1978. In December, 1978 and January, 1979, the parents signed agreements by virtue of which the father had custody of the children and the mother access. . . . In March, 1979 the father filed a petition of divorce on the ground of the mother's adultery with the stepfather.

In September, 1979 . . . by agreement, custody was committed to the father. The divorce was made absolute in November, 1979. The father and stepmother married. The mother and stepfather also went through a ceremony of marriage believing that they were free to do so. In fact, the stepfather's divorce had not gone through. . . .

. . . In May, 1980 there began a hearing by the Scientology "Chaplain's Court" concerning the custody of the children. The decision, inaccurately described as an "Agreement," was that custody should remain with the father.

The mother and stepfather subsequently left Scientology, and decided to take the matter to law. Justice Latey continued:

As to the separation in 1978, the father said in his Affidavit that this was caused by the mother's relationship with the stepfather. In his oral evidence the father accepted that he had drawn up what in Scientology language is described as a "Doubt Formula" ["Doubt" is one of the "Ethics Conditions"] in which he said that he considered himself the mother's intellectual superior, that he had doubts about the wisdom of the marriage and that separation had been discussed on a number of occasions. . . . It is scarcely surprising that with a husband who so regarded her, she became attached to a man who held her in full regard and affection.

As to the custody agreements in 1978 and 1979: The father naturally attaches much weight to them. The mother says that throughout she wanted the children and believed that it would be better for them to be with her. She was a committed Scientologist at the time. Scientology forbids recourse to the law courts of the country save in special circumstances with permission. . . . The mother says that she agreed to the father having custody because of the pressure brought to bear on her by the father and the Scientologists concerned. The father accepts that she agreed very reluctantly. . . .

At the time of the separation B was aged just five and G not quite three. Had the dispute come to court one cannot be sure, of course, what the decision would have been, but it is not unlikely that children so young would have been put in the care of a good and devoted mother as this one is and always has been.

. . . As to the "Chaplain's" decision: There were written submissions and some oral hearings. It is noteworthy that from start to finish the father's submission is couched in Scientology terminology and stresses all he and the stepmother have done for Scientology, how correctly they have complied with Scientology "ethics" and how the mother has offended against those "ethics." The Chaplain of course was a Scientology official.

Both the mother and stepfather wanted to come to Court and in about May 1980 she was given permission to do so by the "Assistant Guardian" on condition that Scientology would not be involved. But the father intervened with the Guardian and the permission was withdrawn.

In the summer of 1982, the children stayed with the mother, and she decided to keep them, despite the previous "agreements." She fled to the United States, and the father followed her, taking the children back to England with him. Justice Latey continued, having admitted that were it not for the father's adherence to Scientology he would have ruled that the children stay with him:

What then is the Scientology factor and what weight should be attached to it? "Horrendous." "Sinister." "A lot of rotten apples in it." Those words are not mine. They are the father's own words describing practices of the Cult and what it does to people inside it and outside it. "A lot of villains in it." "Dreadful things have been done in the name of Scientology." These words are not mine. They are the words of the father's counsel.

Justice Latey went on the describe Scientology as he saw it, and added:

Some might regard this as an extension of the entertaining science fiction which Hubbard used to write before he invented and founded the cult. . . . But in an open Society, such as ours, people can believe what they want to and band together and promulgate their beliefs. If people believe that the earth is flat there is nothing to stop them believing so, saying so and joining together to persuade others.

He then quoted the evidence given by American psychiatrist Dr. John Gordon Clark, during the trial:

Auditing is a simple, thoroughly designed means of concentrating the mind to a state of a controlled trance. The aim and result is progressively to enforce loyalty to, and identification with Scientology to the detriment of one's natural awareness of divergent ways of thinking and outside cultural influences. Love and allegiance are more and more given to Scientology and L. Ron Hubbard.

Justice Latey further wrote that "In blunt language 'auditing' is a process of conditioning, brainwashing and indoctrination."

Justice Latey compared the truth about Hubbard with the Church's published claims:

To promote himself and the cult he has made these, among other false claims:

That he was a much decorated war hero. He was not.

That he commanded a corvette squadron. He did not.

That he was awarded the Purple Heart, a gallantry decoration for those wounded in action. He was not wounded and was not decorated.

That he was crippled and blinded in the war and cured himself with Dianetic technique. He was not crippled and was not blinded.

That he was sent by U.S. Naval Intelligence to break up a black magic ring in California. He was not. He was himself a member of that occult group and practiced ritual sexual magic in it.

That he was a graduate of George Washington University and an atomic physicist. The facts are that he completed only one year of college and failed the one course on nuclear physics in which he enrolled.

There is no dispute about any of this. The evidence is unchallenged.

. . . Hubbard has described himself as "Dr. Hubbard." The only doctorate he has held is a self-bestowed "doctorate" in Scientology.

. . . Mr. Hubbard is a charlatan and worse, as are his wife Mary Sue Hubbard . . . and the clique at the top privy to the Cult's activities.

Further on Justice Latey spoke of "Confessional auditing":

Contrary to the assurance of confidentiality, all "auditing" files are available to Scientology's intelligence and enforcement bureau and are used, if necessary, to control and extort obedience from the person who was audited. If a person seeks to escape from Scientology his auditing files are taken by the intelligence bureau and used, if wished, to pressure him into silence. They are often so used and uncontraverted evidence of this has been given at this hearing.

. . . It is no surprise that to escape from the clutches of Scientology calls for great courage and resolution. The stranglehold is tight and unrelenting and the discipline ruthless. And of course there is the anguish of conscience in the escaper after usually many years of commitment to Scientology.

Justice Latey went on to read "TR-L" ("Training Routine—Lying") into the record. This is a drill used in the training of Guardian's Office staff members. Its purpose is to enable the trainee to tell a lie in a convincing fashion.

Much of a Hubbard Policy Letter, of August 15, 1960, was also read into the record. It contains the statement: "If attacked on some vulnerable point by anyone or anything or any organization, always find or manufacture enough threat against them to cause them to sue for peace. . . . Don't ever defend. Always attack."

Then Justice Latey read from a Guardian's Order of March 9, 1970, headed "Re: Successful and Unsuccessful Actions." Among the successful actions was seeking out the criminal acts of "traitors" (easy to do if you have their auditing folders).

The Order describes a cross-filing system used to keep track of information on "traitors" (such as myself, I suppose). GO staff were to create a fictitious company (a press agency was recommended), and use letterheaded paper to make inquiries. Information is better discovered through phone calls than through personal visits. Sexual favors to members of governments had apparently also been successful. Hostile groups could be infiltrated and documents stolen. Letters can be forged for purposes of character assassination. Anonymous reports can be made to the tax authorities.

Justice Latey moved on to life inside Scientology:

> Discipline is ruthless and obedience has to be unquestioning. Scientologists working on the staff are required to work inordinately long hours for their keep and a pittance . . .
>
> Scientology must come first before family or friends. Much evidence has been given and not disputed of how it leads to alienation of one spouse from another, of alienation from children and from friends.
>
> Another witness, Mrs. B, was a Scientologist from 1972 and rose quickly in the organization. She had a three year old daughter. Nonetheless, for a period of months she was required to work from 8:30 a.m. to 1 a.m. She was allowed only fifteen minutes daily to put her daughter to

bed. On one occasion when the child broke her arm and she took her to the doctor she was directed to work all night as a penalty.

In January 1982, Mrs. B was made Commanding Officer of the Organization, Saint Hill U.K. Foundation. At around this time the Commodore's Messenger's Org . . . in the United States were originating an increasing number of international directives which seemed to her wrong or bad. She wrote a report addressing it to L. Ron Hubbard. Eight days later in November 1982, she was removed from her post and assigned to the "RPF" (Rehabilitation Project Force). She was refused counselling, required to do at least twelve hours physical work a day (shifting bricks, emptying bins etc.) [sic] and to communicate with no one, except to receive orders. The work aggravated a chronic back condition. When she protested she was threatened with being declared a "Suppressive Person". . . . Her time with her children was limited to one half hour per day.

Another witness worked at Flag [in Florida] and became an "L. Ron Hubbard Public Relations Officer," one of only three in the world and a high appointment. In 1977 she declined to undertake a mission that would cause her to leave her young daughter for at least two months. She was shouted at and abused because she put the care of her child first. She was subjected to a Committee of Evidence (disciplinary tribunal): She left Flag.

Those are a few of many illustrations, proved in evidence, of the ruthless and inhuman disciplinary measures.

Justice Latey then quoted from an Ethics Policy Letter, and from the 1968 cancellation of "Fair Game." He gave the following example to demonstrate that the "Fair Game Policy" (that a Suppressive can be "tricked, sued or lied to or destroyed") was still in force after its apparent cancellation:

Beginning in 1977 the Church of Scientology has conducted a campaign of persecution against Dr. Clark. They wrote letters to the Dean at the Harvard Medical School and to the Director of the Massachusetts General Hospital. They [the Dean and the Director] refused to gag him. Their [the Church's] agents tracked down and telephoned several of his patients and interviewed his neighbors looking for evidence to impugn his private or personal actions. They submitted a critical report to a Committee of the Massachusetts State Senate. On three occasions during the last five years a Scientology "front" called the Citizens' Commission on Human Rights have brought complaints against him to the Massachusetts Medical Board of Registration alleging improper professional conduct. In 1980 he was declared a "Number One Enemy'' and in 1981 they brought two law suits against him (summarily dismissed, but costly and worrying). They distributed leaflets at the Massachusetts General Hospital offering a $25,000 reward to employees for evidence which would lead to his conviction on any charge of criminal activity. They stole his employment record from another Boston hospital. They convened press conferences calculated to ruin his professional reputation.

Justice Latey quoted Hubbard: ''The law can be used very easily to harass,'' and continued:

A sad episode during the hearing was the evidence of a young man. He is greatly gifted and did exceptionally well at School and University. His parents are Scientologists as are his brother and sister. They are all totally committed. He did his first simple course at the age of six, and a further basic course, ''The Hubbard Qualified Scientologist Course,'' two years later. Since then he has continued with course after course. . . . It became apparent that he simply could not accept that there was or could be anything wrong with Scientology. The part of his mind which would otherwise have been capable of weighing objectively the criticisms of Scientology had been blocked out by the processing. He has indeed been enslaved.

In his conclusion as to Scientology itself, Justice Latey had this to say:

Scientology is both immoral and socially obnoxious. . . . In my judgment it is corrupt, sinister and dangerous. It is corrupt because it is based on lies and deceit and has as its real objective money and power for Mr. Hubbard, his wife and those close to him at the top. It is sinister because it indulges in infamous practices both to its adherents who do not toe the line unquestioningly, and to those who criticise or oppose it. It is dangerous because it is out to capture people, especially children and impressionable young people, and indoctrinate and brainwash them so that they become the unquestioning captives and tools of the cult, withdrawn from ordinary thought, living and relationships with others.

Mr. Justice Latey awarded custody of the children to the mother. Late in the hearing the father had made a heart-rending proposal: he and his new wife would abandon Scientology until the children had grown up. It was moving, not because he would have to abandon Scientology, but because for making such a suggestion in court he risked being ostracized by the Scientology Church and community, whatever the outcome. The Justice felt that because the father and his wife were committed Scientologists, their removal from East Grinstead, and from the Church, would not be enough: "The baleful influence of the 'Church' would in reality still be there and the children would remain gravely at risk."

The Justice also gave two very telling examples of that "baleful influence":

> Recently B asked his mother whether he could have a certain friend to stay for the weekend with him "because he's the only one whose parents will let him come to your house."
>
> Recently G asked her mother why she was not a Scientologist. Her mother pointed out that people could be good people without being Scientologists and observed that two widely respected personages in whom G is interested were not Scientologists. To this G replied "they would be better if they were."

CHAPTER THREE

Signing the Pledge

L. Ron Hubbard seemed oblivious to the drubbing he was receiving in the courts, and as the Armstrong trial was nearing its conclusion bulletins relating to a new "Rundown" started to appear. However, the "False Purpose Rundown" did show some awareness that all was not well in the Scientology world. Added to the usual list of items preventing gain in counselling—"overts" (transgressions), "evil purposes" and connection to real or imagined Suppressives—were "false purposes." These were defined as "non-survival purposes." In the first Bulletin Hubbard took one of his perennial swipes at psychiatry. By now the association between the "implanters" who created OT3, seventy-five million years ago, and the modern day psychiatrists was complete. He also said that "psychs" and "priests" are "the same crew," so dismissing all mental therapy and all religion (with the exception of Scientology, of course) in the same breath.

In the wake of their resounding defeat in the Armstrong case in California, and the damning decision in the English child custody case, the Church published an Executive Directive called simply "Squirrels," naming Armstrong, two former members of Hubbard's Personal staff who had given evidence during the Armstrong case, and David Mayo along with two of his associates. The Directive contained the usual hyperbole about enemies of humanity, and accused the named individuals of retailing insanity.[1]

A few days later, on September 24, 1984, the Church of Scientology lost an appeal against the Internal Revenue Service. In a 222-page decision, the Tax Court judge gave a remarkably detailed account of the Church's financial dealings from 1970–1972, showing the movement of huge sums out of Scientology and into Hubbard's control. The judge also described the tactics of evasion ordered by Hubbard, for example, the deliberate jumbling of two million pages of tax related material, so that IRS officials would have to sort it out, at the expense of the U.S. tax-payer.

On October 9, a group of Scientology dignitaries, including David Miscavige, flew to Saint Hill by helicopter, to sign the "Pledge to Mankind" and to form the "International Association of Scientologists." The Pledge contained the usual rhetoric, clumsily written out by an inexperienced calligrapher:

> New religions have been born in blood at the cost of great sacrifice and suffering by adherents. . . . Scientology has survived and expanded because . . . it is a force for goodness and freedom . . . which is easily recognized by men of goodwill; despite the vicious lies which are spawned by those who would enslave mankind and which are carried by the media. . . .
>
> In the United States . . . we are the targets of unprincipled attacks in the court system by those who would line their pockets from our hard won coffers. Bigots in all branches of government . . . are bent on our destruction through taxation and repressive legislation.
>
> We have been subjected to illegal heresy trials in two countries before prejudiced and malinformed judges who are not qualified or inclined to perceive the truth. . . .
>
> The detractors of Scientology know full well that it is a proven, effective and workable system for freeing mankind from spiritual bondage. That is why they attack. They fear that they will somehow be threatened by a society which is more ethical, productive and humane.

Scientologists paid $2,000 to become lifetime members of the Association.

In addition to the Pledge, the Church filed yet another law suit against attorney Michael Flynn, this time demanding $20,600,000 in damages. In the Complaint, it was alleged that Flynn had engineered the forgery of a $2 million check presented to a New York bank in 1982, to be drawn on the account of L. Ron Hubbard. Obviously, they had failed to find evidence which would interest the FBI or a District Attorney. Undeterred, the Scientologists published an issue of its

Freedom magazine, which is handed out by the thousand on the streets. They quoted from affidavits made by the two brothers who had perpetrated the check fraud, in which Flynn was accused of setting up the whole operation. After months of such libels, one of the brothers, who was being held in custody by German police, signed another affidavit, in which he claimed the Scientologists had paid him for the first affidavit. Eventually, the Church withdrew their ill-founded Complaint.

In December 1984, came another bombshell. Following the massive raid on the Toronto Scientology Church of March 1983, charges were finally brought against eighteen high-ranking Church officials and former members, and the Church of Scientology itself. Among the charges was one of conspiracy to attempt murder, though this was dropped a few months later.

On the last day of January 1985, the Scientologists filed a lawsuit against the Advanced Ability Centers in Santa Barbara, Aberdeen and East Grinstead, along with several of these Centers' principals, including David Mayo, Robin Scott, Morag Bellmaine and Ron Lawley. Jon Zegel, whose tapes recounting the CMO takeover were so popular, was also included. The Complaint was for "racketeering; false description of origin; common law unfair competition; statutory unfair competition; receipt and concealment of stolen property; breach of trust; breach of contract; trade secret misappropriation; injunctive relief and damages." Scientology attorneys were invoking the Racketeering Influence and Corrupt Organizations Act, enacted to curtail the activities of organized crime.

A Washington, DC, judge signed an order on March 13, 1985 (the Commodore's 74th birthday), requiring L. Ron Hubbard to appear in the long-standing case of the Founding Church of Scientology of Washington, DC, versus the Federal Bureau of Investigation. The judge deemed Hubbard a "managing agent" of the church despite all protestations that Hubbard had resigned from management in the 1960s. Hubbard failed to appear, and the case was dismissed. One of the Church's suits against Michael Flynn was also dismissed for Hubbard's failure to obey a court order to appear.

Also in March, Julie Christofferson-Tichbourne's case against Hubbard, the Church of Scientology of California, and the Scientology Mission of Davis came back into court in Portland, Oregon. The suit had originally been filed in 1977, and arose out of a claim for a refund of some $3,000 dollars. Julie Christofferson had become involved with

Scientology in 1975, when she was seventeen. She had taken Scientology courses in place of a college course in engineering, and had spent her college money in doing so. She claimed that fraudulent representations had been made to her about the value of Scientology qualifications, and the benefits that Scientology counselling and training would bring to her. Her original Complaint charged outrageous conduct, the infliction of severe emotional distress and fraud.[2]

It was the third time that the case had been brought to trial. In 1979, Christofferson-Tichbourne had been awarded $2.1 million. In 1982, the ruling had been overturned by the appellate court, dismissing the claim of outrageous conduct, but also striking the evidence of several Scientology witnesses.

The 1980s rift in Scientology had started after the appellate decision. Thousands had either left or been expelled from the Church. Among them were many valuable witnesses, and since the Armstrong case there was a greater willingness to go on record. Bill Franks, who had been Executive Director International in 1981, and had controlled the purge of the Guardian's Office, took the stand and when asked by the Church's attorney whether he had thought Scientology created "mindless robots," he responded, "not at the outset." When asked his current opinion he replied, "Absolutely." He complained about the manipulation of members, and the ludicrously high cost of Scientology. Franks said abandoning Scientology had been the hardest move of his whole life. He maintained that most Scientology staff members are decent people, but added, "Scientology plays on decency. That's the whole hook."

The details of a Guardian's Office operation were put into evidence. "Operation Christo" had been aimed at Julie Christofferson-Tichbourne, her family and even a Lutheran minister.

In an attempt to discredit Armstrong's testimony, the Church produced surreptitiously made videotapes. One of Armstrong's former friends had been ordered to see him, claiming to have left the Church. He encouraged Armstrong to talk about potential methods of taking over and reforming the Scientology Church. The conversations were recorded. Judge Donald Londer refused to admit them as evidence, and said, "I think they are devastating, devastating against the church." He expressed doubts that the tapes were made with proper legal authority, and added that the method used to make the tapes "borders more on entrapment than anything else."

However, a few days later, Londer allowed the jury to see the entire 108 minutes of videotape, so the context could be seen, rather than allowing cross-examination based upon excerpts. He overruled Tichbourne's attorney, Garry McMurry, who said the tapes had been made in violation of civil and criminal laws in both Oregon and California (where they were actually recorded). During the taped conversations Armstrong had admitted that he was *capable* of "creating documents" relating to the actions of the current management, and placing them in Church files. There was no evidence that he had ever undertaken such a project.

Three more hours of tape were submitted by the Church, and viewed by the jury. In a twist of fate, the day after the last tape was played, the Internal Revenue Service was given authorization to use the tapes in its case against Scientology.

Martin Samuels gave devastating testimony. As the head of the Mission involved in the case, he had been a principal witness in the original trial. His life had been torn apart after the San Francisco Mission Holders' Conference in 1982. By the time of the new trial, he had brought his own case against Hubbard, also in Portland, for $72 million. Before testifying, he was denied immunity from criminal prosecution for committing perjury at the 1979 Christofferson trial. On the stand, he said representations made by him that his Portland Mission had not been connected to the national Scientology organization were false. He also said that Scientology witnesses had been coached to lie before the original trial, in what he called a "witness college." In the original trial, the Church had carefully constructed a fabric of lies, just as they had proposed to do in the Guardian's Office trial before Meisner's surrender to the FBI.

Defense witnesses testified to the benefits of Scientology on their lives. The Church claimed that their First Amendment rights were being violated, and that religion was being put on trial. On May 18, 1985, after two days of deliberation, the jury awarded $39 million dollars in damages: $20 million against Hubbard, $17.5 million against the Church of Scientology of California, and $1.5 million against the Church of Scientology Mission of Davis.

During the trial, the Scientologists had waged an advertising blitz in newspapers and on local radio and television stations, and this continued with the "Crusade for Religious Freedom." Two jurors told the press that the advertising had not influenced their decision. Jurors also claimed that they had not been influenced by threatening phone calls they had received during the trial from callers claiming to be Scientologists.

A Church spokeswoman told the press, "This is a bizarre plot to destroy the Church. They [the jurors] decided that religion as practiced by Scientology is not protected by the Constitution. Throughout the case we demonstrated beyond a doubt the government's involvement in a conspiracy against the Church."[3]

Scientology attorneys immediately moved for a mistrial. Within a few days, busloads of Scientologists were arriving in Portland to protest the decision. A candlelit parade was arranged, and Scientologist celebrities, including John Travolta, gave talks. A Church spokesman's estimate that half a million protesters would turn up proved to be grossly exaggerated: Chick Corea performed to a crowd of about 2,000 Scientologists in Portland. For weeks, protesters marched in front of the Courthouse, calling themselves the "Crusade for Religious Freedom," and carrying banners proclaiming "Save Freedom of Religion" and "Restore the Bill of Rights." The protesters listened to vehement speeches given by Scientology officials, and punctuated them with choruses of "We shall overcome." The rhetoric of Church spokespeople was strident: "This is akin to burning a witch, to nailing somebody to a cross—an outright attempt to exterminate a religious group," for example. It was said that deprogrammers had turned Julie Christofferson-Tichbourne into a "mindless robot."

The Scientologists kept up what seemed to be senseless pressure. Nonetheless, trial Judge Donald Londer's decision, given two months after the jury ruling, came as a surprise. He declared a mistrial, on the grounds that he had failed to strike remarks made by Christofferson-Tichbourne's attorney that Scientology was not a religion from the record. Consequently, it had been represented to the jury that they could punish Scientology for purely religious beliefs. He also criticized the attorney's characterization of Scientology as a terrorist group and of Hubbard as a sociopath.[4]

The Church was triumphant. In October 1985, the International Association of Scientologists (IAS) celebrated its first anniversary with a rally in Copenhagen. It was announced that the Church had an international staff of over 8,500, many of whom were members of the Association; the Association's total membership numbered 12,000. Even before the rift the Church probably had less than 50,000 members, despite its claims of seven million. As membership of the IAS is the official membership of the Church of Scientology, the figures are very revealing. They had probably lost at least half of their membership in the schism.[5]

In November, the Scientologists named David Mayo in another suit. Larry Wollersheim, a former member, had brought litigation against the Church in Los Angeles. In the case, the Judge had ruled that the OT3 materials should go into evidence. In the United States, documents put into evidence generally become publicly available, and on the morning of November 4, about 1,500 Church Scientologists crammed three floors of the Courthouse in an attempt to block public access to their confidential "scriptures." The *Los Angeles Times* managed to thwart the blockade, obtained the materials, and published a brief account of OT3, which was enthusiastically taken up by newspapers throughout the U.S. The Church filed suit against Wollersheim and Mayo in the U.S. District Court to prevent further distribution of "confidential" materials.

On November 23, 1985, to the amazement of many, the Court issued a temporary injunction enjoining defendants from the use or distribution of any of the OT levels beyond OT3, in any way whatsoever. It meant little to Larry Wollersheim, who had no use for materials which he asserted were brainwashing, but Mayo's Advanced Ability Center relied upon his version of these levels for a fair proportion of its income. The Santa Barbara AAC was thus prevented from practicing what the Church had insisted was the "religion of Scientology." Ironically, Mayo had pioneered the development of these particular forbidden scriptures in an attempt to save Hubbard's life. It took almost a year for the injunction to be removed, by which time Mayo's group had been driven out of business. In Hubbard's words, "the purpose of the suit is to harass and discourage rather than to win." When the injunction was finally overturned, the Appeal Judges ruled that "the Church's contention that the disputed materials are 'religious scripture' was not reconciled with the California statute's reference to 'economic value' as an element of a protectible trade secret.'"[6] In other words, the Church could not have it both ways, religious scriptures are not business trade secrets. Subsequently, however, a judge has ruled that even this issue can be tried in a court of law.

CHAPTER FOUR

Dropping the Body

The Independent Scientology movement owed its origins in part to the uncertainty surrounding Hubbard's disappearance in 1980. There was an unwillingness to ascribe the bizarre actions of Church management to the Founder. Many Independents thought Hubbard had died, or even been murdered, and that his name was being used to maintain the authority of the young rulers. It was the new management's apparent betrayal of Hubbard's principles that persuaded many to leave the Church, so that they could better realize what they considered to be Hubbard's aims. Conversely, many of those who stayed in the Church must have believed that the new management really did represent Hubbard. They were almost certainly right.

Rumors of Hubbard's whereabouts circulated freely. He was on Catalina island, or in Missouri; he had taken to the sea again, or was in Ireland. News of repeated applications for entry to Britain (which were always turned down) led to the belief that he was trying to return to Saint Hill. In 1985, two *Los Angeles Times* journalists bruited it about that Hubbard was just north of Santa Barbara. They came closer than anyone else.

Hubbard died at 8:00 p.m. on Friday, January 24, 1986, at his ranch near Creston, in California. He was attended by his doctor, Eugene Denk, and at least two other Scientologists. Church attorney Earle Cooley, who had defended against the Christofferson-Tichbourne suit, was informed. He advised that nothing be done before his arrival from Los Angeles, when he took charge. Cooley was with Hubbard's body

351

from that moment until the ashes were scattered at sea. The body was kept at the ranch for over eleven hours before being collected by Reis Chapel mortuary in San Luis Obispo on Saturday morning. The mortuary notified the coroner's office, concerned that Cooley had made a request for immediate cremation. Dr. Denk reported that Hubbard had died "several days" after suffering a brain hemorrhage, and indicated on the death certificate that the cause of death was a "cerebral vascular accident," a stroke.

George Whiting, the county coroner, said that in such a "straightforward case" there would not normally have been any investigation, but because of the delay in notification, Chief Deputy Coroner Don Hines photographed the body, and took fingerprints. He was accompanied by pathologist Karl Kirschner, who examined the body for marks, and found none. He accompanied Hubbard's physician, Dr. Denk, to a laboratory to test blood samples.

Whiting has said that although the evidence supported a finding of death by natural causes, he would like to have performed an autopsy. He claimed to be prevented from doing so under California law, because four days before his death Hubbard had signed a legal document saying an autopsy would be against his religious beliefs. A will, written the day before he died, was also presented, and the district attorney was consulted, as one of the chapel employees put it, "They wanted to make sure this wasn't a scam."

The blood samples showed acceptable levels of anti-stroke medication, but no "harmful" levels of drugs. Coroner Whiting said the fingerprints were matched with sets obtained from the Department of Justice and the FBI, and concluded: "The person we fingerprinted was Hubbard."

The Coroner's office released the body to Denk and Cooley, who attended the cremation. Cooley said that the ashes had been scattered at sea by 3:40 p.m. that day, Saturday, January 25.

Church officials claimed that although Hubbard had suffered a stroke the week before his death, he was lucid when he amended his will the day before he died. The change was allegedly in favor of members of his family. Cooley told the press that Hubbard had left a "very generous provision" for his wife Mary Sue, and for "certain of his children." He said that the remaining "tens of millions of dollars" would go to the Church of Scientology.

Earl Cooley joined the Church of Scientology while acting as the Church's attorney during the Christofferson-Tichbourne case, less than a year before Hubbard's death. In his talk to the assembled Scientologists who gathered to hear the news of Hubbard's death, Cooley maintained the doctrinaire attitude which governs the Church: "Together you will win total victory and achieve the ultimate goals of Scientology."

Hubbard had been living for several years at the remote 160-acre fenced ranch near Creston, about thirty miles north east of San Luis Obispo. Six other people lived there, among them Eugene Denk, and Pat and Anne Broeker. Hubbard was keeping about thirty-five quarter horses, and there were also four buffaloes, a pair of llamas, and several Black Angus cattle, including Hubbard's favorite bull, Bubba. At the time of his death Hubbard was living in one of his several luxury motor homes, while the main house was being remodeled. The property was guarded by six Japanese Akita dogs.

The Whispering Winds ranch was bought by Pat Broeker, under an assumed name, in summer 1983, for $700,000. Rebuilding the house alone cost $300,000. The Church have tried to give the image of a smiling, gregarious Hubbard wandering around the ranch, chatting with the workers. In fact, the locals saw very little of him, and he complained constantly about work done on the house, and kept changing the plans. For example, a stone fireplace was replaced with a tile one, and then ripped out altogether. That was the pattern, so much so, that in the two and a half years that he lived on the ranch, Hubbard never occupied the house, living instead in his $250,000 Bluebird motor home.

Hubbard eked out his last days working on the presentation of the OT levels beyond 7, taking photographs, designing and redesigning the house, and watching films. "His movie favorites included Hitchcock films, *Star Wars* but not the later movies in the trilogy, *Diva*, *Citizen Kane*, *Slaughter House Five* and *Patton*. He liked Clint Eastwood and Robert Duvall," according to one of the Messengers.

After Hubbard's death, *Rocky Mountain News* journalist Sue Lindsay was allowed to visit both the Whispering Winds ranch and Gilman Hot Springs. In her excellent article the truth was revealed about the luxurious accommodation prepared for Hubbard by the Messengers. The house at Gilman, which he never occupied, was completed in 1983, after three years work. The Clipper ship, which cost about half a million dollars in materials alone, has already been mentioned, and in 1984 a twenty-four track recording studio was also completed for Hubbard at Gilman:

Now, although he is dead, tables throughout the [Gilman] compound are set for one with glasses of water covered with plastic wrap, a flexible, striped straw poking through. Each of Hubbard's personal bathrooms has toothbrushes and identical sets of Thom McAn black thongs ready for him to step into after a shower or bath. Any spot where Hubbard would conceivably sit is furnished with a yellow legal pad and pen, usually placed at an artful slant. . . .

His snappy black, white and chrome office in the movie studio contains a kitchenette with a table set with fresh flowers and salt and pepper shakers. In the adjoining bathroom, equipped as a makeup studio, Hubbard's red wig rests on a mannequin's head. . . .

He owned enough photography gear to stock a large camera store, if not a chain of them. Hundreds of cameras are boxed with lenses ready for use. Another 3,000 pieces of gear are in storage.

The news of Hubbard's death was first given to a sizeable group of Scientologists, who had been peremptorily summoned to the Hollywood Palladium. Here the elusive Pat Broeker made his first public appearance of the 1980s. The audience was told that Hubbard had decided to "leave the body," because it was hindering his OT research. David Miscavige assured them that Hubbard had "moved on to his next level of OT research." Miscavige added, "This level is beyond anything any one of us ever imagined. This level is in fact done in an exterior state, meaning that it is done completely exterior from the body. At this level of OT, the body is nothing more than an impediment." According to Pat Broeker, "LRH expressly stated that there was to be no grief, no mourning . . . 'They know they're not a body. Don't let them be confused about it.' "

Hubbard's last message to his flock, dated five days before his death, was a Flag Order entitled "The Sea Org and the Future."[1] In it he assumed the rank of Admiral, and created the new rank of "Loyal Officer." Pat and Annie Broeker became the First and Second Loyal Officers respectively. Hubbard ended with a cheery message to Sea Org members, speaking of taking Scientology to other planets, and reassuring them that they would be seeing him again.

Heber Jentzsch, President of the Church of Scientology International, announced Hubbard's death to the press at 9:00 p.m. on Monday, January 27, 1986. Jentzsch told the Press that "after completing his life's work to his full satisfaction," Hubbard had "departed his body." Another Scientology spokesman said Hubbard would continue his research, having "learned how to do it without a body."

In March 1986, Scientologists celebrated Hubbard's birthday as usual. In Los Angeles, Annie Broeker made *her* first public appearance since the 1970s. Fumbling with her lines, looking tired and wearing too much makeup, she told the assembled fans a story. She said that Hubbard had once told her that "after the first tick of time" that one "Arp Cola" had invented music. There was a strong implication that Hubbard had been Cola. He had supposedly borrowed some of these early tunes and refashioned them into the modern style. The result was an album called "The Road to Freedom," which was released that night.

The record was made by Scientologist musicians, with Hubbard supervising at long distance through taped messages. Hubbard wrote the lyrics, which are peppered with Scientologese. They provide an insight into his state of mind at the end: "There was a worried being who did secret acts/ He felt he had to hide, hide, hide, hide, hide"; or, as a confession about the OT levels perhaps, "In olden days the populace was much afraid of demons/ And paid an awful sky high price to buy some priestly begones. . . . Oh now here is why that makes the world an evil circus/ No demons at all but just the easily erased evil purpose."

"Thank you for listening," the last ditty on the album, sung in a rumbling growl by Hubbard himself, takes the form of a "thank you" to attack his detractors: "For truth is truth and if they then decide to live with lies/ That's their concern not mine, my friend, they're free to fantasize."

A reviewer at the leading British music paper, the *Melody Maker*, finished his criticism of the album with this quip: "You're supposed to eat vegetables, not listen to them."

CHAPTER FIVE

After Hubbard

Scientology is here to rescue you—L. RON HUBBARD

Hubbard's last will and testament, dated the day before his death, held no surprises. He left an unspecified amount of money, the bulk of his fortune, to the "Author's Trust Fund B." Norman Starkey, a founding Sea Org member, became Hubbard's executor. He had been president of Author Services Inc., which marketed Hubbard's published works, since January 1983.

Hubbard disinherited his oldest son, Nibs, and his daughter by Sara, Alexis. Both were later paid settlements, Nibs having threatened litigation. To Scientologists Hubbard bequeathed only "my love and continued support, and my hopes for a better world." Secret provisions were made for his wife, Mary Sue, whom he had chosen not to see for the last six years of his life, and for her three surviving children. Provision was also made for Nibs' sister, Catherine.

In July 1986, a Los Angeles jury awarded $30 million in damages to ex-Scientologist Larry Wollersheim, who claimed that the Church had jeopardized his mental health and deliberately ruined his business. The jury also ruled that the Church must pay $45 million into the Court before they would be allowed to appeal. In July 1989, the California Court of Appeal upheld a ruling in Wollersheim's favor, repeating the earlier court's statement that he had been subjected to the Fair Game

Law by the Church of Scientology. However, the award was adjusted to $2.5 million.

In a surprise move in December 1986, the Church settled every case brought against them through Boston attorney Michael Flynn. They also settled out of court with former Mission Holder Martin Samuels, and with Julie Christofferson-Tichbourne. In a secret agreement, the plaintiffs agreed not to make any further public statements about Scientology, nor to disclose the amount of their settlements. When the document finally leaked out, it contained an interesting clause, saying that the amounts paid in settlement depended in part upon the ''length and degree of harassment'' each plaintiff had received. The payments amounted to almost $4 million, with Armstrong taking $800,000, and Flynn $1,075,000. For that price the Scientologists bought the silence of their most significant opponents. With the Armstrong settlement, the Hubbard archives material which had been held under seal was returned to the Scientologists. The contents of the Affirmations, the Blood Ritual, and Hubbard's letters to his three wives may never be published; but there is enough historical evidence now in the public record to show Hubbard for what he was. If a piece is broken from a hologram the entire image remains in the fragment. Hubbard too is implicit in every detail of his life, even in some of his most public utterances.

Michael Flynn fought against the Church for seven years. In doing so he spent a great deal of his own money, put his career in jeopardy, faced an unceasing barrage of invective and libel, and had to defend (and managed to win) some fourteen legal complaints brought against him by the Church. He gave succour to many ex-Scientologists. When Flynn settled, he gave all of his Scientology files (apart from client material) to the Church. But he had tried to ensure that the good fight would continue.

Throughout 1986, a group of over 400 former Scientologists gathered to create a Class Action against the Church. They called themselves Freedom for All In Religion, or FAIR. Michael Flynn was closely involved in the initial preparation of their Complaint.

On the last day of 1986, a few weeks after Flynn announced his withdrawal from the fight, the FAIR suit was filed in Los Angeles. It was filed not only against the Church of Scientology, but against its leading executives. There were three causes in the Complaint:

> a. Fraudulent representations have been made by defendants concerning their tax-exempt status and charitable nature, concerning the manner in which monies were obtained and received by L. Ron Hub-

bard and defendants named herein, concerning the confidentiality of defendants' auditing files, and concerning L. Ron Hubbard's background, achievements and character;

b. There has been a breach of fiduciary duty [breach of trust] to all the members of the class;

c. Plaintiffs seek equitable relief and request that a constructive trust be imposed on all pertinent assets of defendants.

A constructive trust would place the Preclear, Ethics and B-1 files of the members of FAIR into the hands of the Court until the case is settled. The suit was filed by a group of six ex-members, and demanded a billion dollars in relief. At the time of writing, after five amended Complaints, FAIR have failed to have a Complaint accepted for trial.

In April 1988, the former Inspector General of the Religious Technology Center filed a suit against various Scientology Organizations. Vicki Aznaran was an executive during the schism, rising to become David Miscavige's immediate junior. She and her husband, Richard, left the Sea Organization in April 1987.

The Aznarans' Complaint criticized the Team Member Share System operated at CMO headquarters, described as:

privately issued money in exchange for food, board, pay, bonuses and liberty. The Team Member System required that the Plaintiffs be given one of each of these cards when the Church administration was satisfied with their work production, and loyalty to the organization. Any dissatisfaction with the work output or 'attitude' of Plaintiffs would result in revocation of the tokens, thereby requiring Plaintiffs to work long hours with no days off, no pay, no board (requiring them to sleep outdoors on the ground [called 'pig berthing' in the Church issue]) and substandard nutrition comprised solely of rice, beans and water. When Plaintiffs had lost all of their cards, as a matter of course, they would be sent to the Rehabilitation Project Force for 'attitude adjustment,' which was comprised of even harsher labor, deprivation of liberty, and psychological duress forcing the submission of Plaintiffs to the power and control of Defendants.

The Aznarans had no reservations about the true intent of Church management, and described their treatment as "brainwashing," and their condition as "slave-like." Further, they asserted that the Scientologists had:

employed the following psychological devices . . . to cause Plaintiffs to involuntarily abandon their identities, spouses and loyalties, and deprive Plaintiffs of their independent free will. . . . Threats of torture; implementation of brainwashing tactics; threats of physical harm for lack of loyalty . . . lengthy interrogations . . . sudden involuntary and forceable separation of spouses from one another for many months, and depriving the spouses of communication with one another or allowing them to know where the other was located; willfully and expressly inducing divorce between Plaintiffs . . . deliberately inducing fatigue by physical abuse and deprivation of sleep; forcing Plaintiffs to be housed in animal quarters; deliberately confining Plaintiffs to premises under the control of Defendants and under threat of physical harm without allowing Plaintiffs to leave of their own free will; and threatening Plaintiffs that failure to submit to the power and control of Defendants would result in their becoming 'fair game.'

Vicki was sent on "mission" to Los Angeles in 1981 "to purge members of Defendants' organization . . . remove assets of Defendant Church of Scientology of California to overseas trusts where they could not be accessed by plaintiffs or the government, and set up sham corporate structures to evade prosecution generally. Richard was sent with Vicki in the capacity of a security investigator who surveilled members of the organizations associated with Defendants for the purposes of determining their loyalty and likelihood that they would testify against Defendants in pending civil and criminal suits, as well as designated 'enemies' of the Church."

In December 1981, Vicki Aznaran was assigned to Author Services Inc., a for-profit corporation using Sea Org personnel. She was "commissioned to reorganize corporate structures and effect sham sales of millions of copies of *Dianetics* to the corporate Defendants named herein as a vehicle for transferring assets among them."

In Spring 1982, Miscavige deprived Richard Aznaran of all his Team Member shares, and sent him to the Rehabilitation Project Force (RPF) in Los Angeles. His pay was reduced to $1.25 per week, and he spent ninety-nine days on the RPF. Meanwhile, Vicki worked directly for Hubbard's deputy, Ann Broeker. Meetings between Vicki and Richard were prohibited, so they met surreptitiously.

The Aznarans allege that the intention in October 1982 (the time of the San Francisco Mission Holders' Conference) was "for all Scientology entities to turn over their profits to . . . Author Services, Inc." When Vicki expressed disapproval of this, she was ordered to the RPF in Hemet where, "for approximately 120 days, [she] was forced to participate in the 'running program.' The running program required Vicki and other persons subjected to the control of Defendants to run around an orange telephone pole from 7:00 a.m. to 9:30 p.m. . . . with ten minute rests every one-half hour, and thirty minute breaks for lunch and dinner.''

In about May 1983, Vicki was ''deemed rehabilitated'' and ordered back to the Religious Technology Center at Gilman. Until Hubbard's death, the Aznarans remained at Gilman, when Richard was ordered to Hubbard's ranch at Creston working there as a security guard for a year and a half: ''Richard was forced to falsify time cards to falsely indicate that he had been working forty hour work weeks, so as to avoid an obligation on the part of Defendants from paying him overtime. . . . Richard was forced to sleep in a horse stable with several . . . other indoctrinated employees. During the course of Richard's stay at the ranch, Vicki was not told of his whereabouts, nor were Plaintiffs permitted to correspond with each other.''

Most important for the future of Scientology, the Aznarans claim that ''in or about February of 1987, a schism arose between Defendant Miscavige and the Broekers, each of whom claimed to possess the 'upper level Holy Scriptures' written by Hubbard.''

Miscavige allegedly saw Vicki's demands for contact with her husband as an ''expression of allegiance'' to the Broekers. Miscavige ordered Vicki to the RPF at ''Happy Valley,'' a ''secret location bordering the Sobova Indian Reservation near Gilman . . . overseen and controlled by Defendant Norman Starkey.''

Vicki was ''not allowed to go anywhere or do anything without her guard being present. At night she was imprisoned by having heavy furniture moved to secure the exit. . . . Defendants kept, and continue to keep all of her physical belongings including a horse and two dogs.''

Vicki claimed she ''had seen in the past other victims of Happy Valley be beaten upon attempted escape, and their personal belongings destroyed. . . . Vicki and others were made to wear rags taken out of garbage cans, sleep on the ground, dig ditches.''

Finally, on about April 9, 1987, ''Vicki and two other victims escaped from Happy Valley onto the Sobova Indian Reservation where they were pursued on motorcycles by guards.'' They were rescued by the Indians.

Richard Aznaran meanwhile was urged to divorce his wife. Instead, that very month they left the Sea Org, though not the Church, and returned to Dallas, Texas, where they started a private investigation business.

The Aznarans received a "Freeloader Bill," for Scientology services they had received while in the Sea Org, amounting to $59,048.02. They say that they did not seek legal assistance until January 1, 1988, because "As a result of the psychological trauma of indoctrination techniques applied by Defendants . . . Plaintiffs were unable to comprehend their legal rights with regard to the actions of Defendants."

Fraud is among their charges: "Defendants . . . knew that the practices of the so-called Church of Scientology . . . were not designed to increase the well being of any of its victims, but where [sic] made to coercively persuade each and every follower to dedicate their lives to Defendants in order for Defendants to increase their wealth derived from an overall scheme to make money founded on the exploitation of free labor. . . . Defendants . . . required Plaintiffs to participate in crimes against the United States Government, including the obstruction of justice and efforts to create corporate structures designed to keep payments from properly being paid to the Internal Revenue Service. . . . Plaintiffs were subjected to humiliation, degradation, physical labor, and imprisonment, all designed to break down their will and free thinking, and convert them into submissive, frightened and dedicated followers of Defendants."

The Aznarans also charge Breach of Contract: "Defendants . . . breached the said agreements [i.e. the provisions of the staff contract] by not providing any spiritual or psychological services, but rather, providing indoctrination, psychological coercion, duress and stress, all designed to break Plaintiffs' will so that they would remain compliant servants to Defendants for the remainder of their lives, and to the use of Defendants in furtherance of illegal conduct and money making schemes."

Invasion of Privacy is a further charge: "Plaintiffs were forced to participate in 'counselling sessions' in which they were forced to reveal that [sic] their innermost private thoughts and feelings." It was, of course, represented that these would be held in confidence, but "In April, 1987 . . . Defendants . . . read the private file of Plaintiff Vicki J. Aznaran. . . . Defendants . . . demanded that Vicki then publicly disclose and give further details concerning further events they had learned from said file concerning various other victims of Defendants. Vicki was advised, warned and threatened that if she did not give further details, Defendants, and each of them, would 'get it out of you one way or another.' "

The Complaint is a devastating indictment of the methods and motives of the current Scientology leadership.

In the month the Aznarans filed their Complaint, April 1988, the truth of their allegations about a rift at the top of Scientology were confirmed. David Miscavige, by this time both a captain in the Sea Org and the head of the Religious Technology Center, issued a Flag Order making the issue clear. He asserted that the Broekers had forged Hubbard's last published Order, promoting themselves to the command of the Sea Org as "Loyal Officers." Miscavige cancelled the new rank, saying that Pat Broeker had simply been part of Hubbard's domestic staff. The Broekers were "under standard justice handling" and were "being dealt with appropriately." However while canceling the supposed forgery, Miscavige made no mention of the rank given to Hubbard in it, so Hubbard remained an admiral, promoted, so it would seem, by a member of his domestic staff.

In June 1988, the Scientologists' new ship, the *Freewinds,* took her maiden voyage, with the first public OT8 students aboard. The *Freewinds* is a 440-foot cruise liner capable of carrying 450 passengers, and is based in Curaçao, in the Caribbean. As yet there is no indication that the Scientologists will return to their earlier shipboard practices.

At the end of June, the Scientologists filed a Complaint against their former attorney, Joseph Yanny, accusing him of "treachery," and saying he had "joined forces with confederates to mastermind and prosecute an action." The preamble to the Complaint says "what follows is a chronicle of betrayal, deception, and conspiracy practiced by members of the bar as a vendetta against a former client, and callous disregard of fiduciary and ethical obligations." Yanny responded with a declaration alleging that he had left the services of the Church because he was asked to participate in an attempt to blackmail an attorney hostile to the Church.

At the same time, an investigating magistrate in Milan started making arrests. By September 1988, seventy-six Scientologists had been committed for trial charged with offenses ranging from fraud to medical malpractice, and taking in criminal conspiracy to extort money and unlawful detention. The Scientology drug rehabilitation group, Narconon, came in for particularly stringent criticism: "Extravagant therapies were applied which yielded no practical results other than extracting huge sums of money from the families of young people who wanted to get out of the heroin trap.''

In November, Spanish police raided Scientology organizations (including Narconons) in Madrid, Barcelona, Valencia, Alicante, Seville, Jerez, Bilbao, Burgos and Ondaroa. Sixty-nine people were arrested, including the President of the Church of Scientology International, Heber Jentzsch. Eleven were eventually detained. The arrests followed a nine-month investigation headed by Judge Honrubia, who described Scientology as ''a multinational organization whose sole aim is making quick money under the guise of doing good.'' The judge concurred with the Italian opinion of Narconon, saying that their establishments were dirty, run by untrained staff and were actually little more than recruitment centers for Scientology. A Scientology spokesman muttered about Spain's ''fascist past,'' and Jentzsch accused Spain of a return to the Inquisition. He and two other non-residents were bailed for a million dollars the next month, pending trial.

P A R T N I N E

SUMMING UP

Scientology's may be the most debilitating set of rituals of any cult in America.—CONWAY and SIEGELMAN, "Information Disease," *Science Digest*, January 1982

CHAPTER ONE

The Founder

It can be said with more than a little truth that a society is lost when it loses its greed, for without hunger as a whip—for power, money or fame—man sinks into a blind sloth and, contented or not, is gone.— L. RON HUBBARD, "Greed," *Astounding Science Fiction*, April 1950

L. Ron Hubbard was an opportunist who lied consistently about his past, as part of a process of self-glorification. He was an arrogant, amoral egomaniac. Incapable of admitting his mistakes, he continually created scapegoats. The pure motives of his followers were exploited to build a secret mountain of cash. Hubbard was an outright plagiarist, who eventually could not bear to acknowledge anyone else's originality. He had a supreme distrust of the motives of all of humanity, despite his bland generalizations about man's basic goodness. This goodness would only be revealed after the individual had achieved some unspecified state of "OT." Hubbard was a paranoid, power hungry, petty sadist who paraded his inadequacies through ever more frequent tantrums. Revelling in his disciples' adulation, he spent his last years in seclusion, surrounded by sycophants. He had an alarming ability to keep all the many compartments of his life and his past separate, even, so it seems, in his own mind. Nonetheless, such a complicated man cannot be confined in such tidy definitions. Although the facts form a comprehensive picture, perhaps we have only caught glimpses of the man behind the many masks.

In February 1983, in written replies to *Rocky Mountain News* journalist Sue Lindsay, Hubbard said his favorite non-fiction book was *Twelve Against the Gods*, by William Bolitho, adding, "the introduction is particularly good." In this statement Hubbard provided a powerful clue to his most potent urge.

Bolitho's book was published in 1930, and consists of twelve short biographies. Its central point is that "adventure is the vitaminizing element in histories both individual and social." Bolitho lauded the adventurer above all others. His twelve chosen adventurers were Alexander, Casanova, Columbus, Mahomet, Lola Montez, Cagliostro (and Seraphina), Charles XII of Sweden, Napoleon, Catiline, Napoleon III, Isadora Duncan and, for topical reasons, Woodrow Wilson. Judging by the tone of the book, had Bolitho written a new edition in the 1940s, Hitler would very probably have replaced Wilson. The following quotations are all taken from the "particularly good" introduction, and clearly state Bolitho's basic thesis:

> The adventurer is within us, and he contests for our favor with the social man we are obliged to be. . . . We are obliged, in order to live at all, to make a cage of laws for ourselves and to stand on the perch. We are born as wasteful and unremorseful as tigers; we are obliged to be thrifty, or starve or freeze. We are born to wander, and cursed to stay and dig . . . all the poets are on one side, and all the laws on the other; for laws are made by, and usually for, old men . . .
>
> The moment one of these truants breaks loose, he has to fight the whole weight of things as they are; the laws and that indefinite smothering aura that surrounds the laws that we call morals; the family, that is the microcosm and whiplash of society; and the dead weight of all the possessors, across whose interwoven rights the road to freedom lies. If he fails he is a mere criminal . . .
>
> . . . the adventurer is an individualist and an egotist, a truant from obligations. His road is solitary, there is no room for company on it. What he does, he does for himself. His motive may be simple greed.

However, as Bolitho said, "these are men betrayed by contradiction inside themselves." With his casual reference to *Twelve Against the Gods*, Hubbard gave his own betraying contradiction: it is a glaring admission of his deep-seated aspirations. His readiness to laud the book shows that he saw nothing reprehensible in Bolitho's sentiments. The quoted passages give concise expression to the underlying pattern of Hubbard's whole life, and to his self-image. Hubbard considered himself an adventurer, a man above morality, who steadfastly followed his goal. It is possible that Hubbard read Bolitho's book when it was published (he was nineteen at the time), and took it as his model. His mention of it in 1983 was not the first. He had already praised it, in a 1952 lecture, at the very beginning of Scientology.[1]

There is powerful evidence to support this thesis. In 1938, at the age of twenty-seven, just after his failure to find a publisher for *Excalibur*, Hubbard wrote a long letter to his first wife. Hubbard told Polly he had received a unique insight into the nature of reality. His understanding made him superior to all of humanity. He was utterly single-minded in his objective: to be remembered in future centuries as the equal of his heroes Napoleon Bonaparte, Genghis Khan and Alexander the Great, even if every word he wrote was lost. He had no other purpose, and became depressed when he was thwarted; but in the throes of the mysterious power which stirred in him, he felt absolutely unbeatable. He spoke of the possibility of becoming a demagogue, a great political leader. He also admitted to his craving for applause.

Hubbard lusted after fame, wealth and power, and was clearly willing to abandon moral restrictions to accomplish his ends.

Hubbard was a natural entertainer, able to captivate some people with his charm. It often took prolonged, close contact for those so charmed to see that he was arrogant, extravagant, eccentric and a liar on a grand scale. Even then many continued to believe in his genius.

Hubbard can be dismissed as a fabulist, a compulsive storyteller, whose exaggerations were harmless. But he was far worse than this. His avarice coupled to deliberate deceit became outright fraud. Hubbard plainly made fraudulent claims about himself and his supposed research. He also made fraudulent claims about the money gathered ostensibly to further the publicized aims of Scientology. This was not harmless puffery: it was conscious deceit designed to make him ever more famous, influential and wealthy. The poverty and suffering of those believers who sustained his opulent life-style must also be taken into account.

Although Hubbard single-mindedly pursued his ambition, he may well have believed throughout that he was doing good. Nonetheless, he laid his "road to truth" on a foundation of lies. Hubbard's long hours and obvious absorption in his work support the view that he believed in the efficacy of his "Technology." Bolitho's idea that "the magician must believe in himself, if it is only as long as he is spouting,'' falls short of the mark. Martin Gardner, well known adversary of parapsychology in general and Ron Hubbard in particular, made a germane observation: "Cranks by definition believe their theories, and charlatans do not, but this does not prevent a person from being both crank and charlatan.'' Hubbard's fraudulent claims undoubtedly make a charlatan of him.

In the mid-1960s, Hubbard began to speak of himself as the "Source" of Scientology. Having initially acknowledged a debt to Freud and a host of philosophers, and having handed out numerous "Fellowships" to Scientologists for their "major contributions," he finally decided that Scientology was his creation alone: "Willing as I was to accept suggestions and data, only a handful of suggestions (less than twenty) had long run value and *none* were major or basic; and when I did accept major or basic suggestions and used them, we went astray.''[2]

Hubbard was not truly the "Source" of Scientology; little, if any, of his work is original. Hubbard pieced together modified versions of existing ideas. Hubbard's peculiar genius was for reframing such ideas so they would fit neatly into his own belief system, and articulating them in a digestible form. For example, Scientology organizations use surveying techniques derived from Motivational Research, which was developed by psychiatrists in the 1950s. The only text referred to by Hubbard in this connection was Vance Packard's *The Hidden Persuaders*. Hubbard failed to acknowledge that Scientology survey methods derive from the psychiatric stimulus-response techniques which Packard was attacking.

Hubbard insisted that Scientology alone could save the world from a holocaust. Scientology would create "a civilization without insanity, without criminals and without war, where the able can prosper.'' His own survival, in an environment conducive to "research,'' was therefore imperative, at least until his work was complete. In his own words: "the whole agonized future of this planet, every Man, Woman and Child . . . depends on what you do here and now with and in Scientology.''[3] Hubbard believed that his was a messianic mission. To quote from his obtuse poem *Hymn of Asia*, written in the 1950s: "See me dead/ Then I will live forever/ But you will/ See/ An Earth in flames/ So deadly that/ Not one will live/ Fail once to stem/ A hand that smites/ Against me and/ I die.''

In his writings, Hubbard made a distinction between morals and ethics; the former being based upon custom and opinion, the latter upon reasoned "pro-survival" decisions. He advocated the pursuit of "the greatest good for the greatest number of dynamics" (the eight "dynamics," or urges toward survival for self, family, groups, mankind, matter, other lifeforms, spirit and infinity). If Scientology was to save the world, and if it depended upon L. Ron Hubbard for its completion, then the "greatest good for the greatest number of dynamics" would always include as its most significant aspect the continued protection and support of L. Ron Hubbard.

To Hubbard, anyone who opposed or even criticized him was evil, their opposition to him inevitably slowing the progress of mankind. It was his published assertion that the "anti-Scientologist" and the "anti-social personality" are one and the same. His obsession with enemies sprang from his evident paranoia. A former Director of the original Hubbard Dianetic Research Foundation told me of Hubbard's overwhelming suspicion about agents infiltrating the organization. A girlfriend of the early 1950s said Hubbard was forever looking over his shoulder. The trait developed, until he came to believe that the American Medical Association, the World Federation of Mental Health, the world bankers, the press barons, and the Western governments were all involved in a multi-million dollar plan to destroy Scientology and, most especially, L. Ron Hubbard.

In his ruling in the Armstrong suit in California, Judge Breckenridge called Hubbard "schizophrenic," but was he really insane? Avoiding the sometimes contradictory definitions of psychiatric authorities, it seems safe to take the legal view that a madman is someone who cannot be considered responsible for his actions. He suffers from delusions, and has no clear sense of right and wrong. Psychiatrist Frank Gerbode, who practiced Scientology for many years, feels that Hubbard was not schizophrenic, but rather "manic with paranoid tendencies" (which is not a classification of psychosis, but of tendencies towards psychosis). However, Gerbode suggests that the best description is the lay diagnosis "loony." Even if Hubbard was manic with paranoid tendencies, he was still sane in the eyes of the law, and therefore still responsible for his actions.

Hubbard borrowed the expression "anti-social personality" from psychiatry, where it is synonymous with psychopath and sociopath. Professor of psychiatry Hervey Cleckley, who became famous with his co-authorship of *The Three Faces of Eve*, was an acknowledged authority on psychopaths. In his book *The Mask of Sanity*, he listed sixteen telling characteristics, the majority of which are found in psychopaths.

Cleckley pictured psychopaths as superficially charming and of good intelligence. Their thinking is logical, and has a basis in reality, which is to say they do not suffer from delusions. They are not nervous or neurotic. They are unreliable, untruthful and insincere. They feel no remorse. They perform anti-social acts without any real motive. Psychopaths do not learn from experience. They have "pathologic" egocentricity, an incapacity for love and are unresponsive in relationships. They cannot comprehend the response generated by their antisocial actions. Psychopaths demonstrate uninviting behavior, and tend to drink or take drugs. Finally, they do not respond to any sort of therapy. According to Cleckley, psychopaths have a remarkable ability to evade punishment. A psychiatrist could construct a powerful case to support the diagnosis that Hubbard was a psychopath, or anti-social personality. At least in Cleckley's terms.

Of course, Hubbard had his own version of the anti-social personalities, Suppressive Persons or anti-Scientologists: they speak in generalities ("everybody knows"); deal mainly in bad news; worsen communication they are relaying; are surrounded by "cowed or ill associates or friends"; habitually select the wrong target, or source; are unable to finish anything; willingly confess to alarming crimes, without any sense of responsibility; support only destructive groups; approve only destructive actions; detest help being given to others, and use "helping" as a pretext to destroy others; they believe that no one really owns anything; and fail to respond to therapy.

Hubbard conforms to a number of the characteristics in both his own and Cleckley's summaries. Hubbard's clinching point for the recognition of an anti-social personality was the inability of the Suppressive to see in himself any of the listed deficiencies. There is no suggestion that Hubbard ever saw himself as a Suppressive Person.

However, as another authority, Robert G. Kegan, has pointed out, the traits of the psychopath are also true of many ten-year-olds (in "The Child Behind the Mask: Sociopathy as Developmental Delay"). Hubbard was very much an overgrown child, and it is easy to see aspects both of his behavior and of Scientology as projections of this dangerous immaturity. Hubbard's self-obsession fits neatly into the psychopathic type known as a narcissist.

Judge Breckenridge called the Church of Scientology Hubbard's "alter-ego," a perceptive comment. Indeed, the whole of Scientology can be seen as an externalization of Hubbard's temperament.

Scientology makes more sense when seen in the light of Hubbard's psychopathic tendencies and his paranoia. His bouts of exhilaration in the belief that he had conquered some deficiency, and his bouts of intense and usually private depression when his deficiencies once more took hold, created a pattern which runs throughout Scientology.

Hubbard had promised a release from stimulus-response behavior through Dianetics, yet most of his work was itself a predictable response to some immediate threat. The Guardian's Office came into being as a consequence of Lord Balniel's 1966 question in Parliament. The "technology" of counselling was an ongoing attempt to cure Hubbard's own ailments. Various early techniques designed to cure what Hubbard called "terror stomach" were surely an attempt to relieve his ulcer. Despite Dianetics, his ulcer, his poor eyesight and his bursitis persisted. In the 1960s, he suffered periodically from pneumonia, probably worsened by his drug abuse, definitely worsened by his chain-smoking. He promised that OT3 would cure such respiratory problems; it certainly did not work for him. Hubbard suffered from a catalogue of disabilities. No matter how much Tech he developed, he continued to suffer from the same difficulties, both mental and physical. Various prescriptions for mega-vitamin therapy, and a bizarre (and potentially dangerous) bulletin about antibiotics came out of his 1972 illness. In 1978, he suffered a second heart attack, and NOTs was developed in an attempt to assist his recovery. It is often possible to trace Hubbard's obsession with a particular new counselling "rundown" to some disability of his own.

Yet from 1950 onwards, Hubbard was to insist again and again that he had the solution to all human problems. When the method of the first book failed to Clear anybody (despite the claims that 273 people had been counselled and many Cleared as part of an exhaustive research program), new methods were released. Alphia Hart, who published his own journal after leaving Scientology in 1953, called the device "This is It," and suggested that each claim should be carefully dated so that "This is it! 1955" could be distinguished from "This is It! 1959," and so forth. There were tens of Clearing procedures, all promoted and sold as The Answer, and all superseded after a few months. Nibs Hubbard says his father produced a new technique every six months. The *Technical Bulletins of Dianetics and Scientology* (available in twelve bound volumes, with half a dozen supplementary folders) prove the truth of his assertion.

Hubbard seems to have believed himself cured every time. There are a series of excuses built in to Scientology to explain each failure, and to justify Hubbard's relapses. These are enshrined as "correction lists" and "rundowns." Where all of these fail, the individual is given "ethics handling" (something Hubbard certainly never received!). The final solution for any failure to improve is that the individual who has received, and paid for, all of these correction lists, rundowns and handlings is a "no case gain case," that is, a Suppressive Person.

All of these responses to stimuli accumulated to become Scientology. They are the incidents (or "engrams," perhaps) which make Scientology: procedures designed to solve Hubbard's own immediate problem, and then used on all Scientologists, whatever their difficulties. Nothing written by Hubbard could be removed from the literature without his approval, and he was too busy churning out new material to revise old, so these ingrained responses were rarely relieved.

Hubbard read voraciously, mostly pulp fiction. There is nothing to suggest that he studied any serious subject in depth. It is doubtful that he read much Freud, or Korzybski (he claimed Heinlein had explained Korzybski to him, though his second wife, Sara, says she did). He read popularizations. In a lecture on study he complained that the contemporary *Encyclopaedia Britannica* was too difficult for him, it was written by experts for experts, so he used the pre-World War One edition. In what appeared to be a joke, he said he intended to use children's textbooks in future. This parallels his self-confessed method of story research, described in a 1930s article called "Search for Research." He would read the *Britannica* entry, and then skim through any readily available books referred to in the entry's bibliography. The story had to be written in a couple of days, so research had to be fast. Whole sections of Scientology also seem to have been fashioned in this way. The original Dianetic techniques can be derived almost entirely from three short Freud lectures. Hubbard's statements about Buddhism also show a lack of study. In fact, he only started to incorporate what he believed to be Buddhist ideas in the early 1950s, after he had been given an extensive library of mystical and religious books. One of his staff read and summarized the contents.[4] Hubbard displayed no specialized knowledge of any subject, except of course Scientology.

Hubbard created a curious amalgam. Dianetics came from Freud (with echoes of Fodor and Rank), Korzybski and possibly from certain wartime, psychiatric work in abreactive therapy. The origins of Scientology are in Aleister Crowley's Magick, a smattering of schoolboy science, demon exorcism and science fiction. The Sea Org derives directly from Hubbard's naval experience; not only does it have uniforms, ranks and campaign ribbons, but also Fitness Boards, Committees of Evidence, Compliance Reports and Commendations. These diverse elements were rounded out with touches of behavioral therapy, Chinese brainwashing techniques, references to Machiavelli (Hubbard said *The Prince* was one of his favorite books, and even claimed to have written it), and possibly some acquaintance with Gustave le Bon's crowd psychology. All of this disparate material was synthesized through the personality of L. Ron Hubbard.

Hubbard spent his life searching for one particular experience. From the early 1950s, he had insisted that "exteriorization," or out-of-the-body experience, was the crucial element of Scientology. He was convinced that he had such an experience in 1938, under the influence of nitrous oxide, which led to the writing of *Excalibur*. Hubbard desperately wanted to repeat that experience and, according to those who audited him, was never able to do so, despite his glib claims about Scientology techniques which would readily and rapidly produce "exteriorization." Hubbard published numerous techniques, and, of course, made elaborate claims for their efficacy. Indeed, the stated purpose of Scientology is to create a "stable" exterior state, whereby the individual consciously achieves immortality.

Having decided in 1952 that most science fiction is actually a recounting of real past-life experience, Hubbard's own preoccupations as a science fiction writer became the cosmology of his religion. He was an egomaniac who generated an egomaniacal philosophy, which had at its core the belief that whatever happens to others is their own fault. Whatever happened to L. Ron Hubbard was the fault of a great Conspiracy. He advocated personal responsibility to his followers, but almost uniformly failed to practice what he preached.

The most alarming aspect of Scientology is the barely concealed thrust towards world domination. Sea Org members are told that *when* World War Three finally happens, they will be the only group which is well enough organized to take over. At various times Hubbard and his followers have courted different governments—in the 1960s in Rhodesia (for which he wrote a proposed Constitution), and in Greece (with the would-be University of Philosophy in Corfu); in the 1970s in Morocco and later Mexico, where members of the government opposition travelled to Florida for counselling. China and several African nations have been approached, with offers of help with educational policy. Ron Hubbard would have liked to rule the world. He believed, and said, that benevolent dictatorship is the best political system, and saw himself as the only natural candidate. His successors possibly suffer from the same conceit.

In the mid-1970s while in Washington, DC, Hubbard inaugurated a secret project to find out all he could about the "Soldiers of Light" and the "Soldiers of Darkness." The notion that people are born either good or evil and engage in a cosmic spiritual war can be found in Zoroastrianism, and in the Dead Sea Scrolls of the Essenes, whence it found its way into certain Gnostic Christian sects. In the early 1950s Hubbard had talked about people being "players," "pieces" or "broken pieces" in the "game" of life. This concept is fundamental to Scientology. He later spoke of "Big Beings" existing in a ratio of one to eighteen compared to "Degraded Beings." Separately from this estimate, he said that Suppressives make up two and a half percent of the population, and Potential Trouble Sources (PTSes) who are in their sway a further 17.5 percent. He categorized some people simply as "robots," incapable of decision. In short, there are a small number of "players," some Soldiers of Light, some Soldiers of Darkness. They are engaged in an eternal battle, using the "pieces" and "broken pieces" to achieve their ends.

In confidential issues, Hubbard dismissed Christian teaching as an "implant." Psychiatrists and Christian ministers are the Soldiers of Darkness, the suppressives, returning life after life[5] to torment the degraded beings, robots, and PTSes, and destroy the handiwork of the Soldiers of Light. Of course, by Hubbard's standards the Soldiers of Light were those individuals currently in favor with the Scientology Church. Hubbard is their Emperor, the "Source." Hubbard believed in the Nietzschean Superman, the OT or Big Being and the right of the "good" and the "just" to abuse the "evil."

Most of Hubbard's thousands of followers regarded him as more brilliant than Einstein, more enlightened than Buddha, and quite as capable of miracles as Christ. Perhaps there was a more sinister motive underlying Hubbard's actions. Some Taoists believe that human beings can achieve immortality by becoming the focus of worship; some of the Roman Emperors had a similar belief. The deification of Hubbard seems to be taking place in the Scientology Church throughout the world. Maybe he thought he was gathering up all of his devotees' shed body-Thetans so that he could use them for magical purposes (in his secret Affirmations, Hubbard asserted that elemental beings were completely in his power). Given his fertile, and often juvenile, imagination, and an awareness of his duplicity, it is hard to decide what Ron Hubbard really did believe.

Hubbard was a fabulist and a mesmerist, a spinner of both tales and spells. A charismatic figure who compelled the devotion of those around him, despite his cruelties and eccentricities. Some who worked with him say he was "compassionate." On the *Apollo* he was seen working remarkable hours on Preclear folders. He spent thousands of hours lecturing and writing about Scientology.

He also masterminded, organized and directed a series of crimes on an international scale, yet escaped punishment completely. Unless his belief in karma (carefully repackaged in Scientology) turns out to be true.

CHAPTER TWO

The Scientologist

But in an open Society, such as ours, people can believe what they want to and band together and promulgate their beliefs. If people believe that the earth is flat there is nothing to stop them believing so, saying so and joining together to persuade others.—JUSTICE LATEY

Hubbard cast his net wide. Scientology has attracted people from most social and intellectual backgrounds, from laborers to lawyers, from plumbers to university professors. Frederick L. Schuman, professor of political science at Williams College, was an enthusiastic convert, and publicly defended Dianetics in 1950, though he soon changed his tack and distanced himself. There were psychologists working in the original Foundations; in fact, the New York Foundation was started by psychologist Nancy Rodenburg. Fritz Perls, founder of Gestalt therapy, defended Hubbard's early work (though insisting that it needed scientific validation), and briefly received Dianetic counselling.

British Member of Parliament William Hamling, and former Lieutenant-Governor of Western Nigeria, Sir Chandos Hoskyns-Abrahall, have already been mentioned. Two Danish MPs were Scientologists at one time. Several NASA scientists have belonged to the Church. Dr. J.L. Simmons, who lectured in sociology at the Universities of Illinois and California, wrote an appendix to Roy Wallis's *Road to Total Freedom* sharply criticizing both the author's approach

378

and his conclusions. At the time, Simmons was a convinced Scientologist; since leaving the Church he probably regrets aspects of his statement. Research physicist, and former Stanford professor, Harold Puthoff, was also a member of the Church. Puthoff, who holds several patents for laser developments, is best known for his books on parapsychology co-written with Russell Targ. Ingo Swann, who was the subject in some of Puthoff and Targs' parapsychology experiments, was a member of the Church for some years. His novel *Star Fire* was a best seller. Another Scientologist also achieved best seller status with a novel about reincarnation.

A group of Oxford graduates were long-term members. A number of medical doctors, dentists and lawyers have been involved. Over the years Scientology has also boasted the adherence of several celebrities. Virtuoso jazz pianist Chick Corea, a member since 1968, is an OT, as is Stanley Clarke, the highly influential jazz bass player. Clarke has left the Church, but Corea remains in the fold. The Incredible String Band were Scientologists, and distributed Scientology literature at their gigs. Actors John Travolta and Karen Black are both Church members, as is "Waltons" star Judy Norton-Taylor. Priscilla Presley has been involved for many years, and Elvis' daughter, Lisa Marie, is a Sea Org member. Van Morrison was associated with Scientology for a short while. The novelist William Burroughs went Clear in the 1960s, but later satirized the movement in several novels. Scientology has also attracted many millionaires, and several multi-millionaires.

Most cults have a single selling feature, and so tend to appeal to a specific public. Scientology claims to be all things to all people: a psychotherapy, a religion, twentieth-century Buddhism, an educational system, a drug rehabilitation therapy, a human rights and social reform movement, or a business management system. It is spiritual, mental or material according to the mind-set of the person being approached. Scientology front groups appeal to different publics. Scientologists are drilled to quickly isolate an individual's concerns and tailor an approach which encourages interest.

The most contentious of these self-made characterizations is that of religion. Whether Scientology is a "religion" is a matter of definition. Because of the very broad nature of the definition of religion in the United States, it has been established that Scientology is a religion in the legal sense. However, in the United States religious status does not automatically give an organization tax-exemption, which Scientology has failed to achieve. In Australia, Scientology is also recognized as a religion, though the court there added "Regardless of whether the members of the applicant [the Church of Scientology] are gullible or misled or whether the practices of Scientology are harmful or objectionable." English law differs, and accords with the dictionaries: a religion is committed to acts of worship. Scientology has none, but claims to be a religion in the same sense as Buddhism, without a deity or deities, and consequently without worship. Lord Denning set a precedent in England by agreeing that Scientology could indeed be compared to Buddhism, which, because it has no act of worship, is not legally a religion, but a philosophy or way of life.

Scientologists are willing to see their practice as a psychotherapy or as a religion, but few would acknowledge that it is a belief system. They are convinced that it is a science, based upon Hubbard's intense research. This is simply untrue. In thirty-six years Hubbard failed to produce a single piece of work which meets acceptable scientific criteria.

The techniques of Scientology are loosely embedded in a sometimes tortuous philosophy. At the core of this is a relatively simple cosmology which starts with the first three "Factors of Scientology." These give Hubbard's explanation of the origin of life:

1. Before the beginning was a Cause and the entire purpose of the Cause was the creation of effect.
2. In the beginning and forever is the decision, and the decision is TO BE.
3. The first action of beingness is to assume a viewpoint.[1]

From this viewpoint the universe is perceived. The first "Axiom" of Scientology is "Life is basically a static," which has "no mass, no motion, no wavelength, no location in space or in time. It has the ability to postulate and to perceive."

The Life Static is most usually called a Thetan. The Thetan is immortal and does not owe its origin to God. It is perpetually individual.[2] After the beginning, Thetans generated "points to view," or "dimension points" which caused space to come into existence. Thetans agreed that other Thetans' dimension points existed, and that agreement brought about Reality. Reality, indeed the entire universe, is an "agreed upon apparency," and all matter, energy, space and time (MEST) exists because Thetans agree it exists. But for continued existence there has to be a lie ("alter-is-ness") in the fabric of these aspects of Reality, for if anything is seen exactly as it is ("as-ised") it will cease to exist. Reality, to the Scientologist, is a communal daydream.

Thetans are all-knowing beings, and became bored because there were no surprises. Hubbard asserted that the single most important desire in all beings is to have a "game." To have a "game" it was necessary to "not know" certain things, so certain perceptions were negated ("not-is-ed"). More and more perception and knowledge had to be abandoned as time passed, and some Thetans started the "game" of creating traps for other Thetans. Believing it possible to harm others, Thetans learned contrition, and punished themselves for their own "harmful" acts. An ongoing part of this self-imposed punishment is dwindling perception.

One universe ended and another began, and there have been many universes, each more solid and entrapping than the last. An essential part of the game was the "conquest" of matter, energy, space and time by the life force, Theta. In each universe Thetans have become more enmeshed in matter, energy, space and time (MEST), to the point where many have identified themselves totally with it, and consider themselves nothing but MEST. Thetans are by now in a hypnoid state, having forgotten their quadrillions of years of existence and their original godly power, barely capable of even leaving their bodies at will.

Thetans nevertheless have the power of "postulate." Whatever they intend comes into being. Negative decisions and opinions, or "bad postulates," generate a negative destiny. For quadrillenia, Thetans have been "implanting" one another with hypnotic suggestions, and clustering other Thetans together (turning most into "body-Thetans"). Scientology seeks to undo "other-determinism," and return the Thetan to "self-determinism," and eventually to "pan-determinism" where he acts for the good of all.

Most of these ideas can be found elsewhere. "Before the beginning was a Cause" is highly reminiscent of the central premise of the Tao Teh Ching. In the Bhagavad Gita, Krishna teaches Arjuna that he is immortal and imperishable, that life is a game, and that in truth no harm can be done to others, as they too are immortal and imperishable. The comparable word for "Thetan" is "atman." The doctrine of reincarnation is common to several major religions. That we reap as we have sown, or karma-vipaka, even more so. The emphasis upon the development of Intention, or the ability to postulate, in Scientology comes straight from Crowley's "thelema" or Will, upon which most magical systems concentrate.

To sum up: Hubbard saw the individual's current state as a fall from grace, but the individual's own grace, not that of God. He saw the Thetan as an all-capable individual, who has gradually restricted his powers, over "quadrillions" of years, in part to have a "game," and in part for fear of hurting others. He called this degeneration the "dwindling spiral." In Scientology counselling, the Preclear is directed back to incidents in his past existences which have shaped his way of thinking (and consequently his current circumstances). A better future is to be obtained by release from quadrillenia of long forgotten conditioning and guilt. Sociologists use the term "neo-gnosticism" to describe such beliefs when they are allied to a supposed system of enlightenment (many of the original Christian gnostic sects spent their time learning the passwords which would give them entry to heaven after death).

The more indoctrination into Hubbard's ideas they receive, the more Scientologists fall in with his view of universal history. When first reviewing "past lives" in counselling, famous lives will be offered. There are many Napoleons and Christs. Several Guardian's Office staff have told me that they felt they were paying for the harm they had done in former lives as Gestapo or SS officers. With more indoctrination, the individual starts to offer incidents which occurred in outer space, and at "implant stations." Even so, no one is required to accept Hubbard's cosmology wholeheartedly until the Operating Thetan levels. OT3 is the point of departure. If you refuse to believe in Xenu or the body thetans you can go no further. The courses leading up to OT3 (specifically Grade 6, the clearing Course, and OT2), are actually part of the same conception, but their mystifying procedures are not explained until OT3, when the individual learns he has been dealing with OT3 implants, which had to be relieved before it was safe to reveal the horrible truth of the entire incident. At any given time, the majority of Scientologists have not done OT3, so will not know its content. To them it is a mysterious and compelling promise of future liberation, but deadly to the unprepared. In over twenty years, only a few thousand people have actually done OT3, many deciding it was of questionable value at least, and mind-bending at worst. The secret OT levels up to OT8 are simply extensions of the Body-Thetan idea (sleeping Body-Thetans, Body-Thetans in parallel universes, and so forth).

Certain tenets are essential to Scientology. The first is the assumption that Man is basically good (although this does not extend to critics of Scientology, even those who helped to create and sustain the movement. Those who criticize Scientology are irrevocably evil). Scientology aims to raise the Emotional Tone Level of the individual to Enthusiasm and beyond. Scientologists believe that any problem, whether physical or mental, exists because there is some distortion in their perception of it (the lie or "alter-is-ness" which brings about persistence). They are positive thinkers, believing that their "postulates" will come true, and seeing their failures in life as simply failures to postulate with sufficient conviction. To paraphrase Hubbard: considerations are senior to the mechanics of matter, energy, space and time. So the Scientologist sees all problems, including his own, as essentially mental, and self-generated. Scientologists have an optimistic persistence, allied to acute gullibility. OTs have died of cancer believing they could postulate it away, avoiding proper medical action.

Despite its claims to be nondenominational, and to welcome members of all religions, Scientology is essentially anti-Christian. In confidential materials Hubbard attacked Christianity as an "implant," and said that Christ was a fiction. He railed against "priests."[3] The belief in reincarnation is also necessary for progress through even the early levels of Scientology. Hubbard's Scientology morality is opposed to Christianity. Certain basic Christian values are despised by the Scientologist, who considers them misconceived. Humility is supplanted by self-pride. Searching self-criticism is considered dangerous ("never disparage yourself," to quote Hubbard).[4] Material wealth is a virtue. Charity creates dependence. In Scientology, there is no concept of God, nor of grace. The Scientologist is in every respect a self-made Thetan.

Nor is Scientology compatible with the beliefs of other faiths. A Buddhist, for example, could not truly be a Scientologist. The core of Buddhism is the disintegration of the self (anatta), where Scientology believes the self to be all-important and perpetual. Hubbard dismissed yoga and all other mystical systems as traps: "Data from India, even that found in the deepest 'mysteries' . . . is knowingly or unknowingly 'booby-trapped.' "[5] While receiving counseling the Scientologist is prohibited from other practices, including meditation. There are specific steps in auditing to erase adherence to other systems and beliefs. Scientology is the only way. Recently, the Scientologists have trotted out one of their number who is a Catholic priest. He says there is no conflict, but has a surprise in store on the OT levels.

Hubbard also insisted upon "exchange." Despite Church claims, no one has ever told me that they received even an hour of charity auditing from the Church. In Scientology, it is considered immoral to do something for nothing. The starving and the crippled are seen as living out self-generated misfortune. Coupling this to Hubbard's philosophy of exchange, Scientologists do not usually give to charity, except to Scientology causes, or in the interests of public relations (the "exchange" being the generation of public goodwill towards Scientology). This can result in an alarming lack of fellow feeling.

On first meeting, most Scientologists have a friendly demeanor, but this is unsurprising in a group so eager to gain converts. To promote a practice which supposedly brings about cheerfulness, it is necessary to appear cheerful. Sea Org members are trained to be friendly to the public, but behind closed doors they are ruthless and scream at their subordinates, giving them "severe reality adjustments." Some have a private conceit that they are the elect, seeing even their own paying public as no more than cattle to be milked.

Scientologists are often self-confident and self-assertive. They are not allowed to discuss their "cases" (difficulties), and are discouraged from even thinking about personal problems outside the counselling room. They are also prohibited from entering into detailed discussions of Scientology ("verbal Tech"), and from voicing criticism of Scientology. This can lead to a suspension of the analytical faculty, especially as it applies to self-observation and self-criticism. Scientologists often take vitamins instead of medicinal drugs, even avoiding aspirin. Hubbard was not averse to sleeping with female students, though he did so discreetly, until the mid-1960s. Promiscuity was not unusual, though by no means the norm in Scientology into the early 1970s. By the time I joined, in 1974, these days were over. I did not find Scientologists especially prudish, though Sea Org members are prohibited from sexual relations with anyone except their legal spouse. Homosexuality is outlawed; Hubbard insisted that the Emotional Tone Level of a homosexual is "covert hostility": they are backstabbers, each and every one.

Scientologist communities have a limited social life; there is simply no time. Staff members are hard at work bettering their stats, and public Scientologists are hard at work to pay off the loans they've taken out for exorbitantly priced Scientology courses. The work ethic prevails. Wealthy people and celebrities are doted upon by Sea Org members.

There are financial benefits in selling Scientology to others. Field Staff Members (FSMs) are paid a ten percent commission on any counselling, and a fifteen percent commission on any training they sell. There are even a few Scientologists who have derived their entire income, and paid for their own Scientology, by working as FSMs. Scientology "Registrars" (sales staff) are openly trained in hard sell techniques. They believe in the power of Scientology to such an extent that they will push individuals into financially disastrous situations, and many people have been financially ruined by Scientology. There is a widespread belief that people will automatically become capable of repaying loans after they have taken the Scientology courses or counselling those very loans paid for. The Registrars receive a sales commission, and are usually the only people in an Org who make anything like a living wage.

Recruitment for staff is a constant pressure on public Scientologists. There is a push to "recruit in abundance," to use Hubbard's expression. Students are carefully routed through various sections of the Organization when starting and finishing a course. Recruitment is built into the "routing form" at the end of every course. The majority of Scientologists spend some time on staff.

Most Scientologists genuinely want to improve society. They fervently believe their ideology is the only hope for a better world. Hubbard's motives are highly questionable, but the motives of the great majority of Scientologists are good. They wish to make people happier and more capable. Nothing in their philosophy jars with receiving a commission for doing so, though most take their commission in Scientology "services."

In some respects, Scientology is a philosophy well-suited to the last phase of the rapacious Industrial Age. It glorifies personal wealth, and teaches people that they are not responsible for the condition of the world. It is geared for the high speed of modern society, raising statistics and increasing production, concentrating on quantity at the expense of quality. It is also claimed to be virtually "instant," though after decades of noisy claims the Scientologists are still incapable of producing anyone who meets the criteria laid out for a Clear in Hubbard's original book, *Dianetics: The Modern Science of Mental*

Health. Some Scientologists have given almost forty years of their lives, and enormous sums of money, without attaining any of the promised abilities of the state of Operating Thetan.

Membership of Scientology is split into distinct categories. Having become involved, some people remain "public" Scientologists. They pay for their auditing and training and do not become staff members. Because they cannot afford the exorbitant cost of Scientology, many join the staff of a Mission or Org. A large proportion go on to join the Sea Organization. The majority leave the Sea Org within a few months, and end up paying huge amounts in "Freeloader Bills" for the Sea Org training they received, before they are allowed to receive any more Scientology. All Scientology staff members are under contract, and a Freeloader Bill is imposed on anyone who leaves before their time is up—whether it be the two-and-a-half- or five-year staff contract, or the Sea Org's round billion. Freeloader Bills often amount to tens of thousands of dollars. Those who fail to join or drop out of the Sea Org often feel guilty or inadequate.

As well as the distinction between public and staff Scientologists, there is a divide between those who have taken OT levels and those who have not. At any given time, the majority of Church members will have no idea of the contents of the secret OT levels. They adulate OTs, believing them capable of all sorts of magical feats or "OT abilities." It is amazing how well this mystique is maintained, as in Scientology there are no credible demonstrations of paranormal abilities. Bathing in this admiration, many OTs begin to feel they really do have psychic powers. Most encourage the uninitiated to believe their fantastic notions about the state of "OT." Dissatisfied OTs usually believe that their inability to perform is their own fault, and avoid disabusing others of the beliefs Hubbard has given them about OT.

After years of claims about the powers of OTs, Hubbard redefined the state in 1982. He said the available OT levels were actually a preparation for *real* OT levels, which were yet to be released. Even so, each level confers a new status upon the recipient, and the OT is convinced he guards a dangerous secret. OTs usually believe they are influencing events through psychic power.

A set of beliefs can create a community which is almost a nation apart. This is certainly true of Scientology. Comparison with real nations, and their agencies, sheds a different light on the behavior of the Scientology community. While the totalitarian system of the Communist bloc provides far closer parallels with the authoritarian and absolutist nature of Scientology, Hubbard's roots were in North American soil. The tremendous virtues of the Freedom of Information Act, and of Congressional hearings, have made knowledge of U.S. government agencies' malpractices available, and individuals have been allowed to speak out against abuses. Watergate, Irangate and revelations about the CIA's violations of international law have drastically altered public opinion. It became obvious in the 1970s that immoral means were being used in an attempt to maintain and extend the American dream of a democratic world of free opportunity. The public Scientologist, and most staff, are in the position of the American public before this information became known. They believe that the Church exists to "Clear the planet," and create an ethical society. As with the pursuit of the American dream, the truth shows an ideal severely tarnished.

While Hubbard was alive, he was more than a president, he was an absolute dictator, controlling Scientology through the Sea Org and the Guardian's Office, using each to check the other. He found that he could direct his organizations to undertake even immoral and criminal acts by claiming them to be the "greatest good for the greatest number of dynamics." Hubbard was also the sole legislator, creating the law for Scientologists. There was no Congress, no democratic body, no independent justice system, no single Church official with real power.

Since Hubbard's death, control seems to have passed to David Miscavige, who directs the Church through the Sea Org. Since its inception in 1967, the Sea Org has been organized as a para-military unit. It concentrates on the expansion of Scientology through the strict application of orders from the executive. Sea Org members sign a Code of conduct which begins, "I promise to uphold, forward and carry out Command Intention." The Sea Org has largely been involved in the creation and maintenance of Scientology Orgs, providing Scientology training and counselling.

The Sea Org manages the Orgs, and, more loosely, the Missions. The Orgs and Missions have no hand in management, and are ill-informed of its activities.

Until it passed into the hands of the Commodore's Messengers, the Guardian's Office was the most powerful organization in Scientology. The GO contained the Legal, Financial, Public Relations and Intelligence (or, euphemistically, "Information") departments, as well as the "Social Coordination Bureau." By 1983, the GO Bureaus had been separated from one another, and absorbed along with the Sea Org under the Messengers' control.

The Public Relations department exists to combat bad press and emphasize successes. It simply does not report any of the many failures to public Scientologists. If a court case is lost, or a government closes Orgs down, Scientologists will generally hear of it only if the media reports it. Moreover, Scientologists are discouraged from reading newspapers. When an event has to be commented on, the PR department follows the time honored practice of "plausible denial" favored by so many politicians. Free nations have the advantage of a free press, this is not so in the Scientology community. Only during the periods of extensive splintering (in the early 1950s, the mid-1960s and the 1980s) has there been anything like an independent press trying to inform Scientologists of the inadequacies and the crimes of the Scientology Church. So, Scientologists outside the PR Bureau have a very incomplete picture.

When PR fails, the Legal department takes over, at least in theory. Its mission is to block any criticism of Scientology. Governments, too, seek to stifle opposition, and leaks of discreditable information. This is particularly obvious in the totalitarian Communist countries, but even Western Europe and the U.S. are not free from such practices. Ex-CIA agent Victor Marchetti's supposed Constitutional right to free speech was withdrawn by the Courts, when he was prohibited from making *any* statements about the CIA without their approval. When it happened this was a novel and a unique situation for the U.S.A. In Britain, it is illegal for any government employee to reveal information gained during his employment, under the draconian Official Secrets Act. The clumsy efforts to prevent the publication of Peter Wright's *Spycatcher* show the lengths to which even a Western government will go to stifle criticism. Scientology, too, uses the courts in an attempt to silence opposition.

Where the Legal department fails, it is time for Intelligence, with its branches of covert and overt data collection. This was Hubbard's personal CIA, and details of its modus operandi came as a shock not only to public Scientologists, Org staffs and Sea Org members, but even to many Guardian's Office staff. As with an Intelligence Agency, information is only distributed on a need to know basis. Intelligence Agencies too perform immoral acts justified as being for the "greatest good for the greatest number."

By keeping the compartments of Scientology separate, Hubbard ensured that no one would have a complete and true picture. An individual can only act on the information he has, the combination of his experience and his belief. The PR department censors and distorts information, and feels justified in doing so on the grounds that passing on bad news is a characteristic of the Suppressive. So Scientologists generally have little accurate information. Whatever their feelings about the Organization, Scientologists are convinced they have experienced psychological and spiritual benefits, and feel more secure than they did before joining Scientology. Scientologists are also convinced that they belong to the only group which can save Mankind.

CHAPTER THREE

Fair Game, Ethics
and the Scriptures

Brainwashing has become so much of a subject that it is very well for anybody having to do with the field of the human mind to be able to understand the intentions behind it and how it is done.—L. RON HUBBARD, Operational Bulletin 8, 13 December 1955

It is paradoxical that people who become involved in Scientology to increase their ''self-determinism'' usually accept a life of increasing self-sacrifice and ''other-determinism'' (control by others) if they join the staff. Sea Org conditions are the worst: atrocious, over-crowded and often bug-infested housing; only half a day of free time each two weeks; almost no time with their children (who have often been kept in deplorable conditions); no medical or dental insurance; months together of a diet consisting solely of rice and beans; long working hours and insufficient sleep. These combine to make a regimen which is not only morally unacceptable, but can violate minimum standards of Health and Labor laws. Guardian's Office staff were slightly better treated and better paid (but still below the poverty line)—presumably their conditions have deteriorated with their absorption into the Sea Org.

Org staff members usually work slightly less than the ninety hours or more of the Sea Org member, although they too are paid only a few dollars a week. Mission staff usually fare a little better. Staff members sacrifice their family life, their financial security and their careers to "Clear the planet." There is a conspiracy of silence about this maltreatment. Scientologists are required to direct their complaints only to Organization executives, using the Ethics Report system. Criticism relayed to any unauthorized person is labelled "natter," and the person who "natters" will soon be reported to Ethics for corrective action.

Scientology is highly compartmented, and an air of secrecy pervades most of its departments and activities. The Guardian's Office restricted knowledge of certain events to B-1. There was tremendous esprit de corps, and B-1 agents remained mute about their work. In nine years, I heard nothing of the criminal tactics they employed, and was incredulous when I eventually read the affidavit of a former agent who had run a cell of infiltrators in Boston. The Sea Org kept their austere life-style secret. The public Scientologist is in a separate compartment. If a major malpractice was reported by a public Scientologist to the Guardian's Office it would usually be brushed aside with a false reassurance. If the Scientologist was insistent, he might be threatened into silence. If there was enough discontent among Scientologists at one of Hubbard's schemes, a scapegoat would be found. Problems often arose because of the conflict between Hubbard's published Policy and his secret orders, which were followed to the letter.

The Guardian's Office maintained a series of front groups. These are now directed by the Sea Org through the Office of Special Affairs, or the Special Activities Corps. Scientology businesses belong to the World Institute of Scientology Enterprises (WISE). Recently, Sterling Management have attracted publicity for their business training schemes. Other front groups used to be managed by the Social Co-ordination Bureau of the Guardian's Office (SoCo). SoCo was established to monitor and direct Scientology educational and rehabilitation groups, and received a tithe for doing so. In 1989, the Association for Better Living and Education (ABLE) replaced SoCo. The Church also runs anti-psychiatry groups, as well as a campaign for Freedom of Information outside the U.S., and a campaign against Interpol. These groups are run by trained Scientologists, committed to Hubbard's principles. There is a bitter irony in the Scientologists' campaign for Freedom of Information, allowing public access to government files: The GO never allowed such access by Scientologists to their B-1 files. There is no evidence that these files have been destroyed, or the system abandoned.

In Britain, the Effective Education Association teaches children "Study Tech." Applied Scholastics and Education Alive function in the U.S., where the Apple and Delphi schools are accredited. Greenfields is the name of the Scientology school near Saint Hill, in England. The headmaster of Delphi, in Oregon, has claimed that children who are not educated in Scientology schools are being "psychwashed" by the educational system. Further, he has said that Delphi wants non-Scientologist children so that the Scientology children, who are being trained to become leaders, can gain experience in dealing with "wogs."[1]

A brief investigation shows that the extravagant claims made by Narconon, the Scientology drug rehabilitation program, are largely false, including claims of endorsement by governments and state authorities. Those who do withdraw from drug abuse are often recruited into Scientology.

In their anti-psychiatry campaign, Guardian's Office tactics included infiltrating hospitals, stealing psychiatric records and spreading libels about psychiatrists during "noisy investigation." The campaign was stepped up when psychiatrists became active in the anti-cult movement. Psychiatrist John Clark and psychologist Margaret Singer were viciously libeled and harassed for speaking out in public, and for their testimony as hostile expert witnesses in cases involving Scientology.

As ever, Hubbard's ultimate motive for the GO's campaigns is questionable, but good came from some of them. There have certainly been psychiatric abuses, and they were rightly publicized. The Guardian's Office played a part in the exposure of "MK Ultra," a long-running and terrifying series of experiments in mind-control funded by Canadian, British and U.S. Intelligence Agencies. GO staff saw themselves as crusaders against dark forces. They encountered enough duplicity in government to dismiss out of hand attacks upon Scientology. And they worked out of commitment to social change; it certainly was not for personal gain. The good Scientologists have done does not compensate for the harm. The campaigns were largely an attempt to manipulate public opinion and divert critics from Scientology malpractices.

It is a Hubbard maxim that Public Relations should provide an "acceptable truth," tailored to fit the "reality" of a given audience.[2] The practice essentially filters all statements given to the general public and public Scientologists. In the Guardian's Office, it brought into being the technique called elsewhere "plausible denial." Using an acceptable truth at first meant avoiding embarrassing aspects of the truth, and later, more simply, lying. The Church of Scientology has the protection of its public image so deeply ingrained that its representatives perhaps believe the lies they tell about their membership, Hubbard's income, and past misdeeds. The WISE and ABLE front groups are a part of this ongoing deception. The "acceptable truth" is their purported autonomy from the Church, coupled with the idea that they act primarily out of social concern.

Church Scientologists also justify their incessant attacks upon critics and perceived enemies through the courts as an ethical practice: the greatest good for the greatest number of dynamics. So, in accordance with Hubbard's dictum, the law is indeed used to harass. Of course, more directly harassive tactics have also been used, usually but not always remaining just inside the law, and bearing a marked similarity to the Campaign to Re-elect President Nixon's "ratfucking," made public during the Watergate scandal. Disrupting meetings, making false allegations in anonymous phonecalls, giving information from confidential counselling folders to the police, stealing medical and psychiatric records, burglary, bugging, and infiltrating government agencies.

The compartmenting of Scientology runs throughout the organization and throughout the literature. And even in the compartments there are hierarchies. Not only does the Scientologist not see Hubbard's statements with the emphasis they have been given here, but some of the references are to obscure and secrete materials. The sequence in which information is presented is crucial. Having given an initially favorable impression, it is easier to persuade someone to believe a slightly irrational statement, and thence gradually to persuade them to believe ever more wildly irrational statements. This all takes place in the setting of peer group pressure: as in most cults, Scientologists are highly solicitous towards new members.

The sheer volume of material obscures Hubbard's true intentions. The Technical Bulletins, the books and most of Hubbard's tapes deal with the procedures of counselling. Most of the Church's public see mainly these issues, and either receive auditing or train to become auditors. Policy Letters deal with the Organization. Some public do "admin" courses, so they can apply Hubbard's administration techniques to their own businesses.

There are many forms of internal directives, some distributed to all staff, others only to Sea Org staff (the 4,000 or more Flag Orders fit largely into this category), others only to Guardian's Office staff. Many are unavailable to the public Scientologist, or indeed to anyone without a high enough position in the Organization for which the directive was written. So there are B-1 directives which were only available to individuals who had passed through a stringent series of filters.

Individuals evaluate information differently, selecting different priorities. In such a quantity of material, there is usually a preferable opinion, which can be used either to avoid or to enforce an excessive rule. Moderate Scientologists will justify excesses as examples of Hubbard's frustration at human incompetence.

Hubbard's utterances can be separated into several categories. He wrote many short essays for release in Scientology magazines in the 1950s and 1960s. These were designated "Broad Public Issue" (BPI), and included "My Philosophy," where he spoke of having worked his way back from being "permanently physically disabled," and said "one should share what wisdom one has, one should help others to help themselves, and one should keep going despite heavy weather for there is always a calm ahead." In "What Is Greatness" he said: "The hardest task is to continue to love one's fellows despite all reasons he should not. And the true sign of sanity and greatness is to so continue." (By this standard, Hubbard could make no claim to greatness: he was petty and vindictive in the extreme.)

Hubbard essays, supplemented by extracts from lectures, are reprinted endlessly in Scientology magazines. They sell Scientology as a cure-all, insisting that there is hope for everyone if they only embrace Scientology. Inside Scientology there are a number of broadly known and often quoted Policy Letters. The most important is "Keeping Scientology Working," where the Scientologist is sternly admonished to police the use of Scientology and ensure that there are no departures from Hubbard's teachings. A list of ten points is given for the protection of "Standard Tech," among them "hammering out of existence incorrect technology." This Policy Letter exists in all but introductory Scientology courses. It is there to inculcate reverence to Hubbard as the "Source" of Scientology, and to show the crucial role of the Scientologist's mission on Earth.

"The Responsibilities of Leaders" is another well-known Policy Letter. It is usually referred to as the "Bolivar," because Hubbard wrote it after reading a paperback biography of Simon Bolivar's mistress, Manuela Saenz. Hubbard discussed Bolivar's mistakes at length, and then presented seven maxims for the retention of power. Among these we find:

> 5. When you move off a point of power, pay all your obligations on the nail, empower your friends completely and move off with your pockets full of artillery, potential blackmail on every erstwhile rival, unlimited funds in your private account and the addresses of experienced assassins and go live in Bulgravia [sic] and bribe the police . . .
>
> 6. . . . to live in the shadow or employ of a power you must yourself gather and USE enough power to hold your own—without just nattering to the power to "kill Pete". . . . He doesn't have to know all the bad news, and if he's a power really he won't ask all the time, "What are those dead bodies doing at the door?" And if you're clever, you never let it be thought HE killed them—that weakens you and also hurts the power source . . .
>
> 7. . . . always push power in the direction of anyone on whose power you depend. It may be more money for the power, or more ease, or a snarling defense of the power to a critic, or even the dull thud of one of his enemies in the dark, or the glorious blaze of the whole enemy camp as a birthday surprise. . . . Real powers are developed by tight conspiracies . . . pushing someone up in whose leadership they have faith.

While this Policy Letter is available to all Scientologists, many others are not. Confidential counselling, or Tech, issues are distributed with care. The public Scientologist taking OT3 knows far less than an OT3 review (Class 8) auditor knows about the supposed OT3 incident. Only Sea Org members have ever been allowed to train as Class 10, 11 and 12 auditors, or as NOTs auditors. Some issues and tapes were restricted to Sea Org "missionaires" going from Flag to raise the stats in the outer Orgs. There were also many confidential Guardian's Office issues. Because of compartmentation, it is likely that no single individual in the Church saw all of this confidential material. Sea Org members were not usually in the GO, so their secret indoctrination was kept largely separate. People who were highly trained in the Tech were not usually involved in administrative work, and almost never in Guardian's Office work. The secret issues included tapes of Hubbard lectures made specifically for a given audience. They differ markedly from the broadly issued material. For example, there are confidential Public Relations issues which explain how to discredit critics. There is no suggestion that the subject of criticism be investigated; only the critic.

The image that Hubbard wished to project becomes clearer to the Scientologist as he receives more counselling and more training, and moves into higher and ever more remote positions in the organization. The cognoscenti, the tiny few who have received all the counselling techniques and reached the heights of management, have a very developed view of the Commodore. He is a great spirit, responsible through the millennia for many (if not most) of the real achievements of history, and, indeed, those of the quadrillennia of prehistory. He was Rawl (the imprisoner of Xenu, perpetrator of OT3), the Buddha, and Cecil Rhodes. He is reborn, life after life, to benefit humanity, and in preparation for the great work of liberating mankind and all intelligent life in the universe, from captivity. Most Scientologists feel that they have served the Commodore in earlier lifetimes. Some even insist that they were with him on his fictitious attacks on German submarines during the Second World War. Hubbard was scientist, philosopher and messiah rolled into one. Scientologists forget that he was not only a science fiction writer, but also a competent hypnotist. A very competent hypnotist.

Epilogue

You think that, if you call imprisonment true freedom, people will be attracted to the prison. And the worst of it is you're quite right.
—ALDOUS HUXLEY, *Eyeless in Gaza*

At the end of May 1989, Scientology's New Era Publications filed suit against the publishers of this book, alleging infringement of copyright. Even the Scientologists could find no precedent in U.S. law for their demand to see the manuscript prior to publication. As Mel Wulf, the defending attorney, expressed the situation, "Such an order would . . . have the inevitable effect of casting a chill upon freedom of speech and of the press." His argument was in vain; in an opinion issued at the end of July, Judge Louis L. Stanton ordered delivery of the final manuscript to the Scientologists.

In January 1990, Judge Stanton prohibited publication of *A Piece of Blue Sky* on grounds of copyright violation. However, the appeal was successful, and the three judges ruled unanimously that the book could retain all 121 passages complained of by New Era.

In April, the residents of Newkirk, Oklahoma, were alarmed to discover that the drug rehabilitation program which had acquired the lease to the nearby Indian School complex at Chilocco was a Scientology front group. Narconon intended to create a 1,000 bed facility at the eighty-building complex. The Association for Better Living and Education (ABLE) announced the donation of $200,000 to Narconon Chilocco, citing Narconon's remarkable success in treating addicts. Nothing in the announcement suggested any corporate connection between the two organizations. In fact, Narconon is a subsidary of ABLE.

The Church of Scientology has recovered from the schism of the early 1980s, and significantly increased its membership. While the Church's claims of seven million is ridiculous, international membership is probably close to 100,000 by now. One of the world's top Public Relations companies has been helping with the recruiting drive for several years, designing slick commercials, and preparing for a weekly half-hour national television broadcast in the U.S.

The Church is a very rich and a very dangerous organization. There is no indication that it will change its ways. Hubbard's policy is now considered "scripture," and according to Scientology Policy Directive

19, of 7 July 1982, Hubbard alone can alter these "scriptures." Unless Hubbard's ghost communicates from one of the distant planets it is supposedly reconnoitering, there is no possibility of change. While promising freedom and claiming honesty, Scientology will continue to practice deception and generate tragedy.

The massive campaign to hype Hubbard's books onto bestseller lists was exposed in the 15 April 1990 edition of the *San Diego Union*. The first volume of Hubbard's last, and supposedly bestselling, science fiction work, *Mission Earth*, received this review in *The New York Times*:

> A paralyzingly slow-moving adventure enlivened by interludes of kinky sex, sendups of effeminate homosexuals and a disregard of conventional grammar so global as to suggest a satire on the possibility of communication through language.

Between June 24 and 29, 1990, *The Los Angeles Times* ran an excellent series of articles on Scientology. The coverage of Scientology related groups, particularly Sterling Management, Singer Consultants, Health Med, the Foundation for Advancements in Science and Education and the National Coalition of IRS Whistleblowers, is particularly enlightening.

In July, several senior officers of the French Church, including its president, were arrested in France. Newspapers reported that charges would concern fraud, financial irregularities and practicing medicine without a license (with regard to the potentially dangerous Purification Rundown).

In 1938 Hubbard's single goal was to achieve immortality in name. In his last few years money was siphoned from the Church to Hubbard. The IRS criminal investigators came on the scene too late. With Hubbard's death the investigation was abandoned, but money continued to gush into Author Services Inc., and from thence to the Church of Spiritual Technology (CST). This Church has as its sole function the perpetuation not of Scientology, but of the name L. Ron Hubbard. CST records presented in a tax case in Washington, DC, show that CST has assets of over $500 million. On 28 January 1990, *The New Mexican* reported that CST had dug a 350-foot tunnel into a mesa to store Hubbard's writings, which are being preserved at enormous expense using state of the art techniques. CST intend this storage facility to survive even nuclear war. There are also storage facilities near Los Angeles and in northern California.

Bibliography

For those interested in releasing friends or relatives from the grip of Scientology, I strongly recommend Steven Hassan's *Combatting Cult Mind Control,* Park Street Press, Vermont, 1988.

For an overview of Scientology beliefs and techniques see *The Volunteer Minister's Handbook.*

See also Reference Summary.

ALDISS, Brian, *Trillion Year Spree*, Gollancz, London, 1986.

ASIMOV, Isaac, *In Memory Yet Green*, Doubleday, New York, 1979.

BEDFORD, Sybille, *Aldous Huxley, a Biography*, Collins and Chatto & Windus, London, 1974.

BOLITHO, William, *Twelve Against the Gods*, Heinmann, London, 1930.

BURKS, A.J., *Monitors*, CSA Press, Lakemount, Georgia, 1967.

CAMPBELL, *The John W. Campbell Letters*, ed. Chapdelaine, Chapdelaine & Hay, AC Projects, Tennessee, 1985.

CAVENDISH, R., *The Magical Arts*, Arkana, London, 1984.

CLECKLEY, Hervey, M.D., *The Mask of Sanity*, Times Mirror, New York, 1982.

CONWAY & SIEGELMAN, *Snapping*, Dell, New York, 1979.

COOPER, Paulette, *The Scandal of Scientology*, Tower, New York, 1971.

CORYDON, Bent, *L. Ron Hubbard: Messiah or Madman?*, Lyle Stuart, New Jersey, 1987.

CROSSMAN, Richard, *The Diaries of a Cabinet Minister*, Vol. 3, Hamilton & Cape, London, 1977.

CROWLEY, Aleister, *The Book of Thoth*, Samuel Weiser, Maine, 1984.

—*The Confessions of Aleister Crowley*, ed. Symonds and Grant, Bantam, New York, 1971.

—*Magick in Theory and Practice*, Castle, New York.

EVANS, Dr. Christopher, *Cults of Unreason*, Harrap, London, 1973.

FODOR, Nandor, *The Search for the Beloved*, Hermitage House, New York, 1949.

FORTE, John, *The Commodore and the Colonels*, Corfu Tourist Publications & Enterprises, Greece, 1981.

FOSTER, Sir John, *Enquiry into the Practice and Effects of Scientology*, Her Majesty's Stationery Office, London, 1971.

FREUD, Sigmund, *Two Short Accounts of Psycho-Analysis*, Pelican, Middlesex, 1984.

GARDNER, Martin, *Fads & Fallacies in the Name of Science*, Dover, New York, 1957.

GARRISON, Omar, *The Hidden Story of Scientology*, Arlington, London, 1974.

—*Playing Dirty*, Ralston-pilot, Los Angeles, 1980.

GRUBER, Frank, *The Pulp Jungle*, Sherbourne Press, Los Angeles, 1967.

HOFFER, Eric, *The True Believer*, Harper & Row, New York, 1951.

HUBBARD, L. Ron, *All About Radiation*, Scientology Publications Organization, Denmark, 1979.

—*The Background and Ceremonies of the Church of Scientology of California, World Wide*, CSC, East Grinstead, 1973.

—*Battlefield Earth*, Bridge Publications, Los Angeles, 1982.

—*The Book of Case Remedies*, Department of Publications World Wide, East Grinstead, 1968.

—*The Book of E-Meter Drills*, Hubbard College of Scientology, East Grinstead, 1967.

—*The Book Introducing the E-Meter*, compiled by Reg Sharpe, Hubbard College of Scientology, East Grinstead, 1966.

—*The Creation of Human Ability*, Department of Publications WW, East Grinstead, 1968.

—*Dianetics and Scientology Technical Dictionary*, Publications Organization, Los Angeles, 1975.

—*Dianetics 55!*, Scientology Publications Organization, Copenhagen, 1971.

—*Dianetics the Evolution of a Science*, AOSH DK Publications Department, Copenhagen, 1971.

—*Dianetics: The Modern Science of Mental Health*, AOSH DK Publications Department, Copenhagen, 1973.

—*Dianetics: The Original Thesis*, Scientology Publications Organization, Copenhagen, 1970.

—*Dianetics Today*, CSC Publications Organization, Los Angeles, 1975.

—*Electropsychometric Auditing*, USA, 1951.

—*E-Meter Essentials 1961*, Publications Organization World Wide, 1968.

—*Have You Lived Before This Life?*, two different editions: Department of Publications World Wide, England, 1968; CSC Publications Organization, Los Angeles, 1977.

—*HCOPL Subject Index*, CSC Publications Organization, Los Angeles, 1976.

—*How to Live through an Executive*, Department of Publications World Wide, East Grinstead, 1968.

—*Hymn of Asia*, CSC Publications Organization, Los Angeles, 1974.

—*An Indexed Summary of Scientology and Dianetic Policy*, 4 volumes, PR & Consumption Bureau of the Flag Bureaux, 1972.

—*An Indexed Summary of Technical Bulletins*, 3 volumes, PR & Consumption Bureau of the Flag Bureaux, 1973.

—*Introduction to Scientology Ethics*, Publications Department, Denmark, 1973 (differs from later edition).

—*The Management Series 1970-1974*, CSC Publications Organization, Los Angeles, May 1975.

—*Mission Into Time*, American St. Hill Organization, 1973.

—*Modern Management Technology Defined*, CSC Publications Organization, Los Angeles, 1976.

—*Notes on the Lectures*, Publications Organization WW, Edinburgh, 1968.

—*Organization Executive Course—An Encyclopedia of Scientology Policy*, volumes 0-7, CSC Publications Organization, Los Angeles, 1974.

—*The Philadelphia Doctorate Course Lectures*, New Era, Copenhagen, 1982.

—*The Phoenix Lectures*, Publications Organization World Wide, Edinburgh, 1968.

—*The Problems of Work*, Publications Department, Denmark, 1972.

—*Professional Auditor's Bulletins*, 6 volumes, Scientology Publications Organization, Copenhagen, 1975 (originals also consulted).

—*The Research & Discovery Series*, volumes 1-9, Scientology Publications, Copenhagen, 1980, New Era Publications, Copenhagen, subsequent years.

—*The Road to Truth*, taped lecture, Golden Era Studios, 1983.

—*Ron's Journal 1967*, taped lecture of 1967, Golden Era Studios, 1983.

—*Ron's Journal 38*, Golden Era Studios, 1983.

—*Ron's Journal 39*, Golden Era Productions, 1985.

—*Ron The Writer*, L. Ron Hubbard Library, USA, 1989.

—*Science of Survival*, Hubbard College of Scientology, 1967.

—*Scientology—A History of Man*, Publications Organization World Wide, Edinburgh, 1968 (originally published as *What to Audit*, with a further chapter, in 1952).

—*Scientology—A New Slant on Life*, Publications Department, Denmark, 1972.

—*Scientology: A World Religion Emerges in the Space Age*, Scientology Information Service, 1974.

—*Scientology 8-80*, Publications Department, Denmark, 1973.

—*Scientology 8-8008*, Publications Organization WW, Edinburgh, 1967.

—*Scientology 0-8*, Scientology Publications Organization, Copenhagen, 1970 (differs from later editions).

—*Scientology—The Fundamentals of Thought*, Publications Department, Denmark, 1972.

—*Self Analysis*, International Library of Arts and Sciences, USA, 1951.

—*The Story of Dianetics & Scientology*, taped lecture of 1958, Church of Scientology, 1977.

—*The Technical Bulletins of Dianetics and Scientology*, CSC Publications Organization, Los Angeles, 1979.

—*Understanding the E-Meter*, New Era, Copenhagen, 1982.

—*The Volunteer Minister's Handbook*, CSC Publications Organization, Los Angeles, 1979.

—*The Way to Happiness*, Regent House, Los Angeles, 1981.

—*What Is Scientology?*, CSC Publications Organization, Los Angeles, 1978.

—*When in Doubt Communicate*, Scientology Ann Arbor, Michigan, 1969.

KAUFMAN, Robert, *Inside Scientology*, Olympia Press, London & New York, 1972.

KING, Francis, *The Magical World of Aleister Crowley*, Wiedenfield & Nicolson, London, 1977.

—*Ritual Magic in England*, Neville Spearman, London, 1970.

—*The Secret Rituals of the OTO*, ed. King, C.W. Daniel, London, 1973.

KOPPES, Clayton R., *JPL and the American Space Program*, Yale University Press, New Haven and London, 1982.

LIFTON, Robert, *Thought Reform and Psychology of Totalism*, Norton, New York, 1961.

MALKO, George, *Scientology: The Now Religion*, Delacourte Press, New York, 1970.

MILLER, Russell, *Bare-Faced Messiah*, Michael Joseph, London, 1987.

NEEDLEMAN, Jacob, *The New Religions*, Crossroad, New York, 1984.

O'BRIEN, Helen, *Dianetics in Limbo*, Whitmore, Philadelphia, 1966.

PERLS, Fritz et al., *Gestalt Therapy*, Pelican, London, 1973.

ROGERS, Alva, "Darkhouse," in Lighthouse number 5, February 1962.

—*A Fan's Remembrance*.

ROLPH, C.H., *Believe What You Like*, André Deutsch, London, 1973.

ST. PETERSBURG TIMES, *Scientology—An in-depth profile of a new force in Clearwater*, Florida, 1980.

VOSPER, Cyril, *The Mindbenders*, Neville Spearman, London, 1971.

WALLIS, Dr. Roy, *The Road to Total Freedom*, Heinmann, London, Columbia, New York, 1977.

WINTER, Dr. Joseph A., *A Doctor's Report on Dianetics*, Julian Press, New York, 1951 & 1987.

Reference Summary

Abbreviations:
8-8008—*Scientology 8-8008*, Hubbard.
AAR—*All About Radiation*, Hubbard.
Adventure, 1935—Adventure magazine, vol. 93 no. 5, 1 October 1935, "The Camp-Fire."
Auditor—"The Auditor—The monthly journal of Scientology."
Brief Biography—"A Brief Biography of L. Ron Hubbard—originally printed circa 1960," [Scientology] Public Relations Office News, Los Angeles.
BTB—Board [of the Churches of Scientology] Technical Bulletin.
ClH—transcript of the Clearwater Hearings, May 1982.
Cooper—*The Scandal of Scientology*.
CSC—Church of Scientology of California.
DMSMH—*Dianetics: the Modern Science of Mental Health*, Hubbard.
Evans—*Cults of Unreason*.
FDD69RA—Flag Divisional Directive 69RA "Facts About L. Ron Hubbard Things You Should Know," 8 March 1974, revised 7 April 1974.
Foster report—*Enquiry into the Practice and Effects of Scientology*.
FSM mag 1—Field Staff Member magazine no.1, Dept of Publications World Wide, Saint Hill, 1968.
GA—transcript in Church of Scientology of California vs. Gerald Armstrong, Superior Court for the County of Los Angeles, case no. C 420153. Volume no. followed by page no.
GA exhibit—exhibit no. in CSC vs. Armstrong.
HCOB—Hubbard Communications Office Bulletin.
HCOPL—Hubbard Communications Office Policy Letter.
HOM—*Scientology—A History of Man*, Hubbard.
Hubbard 1963 interview—Scientology news release "an interview granted to the Australian Press on January 10th 1963. . . ."
Kaufman—*Inside Scientology*.
Malko—*Scientology: The Now Religion*.
MIT—*Mission Into Time*, Hubbard.
OEC—*Organization Executive Course—An Encyclopedia of Scientology Policy*, volumes 0–7, Hubbard.
PDC—*Philadelphia Doctorate Course*, Hubbard taped lectures, 1952.
R&D—*Research and Discovery Series*, Hubbard.
Report to Parliament—*A Report to Members of Parliament on Scientology*, World-Wide PR Bureau, Church of Scientology, 1968.
RJ 67—*Ron's Journal 1967*, taped lecture, Hubbard.

Rolph—*Believe What You Like*.
SOED—Sea Organization Executive Directive.
SOS—*Science of Survival*, Hubbard.
Tech—*The Technical Bulletins of Dianetics and Scientology*, volumes 1–12, Hubbard.
VMH—*Volunteer Minister's Handbook*, Hubbard.
Vosper—*The Mindbenders*.
Wallis—*The Road to Total Freedom*.
WIS—*What Is Scientology?*, Hubbard.

WHAT IS SCIENTOLOGY?

1. *Snapping*, Conway and Siegelman, p.161.
2. "Information Disease," Conway and Siegelman, *Science Digest*, January 1982.

PART 1: INSIDE SCIENTOLOGY 1974–1983

MY OWN BEGINNINGS

1. Flag Operations Liaisons Office East US letter to National Personnel Records Center, 28 May 1974.
2. FDD69RA.
3. FSM mag 1.
4. "The Dissemination Drill," OEC 6, p.112.
5. HCOB "TRs remodernized," 16 August 71R.

ST. HILL

1. Tech 12, p.322
2. BTB "Preclear Assessment Sheet," 24 April 69R.
3. BTB "Drills for Auditors," 9 October 71R.

ON TO OT

Principal sources: RJ 67, Section 3 OT course materials.
1. Hubbard, *Scientology 0–8*, p.134.

THE SEEDS OF DISSENT

1. SOED 2192 Int "Re: List of Declared Suppressive Persons" 27 January 83.
2. Scientology Policy Directive 28 "Suppressive Act—Dealing with a Declared Suppressive Person" 13 August 82.
3. Gerald Armstrong affidavit, 19 October 1982.

PART 2: BEFORE DIANETICS 1911–1949

HUBBARD'S BEGINNINGS

Quotations from and reference to Hubbard and Scientology biographical sketches of Hubbard: MIT pp.4–5; Brief Biography; FDD69RA; Hubbard, *Story of Dianetics and Scientology*; Hubbard, *Dianetics Today*, p.989. Shannon story and quotations from four page article, "A Biography of L. Ron Hubbard," by Michael Linn Shannon.
1. GA exhibit 63, p.24.

2. Affidavit sworn by H.R.Hubbard's true brother, J.R.Wilson, 13 September 1920. Harry Hubbard naval record.
3. Adventure, 1935.
4. Russell Miller interview with Margaret Roberts, Helena, April 1986.
5. Land transfers.
6. VMH, p.284.
7. The Factors, 8-8008.
8. GA exhibit 63.

HUBBARD IN THE EAST

Quotations from and reference to Hubbard and Scientology biographical sketches of Hubbard: MIT, pp.5–6; Hubbard, *Have You Lived Before this Life?* p.298; FDD69RA; WIS, p.xlii; Hubbard, *The Phoenix Lectures*, p.34; Tech 1, p.2; Tech 3, p.470; FSM mag 1; Hubbard, *Dianetics: The Original Thesis*, p.158; Hubbard diaries/notebooks, GA exhibits 62, 63, 65.
1. H.R.Hubbard letter to George Washington University, 19 September 1930.
2. WIS p.xl.
3. R & D 4 p. 2
4. H.R.Hubbard letter to GW University, 19 September 1930.
5. R&D 7, pp.98f.
6. AAR dustwrapper.
7. Mary Sue Hubbard in GA 7, p.1083.
8. Hubbard, *Story of Dianetics and Scientology*.
9. Adventure, 1935.

HUBBARD THE EXPLORER

Additional sources: FSM mag 1; MIT; Report to Parliament; Hubbard's college grade sheets; *The University Hatchet*; *Washington Daily News*, 13 September 1932; Gruber, *The Pulp Jungle*; FDD69RA; "L. Ron Hubbard," by the LRH Public Affairs Bureau, CSC, 1981; *Motion Picture Herald*, 23 January 1937; Hubbard, *Battlefield Earth*, p.viii; *Rocky Mountain News*, 20 February 1983.
1. *Adventure*, 1935.
2. *Look* magazine, December 1950.
3. GA 12, p.1972.
4. GA 11, p.1867–8.
5. Rogers, *Darkhouse*.
6. GA 10, p.1577.
7. GA 10, pp.1581–3.
8. GA 15, pp.2423–4.
9. Dianetic Auditors Bulletin III, no.1; Aberree, December 1961.
10. GA exhibit 500-6J; Hubbard letter to FBI, May 1951.
11. Letter to the author from AMORC, 1984.
12. GA exhibit 500-3H.
13. Letters from Hubbard naval record.
14. Russell Miller interview with Robert Macdonald Ford, Olympia, Washington, 1 September 1986.

HUBBARD AS HERO

Additional sources: Hubbard naval record; Hubbard Veterans Administration file;

Thomas Moulton testimony in GA 22; *U.S.S. PC-815* Action Report; Auditor 63; FSM mag 1; FDD69RA; MIT; Brief Biography; Report to Parliament; Dorwart, *Conflict of Duty*, Naval Institute Press, Annapolis, 1983; Hubbard's service in Australia was with Base Section No. 3, Brisbane—see *U.S Army in World War II—The Technical Services* vols. The Ordnance Dept. and The Corps of Engineers, pp. 114-115.
1. Hubbard 1963 interview.
2. Hubbard lecture "Study: Evaluation of Information," 11 August 1964 (Study tape 5).
3. GA 12, p.1925.
4. Hubbard, Professional Auditors Bulletin 124, 15 Nov 1957.

HIS MIRACULOUS RECOVERY

Additional sources: Hubbard naval record; Hubbard Veterans Administration file; FDD69RA.
1. Ken Hoden, *LA Weekly*, 4 April 1986.
2. *Look* magazine, 5 December 1950.
3. MIT, p.11; Hubbard, *Self Analysis*; AAR.
4. R&D 6, p.409. Tech 3, p.146.
5. Kima Douglas in GA 25, p.4459.
6. GA 12, pp.1925–7.

HIS MAGICKAL CAREER

Additional sources: Rogers, Darkhouse; "L. Ron Hubbard: A Fan's Remembrance," article by Alva Rogers; *Book of Babalon*, Jack Parsons; Hubbard naval record; Allied Enterprises articles of co-partnership; Koppes, *JPL and the American Space Program*; records in Parsons vs. Hubbard & Northrup, Dade County, Florida, case no.101634; letters from the OTO New York Jack Parsons file; Jack Parsons' FBI file.
1. *Sunday Times*, London, 5 October & 28 December 1969.
2. Tech 3, p.31.
3. PDC lectures 40, 35 & 18.
4. King, *The Secret Rituals of the OTO*, p.233.
5. King, *The Magical World of Aleister Crowley*.
6. *Secret Rituals*, p.238.
7. Crowley, *Magick in Theory and Practice*.
8. Burks, *Monitors*, p.99.
9. *Magick in Theory and Practice*, p.310.
10. King, *Ritual Magic in England*, p.161; *The Confessions of Aleister Crowley*, p.693; Crowley, *The Book of Thoth*; Cavendish, *The Magical Arts*, p.304.
11. GA exhibit 3.

PART 3: THE BRIDGE TO TOTAL FREEDOM 1949–1966

BUILDING THE BRIDGE

Additional sources: Winter, *A Doctor's Report on Dianetics*; author's correspondence with a former HDRF director; DMSMH; Freud's Clark Lectures, published in *Two Short Accounts of Psycho-Analysis*.
1. GA exhibit 500-47, GA 12, p.1946–7.
2. *Studies in Hysteria*, vol. 2, Sigmund Freud.
3. Malko, p.52.
4. Tech 1 pp.14 & 22; van Vogt in California Association of Dianetic Auditors Bulletin, vol. 17, no.2.
5. *Astounding Science Fiction*, U.S. edition, August 1950.

6. Bedford, *Aldous Huxley, a Biography*, vol. 2, pp.116–7.

THE DIANETIC FOUNDATIONS

1. Gardner, *Fads and Fallacies in the Name of Science*, p.270; Evans, p.49.
2. R&D 3, pp.20–24; R&D 1, p.696; *Fads and Fallacies*, p.270.
3. *New York Times*, 9 September 1950.
4. Tech 1, p.280.
5. DMSMH, p.168.
6. Wallis, p.71; SOS book 2, p.225.
7. Dessler letters; Russell Miller interview with Richard de Mille, Santa Barbara, 25 July 1986; Sara Northrup Hubbard vs. L. Ron Hubbard, Superior Court, Los Angeles, divorce complaint, no.D414498.
8. Hubbard letter to FBI, 3 March 1951; FBI memo, 7 March 1951.
9. Dessler letters.
10. Hubbard telegram to Dessler, March 1951; Dessler letters.
11. Hubbard letter to Dessler, 27 March 1951.
12. "A Factual Report of the Hubbard Dianetic Foundation," John Maloney, 23 February 1952; Frank Dessler letters file.
13. DMSMH, p.363, 365; R&D 1, p.124.

WICHITA

Additional sources: O'Brien, *Dianetics in Limbo*; author's correspondence with a former HDRF director; Russell Miller interviews with Barbara Klowdan, Los Angeles, 28 July–5 August 1986; Hubbard letters and telegrams to Barbara Klowdan; author's interview with a former executive of various Hubbard organizations; information on publications and conference attendance—WIS pp.289–290, Tech 1, pp.122–3 & 165.
1. Hubbard Dianetic Foundation, Inc., bankruptcy proceedings, District Court, Wichita, no.379-B-2; Don Purcell circular letter, 21 May 1952.
2. Corydon, *L. Ron Hubbard: Messiah or Madman?*, p.285.
3. Hubbard circular letter, 20 February 1952.
4. Letter to the author from Chapdelaine, 1984.
5. Wallis, pp. 84–5.
6. Hubbard circular letter, 20 February 1952.
7. "A Factual Report of the Hubbard Dianetic Foundation," John Maloney, 23 February 1952; Dianetic Auditor's Bulletin vol.3; Hubbard circular letter, 28 February 1952.
8. Purcell circular letter 21 May 1952; "Dianetics Today" newsletter, January 1954; Hubbard circular letter 20 February 1952; Hubbard College Lecture no.21 "Anatomy of the Theta Body," March 1952.
9. Jack Maloney circular letter, 29 March 1952.
10. "The Dispatch Case," Hubbard circular letter 8 April 1952.
11. Hubbard College Reports, 13 March 1952.
12. Elliot circular letter, 21 April 1952; Hubbard circular letter, 25 April 1952; Hubbard circular letter, 21 May 1952.

KNOWING HOW TO KNOW

Additional sources: O'Brien, *Dianetics in Limbo*, pp. vii, 52–55, 73, 76–77; HOM; PDC.
1. HOM, p.6.

2. Auditor 21, p.1.
3. Tech 1, pp. 372 & 409.
4. Auditor 21; Tech 1, pp.218 & 220.
5. Wallis, p.80.
6. Promotional piece, "Announcing the Theta Clear."
7. DMSMH, p.40.
8. Tech 1, p.298.
9. Letter to the author from Helen O'Brien; letter to the author from L. Ron Hubbard, Jr.; letter from an attendee of the PDC; L. Ron Hubbard, Jr., Clearwater Hearings 1, p.283.
10. Hubbard College Lecture, no.21.
11. Tech 1, p.337.
12. Tech 1, pp.343 & 369; WIS p.295.

THE RELIGION ANGLE

Additional sources: Tech 1, p.358; Tech 2, pp.32, 157, 267–9, 353–5; WIS, pp. 142, 154.

1. Professional Auditors Bulletin 74, "Washington Bulletin no.1," 6 March 1956 (only in original).
2. L. Ron Hubbard, Jr., ClH 1, p.286; Wallis, p.128.
3. GA 12, p.1976 & 26, p.4619, GA exhibit 500-4V.
4. Tech 2, p.32; *St. Petersburg Times*, "Scientology," p.17.
5. Tech 2, pp.84 & 124; Purcell quote—"Dianetics Today" newsletter, January 1954.
6. GA 12, p.2008 & 26, p.4643, exhibits 500-5 & 500-5F; Kima Douglas in GA 25, p.4435.
7. Hubbard letter to FBI, 29 July 1955.
8. Hubbard letter to FBI, 7 September 1955.
9. Interview with David Mayo, October 1986, Palo Alto.
10. Tech 2, pp.309 & 312; letter to author from Henrietta de Wolf; interview with former executive at Washington, DC.
11. VMH p.77, part K.
12. Tech 2, pp.378 & 564; Tech 3, p. 27; AAR dustwrapper.
13. Wallis, pp.190 & 128.
14. Foster report, para 118.
15. Donna Reeve in GA 24, p. 4185.
16. PDC 21.

THE LORD OF THE MANOR

1. Tech 4, p.29; WIS p. 142; *East Grinstead Courier*, 16 August 1959; *Garden News*, 8 April 1960; Evans, pp.72f; *Sunday Mirror*, 28 July 1968.
2. Tech 3, p.522.
3. Tech 3, pp.555 & 557; Tech 12, p.245ff.
4. Professional Auditors Bulletin 74 (only in original); Tech 2, p. 474; Tech 4, p. 11.
5. GA 25, p.4617.
6. HASI share certificate; Foster report, para 71.
7. Tech 4, p.161.
8. Wallis, p.191; Cooper, p.102.
9. OEC 7, p.487.
10. Tech 4, p.378.
11. Tech 4, p.337.

12. Tech 12, p.245ff.
13. Wallis, p.202; HCO Executive Letter, 14 April 1961.
14. *The Findings on the U.S. Food and Drug Agency* [sic, should be "Administration"], The Department of Publications World Wide, East Grinstead, CSC, 1968.

THE WORLD'S FIRST REAL CLEAR

1. Cooper, p.118.
2. OEC 0, p.166.
3. Interview, John McMaster, London, May 1984.
4. OEC 0, p.35.
5. Tech 6, p.19.
6. Wallis, p.149; *Daily Mail*, 8 December 1965; Guardian's Office memos on "Squeaky" Fromm, former follower of Charles Manson.
7. Wallis, pp.152 & 150.
8. Foster report, paras 12 & 181.
9. Reprinted in Foster report, para 181, and in Latey.
10. Foster report, para 181.
11. *The People*, 20 March 1966.
12. Auditor 13; interview, John McMaster.

PART 4: THE SEA ORGANIZATION 1966–1976

SCIENTOLOGY AT SEA

1. OEC 7, pp.494ff & 503.
2. *East Grinstead Courier*, 12 August 1983.
3. Foster report, para 32; Evans, pp.85–6; Malko, p.82; Hubbard taped lecture, "About Rhodesia," 18 July 1966.
4. Church of Scientology of California vs. IRS, 24 September 1984 judgment, p.35.
5. Interview, OR, former Sea Org executive; interview, McMaster.
6. OEC 7, p.579.
7. Interview, OR; Laurel Sullivan in GA 19, pp.3222–3.
8. Rolph, pp.39 & 85; *News of the World*, 28 July 1968; Wallis, p.194; Evans, p.88; Cooper, p.61; interview with witness.
9. Foster report, para 73.
10. Letter from the Explorers Club to John Fudge, 8 December 1966.
11. GA exhibit 500-6H, GA 13, p.2036–42.
12. Rolph, pp.39f.
13. Tech 6, p.193.
14. OEC 3, p.63.
15. *Daily Sketch*, 11 March 1967.
16. Interview with Gerald Armstrong, East Grinstead, June 1984.
17. Interview with Virginia Downsborough, Santa Barbara, October 1986.
18. *Modern Management Technology Defined*, Hubbard, p.72; *Clearwater Sun*, 7 February 1986; interview, OR; GA 12, p.2021, GA exhibit 500-5Z.
19. GA 12, pp.1997–8, 16, p.2616, GA exhibit 500-5E.
20. Interview, OR, former Sea Org executive.

HEAVY ETHICS

Additional sources: RJ67; correspondence with Hana Eltringham/Whitfield; interviews with OR, a former Sea Org executive; interviews with McMaster; interview with Virginia Downsborough; also interviews with Neville Chamberlin, Kenneth Urquhart, Bill Robertson, Phil Spickler.

1. *News of the World*, 28 July 1968; Evans, p.88; interview with witness.
2. HCOPL, "Conditions, Awards, Penalties," 27 September 1967 (not in OEC).
3. *Sunday Mirror*, 24 December 1967.
4. HCOPL, "Condition of Liability," 6 October 1967 (not in OEC).
5. HCOPL, "Penalties for Lower Conditions," 18 October 1967 (not in OEC).
6. Garrison, *Playing Dirty*, p.75; Foster report, para 216.
7. *Sunday Mirror*, 18 November 1967.
8. Foster report, para 216.
9. *The People*, 18 February 1968.
10. Articles of incorporation OTC; CSC vs. IRS 24 September 1984.
11. Auditor 32, p.5; Auditor 39.
12. Auditors 37 & 39.
13. Vosper, p.178; Auditor 43.
14. *Sunday Express*, 14 July 1968.

THE EMPIRE STRIKES BACK

Additional sources: Rolph; the Auditor; Forte, *The Commodore and the Colonels*; interviews with Chamberlin, OR, Urquhart and McMaster.

1. Foster report, para 14; Rolph, pp.74ff.
2. *Evening News*, 31 July 1968; *Daily Sketch*, 31 July 1968; *Daily Telegraph*, 7 August 1968.
3. *Evening News*, 1 August 1968.
4. Auditor 17, back page.
5. *The Observer*, 11 August 1968; Kaufman, pp.195–6f; Cooper, pp.81–2.
6. Interview with Phil Spickler, Woodside, California, October, 1986.
7. Kaufman; *The Observer*, 11 August 1968; *Auditor*, "Special South African Issue," c. summer 1968.
8. *Daily Sketch*, 2 August 1968.
9. *Daily Mail*, 3 August 1968.
10. *Daily Mail*, 6 August 1968.
11. *The Shrinking World of L. Ron Hubbard*, Granada Television, 1968.
12. Auditor 43, pp. 2 & 4.
13. *Playing Dirty* p.75; *Commodore and the Colonels*, p.19.
14. Auditor 41.
15. Chamberlin to author, 1984.
16. Chamberlin to author, 1984; *Commodore and the Colonels*.
17. Interview McMaster; Interview Chamberlin; Tech 6, p.276.
18. Tech 6, p.273; OEC 1, p.487.
19. *Sunday Times*, 17 November 1968.
20. OEC 1, p.489.
21. OEC 1, p.486.
22. Rolph, pp.63ff; *Daily Telegraph & Daily Mirror*, 6 August 1968; *Daily Sketch*, 13 August 1968; *The People*, 18 August 1968.
23. Wallis, p.196; *Daily Telegraph*, 25 November 1968.
24. Wallis, p.222.
25. *Playing Dirty*, p.80; CSC vs. IRS, 24 September 1984.
26. HCOPL, "Ethics Penalties Re-instated," 19 October 1971 (not in OEC).

THE DEATH OF SUSAN MEISTER

Sources: "Scientology Said Susan Was a Suicide," article by George Meister; George Meister testimony, Clearwater Hearings, May 1982; letter to the author from George Meister, 13 June 1986; also Urquhart interview, correspondence with Amos Jessup.

HUBBARD'S TRAVELS

Additional sources: "Debrief of Jim Dincalci on NY Trip with LRH"; WIS, pp.154–8 & 184.
1. Sea Org Orders of the Day ("OODs"), 7 June 1971; GA 15, pp.2482–4 & 17, pp.2847–9.
2. Hubbard, *The Management Series 1970–1974*, p.384.
3. Wallis, p.198.
4. Interview with witness.
5. GA 9, p.1436; *Playing Dirty*, p.80.
6. *Playing Dirty*, p.82.
7. GA 17, p.2675f; Schomer in GA 25, p.4480; Tech 8, p.189; Guardian Order 732, "Snow White Program," 28 April 1073.
8. CSC vs. IRS, 24 September 1984, p.66.
9. Kima Douglas in GA 25, pp.4444ff; Laurel Sullivan in GA 19A, pp.3007, 3018 & 3020; Mary Sue Hubbard in GA 17, p.2776.
10. GA 9, p.1436; Urquhart interview.
11. Miller interview with Kima Douglas, Oakland, California, September 1986.
12. Gerald Armstrong affidavit, March 1986, pp.53ff.
13. BPL "Confidential—PR series 24—Handling Hostile Contacts/Dead Agenting," 30 May 1974 (not in OEC).
14. Hubbard, *Modern Management Technology Defined*, definition 3.
15. *Playing Dirty*, p.82; Interview Urquhart; Miller interview with Kima Douglas.
16. *Playing Dirty*, p.84.
17. GA 9, p.1431; Sullivan in GA 19A, p.3190.
18. Miller interview with Kima Douglas.

THE FLAG LAND BASE

Sources: Documents referred to in text.
1. *Playing Dirty*, p.86.
2. Tech 11, p.236.
3. *St. Petersburg Times*, "Scientology," pp. 7, 2 & 27; Armstrong affidavit, March 1986, p.50.
4. GO Program Order 158; Mary Sue Hubbard Stipulation, pp.90f.
5. *St. Petersburg Times*, "Scientology," p.8.
6. *Clearwater Sun*, 4 November 1979; *St. Petersburg Times*, "Scientology."
7. Terri Gamboa in GA 24, p.4238.
8. Interview with witness.
9. Tech 2, p.157.
10. Miller interview with Kima Douglas; coroner's reports.
11. Interview with Frank Gerbode, Woodside, California, October 1986.

PART 5: THE GUARDIAN'S OFFICE 1974–1980

THE GUARDIAN UNGUARDED

Additional sources: Rolph; *St. Petersburg Times*, "Scientology."
1. OEC 7, pp.494ff.
2. OEC 7, p.503.
3. Interview with former Hubbard telex encoder.
4. Tech 2, p.157.
5. Hubbard Executive Directive 55 "The War," 29 November 1968.
6. Rolph p.63; *Daily Telegraph*, 26 November 1968.
7. OEC 7, p.521; Rolph, pp.102 & 52f.
8. SOED, 26 March 1969.
9. Auditor 15, p.7.
10. Sara Hollister to Paulette Cooper, 1972; GA 12, p.1940.
11. GA exhibit 500-4L, GA 12, pp.1946ff.
12. Sentencing memorandum in U.S.A. vs. Jane Kember, District Court, DC, criminal case no., 78-401, p.25.
13. *St. Petersburg Times*, "Scientology," p.9.
14. U.S.A. vs. Kember, p.23.

INFILTRATION

Principal source: Stipulation of Evidence in U.S.A. vs. Mary Sue Hubbard et al., District Court, DC, criminal case no. 78-401.
Additional sources: Sentencing memorandum in U.S.A. vs. Jane Kember; interviews with former B-1 agent; documents quoted in text.
1. Interview, Urquhart.

OPERATION MEISNER

Principal source: Stipulation of Evidence in U.S.A. vs. Mary Sue Hubbard et al., District Court, DC, criminal case no. 78-401.

PART 6: THE COMMODORE'S MESSENGERS 1977–1982

MAKING MOVIES

Additional sources: Tonja Burden affidavit, 1982; Hartwells testimony in Clearwater Hearings, May 1982; interviews with four former CMO executives and one former Sea Org executive.
1. Tech 11, p.259.
2. Anne Rosenblum affidavit, p.22.
3. *St. Petersburg Times*, "Scientology," p.20.
4. ClH 3, p.260; Walters in GA 25, p.4394-7; Douglas in GA 25, p.4437; Nancy Dincalci in GA 20, pp.3530f; Janie Peterson in ClH 4, p.81; Guardian Order 121669, 16 December 1969, by Mary Sue Hubbard.
5. *St. Petersburg Times*, "Scientology," p.20.
6. Tech 11, p.234.

THE RISE OF THE MESSENGERS

Sources: Mayo "Recollections," *AAC Journal*, April 1985; "An Open Letter to All Scientologists from David Mayo," 1983; Armstrong affidavit, May 1983; John Nelson taped talk, 13 August 1983; interview with John Nelson, East Grinstead, January 1984.

1. Hubbard in Clearing Course film.
2. Miller interview with Kima Douglas.
3. Tech 12, p.307; Nelson interview; interview, former CMO executive.
4. Central Bureaux Order 588, "Flag Senior Management Command Lines," 26 July 1979; CMO Executive Directive 92, "CMO Regulations," 11 January 1978; Central Bureaux Order 621, "Bypass of Management Sector Handling Of," 29 November 1979.
5. Mary Sue Hubbard in GA 6, p.876.
6. HCOB, 3 January 1980.
7. Sullivan in GA 19A, pp.3053ff.
8. GA 9, pp.1492ff & 1555; Sullivan in GA 19, p.3246.
9. Mary Sue Hubbard in GA 6, p.886.
10. Armstrong affidavit, 19 October 1982.
11. GA 14, pp.2272ff.
12. HCOB, 30 July 1980.
13. HCOB, 29 July 1980.
14. Omar Garrison in GA 21, pp.3595–7.
15. A.E. van Vogt letter to the author.

THE YOUNG RULERS

Sources: correspondence with a former CMO executive; interview with former Guardian's Office executive; Peter Green, taped talk, 23 June 1982.
1. HCOPL, "The Executive Director International," 11 December 1980.
2. Sullivan in GA 19A, pp.3144f.
3. David Mayo letter, 8 December 1983.
4. Litt in GA 28, p.4734.
5. McKee, ClH 4, pp.397ff.
6. Bent Corydon, taped talk, July 1983.
7. Mayo letter 8 December 1983.
8. HCOB, "The State of Clear," 14 December 1981.

THE CLEARWATER HEARINGS

Principal source: Transcript of the City of Clearwater Hearings re: The Church of Scientology, May 1982.
1. Complaint in M.J. Flynn vs. Hubbard, U.S. Court for the District of Massachusetts, no.83-2642-C.
2. Interviews with two former CMO executives.
3. HCOPL, "Penalties for Lower Conditions," 18 October 1967 (not in OEC).
4. HOM, p.20; Tech 1, p.337.

THE RELIGIOUS TECHNOLOGY CENTER AND THE INTERNATIONAL FINANCE POLICE

Sources: John Nelson; interviews with two former CMO executives; Howard Schomer testimony in Christofferson Titchbourne vs. Church of Scientology Mission of Davis et al., State of Oregon Circuit Court, Multnomah County, case A7704-05184; Schomer testimony in GA.
1. HCOB, 26 August 1982.
2. Jay Hurwitz letter to David Banks, 1983; interviews with Hurwitz, East Grinstead, 1983 & 1986.

PART 7: THE INDEPENDENTS 1982–1984

THE MISSION HOLDERS' CONFERENCE

Principal source: SOED, "The Flow Up the Bridge—the U.S. Mission Holders Conference—San Francisco 1982," 7 November 1982, and a tape of the proceedings.
1. Bent Corydon interview in *Copenhagen Corner*, issue 11.
2. Kingsley Wimbush, taped talk, 1984.

THE SCIENTOLOGY WAR

Sources: Complaint in Martin Samuels vs. Hubbard, Circuit Court, Oregon State, Multnomah County, case no.A8311 07227, November 1983; Bent Corydon, taped talk, July 1983, and interview in *Copenhagen Corner*, 11; Religious Technology Center Conditions Order 1-3.
1. Jon Zegel taped talk, June 1983.
2. Stansfields, "Knowledge Report," 14 March 1983.
3. Zegel talk, June 1983.
4. Interview, former employee.
5. RTC Conditions Order 1-3.
6. Interview with David Mayo.

SPLINTERING

1. Flag Conditions Order 6577-1, "Writ of Expulsion Confirmed," 24 February 1983.
2. SOED, 2192 Int "Re: List of Declared Suppressive Persons," 27 January 1983.

STAMP OUT THE SQUIRRELS!

Sources: Interviews with Ron Lawley and Morag Bellmaine; interview with Gulliver Smithers, East Grinstead, May 1984.
1. HCOB, "Dianetic Clear Solved," 27 March 1984.
2. Central Bureaux Order 746, "Organization Pattern: Continental Commodore's Messenger Orgs," 16 August 1983.

PART 8: JUDGMENTS

SCIENTOLOGY AT LAW

Principal source: Memorandum of Intended Decision in Church of Scientology of California vs. Gerald Armstrong, Superior Court, Los Angeles County, case no. C 420153.
1. *The Times*, London, 4 September 1973; *Evening News*, 5 June 1973.

THE CUSTODY CASE

Source: Decision in "B & G Wards," Royal Courts of Justice, High Court, London, 23 July 1984.

SIGNING THE PLEDGE

Source for Christofferson Titchbourne case—*Oregonian* 12, 21 & 22 March, 5, 11, 13, 17, 20, 23 April, 18 & 20 May 1985.

1. Office of Special Affairs Executive Directive 19, 20 September 1984.
2. *Oregon Journal*, 3 May 1982.
3. *Los Angeles Times*, 19 May 1985.
4. *Clearwater Sun*, 17 July 1985.
5. *Impact 4*, p.12, December 1985; Impact 13.
6. Appeal opinion, 8 August 1986, p.36.

DROPPING THE BODY

Sources: "International Scientology," issue 8; *Rocky Mountain News*, 16 February 1986; *Riverside Press-Enterprise*, January & February 1986; *San Jose Mercury News*, 28, 30 & 31 January 1986; *St. Petersburg Times*, 2 February 1986; *Clearwater Sun*, 31 January 1986; *Los Angeles Times*, 28 & 30 January 1986; Miller interview with Robert Whaley, *Creston*, August 1986.
1. Flag Order 3879, 19 January 1986.

AFTER HUBBARD

Sources: FAIR Complaint in California Superior Court, Los Angeles County, no. CA 001012; Aznaran Complaint in District Court, Central District, California, no. CV 88-1786-WDK; "Flag Order 3879 Cancelled," 18 April 1988; RTC et al. vs. Yanny et al., in California Superior Court, L.A. County, no. C690211.

PART 9: SUMMING UP

THE FOUNDER

Sources: Bolitho; Hubbard letter to his first wife, 1938.
1. PDC 16, transcript, p.145.
2. OEC 0, p.35.
3. Ibid.
4. Interview with witness.
5. HCOB, "Pain and Sex," 26 Aug 82.

THE SCIENTOLOGIST

1. *8-8008*.
2. Hubbard, *The Creation of Human Ability*, p.123.
3. Confidential HCOB, "Resistive Cases," 23 September 1968.
4. *0.8*, Hubbard, p. 63.
5. *8-8008*, p. 135.

FAIR GAME, ETHICS AND THE SCRIPTURES

1. Alan Larson circular letters, 17 June 1985, 19 August 1987.
2. *The Management Series 1970–1974*, Hubbard, p.116.
3. OEC 7, pp.357–8.

Abbreviations

AAA = Advanced Ability Center
ABLE = Association for Better Living and Education
ACU = All Clear Unit
AG = Assistant Guardian
AO = Advanced Organization
ARC = Affinity, Reality, Communication
ASI = Author Services Incorporated
B-1 = Branch One, GO
CMO = Commodore's Messenger Organization
COSMOD = Church of Scientology Mission of Davis
CSC = Church of Scientology of California
CSI = Church of Scientology International
DG = Deputy Guardian
ED Int = Executive Director International
FEBC = Flag Executive Briefing Course
FLB = Flag Land Base
FN = Floating Needle
FOIA = Freedom of Information Act
HASI = Hubbard Association of Scientologists International
HCO = Hubbard Communications Office
HDRF = Hubbard Dianetic Research Foundation
HQS = Hubbard Qualified Scientologist
I HELP = International Hubbard Ecclesiastical League of Pastors
IAS = International Association of Scientologists
IMO = International Management Organization
KSW = Keeping Scientology Working
LRH Pers PRO = Hubbard Personal Public Relations Office
MCCS = Mission Category Sort-Out
MEST = Matter, Energy, Space and Time
MSH = Mary Sue Hubbard
NAMH = National Association of Mental Health
NED = New Era Dianetics
NED for OTs = New Era Dianetic for Operating Thetans
Nibs = L. Ron Hubbard Jr.
NOTs = New Era Dianetics for Operating Thetans
OEC = Organization Executive Course
OT = Operating Thetan

Ops = (GO) Operations
OSA = Office of Special Affairs
OTC = Operation & Transport Company
OTO = Ordo Templi Orientalis
PDC = Philadelphia Doctorate Course
PTS = Potential Trouble Source
Purif = Purification Rundown
RJ 67 = Ron's Journal 1967
RPF = Rehabilitation Project Force
RTC = Religious Technology Center
Scn = Scientology
Sec Check = Security Check
SHSHBC = Saint Hill Special Briefing Course
SMI = Scientology Missions International
SO = Sea Organization
SOCO = Social Coordination Bureau
SP = Suppressive Person
Tech = Technology (of Scientology)
Theta being = Thetan
TR = Training Routine
TR-L = Training Routine—Lying
VGIs = Very Good Indicators
WDC = Watchdog Committee
WISE = World Institute of Scientology Enterprises
WW = World-Wide

Index

419